Rise Above!

Letters from TYRONE GUTHRIE

Guthrie at fifty-five.

Rise Above! Letters from TYRONE GUTHRIE

Edited by **CHRISTOPHER FITZ-SIMON**

THE LILLIPUT PRESS

For
Julia and Dick

First published 2017 by
THE LILLIPUT PRESS LTD
62–63 Sitric Road, Arbour Hill, Dublin 7, Ireland
www.lilliputpress.ie

Texts © Christopher Fitz-Simon 2017

ISBN 978 1 84351 718 4

1 3 5 7 9 10 8 6 4 2

Set in Adobe Caslon Pro and ITC Caslon No. 224
Design by Niall McCormack
Printed in Spain by Castuera

CONTENTS

Annaghmakerrig in 1914.

INTRODUCTION

WILLIAM TYRONE GUTHRIE (1900–1971) was widely regarded in Britain and America as the most important theatrical director of the mid twentieth century, especially in relation to the staging of the 'classics' of the Greek and Elizabethan eras. Joe Dowling, who inherited Guthrie's role of Artistic Director at the theatre in Minneapolis that has been named The Guthrie, has written that he 'was probably the most significant figure in world theater'. Guthrie was particularly noted for liberating Shakespeare's plays from the burden of declamatory performance and elaborate scenic representation and also for the absence of 'reverence' in his approach to plays of the past generally. Indeed, he was often accused of introducing an unseemly frivolity into material that was traditionally considered to require a more solemn approach; his private letters, a broad selection of which appear in this book for the first time, reveal a man who beheld life with unreserved levity, a quality made all the more remarkable when, at moments of extreme emotional stress, he responded with an unexpected depth of serious feeling – as when critics destroyed the confidence of an admired young actor, or when his theatre in London was requisitioned as a refuge for families who had lost everything in the World War II bombing, or when an ageing writer was attempting to complete a promising work while dying of cancer. He was hugely sympathetic and supportive of persons when the moment required.

Guthrie has been – erroneously – categorized as an 'English' director. This is not surprising since he was educated in England and came to prominence in the London theatres. He has also been described as 'Anglo-Irish', a label which he also rejected, for he was Scots-Irish by birth. His father, Thomas Clement Guthrie, was a Scotsman appointed as Senior Surgeon to the General Hospital in Tunbridge Wells, Kent – a town celebrated as the citadel of English suburban fundamentalism of a kind that Tyrone (known as 'Tony') and his sister Susan Margaret ('Peggy') came to despise with exaggerated amusement. His paternal

great-grandfather was the Scottish philanthropist the Reverend
Thomas Guthrie, whose statue
in Carrara marble graces Prince's
Street in Edinburgh. Guthrie's
mother was the former Norah
Power of Annaghmakerrig, County Monaghan, Ireland; her
father was General Sir William
Tyrone Power of the same house;
and Sir William's father was the
brilliant Irish actor and playwright
Tyrone Power, among whose other
descendants was the Hollywood
actor of that name. School holidays
from Tunbridge Wells were spent at
Annaghmakerrig. It is interesting
how greatly Guthrie, as a child,
appreciated this country estate in
one of the poorer regions of Ireland

Norah Power about 1890, some years before she married
Dr Thomas Clement Guthrie.

– not so much for its picturesque quality as for the people who lived
there and worked the land. Even at the age of twelve he would write '…
3 weeks till holidays!!! & Annaghmakerrig – hurrah! …' and at nineteen,
when a student at Oxford, 'I wake up every morning feeling homesick
for Annaghmakerrig.' Members of the domestic staff in Tunbridge
Wells came from the Annaghmakerrig neighbourhood and they too
would return there, like the swallows, every summer. Guthrie's nanny,
Becky Miles, *née* Daley, was one of these; his concern for her until her
death in 1967 gave a highly personal dimension to his inclusive concern
for the Chekovian (or Frielesque) estate and its people.

Annaghmakerrig remained a pleasure (as well as an anxiety)
throughout his life. When many such properties were adversely af-
fected by remorseless cultural and social change, and nearby mansions
such as Dartrey and Rossmore were abandoned to the demolition
ball and the encroaching wilderness, Guthrie persisted in 'keeping
the roof on Annaghmakerrig'. He subsidized his mother's residence
there from his theatrical earnings following the untimely death of Dr

Susan Margaret Guthrie ('Peggy') and William Tyrone Power ('Tony') in 1912.

Guthrie in 1928; after her death in 1956 he made the house his headquarters for professional planning and study, where producers, designers, playwrights, actors, composers and conductors came to visit from all over the world. He was determined not only to preserve the house and farm but also to ensure the livelihood of the working families – the Daleys, McGormans, Burnses, Maguires and Mc-Goldricks. It has been pointed out that employment given by Protestant landlords to both Roman Catholics and Protestants was unusual in this Border region but the fact is that religion was never a consideration. Guthrie was increasingly exasperated by religious intolerance in Northern Ireland – as his public remark in 1964 about the Border being 'a nonsense' demonstrated. It was followed by calls for his resignation as Chancellor of Queen's University by the Protestant/Unionist establishment, calls he blithely ignored.

In 1963, in the hope of alleviating unemployment in his disadvantaged rural area, Guthrie assisted in establishing a fruit-growing and preserving industry with a local entrepreneur, Joe Martin. Substantial development grants were obtained from the government as well as export opportunities mainly to the US and UK where Guthrie's name opened many doors. The enterprise thrived conspicuously well for several years until precisely what Guthrie's brother-in-law Hubert Butler had predicted came to pass: multinational firms made it their business to ensure that the venture did not prosper further. Guthrie undertook several lucrative lecture tours to bolster the firm's finances but this was not enough to save it from liquidation. He told the TV director John Gibson that 'the jam factory was the most important production of my life and it was a flop.'

IMPORTED FROM IRELAND

Irish Farmhouse
SEEDLESS
WILD BLACKBERRY JAM
Ingredients : Sugar and Fresh Wild
Blackberries

NET WEIGHT   12 OUNCES

Made in Ireland by Irish Farmhouse
Preserves Ltd., Newbliss, Co. Monaghan.

Jam label designed by
Antonia Lofting for the
Newbliss factory.

This debacle contributed to the decline in Guthrie's relationship with his much-loved sister Peggy Butler; but his chief offence was his failure to inform her that he had bequeathed the Annaghmakerrig house and lands to his farm steward. After much heated family debate Guthrie reluctantly agreed to the Butlers' proposal that the house be willed to the Irish nation as a workplace for writers and artists; but he insisted in leaving the agricultural land to his steward.

By contrast, Guthrie's theatrical and operatic career prospered increasingly following a late start: from London to New York, from Edinburgh to Minneapolis, to include Belfast, Dublin, Glasgow, Düsseldorf, Sydney, Melbourne, Toronto, Stratford-upon-Avon, Stratford, Ontario – and so on. While he is remembered chiefly for his innovative productions of the classical European repertoire he also enjoyed outstanding success with original plays by contemporary writers, among them W.H. Auden, James Bridie, Paddy Chayefsky, Robert Crean, Robertson Davies, Norman Ginsbury, Eric Linklater, Eugene McCabe, Robert Morley, Sean O'Casey, J.B. Priestley, Barrie Stavis, Thornton Wilder and many others; and new operas by Benjamin Britten and Leonard Bernstein.

While acknowledging that the proscenium theatre was the appropriate place for plays that REQUIRED SCENIC effects as part of their *raison d'être* and also for the kind of plays that required comic business (such as 'people popping in and out of doors and hiding in cupboards') his advocacy of the 'open stage' as created at

Stratford, Ontario, and subsequently at Minneapolis, Minnesota, was immensely influential. He had always held the view that the great European classics should be presented in as near to their original architectural ambiences as possible. The chance of proving this came by accident when he directed *Hamlet* at Elsinore with Laurence Olivier and Vivien Leigh in 1938; the outdoor performance was cancelled due to a rainstorm and restaged in a hotel ballroom with the audience seated 'in the round'. The play took on an intimacy and immediacy that astonished both press and public. The production of a sixteenth-century Scottish morality play in a similar formation in the Presbyterian Assembly Rooms in Edinburgh advanced the theory. The purpose-built theatre at Stratford, Ontario, was created to his specification with the help of the designer Tanya Moiseiwitsch; the director Michael Langham described the Stratford theatre as 'Guthrie's favourite child'. It now appears that his life's work was all the time moving towards this apotheosis. It is likely that Aeschylus' *The House of Atreus*, staged on the magnificent new open stage at the Guthrie Theater in Minneapolis in 1967, provided the triumphant apogee of his career.

The letters in this book, addressed mainly to his mother at Annaghmakerrig, his sister Peggy in Kilkenny and his wife Judith in London (when she was not travelling with him) were not written with publication in view. It has been my aim to balance letters that disclose his career in the theatre – with its dazzling successes and readily acknowledged disasters – alongside the ups and downs of his family relationships. He is probably at his best when describing places visited on professional business – such as the Israel of the much-admired earliest kibbutzim and the burgeoning Habima Theater, or Burnley in Lancashire in the early 1940s where he was in charge of over 200 actors, singers, dancers and musicians from the Old Vic Theatre Company and the Sadler's Wells Opera and Ballet, evacuated there to escape the Luftwaffe Blitz, or New York in the 1950s when he was preparing plays for pre-Broadway tours surrounded by the frenzied activities of producers, agents, casting directors, designers, performers, stagehands and trades-union representatives with the inevitable post-ponements, firings, strikes and shrieking matches peculiar to the theatre life of that city.

Because the letters were *en famille* their style is highly individual both in expression and allusion. The reader who deplores a distinct absence of political correctness may be partially pacified to note the strong use of irony – when the opposite sense to what is written is intended. (Many of the observations, if visible, would be accompanied by a shrewdly raised eyebrow.) Readers sensitive to racial insult will note that flippancies are equally well dispensed in regard to Irish, British, Jewish, American or Australian national characteristics. Guthrie does not pull punches when describing the famous, whether in the theatrical, academic, political or religious spheres, nor in the realm of uncles, aunts and cousins. Though frequently in poor health and seeking medical attention, he ignored advice on long-term diagnosis from his eminent cardiologist. His abhorrence of pretentiousness and pomposity both on the professional and domestic scene is a characteristic that emerges strongly throughout the sequence. He and his wife Judith lived for at least half their adult lives in a tiny flat in an old building in London, described by the actor-author Robert Morley as 'a slum. It was like a dreadful set of a Sean O'Casey play.' The writer Robertson Davies – one of many who enjoyed the Guthries' hospitality after they made Annaghmakerrig their working base – wrote to his wife in Canada that 'the discomfort is of a special quality ... so is the oniony, very greasy food; so is the dirt ...' They never wore expensive or fashionable clothes; yet they looked supremely dignified and impressive when attending important public occasions. They were 'big people' in every respect.

*   *   *

Tyrone Guthrie died in 1971. Judith, in poor health, continued to live at Annaghmakerrig until her death from cancer barely a year later. Guthrie had somewhat reluctantly left the house to the nation as a workplace for writers and artists and clearly did so on account of family pressures. The proposal was that it would be funded jointly by the governments of the Republic and Northern Ireland. After much delay and considerable scepticism in official circles the project was passed to the two Arts Councils in Ireland. Largely due to the energy of the new Director of the Arts Council in Dublin, Colm O Bríain, a Board was formed representative of both jurisdictions and an architect engaged to renovate the mansion, which included the installation of nine bathrooms where previously there had been but two. Bernard Loughlin was engaged as Resident Director and his wife Mary was placed in charge of catering, to great acclaim.

On 10 October 1981 the Tyrone Guthrie Centre was opened by the playwright Brian Friel in the presence of An Taoiseach (Prime Minister) Jack Lynch. It was an instantaneous success, so much so that within a decade the ruinous stables and barns were converted as studios and self-catering accommodation. It is reasonable to speculate that Guthrie would have been surprised and delighted by the new life in the home where he had met and entertained playwrights, producers, designers, composers, conductors and performers from all over the world. Undoubtedly he would have preferred more Spartan living quarters and less fancy *cuisine* than is now provided. He and Judith would certainly be horrified by the health and safety regulations by which country lanes are now illuminated with urban street lamps, a code being required to enter the property and little green electrified men efficiently pointing out the emergency exits.

*   *   *

I have not attempted to 'correct' Guthrie's idiosyncratic spelling, grammar or syntax except when a word or phrase is clearly a misprint. The reader will have to make the best of invented words such as 'unhumiliating' or 'forrader' and abbreviations like 'y'day' for yesterday or 'biz' for business. He also uses phonetic spellings – such as 'in tahn' for 'in town' to suggest a person's accent. I have only tried to impose a kind of consistency on the headings of letters – for example, for Annaghmakerrig he sometimes writes the full word, sometimes places hyphens between the syllables, sometimes abbreviating to A'kerrig or, more often, AK. The two 'Wells' are liable to confusion: 'Tunbridge Wells' is the town where the Guthries lived at the turn of the twentieth century; 'Sadler's Wells' is the name of a London theatre where Guthrie later worked. He rarely begins letters with a formal 'Dear So-and-So' and he usually signs off with a simple 'T'. (This would not, of course, have been the case in business correspondence.) For reasons of clarity dates have been standardized as, e.g., 8 May 1951. Here and

there I have inserted short paragraphs in order to provide context and
in some cases to explain outcomes not covered in the letters, or to fill
in for periods from which few or no letters have survived. I have kept
footnotes to an absolute minimum. Readers will find short descriptions
of family members, close friends and professional colleagues in the list
of Dramatis Personae; the names of less frequently mentioned persons
are given in the Index.

DRAMATIS PERSONAE

Tyrone Guthrie, his relatives and family friends prominent in the letters

WILLIAM TYRONE GUTHRIE (TONY; 1900–1971), theatre director of Scots-Irish parentage, born Tunbridge Wells, Kent, England; inherited his mother's estate at Annaghmakerrig, Monaghan, Ireland. After 1961 **SIR TYRONE GUTHRIE**

JUDITH GUTHRIE (JUDY), his wife, *née* **BRETHERTON**, of Tunbridge Wells, Kent, England. After 1961 **LADY GUTHRIE**

THOMAS CLEMENT GUTHRIE, Tyrone Guthrie's father, senior surgeon of Tunbridge Wells General Hospital; (grandson of Scottish philanthropist Thomas Guthrie, 1803–73)

NORAH GUTHRIE ('MRS G'), Tyrone Guthrie's mother, *née* **POWER**, of Annaghmakerrig; (granddaughter of Irish actor-playwright Tyrone Power, 1797–1841)

SUSAN MARGARET GUTHRIE (PEGGY), Tyrone Guthrie's sister; married Hubert Butler

HUBERT BUTLER, of Maidenhall, Kilkenny, Ireland; market-gardener and distinguished author

JULIA BUTLER, Hubert and Peggy Butler's daughter; married **DR RICHARD CRAMPTON** of New York; **CORDELIA, SUZANNA** and **THOMAS,** their children

JOE HONE, reared by Hubert and Peggy Butler; later journalist, novelist and memoirist

SUSAN POWER (AUNT SUE) Norah Guthrie's sister, of Crossways, Tunbridge Wells; suffragette; supporter of Carson's Ulster Volunteers

GORDON & NELLIE BRETHERTON, Judith Guthrie's father and mother, and **MARTIN BRETHERTON,** her brother, of 'Peacemeal', Tunbridge Wells

NORAH ('PETER') Kesteven, Norah Guthrie's niece, of Sevenoaks, Kent, England

MOLLY DEWHURST, Norah Guthrie's niece, and her husband **DR MICHAEL DEWHURST,** of Havant, Hants, England

ETHEL WORBY ('BUNTY'), Norah Guthrie's companion-housekeeper at Annaghmakerrig following Dr Guthrie's death and her blindness; former nurse at Tunbridge Wells General Hospital

AILISH FITZ-SIMON (*née* **KILLEN**), a connection through the Fosters of Newbliss; her husband **COLONEL 'SIMON' FITZ-SIMON**, sometime overseer of Annaghmakerrig estate; their sons **CHRISTOPHER** and **NICKY**

MAY DAVIS ('**MIGSIE**'), of Holywood, Co. Down ('Davisville'); enduring family friend; her brothers **FRED** and **HARRY**

CHRISTOPHER SCAIFE, Guthrie's lifelong friend from Oxford University; lecturer in Beirut; retired to Italy

Annaghmakerrig 'retainers', their family members and other Monaghan persons prominent in the letters

BECKY MILES (*née* **DALEY**), of Annaghmakerrig; Tony and Peggy's nanny at Tunbridge Wells; 'Mookie' in Guthrie's play *Top of the Ladder* based on her; later returned to Annaghmakerrig

EDDY DALEY, Becky's brother; farm steward at Annaghmakerrig; **ANNIE**, his wife; their children: **LILY**, later a schoolteacher (Mrs Hawthorne); **SUSIE** (Mrs McEndoo); **ETHEL** (cared for ageing 'Aunt Becky'); **LORA** (Mrs Williams); **JOAN** (Mrs Lee)

EUGENE MAGUIRE, gardener; his children who worked at Annaghmakerrig: **ANN** (Mrs McGuirk), **MICHAEL** (later chauffeur) and **JOHN**

BOB BURNS, chauffeur; **MARY BURNS**, (*née* **MORGAN**, of Clones), his wife, one-time parlourmaid; **CHRISTINE** and **MAUREEN**, their daughters; **JIM** and **TEDDY**, their sons; after Mrs Norah Guthrie's death the Burnses ran the domestic side of Annaghmakerrig

CHRISSIE MORGAN, of Clones, Mary Burns' sister, one-time parlourmaid

SUSAN MURRAY, of Smithborough, one-time cook-general

GRETTA MULLEN, of Newbliss, one-time parlourmaid

MARY KELLY, of Newbliss, one-time parlourmaid and cook-general; **ANNA KELLY** her sister, one-time parlourmaid and cook-general

SEAMUS McGORMAN, farm worker; estate steward following death of Eddy Daley; Tyrone Guthrie willed the Annaghmakerrig lands to him; **MARY**, his wife

BRIAN McGOLDRICK, farm worker; **MARY**, his wife, laundress at Annaghmakerrig

FRANK McDERMOTT worked on the farm for several years

JOE MARTIN, of Newbliss; manager of Irish Farmhouse Preserves, 'the jam factory'

Clockwise: Peggy and Tony in 1908 and with their mother in 1906. Peggy with Hubert Butler at Annaghmakerrig at the time of their engagement in 1929. Tony and Judy shortly after their wedding in 1931.

Professional friends and colleagues most frequently mentioned in the letters

GEORGE CHAMBERLAIN, actor, later stage manager, later administrator, Old Vic Theatre, and his wife **ANNETTE** (*née* **PRÉVOST**)

EVELYN WILLIAMS, of Castlerock, Co. Derry, secretary of the Old Vic Theatre for many years

KENNETH RAE, Oxford University friend who held many theatre positions including secretaryship of the British Theatre Institute, and his wife **GWENETH**

EUGENE McCABE, of Clones, Co. Monaghan, neighbour and playwright; and his wife **MARGOT**

BRIAN FRIEL, of Muff, Co. Donegal, playwright; and his wife **ANNE**

JAMES FORSYTH, of Ansty, Sussex, playwright; and his wife **LOUISE**

OSBORNE MAVOR, of Bearsden, Scotland, playwright ('**JAMES BRIDIE**'); and his wife **RONA** and son '**BINGO**'

FREDERICK BENNETT, DOUGLAS CAMPBELL and his wife **ANN** (*née* **CASSON**), **LEWIS CASSON** and his wife **SYBIL THORNDIKE, ROBERT DONAT, ALEC GUINNESS** and his wife **MERULA, MURRAY McDONALD, JAMES MASON, ANTHONY QUAYLE, FLORA ROBSON, EMLYN WILLIAMS, DIANA WYNYARD, FREDERICK VALK** and his wife **DIANA**; early theatre colleagues with whom he frequently worked thereafter, maintaining close friendships

PEGGY ASHCROFT, JOHN GIELGUD, ROBERT HELPMANN, JOHN MILLS, LAURENCE OLIVIER, RALPH RICHARDSON, MICHAEL REDGRAVE, CHARLES LAUGHTON and his wife **ELSA LANCHESTER**; actors from the early Old Vic period with whom he remained constantly in touch

NINETTE DE VALOIS, Irish choreographer, founder of Sadler's Wells Ballet and later The Royal Ballet

BENJAMIN BRITTEN, composer, and his partner, **PETER PEARS**, tenor

JOAN CROSS, soprano from the early Sadler's Wells period, later director of Phoenix Opera

TANYA MOISEIWITSCH, the set and costume designer with whom Guthrie was most often associated; and her father **BENNO**, pianist

HUGH BEAUMONT ('**BINKIE**'), leading London impresario

MICHAEL LANGHAM, director, subsequently Guthrie's successor at the Stratford Shakespeare Festival, Ontario, and the Guthrie Theater, Minneapolis

ROBERTSON DAVIES, Canadian author, and his wife **BRENDA; DORA MAVOR MOORE; A.M. BELL;** and **TOM PATTERSON**, all central to the foundation of the Shakespeare Festival at Stratford, Ontario

RUPERT CAPLAN, producer, CBC Radio, Montreal

OLIVER REA, American entrepreneur of Ulster descent; central to the establishment of the Guthrie Theater, Minneapolis

PETER ZEISLER, American stage director and administrator; also central to the foundation of the Guthrie Theater

LEONID KIPNIS, Russian writer living in New York, and his wife **SONIA**

RUTH GORDON, American actor, and her husband, **GARSON KANIN**, director

ELLIOT MASON, Scottish actor, to whom Guthrie was temporarily engaged

JOHN GIBSON, BBC TV producer in Belfast, and his wife **AMIE**

JOHN BOYD, BBC Radio producer in Belfast

LILIAN BAYLIS, co-founder of the Old Vic Theatre

MICHEÁL MacLÍAMMÓIR, actor and co-founder of the Dublin Gate Theatre

PAMELA TRAVERS, author of Mary Poppins; friend of the Butlers who advised on the future of Annaghmakerrig

Synopsis of Principal Domestic Scenes

ANNAGHMAKERRIG, DOOHAT, NEWBLISS, CO. MONAGHAN, IRELAND. House and country estate of the Power family (see above); inherited by Tyrone Guthrie from his mother; on the suggestion of his sister and her husband, Peggy and Hubert Butler, bequeathed to the Irish nation as a workplace for artists and writers

BELMONT, and subsequently **WARWICK LODGE, TUNBRIDGE WELLS, KENT, ENGLAND.** Homes of Dr Thomas Guthrie and his wife Norah, where Tony and Peggy were brought up

23 OLD BUILDINGS, LINCOLN'S INN, LONDON WC2. Diminutive flat occupied by Tyrone and Judith Guthrie from 1931 until 1956 in a seventeenth-century city development originally created for the legal profession

MAIDENHALL, BENNETTSBRIDGE, CO. KILKENNY, IRELAND. Country house of the Butler family, inherited by Hubert Butler in 1941 and thence his and his wife Peggy's home and that of their daughter Julia and their protégé Joe Hone

My Dear Mummy
we are all quite well.
we had a nice time
at Grandfathers and
we are going to up.
to day Roby is coming.
to tea. Miss Bloom
gave me a we read
some of it, it is so
nice.. much love and

kisses from Peg

and Tony

Earliest-known letter from Tony, visiting his grandfather in London, to his parents in Tunbridge Wells, c. 1907.

I A RESPECTABLE EDUCATION:
TEMPLE GROVE, WELLINGTON AND OXFORD

In 1911 William Tyrone Guthrie was sent to Temple Grove, a preparatory boarding school for boys in Eastbourne. His apparent interest in the religious/political demography of Ulster at the age of fourteen was undoubtedly influenced by his aunt, Susan Power, an devotee of Carson's Ulster campaign against Home Rule for Ireland. If he felt at a loss being away from home his letters do not show it. He writes copiously about cricket and football. The following short extracts are typical.

No dedication, presumably to his parents, at Belmont, Tunbridge Wells, Kent, England
Temple Grove, Eastbourne. Undated, 1911

> I got here alright yesterday and like it awfully. I like Mr Waterfield [Headmaster] very much and Mrs Waterfield is very nice. Most of the boys are about 11 or 12 but I am bigger than most of my age.
>
> I think I must have been asked a million times "Who are you?" – "What is your name?" – "Where do you come from?" etc etc. I am beginning to know them by sight & one or two I know the names of, but the rest ought to have labels pasted on in front – "Smith" – "Jones" – "Robinson" etc. We had prayers in the chapel which I like awfully. There is 1 matron and then there are what is called Dormitory Maids who wash up and help generally. The matron is not bad, I don't think she is a lady though she speaks like one! This is a huge place the schoolroom is about as large as Aghabog Church [in County Monaghan, Ireland], larger if anything.

No dedication, presumably to his parents at Belmont, Tunbridge Wells

Temple Grove, Eastbourne. Undated, 1912

> I really am having a very good time so far, it is quite different to the beginning of last term as everybody knows me and I know everybody else. This afternoon we did Cadet Corps drill all in uniform which looks awfully nice. Would you send my tennis racquet but I *can* do without it.

To Mrs Becky Miles [nanny] at Belmont, Tunbridge Wells

Temple Grove, Eastbourne. Undated, 1912

> Just a line to ask if you would get some flowers for Mummie's birthday, anything up to 2/-, roses or carnations or really nice lily-of-the-valley I prefer but get whatever you think looks fresh and nice and put them with the card which I have enclosed. I hope your rheumatism is better.

No dedication, presumably to his parents, at Belmont, Tunbridge Wells

Temple Grove, Eastbourne. Undated, 1912

> I was top of the class this week with 171 marks. I have very little news. I played in a match and made two os!

No dedication, presumably to his parents, at Belmont, Tunbridge Wells

Temple Grove, Eastbourne. Undated, 1912

> There is less than 3 weeks till holidays!! & Annagh-ma-kerrig – hurrah! Won't it be just heavenly!! I am already hungry for the eggs and bacon on the Dundalk train – I think it is the most delicious meal possible, don't you?

To Mrs Norah Guthrie at Belmont, Tunbridge Wells

Temple Grove, Eastbourne. Undated, 1904

> Shall I go on with the Kepler tonic? I have just finished the second bottle and I have long finished the Jelloids. I enclose the populations of R.C. to Protestant in the counties of Ulster, they appeared in the Daily Graphic a day or two ago and they are rather startling.

Aunt Sue Power presenting the colours to Carson's Volunteers, Monaghan, 1913.

| | Per 1000 of the total population | |
	Protestant	Roman Catholic
Antrim	80	20
Down	68	32
Armagh	55	45
Derry	54	46
Cavan	19	81
Donegal	21	79
Monaghan	25	75
Fermanagh	44	56
Tyrone	45	55

Wellington College, Crowthorne.

Guthrie entered Wellington College in September 1914. The majority of letters preserved describe numerous sporting activities. There are many references to injuries to a toe and a knee, and to 'neuralgia', all of which reappeared frequently throughout his later life and included many hospitalizations. He did well academically but found mathematics troublesome. The Officers Training Corps was central to school life; the probability of 'joining up' in the Great War was met with complete absence of anxiety and no feelings of 'conscientious objection' whatsoever. The short extracts below, mostly from undated letters, give some sense of the times he was living in.

To Mrs Norah Guthrie, Warwick Lodge, Tunbridge Wells
Hardinge Dormitory, Wellington College, Crowthorne, Berkshire, England. September 1914

When you had gone I went back to the College. I fell in with another boy, Duncan, & we went round exploring together till about 6.50. I have put your photo by the window and the other two on the other side. This morning I was taken in to breakfast by a boy called Allom – he has to show me & Duncan & Crozier about. After breakfast we went down to the town & got dormitory caps. Hardinge is brown & blue. The work is no harder than at Temple Grove & I'm in a fairly small class. We new boys get off fagging till next Saturday so as to give us time to learn the way about.

To Dr and Mrs Guthrie, Warwick Lodge, Tunbridge Wells

Hardinge Dormitory, Wellington College. Extracts from undated letters, 1914–15

We are practising a short anthem about "the departed" for a service to the memory of the soldiers who have fallen in the war; I am one of the soloists.

Major Blacker's son has been on the wounded list for some time but to-day his name was followed by an asterisk which means "Died of his wounds". I *am* sorry for his parents. Isn't it ghastly.

There is no heating in the dormitory and no hope of it before mid-winter. We sit in our coats, and skip from time to time.

Our chief event has been a Zepp scare.[1] I happened (very oddly) to be awake when the alarm went at 2 A.M. Then Stocken [housemaster] rushed into dormitory, raised the "pres" [prefects] who roused us. We shut our windows etc & arranged ourselves. Down the stairs to a classroom where we remained for 1½ hours. We got to bed. Nearer 5 before I was asleep. In consequence of which, and the snow, I have had a revisitation of my Neuralgia.

I don't think I ever wrote you of two honours conferred on me this term: (i) my Lance Corps. stripe; (ii) I am elected a member of the Literary Society – which is rather an honour as the members are chosen strictly for merit.

The Music Competition is again on the tapis. This time for the piano: the piece is to be any movement from Beethoven. I am going to play the Funeral March. There is now a boy in dormitory who plays the piccolo quite nicely. I shall accompany him probably in one of Bach's minuets. This is indeed the term for Competitions. We've begun practising for the Drill Competition, also the Gym., while it was in a 2ⁿᵈ XV match that I hurt myself in yesterday.

Being near Aldershot we hear a great deal about the German prisoners – and the other night they mutinied and the soldiers guarding them had to fire among them, one man was killed.

---

1   The Zeppelin airship raids on the south-east of England, starting in the winter of 1915, caused much damage but comparatively little loss of life.

To Mrs Norah Guthrie at Warwick Lodge, Tunbridge Wells

Hardinge Dormitory, Wellington College. Undated, spring 1916

I'm laid rather low with a badly bruised knee. I did it yesterday on the [rugby] game, it has swelled up a good deal & is very stiff & rather aching. I saw the doctor who said he couldn't do anything: he offered me a bed in the Sani. I didn't want to go to bed tho', so am hobbling about.

To Mrs Norah Guthrie at Warwick Lodge, Tunbridge Wells

Sanatorium, Wellington College. Undated, autumn 1916

I came down here last night having again hurt my knee in a game of hockey. I was running quite peacefully along when it just gave and I came down like any old cart horse! It was so painful that I left the game at once & after changing got leave to come down here, where they took the strapping off and put me to bed. The doctor seemed rather angry at my playing at all.

To Dr Thomas Guthrie at Warwick Lodge, Tunbridge Wells

Hardinge Dormitory, Wellington College. Undated, 1917

Bryant [Officer Training Corps sergeant] says that by far my wisest plan is to go into an O.T.C. That will mean my staying on at college until I am 18½ years old. Then I should try for my scholarships. I've passed the Maths in the Oxford & Cambridge certificate! Please tell Miss P [his sister] that my passing was largely due to her assistance. I've arranged to give as much time as possible to History, & unless I hear to the contrary from you shall take it for granted that you approve. I'm going to begin at the beginning of the History of England this term & work right ahead. Please send *Utopia* [Thomas More] by return post, I have to read it for the exam.

To Mrs Norah Guthrie at Warwick Lodge, Tunbridge Wells

Hardinge Dormitory, Wellington College. Undated, 1917

Please tell the "Dear Doctor" that Master Guthrie's second toe from the right on the left foot has been really quite a bore – I have painted it with iodine but wonder if here is any other nostrum that I could apply. I have spoken to Stocken [housemaster] about the [Oxford] History Scholarship.

To Mrs Norah Guthrie at Warwick Lodge, Tunbridge Wells

Hardinge Dormitory, Wellington College. Undated, 1918

The field day was a great success. We got up at 7 o'clock, Chapel 7.30, breakfast 7.45, parade 8.50 when we set off on our march. We were fighting with the Munster Fusiliers against Eton & Royal Irish Rifles. One side had to defend a ridge. However, altho' the enemy got onto the ridge the result was a draw as the chief umpire said that some of the assistant umpires ought to have let the other side come on as they ought to have been shot long before! In all we covered 15 miles.

To Mrs Norah Guthrie at Warwick Lodge, Tunbridge Wells

Hardinge Dormitory, Wellington College. Undated, 1918

I'm afraid I was bitterly disappointed Dad did not think better of my knee. I can't help feeling that if he had seen the gym instructor he would have thought differently. He wrote that I should be alright to play [hockey] when the leg became as strong as the good one – well it is. I am glad that Dad is so much better. He certainly was miserably seedy here but I must say the change and the rest did him good. We've started gargling and nose-douching with "sort of" disinfectant as a preventative for flu.

To Mrs Norah Guthrie at Warwick Lodge, Tunbridge Wells

Hardinge Dormitory, Wellington College. Undated, 1918

I shall finish the Mediaeval History this week – revise rapidly and have a paper to see how much (or little) I remember – then to European! I shall begin by doing the French Revolution & XIX Century as being the most momentous & interesting, then back to the Reformation in Europe.

You ought to be made a super-grande-dame of the British Empire, with stars, garters, stripes & spangles attached. Seriously, though, I think it is awfully good – you & Dad have really done your bit in the "Great War". I'm very glad the Kitchens are such a success, I think they are the most interesting of your works.

I'm settling in as a "pre" now & get on alright with the other 3.

To Dr & Mrs Guthrie at Warwick Lodge, Tunbridge Wells

Hardinge Dormitory, Wellington College. Undated, summer 1918

My great piece of news is that on Tuesday we went to Reading for the army medical exam and I passed A.1. Isn't that splendid? I'm most frightfully glad about it. We (i.e. all those who will be 18 this term, about 8 in all) journeyed to Reading on the 1.56 train in uniform (so that our ticket cost nothing) under the charge of the senior in the O.T.C. We were conducted to the Town Hall where the examination took place. There were quite a good many other people there as well; a few boys about our own age but mostly men of about 40–45. We went into a large room screened off with canvas where we undressed and put on the rather unsavoury blue wraps provided for the purpose! I was in terror that my knee would get me ploughed but nothing came of it. The Eye Man said I was rather short-sighted. It is such a relief to feel that I have passed alright.

To Mrs Norah Guthrie at Warwick Lodge, Tunbridge Wells

Hardinge Dormitory, Wellington College. Undated, September 1918

Self and youth called Wentworth set forth early this morning at 8.30 in our best attire and with our whole fortune in our pockets. We caught our train quite easily at Wokingham and arrived safely at Waterloo. Then we made direct by Underground to "The Adjutant, Irish Guards, Buckingham Gate". After parleyings with a sort of clerk person were shown the dread adjutant. He was in a small office – an old, very tall man with a stoop and a high cracked voice. With him was another officer about 45–50 very handsome and pleasant looking. I went in first. He asked me a few questions about myself then handed me over to the younger man, and it was arranged that I should join at Bushey [Barracks] all being well, in January.

Fortunately (it must be assumed) for the peace of mind of Norah Guthrie – heavily involved in caring for Belgian refugees – and Dr Thomas Guthrie – unwell, and overworked by war casualties – the armistice of 11 November 1918, put an end to recruiting and young Guthrie's 'call up' was cancelled. He received news of his Oxford history scholarship in December and remained at Wellington until the end of the academic year. Curiously, there is no mention during his five years at Wellington of his ever having taken part in a school play. He was an unofficial 'nurse' during the international 'flu' epidemic when more people died than on the battlefields. Dr Guthrie was clearly in declining health; several otherwise conventional letters in 1918 refer to 'poor old dad'.

To Dr & Mrs Guthrie at Warwick Lodge, Tunbridge Wells
Hardinge Dormitory, Wellington College. October 1918

> Wasn't the Leinster affair hideous?[2] I did not know the names of those lost even by name except Lady Abercorn's daughter: even so the business seems more horrible than others of the same kind knowing the ship so well – and all the circumstances of the voyage.

To Mrs Norah Guthrie at Warwick Lodge, Tunbridge Wells
Hardinge Dormitory, Wellington College. Undated, presumably 10 November 1918

> Isn't the news marvellous? I suppose this November will be remembered as one of the most, if not the most, momentous months in history. I think the Germans cannot but accept our terms. Vaughan [Headmaster] thinks the revolution in Germany is a disaster for *us* because the collapse of orderly government means there will be nobody to make peace with, consequently the war will smoulder on indefinitely. Then, though Germany will be too broken & divided to molest us again she will never be able to make reparation, i.e. restore Belgium's pay indemnity, etc. But these reasons do not either of them convince me.

To Dr Thomas Guthrie at Warwick Lodge, Tunbridge Wells
Hardinge Dormitory, Wellington College. Undated, presumably 12 November 1918

> A perfectly delirious day here. Vaughan standing up on a bench in the middle of the Quad led 3 cheers for the armistice himself, throwing his cap and yelling with the best. A general rag in the front quad culminated in the decoration of Wellington's bust with a bowler hat and a neckerchief and the turning of 3 separate fire hoses on the helpless

---

2   Torpedoing of the Holyhead-Kingstown steamship, 10 October 1918, with the loss of 501 lives, the greatest disaster ever recorded on the Irish Sea.

bursar! The Hardinge created a sensation by flying my counterpane on the end of a broomstick – on it in vast characters traced in red ink by my nimble white fingers was inscribed "PEACE"! Later on we had an illumination – each window, by an ingenious arrangement of brown paper and cloth hanging displaying one letter each of "glorious victory" – also my idea and a crowning success!

To Mrs Norah Guthrie at Warwick Lodge, Tunbridge Wells
Hardinge Dormitory, Wellington College. Undated, late 1918

I *am* sorry Dad has had another relapse. Surely he ought to take a real holiday right away from T.W. & stay away for some time. I'm sure he must be played out after 4 years of strain. The Spanish influenza is certainly bad at T.W. I only hope Dad won't get it from seeing cases.
I have sent up my application form to Oxford with a letter saying that supposing I won the scholarship the money should go to the next candidate who without it would be unable to go to the university. You said I should be able to go anyway. I was advised to write the letter but did not have time to let you know first.

To Mrs Norah Guthrie at Warwick Lodge, Tunbridge Wells
Hardinge Dormitory, Wellington College. Undated, 1919

We have had a day of utter chaos. Last Wednesday a boy got flu. By [this] Wed. all his house except 4, & all his form & master, were in bed. By Thursday there were 80 cases and the Combermere [Dormitory] was turned out to provide a sanitorium overflow. Today I should say there will be well over *150 cases*! Hardinge received orders to pack up and move out this morning. [Later:] There are now about 350 cases so that when one is ill one just lies down in one's room telling one of the nurses who are hovering about. Directly after breakfast I and a lad called Holdsworth Hunt, set to and made all the beds, emptied baths, etc. Having set the rooms to right we had to keep the nurses supplied with hot water for washing their patients; bring tea round and biscuits. We had to fetch all the food up from the kitchens (up 61 steps) 3 journeys. Now Mrs Cott [a parent] is away for her lunch and I am in charge.

To Mrs Norah Guthrie at Warwick Lodge, Tunbridge Wells

Hardinge Dormitory, Wellington College. Undated, 1919

> Certainly we live in the most marvellous times since the Reformation – if not since Christ. I do not know whether we're "lucky" or the reverse. I think for the older generation who see all things they have known and loved crumbling to dust it's *too appalling*: but for the young who will live to see the wounds heal and help in the reform and reconstruction to come, it's an opportunity such as the world has never known before.

Guthrie was enrolled at St John's College, Oxford, in the autumn of 1919. Without delay he joined the tennis and hockey clubs, the Folk Music and Dance Society, the Oxford University Dramatic Society and the Oxford Union Society. He attended a Mr Garcia for singing lessons. He formed a lifelong friendship with Christopher Scaife, also of St John's, a talented dancer and actor and winner of the Newdigate Poetry Prize. Several undergraduates – such as Kenneth Rea and Henry Havergal – would appear significantly in later life. He also became friendly with Hubert Butler from Kilkenny, Ireland, who, in 1930, would marry his sister Peggy.

To Dr & Mrs Guthrie at Warwick Lodge, Tunbridge Wells

St John's College, Oxford. Undated, October 1919

> My tutor for History is called Last – I'm not sure at all whether I like him! He is very young, about 23–24. He has been in the army but it doesn't seem to have brightened him up very much. His hair is very long & falls in great lank curls over his eyes. He speaks in a tired – very tired – drawl. On the other hand he is excessively brainy!

To Mrs Norah Guthrie at Warwick Lodge, Tunbridge Wells

Union Society, Oxford. Undated, probably October 1919

> My opposite neighbour, [Henry] Havergal, has arrived. I like him very much which is satisfactory as it would be so boring to live near someone objectionable! Kenneth [Rae] is really funny – a clown who contrives not be exhausting by knowing when to stop.

To Dr & Mrs Guthrie at Warwick Lodge, Tunbridge Wells
St John's College, Oxford. Undated

> Went to see Beaumarchais' *Barbier de Séville* done by the French Club quite badly but pleasantly. A che-arming piece – I fell completely in love with it & mean to translate it as soon as I have time. It's the most ridiculous piece of XVIIIth century fun, very artificial but exquisitely finished and witty.[3]

To Mrs Norah Guthrie at Warwick Lodge, Tunbridge Wells
St John's College, Oxford. Undated

> Yesterday Kenneth took me up to tea with the Masefields. Lovely walk thro' bluebell woods. M's themselves are charming. Alas! the place was positively besieged by richly dressed & rapidly motored Americans who came to "do" Masefield as one of the sights of Oxford. Mrs Masefield is ugly beyond belief – dressed in fusty brown wool, not over-clean – with muddy boots. The children are ugly & intelligent & not the least precocious. The house is full of interesting and beautiful things but looks as if a herd of cows had just slept in it.

To Dr & Mrs Guthrie at Warwick Lodge, Tunbridge Wells
St John's College, Oxford. Undated

> I wake up every morning feeling homesick for Annagh-ma-kerrig and lie in bed picturing my favourite views. The White Walk and the big trees from the front door; the view over the country from Mullenagraw – the lake from the gap in the planting on Macullan's land. With a very little effort I can feel the feel in the air and the smell of the grass and the feeling of brushing against spruce and fir branches after rain – and the smell of a turf fire – and the silence and the little birdy noises down by the lake when it's nearly dark. Oh! if only we would be there!

---

3   Rossini's *The Barber of Seville* for Phoenix Opera turned out to be Guthrie's final production before his death in 1971.

Guthrie as an undergraduate at St John's College, Oxford, and in the cast of *Le Bourgeois Gentilhomme* with the Oxford University Dramatic Society, 1920.

To Peggy Guthrie at Warwick Lodge, Tunbridge Wells

St John's College, Oxford. Undated

I'm thinking of going to Germany for about a fortnight. The idea is that Christopher & I should go to Dresden chiefly to hear opera. The rate of exchange makes it possible to do the trip ever so cheaply and I think it would be wise for me to hear some decent opera especially Wagner if there's any possibility of my taking up a musical career.

The Morris & country dancing continues to be monstrously diverting. Morris dancing is so strenuous that females don't do much of it!

To Mrs Norah Guthrie at Warwick Lodge, Tunbridge Wells

St John's College, Oxford. Undated

Christopher [Scaife], Miss Bailey [Folk Dance instructor] & I went off in Miss B's little car to see the "Boar's Hill Players" do *Macbeth*

Christopher Scaife, Guthrie's lifelong Oxford friend.

in a village hall 2 miles beyond Abingdon & we nearly died of cold getting there. The play was enormously amusing: produced by [John] Masefield, who acted 2nd Witch and acted by high-class intellectuals; high-class low-class sons of shop assistants and (for the most part) yokels. The curtain (of course) went wrong – sometimes wouldn't draw at all. The same helmets were worn by all the company in turn; & a red velvet cloak was observed to have a row of curtain-rings attached. Macbeth's second costume consisted of a lady's black silk bodice on top of a skirt that had evidently been Cleopatra's in another production. The whole effect was really no sillier than most professional Shakespearian costumes. The acting was mostly bad but spirited and intelligent. Lady Macbeth was jolly good.

To Peggy Guthrie at Warwick Lodge, Tunbridge Wells

No letterhead. Undated

You'll be interested and alarmed to hear that in my first disguise in the play [*Le Bourgeois Gentilhomme* in the garden of Holywell Music Rooms] I look a caricature of you. I sing a trio as an Arcadian Shepherd & have a longish bobbed wig, rather fluffy, of the most virulent red. The appearance is fearful.

To Mrs Norah Guthrie at Warwick Lodge, Tunbridge Wells

St John's College, Oxford. Undated

I've been asked to play Antonio in Gyles Isham's *XXII Night*. They're doing it in Essex somewhere and can put me up. I conveyed the Scaife relations to the Keble Week concert as Christopher had to attend a sword-dance rehearsal. Ma Scaife is a vast female of *limitless* bel air, very extravagant, with grand views but vague, and a heart of gold. Gillian [Christopher's sister, actress], who is hideous in feature – a discoloured mottled little marmoset, but very sweet-looking because so animated: not the least stagey or self-conscious; Gillian & Christopher are quite ridiculously devoted to one another.

To Mrs Norah Guthrie at Warwick Lodge, Tunbridge Wells

Oxford University Dramatic Society. Undated, summer 1923

> Casting reading for *Henry IV* at the O.U.D.S. last night. I had good parts to do – a scene of Prince Hal, another of Falstaff & another of Hotspur: was indifferent as the Prince, hopeless as Falstaff and quite good as Hotspur. In the end I got Glendower.

To Mrs Norah Guthrie at Warwick Lodge, Tunbridge Wells

Oxford University Dramatic Society. Undated

> So glad Pop is better now – I do hope he will take things easy for a few days. No chance of his coming here, is there? He could have Xopher's room for C. goes off to Somerset. He has just been elected President of the Union – great triumph!

To Peggy Guthrie, visiting Edinburgh

St John's College, Oxford. Undated, July 1923

> The play [*Henry IV*] has been voted a great success – many people "who know" say it is the best the O.U.D.S. have ever done & certainly the best since the war. The Sunday Times gave a sensible but decidedly sniffy review & blew up every member of the cast except Hotspur, Kenneth & me.

Guthrie's final examination results at Oxford were poor and he had to stay on to repeat. He may have been considering his interesting experience in *Henry IV*, which was directed by a distinguished professional, J.B. Fagan, and played a week in London. As it happened Fagan was setting up The Oxford Playhouse Company; evidently impressed by Guthrie, he invited him to join as an Assistant Stage Manager, playing supporting roles.

To Dr Thomas Guthrie at Warwick Lodge, Tunbridge Wells

Letter is headed Warwick Lodge. Undated, autumn 1923

> Exam results are out & I fear I have done pretty frightfully. I have "satisfied the examiners in Group A2" – that means I was not good enough to get honours but whether or not I can take a degree with

that is not quite clear. I had an awfully nice letter from Last in which he says my papers were "not bad at all" but the Latin & Greek was so appallingly bad they could not give me a class. A decided blow and I'm so afraid you and Mum will be grieved. I must abandon all intention of being a pedagogue, a career I have no desire to embark upon except as a means of procuring bread.

To Mrs Norah Guthrie at Warwick Lodge, Tunbridge Wells

No address. Undated, mid October 1923

I think all things considered we [Playhouse Company] did very gallantly. So far as stage management [Shaw's *Heartbreak House*] was concerned there were no hitches at all – the only disappointment being the big explosion which was the tamest of affairs, a mere popping of a cork in a medicine bottle! My make-up & beard & moustache [as Hector] is inclined to be wax-worky & I acted very badly yesterday. I wasn't nervous in the least when the moment came, just conscious that it was "an occasion" which was of course disastrous. There was a full house & enthusiastic applause. The two great successes were Dorothy Green [Hessione] who looked perfectly magnificent and Richard Goolden [Mazinni Dunn] who simply brought the house down he was so sweet & funny. Flora [Robson] makes a lot of Nurse Guinness.

To Mrs Norah Guthrie at Warwick Lodge, Tunbridge Wells

Oxford Playhouse. Undated, November 1923

The Importance of Being Earnest after an utter fiasco on the opening night came into its stride and finished very strong indeed. Over 200 people turned away at the door. We are at present rehearsing *The Return of the Prodigal* [St John Hankin] & tonight is the dress rehearsal of *Mirandolina* [Gregory, after Goldoni].

To Mrs Norah Guthrie at Warwick Lodge, Tunbridge Wells

29 Holywell, Oxford. Undated, late November 1923

Mirandolina finished fairly strong on Sat. & more than paid expenses of the week. The press was very favourable & with the exception of the Morning Post gave me good notices. *The Prodigal* opened yesterday to a minute audience – under 100, I should say. Personally I think they can't expect to have full houses unless they put on hackneyed plays. The stage managers have had a bad time as both Herbert [Lugg] and I are acting & have a change of costume & the changes of scene & furniture are the heaviest of the season.

To Mrs Norah Guthrie at Warwick Lodge, Tunbridge Wells

Oxford Playhouse. Undated, January 1924

I wish you had seen *Captain Brassbound's Conversion* [Shaw] as it's not at all a bad show. As Sidi I have not been very good – I don't quite know why because tho' small it's an effective part & I ought to be able to make something of it as I look quite impressive in a black beard – but except for the Morning Post who called me "stiff-jointed and high-pitched" none of the press has mentioned it. I'm disappointed it hasn't succeeded because I think it's the best thing I've done. *Love for Love* [Congreve] is still in chaos – how it will ever be produced on Monday I can't begin to imagine but I suppose we shall muddle through somehow. I am dire as Jeremy – too gawkily spry & laboriously arch for words! By the way, Mrs Gielgud is coming up next week to see young Jack [John Gielgud] in *Love for Love* on Sat. and *Rivals* [Sheridan] on Mon. Jack isn't at all bad – conceited and a little "artistic" but I think he will improve a lot. He's only 19 & is just a bit full of himself at the moment – but when being natural & not showing off he's very intelligent & genuine & friendly. I think he will do very well.

To Peggy Guthrie at Warwick Lodge, Tunbridge Wells

40 St John Street, Oxford. Undated, February 1924

The chief event in my history this week occurred on Sunday when Christopher & I were asked to sing at the prison. It was an awesome moment when the gates clanged to behind us & were padlocked by a warder who had a jingling bunch of keys at his girdle. We were conducted by the governor up a corkscrew staircase in a sort of cast iron café into the prison chapel. A gloomy place with benches like a schoolroom & heavily barred windows. Seventy convicts – one in broad arrows: we sang a rather under-rehearsed programme of folk songs. The poor things obviously enjoyed it thoroughly – and well they might for the alternative was just pacing their cells. It was a depressing experience – most of the prisoners were very young and ordinary-looking – no typical Bill Sykes faces at all – & one felt terribly sorry for them: when we were putting on our coats they were flung back to their cells. There was one particularly nice looking youth in the front row and we asked about him. He was the youngest of a big family & the sole support of old parents, stole some lead piping & sold it to a "receiver" for 4/- . As a result of this "crime" he's doing 3 months. Of course he was caught & proved guilty, he had to be punished, but individual cases like that do bring home to one the fact that civilisation is a miserably clumsy machine.

I was up in town last week choosing the clothes for *She Stoops*. My part is rather a bore because it involves so much waiting about – I keep popping in & just saying "The carriage waits!" but it's a delightful play & Mrs Hardcastle is a joy, a stout old female called Minnie Rayner – divinely comic & vulgar. The latest fuss is caused by several people writing to protest against the production of the Congreve play. Everybody knows that Congreve's plays are not "pour la jeune fille" & there isn't a scene in the play that one doesn't see enacted daily in real life, only Congreve holds up to nature a mirror of real genius – the wit of Voltaire, satire as sharp as Swift & language that Shakespeare could not better. It's far less unwholesome than Wilde & takes a far more lenient view of humanity than Shaw.

To Mrs Norah Guthrie at Warwick Lodge, Tunbridge Wells

40 St John Street, Oxford. 5 March 1924

The Land of Heart's Desire [Yeats] has had very good notices and most people seem to like me in it [as Shawn] but I fear Fagan doesn't. It was a tiny audience but the applause was very hearty.

J.B. Fagan indicated that Guthrie – and also Flora Robson – would not have their contracts renewed for the following season. In any case Guthrie was looking around for other work. He applied for a post as 'Studio Assistant' with the British Broadcasting Corporation. He had repeated his university exams and achieved a poor degree.

To Mrs Norah Guthrie at Warwick Lodge, Tunbridge Wells

40 St John Street, Oxford. 24 March 1924

> *Monna Vanna* [Maeterlinck] has been a cope as the scenery is more elaborate than usual. It's a terrible play – a wallow in sex-sentimentality with a vague attempt at metaphysics which is very boring. All news has paled before the announcement that young Jack Gielgud has succumbed to mumps! Isn't it fierce! His very important part was read tonight by old Fagan – quite a gallant and sporting attempt. I don't know if it's the coming of spring but I wake every morning feeling homesick for Annaghmakerrig.

To Mrs Norah Guthrie at Warwick Lodge, Tunbridge Wells

40 St John Street, Oxford. Undated, spring 1924

> Was tied up over the weekend owing to Fagan's mismanagement. *Oedipus* [Sophocles] was a fierce tussle to get ready. It has so far drawn £7, £8 & £10 & hasn't had a good press. I personally have had quite a success but have played so many buffoons that some of the notices expressed surprise rather than interest in my performance. "Mr Guthrie plumbed unsuspected depths of tragedy" – "The outstanding performance of the evening was certainly that of Mr Tyrone Guthrie as Tiresias, he alone of the players raised the drama to real heights of tragedy and passion".

To Mrs Norah Guthrie at Warwick Lodge, Tunbridge Wells

Oxford. Undated, June 1924

> I was interviewed by the [BBC] Controller, who seemed nice – an ex-admiral with a son at Wellington. At all events I've been offered a job. My business will be to assist in the arrangement of programmes & engagement of artistes (almost entirely musical). I shan't have to mend the machines at all! I will be given a preference of station – i.e. there's a good chance of working either in London or Edinboro' as opposed to Cardiff or Hull. What I feel is this is about the best chance I shall ever get of would-be "artistic" work that is yet a career. As such I incline to take it. The pay is good – promotion likely. Broadcasting obviously has a big future & the B.B.C. has a monopoly

for 3 more years by which time they expect to be so firmly entrenched that unless they degenerate frightfully it won't be worthwhile for any other company to compete. Now shall I – shall I take it?

2 BELFAST AND GLASGOW:
BEGINNER'S RADIO AND FIT-UP THEATRE

In 1923 the British Broadcasting Corporation engaged Guthrie at £280 per annum as the earliest 'junior assistant' in the new regional studio in Belfast, which broadcast each evening with the call-sign '2BE'. Much of his work would be in commissioning 'experts' to give live talks and to have local drama groups present plays; but he had more advanced ideas of what 'real' radio drama should be. In a very short time he was authorized to engage professional actors from Dublin and London. Hubert Butler, an Oxford college friend, was by now Carnegie Librarian in Coleraine, Co. Derry.

To Mrs Norah Guthrie at Warwick Lodge, Tunbridge Wells
Midland Station Hotel, Belfast, Northern Ireland. Undated, August 1924

Major Walker Montague Douglas Scott, Director of Broadcasting, seems quite nice & easy to get on with. He doesn't appear to be the least efficient but probably that is only manner – time will show. [Godfrey] Brown, who is the musical director, seems to be a decent lowish class body with none too much gumption but very kind and has asked me out to tea in Holywood. Ingram the head engineer is five years of age & peers with baby wonderment but mechanical acumen from behind the vastest "horn-rims".

My job is going to be running the dramatic side: engaging people to give "Talks" – and doing my share of announcing.[4] We are going

---

4   Guthrie's voice was the first to be heard from the station, announcing its initial transmission on 15 September, 1924, some weeks prior to the official opening. Subjects for broadcast talks included 'Ulster's Contribution to the Empire', 'Ulster's Contribution to the Breakfast Table', 'The Building of a Liner' and 'The Romance of Flax Seed'.

to have a "Children's Hour" – I shall try to be firm on the subject of avuncular archness but don't expect my opinion will count for much for some time yet. B.B.C. address: 31 Linenhall Street.

To Peggy Guthrie at Warwick Lodge, Tunbridge Wells
c/o Mrs Hunter, 82 Cromwell Road, Belfast. Undated, 1924

The offices are still in the hands of plasterers, painters etc: and no furniture has arrived: so we are all gathered in one room (what will eventually be the engineers' room) with two tables and a few chairs. As far as I can see there will be very little for me to do until the actual transmission begins, i.e. Sept. 15th. There will not be much to do in the dramatic line – less than one show a week – and most of the talks are sent from London.

My landlady seems very nice and cooked me a very nice supper last evening and breakfast to-day. The sitting-room is poky and hideous and crammed with ugly furniture but I shan't be there much. It is very convenient – only 12 minutes walk. I think I'll have a shot at Annaghmakerrig next week-end or if you could manage to arrive here the following Saturday we might travel down there that afternoon which would be fun.

To Mrs Norah Guthrie at Warwick Lodge, Tunbridge Wells
BBC Belfast. Undated, August 1924

The weekend at Annaghmakerrig was simply splendid & made all the difference to me due to the rather trying launching-forth in a new place. You won't forget to send me my hockeying-ing costume – girls like me can't be too careful what they wear. I've begun singing lessons again with a man called Herbert Scott. He's a delightful person – very enthusiastic & energetic. He's one of the leading teachers here & being very go-ahead & brusque he has many enemies.

To Mrs Norah Guthrie at Warwick Lodge, Tunbridge Wells
BBC Belfast. Undated, late October 1924

I caught a cold sitting in a draught among hydrangeas last Friday at the Official Opening [of the BBC]. It was a dire function: one of

The earliest executive and studio staff (*Guthrie third from right*) at the British Broadcasting Corporation (then 2BE) in Belfast, 1925.

those "brilliant occasions" when nobs stand on red carpets and pay trite compliments to one another. The d. [Duke] of Abercorn is a big fuzz-buzz with a well-preserved Duchess. Millar Craig [BBC Glasgow Controller] was there like an old cattle dealer but a most *charming* speaker with a most admirable "delivery". There was boundless enthusiasm about things like The British Empire or The Duchess of Abercorn.

We've had quite a deluge of appreciative letters & I've come in for my share of verbal bouquets. I feel an awful fraud as I can't take it quite seriously. Thompson [Assistant Director] & worthy Godfrey Brown are so in earnest & really think they are educating the masses, but until the whole thing improves enormously or I become saturated with B.B.C. ideas the tongue will remain firmly pressed into the cheek. Major Scott, I'm sure, feels like I do, but of course one can't admit it openly. I am quite busy but nothing like [Oxford] Playhouse scrimmages. Am anxious to get as much into my hands as possible & then ask for more money.

Having 4 rival females coming to make microphone tests for the post of "Auntie". It will be appallingly funny. I'm rather afraid of behaving indecorously.

To Mrs Norah Guthrie at Warwick Lodge, Tunbridge Wells

BBC Belfast. Undated, November 1924

The Land of Heart's Desire [Yeats] went very well and made a great impression on the dozen or so of audience in the studio & the elect outside. I thought it lovely but, as expected, Belfast "hadn't much use for something so unusual". Dance music & comic songs are the most popular, I think, especially if the comics are reinforced by patter of the kind:- "I was walking down the street and I saw a pretty girl – oh boys! she didn't half give me the glad eye, etc" – bad enough in Cockney or Lancashire but intolerable in Belfast accent by a comedian with about as much vitality or sparkle as a whelk. This sort of thing is run extremely close by sentimental hymns sung yearningly at twilight on Sunday evening.

To Mrs Norah Guthrie, Warwick Lodge, Tunbridge Wells

BBC Belfast. Undated, November 1924

This afternoon we wrestle with a Radio League children's party – such an unmitigated embarrassment & bore. Mercifully only about 50 or 60 are coming but you can imagine my feelings when on ringing the Restaurant (where we're holding it) to make final arrangements about food the manageress lightly informed me that due to a misunderstanding she had not booked the room. I swooned but on recovery rushed around & after 20 minutes of alternate threats and coaxing induced her to arrange for us to have it instead of a Presbyterian whist drive! The party will be dreadfully bright … Now children, let's form a big ring and you – yes, you, that little girl with ringlets and a red plush dress – you be in the middle, you've got to catch the handkerchief, see? I shall be glad when it's all over and I'm seated in 3rd class plush gliding towards Hubert & Coleraine.

To Peggy Guthrie at Warwick Lodge, Tunbridge Wells

BBC Belfast. 24 November 1924

I have just returned from a delightful week-end spent with that Hubert Butler who runs the Carnegie Libraries in Ulster: he was staying at Portstewart & invited me up there. His mother was there too – charming person – real lady – with a great sense of humour & very intelligent. We took a chariot-bang on Sunday afternoon via Portrush which is rather "little low-class resorty" to the Devil's [sic] Causeway which is very interesting & queer. It is a wonderful coast & we must go up there some time.

To Peggy Guthrie, Warwick Lodge, Tunbridge Wells

BBC Belfast. Undated, December 1924

Herbert Scott suddenly discovered what a tremendously loud voice I've got. I'd never had really to sing out my loudest for him before. He said, in *awesome* tones, "Do you realise you've got a bigger voice than Jimmy Newell?" Jimmy Newell is Belfast's King of Song. Have been asked to go motoring on Sunday by Bertie Scott to make up a party of 4 – Bertie, Jimmy Newell, self & Plunket Greene (who is coming over to judge at musical competitions). I think it will be rather awful & have not definitely accepted. If stuck in Belfast I'll go but would greatly prefer Annaghmakerrig. One would like to know P. Greene but I think a whole day in a hired motor listening to Artiste's talk would be profoundly enervating![5]

To Mrs Norah Guthrie at Warwick Lodge, Tunbridge Wells

BBC Belfast. Undated, December 1924

Am in the throes of anti-Belfast reaction. Oh! the insufferable all-suffusing bigotry. It's almost impossible to find moderate opinion on any subject. The intolerance & excess seem to permeate from religion & politics into every department of their civilisation – so few of them seem to be capable of taking a detached & disinterested point of view & so few of them have any sense of humour.

---

5   Herbert Scott and Jimmy Newell were much-admired Belfast musicians. Harry Plunket Greene was a celebrated Dublin-born baritone based in London; in later life he made worldwide trips to adjudicate at music festivals.

To Mrs Norah Guthrie at Warwick Lodge, Tunbridge Wells

BBC Belfast. Xmas 1924

I had a busy Christmas Day. We'd a long Concert in the afternoon & the Children's Hour at 5.15 – & be sure the Aunties & Uncles of 2BE made heroic efforts to be sprightly & make Yuletide Jollity for their thousand and one tots. Dec. 23 we had an Ulster Ceidlith [sic], pronounced Caley, – "Folk" conversation, songs, stories & dance music; scene a Farmhouse Kitchen; characters the farmer's family, friends & neighbours. Then on Xmas Eve we had a specially made radio version [script] sent over for us from London. It was very cleverly adapted & seems to have been quite a success but was the devil's own cope to produce as there were 15 billion characters in it: then, to make matters worse, my leading lady couldn't play – at 3 o'clock on the day of the show she got word (poor soul) that her brother had died v. suddenly. So I spent 3 – 8 solidly rehearsing an understudy. Good experience but very tiring: more than stage rehearsing because more concentrated & 3 hours over and over just with the voice alone is quite the equivalent of 4 or 5 on the stage.

The Glittering Gate [Dunsany] went off quite well I think. The Players at all events were quite pleased about it. Jimmy Mageean wants me to do a show for the Ulster Players which is flattering & unlikely to occur.

I saw the Ulster Players last night. They played *The Drone* which is their chef-d'oeuvre excellent! Rather on the lines of *The Whiteheaded Boy* & really I think quite as good, both play and production.[6]

To Mrs Norah Guthrie at Warwick Lodge, Tunbridge Wells

BBC Belfast. Undated, January 1925

Went on Tuesday to Queen's Island [Harland & Wolff, Shipbuilders] to hear the Q.I. Dramatic Society give a performance of Milne's *Stepmother* in hopes that I would engage them to broadcast. They were

---

6   The Ulster Players in Belfast were inspired by the twenty-year-old Abbey Theatre in Dublin. Rutherford Mayne's comedy *The Drone* was one of its staples. Lennox Robinson's Abbey play *The Whiteheaded Boy* had been hugely successful internationally. In 1950 Guthrie directed three plays with the Ulster Players for the Festival of Britain.

very nice & the play quite suitable, only, alas! they were so bad and the English "nobs" spoke with terrible Belfast accents. It was a trifle embarrassing for me and for them when they asked at the end "What do you think of it?"

To Mrs Norah Guthrie at Warwick Lodge, Tunbridge Wells
BBC Belfast. Undated, early 1925

We [with his sister Peggy] are just off to Dublin – where we lie tonight at Jury's Hotel – such fun! Peggy has had a very charming welcoming letter from Mrs Butler to which we concocted a reply of laborious naïveté! We propose to spend tomorrow morning at the Harcourt Street Galleries & Royal Irish Academy – we are to meet the Butlers at midday at the Bonne Bouche.

To Mrs Norah Guthrie at Warwick Lodge, Tunbridge Wells
BBC Undated, early 1925

I'm glad you think my letter [to BBC London] demanding more pay is "couched" appropriately. As you say, it is a little early to being fussing for more, but what I feel is if I go toiling and moiling here they may lose sight of me. So I feel if I set a high value on my own services (without actually being impertinent) it will tend to keep me in mind if not actually to produce more cash or a better post at the moment.

To Mrs Norah Guthrie at Warwick Lodge, Tunbridge Wells
BBC Belfast. Undated, March 1925

I recd. a note yesterday to say that at the annual meeting for the revision of salaries the Board of Directors of the B.B.C. had raised me to £350 per annum. I shall soon be quite rich & am seriously considering the question of buying a gent's umbrella, a luxury I have always yearned for.

I wonder what your plans are for Annagh-ma-kerrig? Aunt Sue wrote that she thought you would all come over & hold a conseil-de-famille on the spot. I should love to try asking the B.B.C. to give me a job that would enable me to run Annaghmakerrig as well. I think it would be worth my while to ask.

Guthrie met the Davis family of 'Abingdon', Holywood, Co. Down, through his Belfast hockey club. An arrangement was made to live with them as a 'p.g.' – paying guest. May, also known as Migsie, became a lifelong friend. The Davises began to visit Annaghmakerrig with him. On one such weekend his Oxford Playhouse colleague Flora Robson, who Guthrie had brought over for a radio production of *Iphigeneia*, joined them. At the same time he was writing a musical entertainment called *Victoriana* based on a family evening with songs and recitations.

To Mrs Norah Guthrie at Warwick Lodge, Tunbridge Wells
BBC Belfast. 26 March 1925

> The Davises: May, who is about 40, Fred 35 & Harry about 30 – they are all very intelligent & full of character if a trifle odd. Fred & Harry suffer from a mysterious & dreadful ailment called Hymophylia [sic] which means that if they cut their fingers they bleed to death. They suffer periodic bouts when they swell up like zeppelins & suffer intense agony. They are S. of Ireland & very witty & literary & will be a great relief from Bal-fast. There will be great advantages in living in Holywood. Being a p.g. might be rather awkward & trying but the Davises are sufficiently unconventional & I know them well enough, & shall be so seldom in, that I think it will be alright. They are nice enough not to be embarrassing about money & water closets & so on.

To Mrs Norah Guthrie at Warwick Lodge, Tunbridge Wells
BBC Belfast. 30 March 1925

> I saw very little of Abingdon & the Davis family yester. as I left for rehearsal of *The Merchant of Venice* & didn't get back till nearly midnight – very tired. *The Merchant* is pretty boring: William Macready & his wife got over from Birmingham, they are the stars and the "Belfast Radio Players" provide the support. Well – Macready is very good as Shylock but his wife is hopeless as Portia. I'm not looking forward to the show – I think Shakespeare acted without the stage is a little lifeless.

Guthrie in a rowing boat on Annaghmakerrig Lake with Flora (later Dame Flora) Robson and 'Migsie' Davis, 1925.

To Mrs Norah Guthrie at Warwick Lodge, Tunbridge Wells

Annaghmakerrig, Newbliss, Co. Monaghan. 3 May 1925

I am here with Hubert [Butler] – it's been a soaking day so brisk walking has been the programme – over the hill behind Reilly's and round the glen road, thro' Drumgole & home via Crappagh & the Bog Garden. Primroses still marvellous. Did you hear *Victoriana*? The actors thought it very funny but I'm not certain that it quite "got across".

Flora [Robson] arrives first thing on Mon. & stays on until the show [*Iphigeneia*] on Thurs. Rehearsing will be endless. I'm having a sort of Répétition Générale on Wed. & inviting about 6 people to listen on a loud speaker & criticise – 2 of the university professors, Bertie Scott, two of the wireless traders & some other zany not yet decided upon. Prof. Henry of Queen's University will broadcast a lecture on the play the day before the show. The Davis ménage is still the greatest success – they are quite my style!

To Mrs Norah Guthrie at Warwick Lodge, Tunbridge Wells

BBC Belfast. 16 May 1925

Iphigeneia passed off very well, I think. Having left at once [for Annaghmakerrig] I heard very few comments; but if not popular it was undoubtedly beautifully acted. Professor Henry came to several rehearsals & helped me with advice & he was delighted with it & paid Flora a very charming & quite sincere compliment. Flora was splendid and fully justified having her over. All the Company were most enthusiastic about her perf. and she has also gone down extremely well at Davisland.

The Davises & Flora just raved about everything [at Annagh-makerrig] & enjoyed it immensely, as I did. We took a lot of photos which May developed the moment we returned yesterday (characteristic, that is!). Flora departed via Liverpool last night having much enjoyed the trip & having been a complete success.

To Mrs Norah Guthrie at Warwick Lodge, Tunbridge Wells
BBC Belfast. Undated, June 1925

I wish you had heard the "Shakespeare Night". In the Studio the actual acts went off quite decently but the ensemble was killed, to my mind, by the slowness of Thompson (announcer) & Godfrey Brown (conductor) who waited ages & just let all the swing & pace out of the show. I had arranged music [BBC Belfast Wireless Orchestra] to introduce & conclude each scene so that the speaking should not come quavering in indefinitely & peter off into silence at the end – well! between them Brown & Thompson caused pauses of 20-25 seconds between acting & music so that all the pace & verve which I had worked hard to force upon the players was negatived by these delays. But it was very well thought of in 31 Linenhall Street & my stock has risen considerably in the eyes of Brown, Thompson & Co!

To Mrs Norah Guthrie at Warwick Lodge, Tunbridge Wells
BBC Belfast. Undated, June 1925

The *Victoriana* has absolutely hit the mark! There have been floods of letters from all types & classes, well over 300 most of which say "On behalf of my family" or "At the request of a party of listeners". Am trying to brace myself up to the bold venture of asking "Head Office" [BBC London] to give me a job as a free lance to exploit new ideas.

To Mrs Norah Guthrie at Warwick Lodge, Tunbridge Wells

BBC Belfast. Undated, June 1925

> Haven't heard from Jeffrey, the Dramatic Man [BBC London]. I sent back his 8 rubbishy plays with a very brief note saying that "none of them seem suitable".

To Dr Thomas Guthrie at Warwick Lodge, Tunbridge Wells

BBC Belfast. Undated, June 1925

> Rushed down to the "city" to keep an appointment with Herbert Scott to drink midday coffee at his Club. This was in order to have a confidential chat about my future. He thinks that I have the qualifications to make me "A Great Singer" – all the same thing that Gustave Garcia said. Well! I think he's genuine because he very much endorsed my feeling that I should be a great goat to chuck the B.B.C. overboard to follow a will o' the wisp hope of becoming a successful singer. But it's encouraging to know he thinks I have a gift that's worth developing seriously.

A difficulty was emerging with Jeffrey, the head of drama in London, who was prevaricating about giving national airtime to Guthrie's *Victoriana* programme, the unofficial story being that he was loath to promote the work of junior colleagues. In due course *Victoriana* was broadcast in all regions to much acclaim. Guthrie's portrait by James Sleator, exhibited at the Rodman Gallery, Belfast, cannot be traced.

To Peggy Guthrie at Warwick Lodge, Tunbridge Wells

BBC Belfast. 1 July 1925

> Isn't it fearful to think I shall be a quarter century old tomorrow – all my girlish bloom is fast disappearing. My portrait is intensely exciting – such a nice little high-class low-class individual called Slater [James Sleator, later RHA], Orpen's favourite pupil, dressed like a musical comedy "Bohemian". The portrait is like all my pictures – distressingly Noble!! Such a fine, healthy, good young man: one who would only say the traditional "boo" if the goose were pecking his little lame mother's bad legs.

To Peggy Guthrie at Warwick Lodge, Tunbridge Wells

BBC Belfast. Undated, June 1925

My rumpus with the awful Jeffrey is assuming titanic dimensions. My request for an interview in London has not been granted. I wrote & got Major Scott to sign a long document politely summing up the situation, stating grievances and asking for advice & remedies. A week elapses & then the creature sends most unsatisfactory replies. Meanwhile Godfrey Brown on a visit to Glasgow blew my trumpet to Millar Craig [BBC Controller] & hinted that Jeffrey was being difficult. Miller told him that Jeffrey is an impossible person and the only thing was to have a row with him.

To Mrs Norah Guthrie at Warwick Lodge, Tunbridge Wells

BBC Belfast. Undated, autumn 1925

"The Season" in Belfast begins about September – the Lady Mayoress gives a reception (lemonade & Bath buns), there's a subscription thé-dansant in The Carleton Café & the Police Temperance Fife Band gives a recital in the Cripples' Institute, so you see it is all very gay. Belfast is wonderfully repulsive. It has neither the smartness of Brighton nor the un-vulgarity of Doohat. It's just immensely semi-educated & undistinguished. Kind hearts are all very well but one longs for an occasional Coronet and Norman Blood to mitigate the oppressiveness of the Simple Faith of the Belfast Presbyterians! Fortunately I live (as paying guest) with absolutely charming people who make an entire difference to the landscape.

I wonder if you want to come over to Annaghmakerrig sometime? I was there the Sunday before last & I don't think I have ever seen anywhere in the world so beautiful. Melancholy it certainly is, but that really enhances its charm. It would be frightful if there were smart manservants and bobbing lodge-women & individuals who kept things clean – you can get all those at the Metropole at Brighton. Whereas half the "atmosphere" of Annagh-ma-kerrig is the inevitable resignation of artificial things to their decay.

To Dr Thomas Guthrie at Warwick Lodge, Tunbridge Wells

BBC Belfast. Undated, probably late 1925

The whole place [Annaghmakerrig] cries aloud for a resident owner who will keep things up to the mark. Personally I think you and Mum could be very happy there & would find it an absorbing occupation – & not by any means such a desperate fight with nature as Mum seems inclined to imagine. But, honestly, if you retire in 1927, *what* is the alternative? – a "little place" in Surrey or Hampshire near a golf links with colonels'-club talk & bridge parties: or a very small country Residence in some remoter part? This latter seems to have all the disadvantages of A-kerrig as regards inaccessibility & none of the ties of association. Honestly, with motors, radio, etc, living in Annagh-ma-kerrig is not going to be at all remote and presumably you aren't going to be so poor that you won't be able to afford frequent trips to London, abroad, etc. Then you will have constant occupation even when you are both old.

Eddy Daley [farm steward] is, as you probably know, just married to the eldest Potts niece and I was introduced to the bride who looks like a Sunday School child & was so overcome with coyness she just turned away her head & held out a hand to be shaken like a small infant – rather sweet!

Finally, there is what is to me most important of all – the attachment of ownership. Annagh-ma-kerrig is a definite "living with the soil". I wish you were over here to discuss.

To Mrs Norah Guthrie at Warwick Lodge, Tunbridge Wells

BBC Belfast. 20 September 1925

Christopher [Scaife] is due here tomorrow. He is going straight to Cambridge to play in a Repertory Company under the banner of Mr Horne. I feel if it prospers there may in time be an opening for me there because A.B. Horne was quite impressed by my production of *Mirandolina* [Oxford].

Guthrie with Christopher Scaife and Cousin Norah ('Peter') Kesteven at Annaghmakerrig, 1926.

To Mrs Norah Guthrie at Warwick Lodge, Tunbridge Wells

Abingdon, Holywood, Co. Down. Late September 1925

> Luckily, Christopher & Davisland took to each other like anything: but he spent nearly all his time "in town" with me – and we talked and talked indefinitely – trying to exchange the impressions of two years – great fun & very tiring: fortunately our friendship seems to wear well!

To Mrs Norah Guthrie at Warwick Lodge, Tunbridge Wells

BBC Belfast. Undated, post 11 November 1925

> The Armistice business in Whitehall [Dedication of Cenotaph] must have been very impressive. But I do wish people would really make it a commemoration for *all* those who died doing their duty faithfully instead of blowing about "Our Glorious Dead" – the German dead were just as glorious & it makes me so cross to see the whole thing made of thinking hatefully of "those Germans".

To Dr & Mrs Guthrie at Warwick Lodge, Tunbridge Wells

BBC Belfast. 10 March 1926

> I really have had enough of Belfast & feel it's beginning to permeate me & steep me in provincialism & rather bitter dullness. My ideas as

to what I want are definitely crystalising. As always, I want – and am fully determined to be – a dramatic producer. It's the one job I really feel I could do well. I believe if I go about it sensitively & persistently I can get producing work from the B.B.C. I believe if I get the work I can make a success of it. If the future of b'cast plays is as interesting as I imagine it will be, I shall stick to Radio. If it's likely to be a dead end artistically I ought – given adequate luck & supposing I'm not overestimating my own talent – at the end of 10-15 years to step over to theatre or films; and to have saved enough money to be able to pick and choose a little.

To Mrs Norah Guthrie at Warwick Lodge, Tunbridge Wells

BBC Belfast. Undated, probably June 1926

My new play [for radio, untitled] is getting on – I'm not sure if it's any good. I seem to write farce much better than comedy or "drama" – as soon as I try to be serious my dialogue becomes tedious or rhetorical & melodramatic. I have a desperate tendency to caricature & exaggerate. Am inclined to wonder whether I should try to suppress this or whether it wouldn't be more reasonable just to allow my enjoyment of the fantastic and grotesque to express itself to the full.

Guthrie was finding Belfast confining and was watching for opportunities elsewhere. He made a trip to Glasgow to talk to the congenial BBC executive Millar Craig: there were no vacant positions but he was introduced to Glen MacKemmie, chairman of the Scottish National Players who were looking for a new producer. In due course Guthrie was offered the position. Curiously, his recent meeting with Christopher Scaife led to his appointment as A.B. Horne's producer at the Festival Theatre in Cambridge in 1928.

To Mrs Norah Guthrie at Warwick Lodge, Tunbridge Wells

BBC Belfast. Undated, July 1926

Heard today from Scotland. Nat. Players definitely offering – so am writing to resign from B.B.C., still registering reluctant departure & tremendous nobility! Oh I'm so pleased & still think it's the best thing to do.

To Dr & Mrs Guthrie at Warwick Lodge, Tunbridge Wells

BBC Belfast. Undated, probably August 1926

At ¼ to 4 I arrived at The Wire[7] for the Presentation Scene to find the place humming with people. I don't know who wasn't there – the entire orchestra – most of the acting people – most of the Childrens' Hour people – & various odd singers, pianists & the like: most touching. The ceremony was fearful – there were speeches, semi-arch semi-sentimental by Godfrey Brown on behalf of the Station Director who couldn't be present. By Richard Hayward & Charley Kerr on behalf of the Players & by Jack Chambers on behalf of the Ch. Hour. The suitcase was presented by Mrs Eve Kerr with a charming little speech, obviously spontaneous & worth all the others put together. Then I had to reply, & said a few well chosen words which I trust were neither facetious, pompous nor stagily "sincere". It was a devastating ordeal – I have never been so embarrassed in my life – & the only satisfaction gained was from the material splendour of the Suitcase. It's of handsome real leather & strong workmanship – & glitters with an array of dainty toilet requisites.

The Scottish National Players were founded in 1921 in an attempt to do for Scotland what the Abbey Theatre had done for Ireland, producing original plays. It was mainly a touring company undertaking one-night 'stances', mostly evenings of three or four one-act plays; in Glasgow it appeared regularly at the Lyric Theatre for runs of two or three weeks, often with full-length plays. Among the players were Meg Buchannan, Nell Ballantyne, Elliot Mason, Jimmy Allen, James Anderson, Charlie Brooks, James Gibson, Morland Graham, Moultrie Kelsall, Tom Maley and Andrew Stewart, many of whom continued to work with Guthrie in later years; also Ethel Lewis who sang in their 'revues'. Guthrie immediately staged four of their one-act plays – *King of Morven* (A.J. Ferguson), *The Poacher* (John Corrie), *C'est la Guerre* (D. Morland Graham) and *Ayont the Hill* (Corman Simpson).

---

7   Guthrie's name for the British Broadcasting Corporation, i.e. 'wireless'.

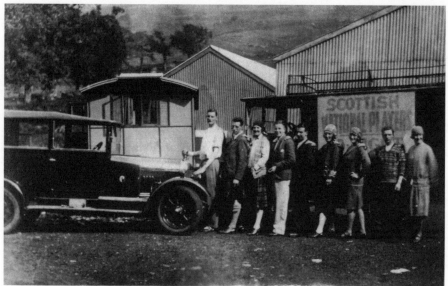

Guthrie with members of the Scottish National Players at an unidentified village hall, 1926.

To Dr & Mrs Guthrie at Warwick Lodge, Tunbridge Wells
No address. Glasgow, Scotland. Undated, September 1926

Glasgow is immense – one had no idea it was so huge – & it struck me as being much more prosperous & glittering than poor Belfast – which, with linen, ships, both so bad is in very dicky condition. It was such fearful fun coming up the Clyde, and just as we were near Glasgow down came a vast Cunarder towed by some impudent tugs. We all stood on the deck of my little steamer & said "Oo! did ye ever? – isn't she big? – thon'd be one of them flootin sullahs (floating cities – Tr.)"

To Peggy Guthrie at Warwick Lodge, Tunbridge Wells
120 Kent Road, Glasgow. Undated, September 1926

The Creative Fatherland mellows on acquaintance & I think we shall get on very well. The lodgings too are being a success – very central (only 5 minutes walk to my office & I'm 10 minutes from the Heart of the great city) clean & not too ugly – food fully adequate – attendance by the landlady herself (Mrs Patterson) & her sister (Mrs Wilson) very adequate too – the whole including full board for 42/- a week. They seem very "decent bodies" – both widows of eminently respectable &

beaming appearance. There is also a piano – not too bad a one. My little office at 120 Douglas Street is comfortable and secluded. I expect I shall be there a good deal.

To Mrs Norah Guthrie at Warwick Lodge, Tunbridge Wells
140 Kent Road, Glasgow. 23 September 1926

The Players have *great talent* – no doubt about it – but they are very badly organised & there is a dearth of good plays. But I am full of enthusiasm & still very glad I took the job. I think I'm going to like MacKemmie [Chairman] which is important. Have got two engagements with the B.B.C. & have a good chance of more.

To Mrs Norah Guthrie at Warwick Lodge, Tunbridge Wells
140 Kent Road, Glasgow. 26 October 1926

The plays were really quite a success – the public were quite enthusiastic – on Saturday the house was full to the door & several people had to be turned away. The only failure was *Morwen* which went a bit flat but the other 3 were received riotously, in fact *The Poacher* simply lifted the roof – most satisfactory. Did I tell you that we were doing a special perf. of *Morven* & *C'est la Guerre* for an American [in fact Canadian] newspaper man? Tomorrow will be taken in making arrangements for touring the 4 plays – scenery, lights, props, etc, & rehearsing understudies – all rather tiresome. On Monday the first of the Xmas plays goes into rehearsal.

To Peggy Guthrie at Warwick Lodge, Tunbridge Wells
140 Kent Road, Glasgow. 30 October 1926

Glasgow is immeasurably colder than Belfast – it's uncomfortable but bracing – but it's rather awkward being so short of coal.[8] It means we can only have occasional fires in the lodgings. However, by breakfasting in bed & lunching in overcoats we get over the difficulty. Davisland are cutting down trees in their garden for firewood. I wonder if we should be sending up trees from A'kerrig & selling firewood in Belfast?

---

8   The General Strike was affecting transport and supplies.

To Peggy Guthrie at Warwick Lodge, Tunbridge Wells

140 Kent Road, Glasgow. 4 November 1926

The Provand's Lordship [ancient city building] performance was quite a success. The Canadian newspaper critic [Lawrence Mason] declares himself more impressed by anything since his first acquaintance with the Irish Players – but I think that is largely gush. He was a fat little commonplace person & made a little speech about Bonds of Empire & The Old Country & Fine Old Traditions – just the normal muck. Really the plays went quite well & with ingeniously "natural" lighting (rigged with safety pins, elastic bands by self & Elliot M.) in that lovely old room it all looked very stylish & tasty.

To Mrs Norah Guthrie at Warwick Lodge, Tunbridge Wells

On tour at Bridge of Allan. 5 November 1926

We – Andrew Stewart, Elliot Mason & I – have been here since morning getting things ready for our show tonight. Quite a good hall & quite a decent stage, only serious set-back being no electric light – only gas footlights & a bunch in the centre high up, eked out by an acetylene lamp used as a "spot". We're resting in the hotel awaiting the arrival of the company – then High T & off to the show. We are playing *Morven* & *C'est la Guerre* – the latter put in at the last moment owing to illness.

To Peggy Guthrie at Warwick Lodge, Tunbridge Wells

140 Kent Road, Glasgow. 12 November 1926

So glad Hubert's visit has been so pleasant – he is a terribly nice creature: you seemed to be having fun. It seems I've been in Glasgow for *months*! Am so happy & can't think how I tolerated The Wire for 2 years – it *was* rather an effort.

To Mrs Norah Guthrie at Warwick Lodge, Tunbridge Wells

140 Kent Road, Glasgow. 21 November 1926

Kilmarnock – a big industrial town S of Glasgow. "The Staff", i.e. Elliot, Andrew Stewart, a scenery man and I left at 9.30 & spent a terrific day marking and tearing in the "Co-Operative Hall". There was nothing – no curtain, lights, not even a place to drive nails into! Everything that could go wrong did go wrong, & as the people were beginning to surge into the hall we were still swarming about on beams – a dire day, maybe at the time, but amusing in retrospect.

On Wed. I had a long rehearsal of *The Sergeant Major* [by William Chapman] for Xmas – not a good play but I think it will be quite possibly a popular success – it's "so natural"!

Thursday addressed the "Glasgow Business Club" at a luncheon. It "went" excessively well in the room – peals of laughter at the right points. Unfortunately "the press" were there & my "little remarks" – "Producer slags Glasgow refinement" – emerged next day in a blaze of publicity, even a reference in the News on the wireless! All the highly-coloured bits picked out omitting the bits that showed I was being arch! Really very embarrassing & will doubtless have made enemies. Moreover, I have learnt my lesson – the moral is twofold: (a) Always ascertain if reporters are present before speaking; (b) Don't be arch in Scotland.

To Dr & Mrs Guthrie at Warwick Lodge, Tunbridge Wells
c/o Scottish National Players, Glasgow. 2 December 1926

This is to wish you a happy Xmas. I wish we could be together but it can't be helped. I'm afraid I shall enjoy coping at the Lyric Theatre but I do wish we could have been at Annaghmakerrig. Hubert is coming to spend Xmas with me. I've no gifts for any of you! When this tyranny is over & my brain begins to work again on everyday lines I shall think of some tasteful novelties, meanwhile you will just have to make shift with my *fondest love*.

To Dr & Mrs Guthrie at Warwick Lodge, Tunbridge Wells
c/o Scottish National Players, Glasgow. 30 December 1926

Well I had the most hectic Xmas on record. Hubert arrived on Thurs. evening – he sleeps in the second bed in my room. On Friday we coped from 9 a.m. at the [Lyric] theatre, most fatiguing & cold & dispiriting. Everyone knew *The Sergeant Major* was boring in the extreme & my setting wasn't a high success either – rather too bleak & modern & out of key with the play. Next day (Xmas Day) we were again at the theatre all morning. I had a lunch engagement – a vast turkey meal in the middle of which I had to leave for the theatre for the dress rehearsal of *The Glen is Mine* [by John Brandane], another cold dispiriting affair. At night we played *C'est la Guerre* and *The Glen* to an absolutely packed & enthusiastic house. The last act of *The Glen* nearly killed the staff as when changing the set the roof scenery collapsed. It might have been a very nasty accident but mercifully ropes & things held & we were able to ring up after 22 minutes (instead of 12). Rehearsed *Count Albany* [by Douglas Carswell] at night & we finished up with very pleasant supper at Masonland.

To Mrs Norah Guthrie at Warwick Lodge, Tunbridge Wells

c/o Scottish National Players, Glasgow. 11 January 1927

Christopher [Scaife] has been up – & Hubert is still here. C. goes to Egypt for a year, next week, as asst. Editor of the Egyptian Gazette, at Alexandria. I think he's mad to go – he doesn't really expect to like the work much, it's mainly to see Egypt. He seems quite resigned to worldly unsuccess & I really think he may justify himself as a writer. He arrived (from Dublin) on Fri. morning – in the evening he and Hubert went to a panto, I to the S.N.P. and thence to the B.B.C. Fancy Ball. Elliot wore a white shroud & I wore Death & the Demon Vice & operating gloves & a long black trailer attached to one finger. The appearance made a profound sensation. When we arrived at the Dance Hall the page boy shrieked aloud (in real fear!). We won the prize for the Best Gent & Best Lady.

Christopher came & saw the plays & was much impressed by the good acting, & then I read him my play [probably the unperformed *Emmy*] & discussed it at length and were not bedded till 3.

To Dr & Mrs Guthrie and Peggy Guthrie at Warwick Lodge, Tunbridge Wells

c/o Scottish National Players, on tour. Undated, early 1927

This is a dreadful day of wrath – dress rehearsals are so terrifying – & the awful cope of getting the stage ready – panicking about time, about falling scenery, gaping curtains, borders hung askew, lights that are not masked. A million things to remember & to do & only one day to do it in: you see, we can never get into the theatre till the day before the first performance. They're ready for me on the stage so I must go. *Mirandolina* greatly spoiled by having to manage with a substitute Captain Ripafratta – Xopher's part at Oxford.

To Peggy Guthrie at Warwick Lodge, Tunbridge Wells
140 Douglas Street, Glasgow. 9 February 1927

I am in the dumps as *Mirandolina* [Lady Gregory after Goldoni] & *Lover* [Sierra] have been a failure. A damning – & quite intelligently damning – press, little enthusiasm in the audience & just appalling booking – we're going to lose lots of money. *Mirandolina is* rather bad. M. herself is charming; the wee servant most amusing & I like Fabrizio (though the press slag him) but the rest are pretty bad. But *The Lover* is, I think, beautifully done – both amusing & touching – yet the people last night *didn't laugh once.* It's very disappointing & financially may cripple us for development next season. I'm a trifle vexed too that none of the papers mention my settings – which are, in my opinion – pretty, and *The Lover* one rather clever. It's all rather depressing but these things are, as we know dear, sent by a higher power to try us, & in 2 years, or even 2 months, time will not seem terribly significant. But of course we are going ahead this summer. I'm free in May – do let us spend some time together – Annaghmakerrig if possible.

To Mrs Norah Guthrie at Warwick Lodge, Tunbridge Wells
140 Douglas Street, Glasgow. Undated, April 1927

We broadcast *The King of Morven* from Edinboro' – it didn't go very well – but John Rae drove us back in the motor which was jolly. *Victoriana* is due on Monday – it is very under-rehearsed but will, I think, be quite funny. *Ayont the Hill* [by Cormac Simpson] & *The Curtain Raiser* [Anon] open on Tues 22. And Greenock begins on April 18.

To Peggy Guthrie at Warwick Lodge, Tunbridge Wells
King's Theatre, Greenock, Scotland. Undated, April 1927

We're having a simply *disastrous* time at Greenock – an immense theatre – & the returns tonight were £16.10.03 of which we get 50/- –

isn't it calamitous? Our play [*The Glen is Mine* by John Brandane] is considered too highbrow, too quiet for Greenock! Things are so bad that they can but mend!

To Mrs Norah Guthrie at Warwick Lodge, Tunbridge Wells

c/o Masonland, Emslee, Hillhead Street, Glasgow. Undated, autumn 1927

It was just beastly going off [from Tunbridge Wells] & leaving you so seedy. Not since schooldays have I hated leaving home so much – & wished so much that I were working near at hand & could just be in and out quite frequently.

The new Scottish National Players office is a great improvement on Douglas Street. As far as I can see it will be a pretty strenuous season. Rehearsals begin tomorrow evening. *Weir of Hermiston* [by A.W. Yuill after Stevenson] on Oct 14. *Britain's Daughter* [by Gordon Bottomley] a month later; &, as well as that, Belfast for 3 nights with the summer show and 4 performances in different towns of *Ayont the Hill* and *The Glen is Mine* to be rehearsed for a week and then launched on tour. Indeed I hardly know how we can get through such a complicated programme.

This tour is being enormous fun & quite invaluable theatrical experience. I now feel that nothing will daunt me in the way of halls. We rise at 6 a.m. & are seldom bedded by 1 a.m. The lorry has to be loaded with the camp things – then reloaded again on leaving the theatre – then at the camp – then reloaded again on leaving the theatre. This week has been a financial success though we had a fearful flop at Pitlochry (only £7) & at Killen, although the hall was full it was so tiny that we only drew £12. However, Grantown-on-Spey brought us £30 & Cullen & Callender £20 apiece. Everywhere audiences have been most appreciative & the show improves a little each night.

It's amusing how the wireless has helped us. Everywhere in these country places people have come because they have heard either the Players or Ethel & me on The Wire. It has all gone just much better than I expected.

To Dr & Mrs Guthrie and Peggy Guthrie at Warwick Lodge, Tunbridge Wells

c/o Scottish National Players, on tour. Undated, 1927

No, we didn't go to Annaghmakerrig – there wasn't a chance, we were far too much entertained in Belfast. All Sunday we were down on Strangford Lough in Bertie Scott's boat – lovely.

On Tuesday we triumphed at Lossiemouth – delightful & vast audience which included Ramsay MacDonald [Prime Minister]. He came round afterwards & was most affable, & may, I think, be rather a help in screwing future monies out of Carnegie! Last night at Braemar was a great success, tons of guests from Five Arms Hotel in sapphires who thought it *so* quaint & artistic, & the back benches full of rustics who gave loud screams at *The Poacher* [by John Corrie]. Am writing far too much about this tour but, as you can imagine, it is pretty much on the brain. It *has* been such a good experience.

I was so distressed to hear your eyes were same as ever. Don't give up heart – just go on determining that they will improve.

To Mrs Nora Guthrie, Warwick Lodge, Tunbridge Wells

120 Kent Road, Glasgow. Undated, 1927

Weir of Hermiston [after Stevenson] draws alarmingly near – fortnight on Monday & it isn't beginning to be ready – the booking is very poor and I think they've managed the advertisements atrociously. I don't think it'll be a bad show but I've worked at it too long now to have any sense of proportion left. I know it now for a poor, but possibly effective, play – just "costume": where it quotes from Stevenson it has style and sweep; where the adapter [A.W. Yuill] relies on himself it is very fustian. I'm putting in a new number, "The Two Crows", a macabre ballad & tune.

Went Tuesday night with David [MacKemmie] & Elliot [Mason] when there was no rehearsal to the theatre – *Their Wife*, with a very brilliant cast "prior to London". It was just awful – not the least funny, not even vulgar. Even Glasgow wasn't very much amused. Athene Seyler was brilliant in the stupidest part. [Nigel] Playfair's production just seemed to me to fall utterly between two or in this case three stools.

Guthrie with the actress Elliot Mason on tour with the Scottish National Players, 1927.

I do not like Glasgow – & I don't think I like the Scotch. I respect their logicality, their candour & pertinacity. And above all their energy – people here never seem to flag – Elliot really isn't very exceptional – but then I think they only keep going so long because never at any one moment do they exist very violently – they do not indulge themselves in bursts of enthusiasm, or use any of their vitality in emotional concentration. They are certainly admirable but not on the whole very likeable. Oh the stodginess of their innumerable poky flats! – so safe! The climate makes existence such a struggle that it's no wonder the inhabitants are hard & dour & materialistic; & no wonder that they look (& are) so coarse. And it's so repellent to know that these squalid precipitous streets are just a filthy crust upon the hills of the Clyde. And yet it's *alive*.

To Christopher Scaife in Alexandria, Egypt

c/o Scottish National Players, Glasgow. 19 November 1927

We have suddenly plunged catastrophically into the whirlwind. My father is very, very ill and the doctors do not think he will recover – it may be weeks, months, possibly three years – a growth in the lung.

My mother is going blind, suffering from the same mysterious disease that has been troubling her for some years. It has finally lodged itself in her eyes – she can hardly see now – cannot read, can barely write and cannot go out in daylight even in black goggles without real suffering. I was down in Tunbridge Wells last week. One can do absolutely nothing.

One of Guthrie's many productions at the Cambridge Festival Theatre: Flora Robson in Pirandello's *Six Characters in Search of an Author*, 1929.

3 SCOURGE OF THE LEADING LADIES

Dr Thomas Clement Guthrie died of cancer on 18 February 1928. Two years later Mrs Norah Guthrie, now partially blind, returned to her family home, Annaghmakerrig, in Co. Monaghan: this was also a return to their roots for the Irish domestic staff. She engaged a companion-housekeeper: Miss Ethel Worby, known as 'Bunty', a nurse from the Tunbridge Wells Hospital, who remained a household member till her death in 1962. Tyrone Guthrie left the Scottish National Players at the end of 1927, partly to be near his ailing parents, accepting a contract with the philanthropic impresario A.B. Horne (aka 'Anmer Hall') at the Cambridge Festival Theatre, where he directed plays by Chekov, Euripides, Ibsen, Molière, Pirandello, Shakespeare, Toller and others. He engaged Flora Robson and Robert Donat among his leading players. The paucity of letters suggests that he visited his parents frequently; and after his father's death was often with his mother and sister Peggy until their move to Ireland. He accepted a six-month engagement in Canada to produce a radio series on Scots and Irish immigration. In 1930 Peggy married his friend Hubert Butler at Aghabog Church in Co. Monaghan.

To Mrs Norah & Peggy Guthrie, probably still at Warwick Lodge, Tunbridge Wells
Festival Theatre, Cambridge. Undated, early 1929

> Cambridge is not, I think, a very attractive town. The colleges & "backs" are heavenly but the actual town isn't nearly as fine as Oxford. It's poky – never any coup d'oeil and the country around is so dismally dull and flat and seeded with bungaloathsome architecture – one yearns for Ireland, for greenness and dampness and turf smoke and – above all – silence. But oh I am enjoying being back to regular work; but I'm afraid tho' manually incompetent and mechanically subnormal

my brain is really a *technical* one – I am fertile of ways and means of expression but not of ideas to express.

Trying in the extreme laboriously to prepare a roaring farce – trying over and over again and over again that seemingly funny business with the soda-water syphon and the ear-trumpet so as to get the timing exactly right – yesterday we did literally spend a solid ¾ of an hour rehearsing one bit of business that in performance may possibly take 2½ seconds.

Have had one or two nice letters about *Squirrel's Cage* [radio play] but as yet no sign of a cheque from the B.B.C.

To Mrs Norah Guthrie, probably now at Annaghmakerrig, Newbliss, Co Monaghan, Ireland
Festival Theatre, Cambridge. Undated, autumn 1930

The Canadian National people came on Saty. & I had hour-long chats with them – Mr England & Mr Weir, the very grand boss. They were flatteringly anxious to have me & to hear views & opinions but think it almost essential that whoever goes should go at once. In any case I think it would be unwise to go to Canada at this juncture because there's quite a likelihood of Anmer Hall starting up a show "in tahn".

To Mrs Norah Guthrie, probably at Annaghmakerrig
Festival Theatre, Cambridge. Undated, autumn 1930

They (Canadian duo) came down yesterday & really it all seems very possible. Six months is really a very different kettle of fish than a year & they promise a certain amount of travelling about. I discussed it all fully with Anmer Hall. He is very seriously considering taking over & converting the St James Picture House [Westminster] but would not likely be opening till autumn – so you see if I got back in July that would be perfect, in fact too good to be true.

To Mrs Norah Guthrie at an unspecified address in England
Festival Theatre, Cambridge. Undated, 1930

Now I'm going to write what will be difficult for the person who reads you this letter because it's so private, but I must say it. You are *never, never, never* to feel that your work in the world is done because it *isn't.* Just because you can't be doing all the things you do so well and that you long to be doing, it doesn't mean for a second that you are useless. Peggy and I and Aunt Sue and others too – many others – are extraordinarily dependent on you – not for what you do but for what you are. P & I are quite strong dominant personalities but you wouldn't believe how much we lean on you; just because we are now (isn't it awful?) "grown ups" and no longer need to be given our baths and have Benjamin Bunny read to us (oh I know how often you wish those days were back again) that doesn't mean we don't need you; and just because we're Awful Modern Young People who argue and don't wear gloves, you know it doesn't mean that we think we can stand on our own legs. You can and do give us so much with your love and belief in us; and just because you have lost so much you have so much to give. Partly by example: your grit and courage has truly inspired us – yes! inspired – tho' I wish the results of the inspiration were more apparent. And partly because suffering has made something wonderful of you and given you a power and influence that I see can only belong to people with hearts that are warm enough to be terribly sensitive to sorrow but who have the fortitude and the faith to resist being broken or embittered by their suffering.

I'm saying all this so that you may know that you can never be "useless" – and when you feel old and depressed and lonely try and remember. And when (as I know I often do) I seem to be hard and unsympathetic and angular and impersonal and a lot of other beastly things – it doesn't mean that underneath I don't just dote on you, and admire you, and depend on you. And remember this too, when I feel depressed and hate and despise myself I feel – and I know – that I must be *some* good because I have yours and Daddy's blood in my veins.

To Mrs Norah Guthrie at Annaghmakerrig

Radio Dept, Canadian National Railways, McGill Street, Montreal. 26 January 1931

I am very rich so if the [Annaghmakerrig] farm ac/s are really very low and the dividends not paying, will you not borrow some money. I have about £100 on hand at the moment and I think it would be a pity to "draw in our horns" over the farm as it is not being extravagantly run and any horn-drawing on our part will mean either men out of employment or letting the land go even worse to rushes and ruin than it has already but please don't allow economy to either the place or the employees, because I have the money & would *like* it to be spent that way.

To Mrs Norah Guthrie at Annaghmakerrig

Radio Dept, Canadian National Railways, McGill Street, Montreal. 5 February 1931

Merill [Canadian writer] slow with scripts. I've just interviewed processions of the most unlikely & astounding would-be artistes: dumpling curates from Presbyterian college; faded "lady elocutionists"; the Gaelic professor at McGill (a sort of modern dress Rob Roy with a red beard & thick thick spectacles); pallid bank clerks from Inverness; roundabout wee buddies from the suburbs whose childhood was spent "among the pecks on Skay"; tipsy retired music-hall artistes who breathe great gusts of gin & swear they can sing Harry Lauder songs "so ye'd juist swear it was Lauder himsel'"; homesick Glaswegians whose eyes shine with pleasure to hear that I know Queen's Park, etc etc. Out of all I've collected a cast *of sorts*.

To Miss Peggy Guthrie at Annaghmakerrig

Radio Dept, Canadian National Railways, McGill Street, Montreal. 13 February 1931

My *Scots Settlers* [radio instalment] went off last night with *éclat* – but mercy me the tussle! The Scots did gallantly – my wee leading man was very sweet – a small dark meagre insurance clerk – intelligent in an infinitely plodding way – utterly determined to do well – wholly sincere. Technically his performance was entirely spoon-fed by me – every pause, every change of inflection, every change of tempo, every *spark* of *imagination* was mine but he had the gift of making the ideas his own & imbuing them with his own loveable sincerity & grit & sweetly stodgy Scottish Burr quality & in the end gave a really creditable show. The culminating bother was when at 11 yesterday morning (the day of the show) a strange doctor phoned to say that Mr Young (one of the cast) had rheumatic fever & he could not think of allowing him to appear. Young was only playing a small part & the gap could have been filled easily in London or Glasgow but here it was a very different kettle of fish. However, about after 20 phone calls & 8 interviews I filled the gap & rehearsed the man from 4 – 6; dress rehearsal 6.30–9.30 & perf. from 10 – 11. On to a party given by one of the cast & bed at 2.30. Today is not awfully biz. I've an interview with the Christian Science Monitor, about 12 auditions this afternoon, a singing lesson at 4.30 & am dining with people called Aylmer at 7.0. You see I'm getting quite social!

Did you listen to the Pope b'casting yesterday? A wee bit thrilling to think of it ringing all round the world & to think of the myriad groups of wondering, interested, expectant, disappointed auditors.

To Mrs Norah Guthrie at Annaghmakerrig

Radio Dept, Canadian National Railways, McGill Street, Montreal. Probably 13 February 1931

Have heard from Anmer Hall – definitely he is going ahead; definitely wants me to continue with him. It's all very thrilling, dates still uncertain. Flora [Robson] had two offers & is going to play in *Desire under the Elms* by O'Neill – an extremely fine part; it's only at the Gate but still it is quite a good opportunity. I think she's sure to go a long way in spite of not being pretty.

To Mrs Norah Guthrie in London

Radio Dept, Canadian National Railways, McGill Street, Montreal. 18 February 1931

Went to *The Apple Cart* [Shaw] yesterday afternoon, more from a sense of duty than anything else. But in the end I loved it. The play didn't really seem so bad – it's shamelessly careless but has a lot of witty interesting observations on current events & opinions. One realised how cruelly the London show had suffered from those appalling scenes & common silly costumes – also how bad the production had been. This was beautifully put on & very adequately produced & some of the acting was excellent. An English & Canadian Coy. – packed house, screams of mirth, great enthusiasm – isn't it wonderful – isn't he clever – hasn't he a wonderful wonderful wonderful *brain*! They always speak of him here in full as George Ber*nard* Shaw.

To Peggy Guthrie at Annaghmakerrig

Radio Dept, Canadian National Railways, McGill Street, Montreal. 18 February 1931

Please tell Mrs G her typing is well improved & spacing *very* well. She still has a slight tendency to hit any letter but it doesn't make it in the least hard to make out the sense – indeed it's rather endearing to read that "Poggy & Jibert are djinp preat wort 6n thu bog graden [Peggy & Hubert are doing great work in the bog garden]"– it has all the trill of a translation from the Russian via the German.

To Mrs Norah Guthrie at Annaghmakerrig

Radio Dept, Canadian National Railways, McGill Street, Montreal. Probably 25 February 1931

Monday I lunched with Rupert Caplan who acts for us here. He is Jewish – very clever; has played in N.Y. – was engaged for *Street Scene* [play by Elmer Rice] in London but had to come back here owing to family illness. I find him extremely interesting – quite a new social, religious, racial background.

To Mrs Norah Guthrie at Annaghmakerrig

Radio Dept, Canadian National Railways, McGill Street, Montreal. 28 February 1931

They want me, if here in summer, to go all over Canada arranging broadcasts of local folklore. It would be wonderfully interesting work & a great chance to see the country. I've written Anmer Hall fully.

To Peggy Guthrie at Annaghmakerrig

Radio Dept, Canadian National Railways, McGill Street, Montreal. 10 March 1931

Isn't it a thrill about Anmer Hall's plans? Offer to direct Bridie's *Anatomist* at the Westminster & a great matter that I won't have to race away from here!

To Mrs Norah Guthrie at Annaghmakerrig

New York, no address. Undated, early June 1931

Tyrone Power II [cousin] came in & lunched with me. He was more than half drunk & is now, I gather, rarely otherwise. The conversation was mildly maudlin reminiscence of "the old days" or boastful theatrical talk – "When I played the moody Dane, laddie, they cheered me to the echo – the students drew my carriage home". Very sad & dreadful. He reminded me very much in appearance of Uncle Jack.

Tyrone Guthrie and Judith Bretherton at the time of their engagement in 1930.

Guthrie spent some weeks travelling in North America at the expense of his sponsor, Canadian National Railways, incidentally making valuable contacts for the future. His correspondence with Judith Bretherton of Tunbridge Wells does not survive but on his return in August 1931 they were married at Aghabog, Co. Monaghan, ending speculation about both Elliot Mason and Flora Robson. They took a small apartment in Lincoln's Inn Fields, London. He directed four plays for Anmer Hall at the Westminster Theatre, three plays at the Arts Theatre, the first production of J.B. Priestley's *Dangerous Corner* at the Lyric and *Richard II* at the Shakespeare Memorial Theatre, Stratford-upon-Avon. In 1932 he received an approach from Lilian Bayliss, co-founder of the Old Vic Theatre, to direct a series of Shakespeare plays there, starting with *Henry VIII* and *Twelfth Night.*

To Mrs Norah Guthrie at Annaghmakerrig

23 Old Buildings, Lincoln's Inn, London WC2. Undated, 1932

> *Dangerous Corner* is coming on all right. On Thursday the young
> man, Derek Williams, decided to give up his part – quite a blessing

as he obviously wasn't happy and wasn't being good – it was all quite gracefully & nicely done & there was no ill feeling either way. We've replaced him with a young man called William Fox who will be v.g. I think, but it meant that rather a lot of time was wasted.

To Mrs Norah Guthrie at Annaghmakerrig
23 Old Buildings, Lincoln's Inn, London WC2. Undated, 1933

We "kept" Judy's birthday yesterday owing to a mistake in the calendar! We had a v. elegant buffet luncheon in the flat – Mr & Mrs Bretherton, Mrs Hubert Butler, & Mr Kenneth Rae were guests – such a success; then we all went to the new René Clair film *A Nous la Liberté* & ADORED IT.

To Mrs Norah Guthrie at Annaghmakerrig
23 Old Buildings, Lincoln's Inn, London WC2. Undated, autumn 1933

Well, *Henry [VIII]* really passed off with great éclat. Not all unqualified success for Charles [Laughton] – personally I think he is excellent in it but Henry is a poor part and few of the critics know enough to dissever the quality of a performance from the quality of a part. Wolsey [Robert Farquharson] not good. Buckingham [Nicholas Hannen] excellent. Athene [Seyler] excellent in a tiny part. Flora [Robson] had a real triumph as Katherine. Her big exit from the trial scene was applauded – and cheered – to the echo, completely held the play up, very disconcerting for poor Charles who had to play the rest of the scene with a slight feeling of anti-climax. On the whole it looks very handsome and grand.

Oh! a nice thing: I slipped into the back of the gallery at yesterday's matinée in Flora's death scene just to see if it was properly audible. Up there I found a great policeman who had looked in to see if all was well – hadn't been able to tear himself away & was standing there weeping – great pear-drops – at the poor dear dying Queen! The Duchess [of York; future Queen Elizabeth] came to a matinée of *The Cherry Orchard*, fairly unofficially but it evidently leaked out because excited women stormed the Ladies' Cloakroom while the Royal Personage was visiting a c*rt**n ap*rtm*nt! Miss Bayliss sent a policeman into the "Ladies" to drive out the excited women. At

The Old Vic Theatre, London, in 1930.

the end we were all lined up on the stage – curtain down – around came Bayliss with H.R.H. I was called out to introduce H.R.H. to all the Company – "This is Miss Athene Seyler. Miss Flora Robson, Mr Charles Laughton" & so on. Quite a nice little thing – very small and rather undistinguished, but a bright & intelligent little face. She was quite nicely and quietly dressed in blue chiffon with a pearl necklace.

To Mrs Guthrie at Annaghmakerrig

23 Old Buildings, Lincoln's Inn, London WC2. Undated, autumn 1933

Katie's [Gielgud][9] criticism of *Henry VIII* very interesting and, from its standpoint, very just. The point she raises is what will always prevent her and people like her from enjoying productions of mine. It's the very "sonority" of "traditional" productions of Shakespeare that I cannot abide – that, to me, robs it of humanity and real meaning. I feel that Shakespeare is essentially a naturalistic writer, that Shakespearian blank verse enables the speaker to slip imperceptibly from prose-speaking to verse-speaking and that

---

9   Katie Gielgud was mother of the actor Jack, later Sir John, Gielgud.

therefore a naturalistic method of verse speaking is indicated. The "traditional" declamatory, rhetorical method is, I think, of French origin derived from Racine who, unlike Shakespeare, was not a naturalistic writer at all, but wrote for a stylized method of delivery. Katie implies that the performance of *Henry VIII* was "undignified" – even rather common. This may be true; personally, I don't think it is in the least common but definitely and consciously avoids that kind of elaborate solemnity that dehumanises the characters & makes them merely very grand dolls. And *I* feel the loss of dignity is more than repaid by the gain in intelligibility, humanity and humour – & is quite justified by the text. Katie says of Flora [Robson] that she seemed merely to "talk" to the Cardinals – instead of declaiming at them – human instead of super-human diction. That implied censure seems to me to be deserving of praise.

Every performance is packed out. I fear the only reason is the personal glamour of Charles Laughton – such is film fame.

To Mrs Norah Guthrie at Annaghmakerrig

Palace Hotel, Zagreb, Yugoslavia. Undated, probably winter 1934–5, Guthries on holiday with Hubert and Peggy Butler

Snow everywhere. And a very low temp. but it is dry & bright. The mountain was a fairyland of crisp snow & trees – Spanish chestnut first, then, higher up, beech and spruce. We have been to a performance of ballet (execrable) at State Theatre & a German film of *Peer Gynt* (enjoyable but not really good; one wouldn't have liked it nearly so much if it had been in English!) as well as endless meetings with friends & acquaintances & visits to museums, cemetery (amazing), churches, etc etc. Our hotel is comfortable & reasonable. The language is quite a tease (not to us especially as Hotel Desk manages a little English & Hubert & my dog German do the rest) but German is by no means universally understood; & the Croatian, contrary to Hubert's expectation, isn't a bit like Russian nor a bit easy to learn. We leave here on Friday evg. I expect Peggy will stay week-end at T. Wells. But the main thing is Peggy does seem OK [expecting Julia]. I don't know what their future plans can be; but it is of course more than one's life is worth to ask.

Having completed his contract with the Old Vic, Guthrie accepted several offers in the West End; although he despised the commercialism and 'star' ethos, the widening of horizons had the beneficial effect of introducing him to leading actors with whom he later enjoyed much rapport. His early West End productions were: *Sweet Aloes* by Joyce Carey with Diana Wynyard; *Viceroy Sarah* (aka Sarah Churchill, Duchess of Marlborough) by Norman Ginsbury with Edith Evans; *Mary Read* by James Bridie with Flora Robson and Robert Donat; *Hervey House* by Jane Cowl with Gertrude Lawrence, Fay Compton and Margaret Rutherford; and *Mrs Nobby Clark* by Murray MacDonald with Marie Ney, Esmé Church and Elliot Mason.

To Mrs Norah Guthrie at Annaghmakerrig

23 Old Buildings, Lincoln's Inn, London, WC2. Undated, late August 1934

> Things here are fairly humming with activity. *Viceroy Sarah* is coming on quite shortly – it is to open at Opera House, Manchester, the week after *Sweet Aloes* which also opens there. The idea is that Murray MacDonald & I should produce *Viceroy* conjointly, he will rehearse mornings & I evenings. Then the company will go to Manchester (where I shall be for *Sweet Aloes* opening in last week of Sept.) for final week's rehearsal. It means a very heavy three weeks for me – *Aloes* rehearsals morning, *Viceroy* in the evening. I feel very perk and equal to it. And it is satisfactory because when the Bridie play [*Mary Read*] is launched we can pack up and leave right away with (D.V.) sufficient money in the pocket to justify a really good holiday & still (D.V.) sufficient Kudos to make it possible to be away for a good spell without dropping right out of the running.
>
> I'm liking Miss Diana Wynyard [in *Sweet Aloes*] – she is compounded of soft chinny chinny ways & dimpled elbows and pouting smiles. But she's a sensible, good-humoured great girl & doesn't put on airs – drives herself about in a small battered lizzie of a car & wears dowdy little Swan & Edgar fwocks which is wise & creditable considering her success is recent and her salary in three figures per week. Her real name is Dorothy Cox & before she became Diana Wynyard Dorothy Cox used to be a games mistress!! Perfect, isn't it? I'm *hating* the management; they are oily & unscrupulous and have no interest except to earn dividends for their foul shareholders.

To Mrs Norah Guthrie at Annaghmakerrig

Harwood, Bonchester Bridge, Hawick, Scotland. Undated, October 1934

Here I am for the week-end! The Mavors are here and I've come up to work with Osborne ["James Bridie"] – a hectic dash. Osborne & I have worked all morning on *Mary Read* which is nearly terrific – I'm a little frightened about it, it's on the verge of being a *great* play, I really believe; but needs a deal of tweaking about – I feel it can be made or marred in production & am feeling a wee bit over-conscious of responsibility.

Sweet Aloes had a v.g. reception in Manchester – they go on from there to Leeds, Glasgow & Edinboro', opening at Wyndham's Theatre in London on October 31st.

To Mrs Norah Guthrie at Annaghmakerrig

23 Old Buildings, Lincoln's Inn, London WC2. Undated, October 1934

I have had such a busy week casting *Mary Read* and going down to B'ham on Friday night to see *Sweet Aloes*. It was v. nice to get a glimpse of Hubert and two glimpses – but no more – of Peggy on their way thro'. The journey seems to be a straightforward affair on main lines all the way. I do hope it turns out to be a successful and happy venture. *Mary Read* promises well – I hope. We have a good cast, I think – Flora Robson & Robert Donat in the leads and v. suitable people in the host of character parts – soldiers, pirates, barmaids, sluts & so on. *Sweet Aloes* comes to Wyndham's on Oct 31. *M. Read* opens at Opera House, Manchester, for a week on Nov 12th and probably during the week after at His Majesty's.

To Mrs Norah Guthrie at Annaghmakerrig

No address or date; towards the close of 1934

I leave for America on Wedy. morning!! Over on one boat (the Berengaria) & back on the next (the Bremen) with five days in in between to cajole & beat Miss Cowl [Jane Cowl, author of *Hervey House*] and I believe I have to chase her either to Chicago or Philadelphia. It's rather amusing & also rather fussing as there's so much on, for instance today I had lunch with Charles Morgan, tea with Maynard Keynes and am dining with Bronson Albery all in a frantic effort to get things moving. However the boat will be a rest if one ain't sick on the way.

To Mrs Norah Guthrie at Annaghmakerrig

His Majesty's Theatre, Haymarket, London. Undated, May 1935

Hervey House passed off with real éclat. There was a brilliant first night audience – all the habitués, a great many theatrical lights + film people, and a large array of countesses & such. Even the newspaper critics have been taken in by it because so much money has been spent. It has been enormously helped by the scenery & the infinite pains we took have been worth while. Much of it does look distinguished and atmospheric – & the quickness of the changes was breathtaking. The curtain would fall and go up again only 20 seconds later on an entirely new elaborate room jammed with props and furniture. It has a sort of miraculous feeling that was exciting; & gave the whole show an air of efficiency and vim.

Jane [Cowl, author and celebrated actress] has been a great worry. She arrived at Paddington from Plymouth on Wednesday at lunchtime. We were all as nervous as if we were to go under gunfire. The train steamed in. Out stepped Lily Cahill – another American actress accompanying Jane – smothered in orchids, gaily waving … greetings, more greetings – no sign of Jane – more greetings – still no sign – more and more greetings not unmixed with anxiety – where is Jane? – Oh still in there, she wasn't quite ready. By this time the platform was empty except for our group and half-a-mile away Jane's enormous pyramid of cabin wardrobes. We all stood breathlessly facing a compartment with closely drawn blinds … pause. Suddenly the blinds flew up – enter a negro maid carrying two jewel cases. Pause. Enter a secretary carrying two more jewel cases. Long pause. Enter Jane – made up as for grand opera – very very very quietly dressed in dark dark grey with a silver fox fur.

She came to rehearsal that night – & considering it was a terrible rehearsal I suppose her behaviour wasn't bad. We had made preparations for coping with her as for a wild beast but she chose the wise & more devastating course of just being Very Beautiful and Very

Sad – horribly and sweetly rude to Joyce [Guthrie's agent] and me about our alterations to her script (which indeed have been drastic), odious about Fay [Compton] who is playing the part she wrote for herself, and would not admit that she liked any of it. However there were no actual scenes or yells or weepings. The company were told (by me) that she was *just delighted* with *everything*. Much the same happened on Thursday over the dress rehearsal. On Friday we again make arrangements for coping with a wild animal. Either Binkie [Beaumont, impresario] or I never left her box – she was practically clamped to her chair except when let out into a special "retiring room" provided behind the box for Royalty. During the interval whiskey in a teacup was brought out of the secretary's bag. Afterwards (at a party given by Binkie) she literally fell upon the supper as if she'd been on a desert island for two days.

We decided that unless the reception were really enormous she mustn't be allowed to take a call. "When the audience starts tearing up the seats", said Binkie, "not before". Eventually the calls for author did become insistent so we shoved her on – Jane acting modest in the wings & saying Oh I simply couldn't, oh I shall die, I'm shaking all over – & then sailing on majestically & making a very egotistical emotional diva's speech of thanks – didn't thank the company, didn't take hands with her leading ladies or pay them any graceful compliment, just primly took the centre of the stage & did Portrait of Beautiful (and gifted) Creature Accepting Homage. But for all her capers she is a highly-coloured and diverting personage that one can't help being grateful for.

To Mrs Norah Guthrie at Annaghmakerrig

23 Old Buildings, Lincoln's Inn, London WC2. Undated, 1935

A propos *Viceroy Sarah* [Norman Ginsbury]: at the Ginsbury's there were never less than 11 of us in the Tudor "Lounge" which is shaped like a coffin & feels about as cold & damp. High Lights: where Miss Rose Ginsbury – one of the younger of the innumerable hook-nosed black-eyed limp tragic sisters – suddenly got up, like a character in Tchekov, apropos of nothing, and said "If I stay in this environment I shall die – die!" in a throbbing contralto. Judy, on being shown over the house, indiscreetly pulled open the drawer of a pretty little bureau, disclosed six live bombs. Believe it or not, *this is true*. But as in Tchekov the general effect was gay – far from gloomy – though the nervous strain of so many gifted and highly temperamental people jammed together in one flimsy villa is very frightening & makes one realise how terribly terribly comfy and padded and sheltered all our lives have been.

Early in 1936 Guthrie was in New York to direct his first production there, *Call It a Day* by Dodie Smith, at the Morosco Theater with Gladys Cooper. The same management engaged him for the Broadway production of *Sweet Aloes*, which had been his greatest financial success in London to date, with a new cast. Back in London he was invited by Hugh ('Binkie') Beaumont to direct *Short Story* by Robert Morley with 'the Queen of the London theatre', Marie Tempest. He also fitted in a work more to his taste, a satirical musical play *The Dance of Death* by W.H. Auden, in London and elsewhere, and some filming for Alexander Korda, which helped pay the bills. He had expectations of being recalled to the Old Vic, and was indeed appointed in the late spring after which he immersed himself in the Old Vic's 1936–7 programme, directing *Love's Labour's Lost*, *The Country Wife* and *Hamlet*, simultaneously tussling on tour with the wayward Miss Tempest.

To Mrs Norah Guthrie at Annaghmakerrig
Hotel New Weston, 34 East 50th Street, New York. 11 January 1936

> We waken around 8 and brew tea on a little spirit lamp contraption in a kettle that J. bought in Macey's (one of the huge department stores) then bathe & dress & go out to b'fast (it's not inclusive and very dear in hotel) so we usually go to a cheap restaurant or drug store. I rehearse *Call it a Day* from 11 till about 6 and have snack lunch. Then we either dine out or have dinner up here in the room (it costs no more to have meals brought up than to have them in the dining room). Have been to quite a few theatres – much the best being *Porgy and Bess* directed by Mamoulian who did the play – marvellous negro acting, singing & mime – the whole thing is really a very exciting theatrical experience. It's better as an opera than a play – the removal from a realistic convention & the heightening of emotional qualities by music

all helpful. I adored it, wept with pleasure and emotion all the way through the evening. It's had a raving, screaming chorus of enthusiasm from the press and the public stay away in thousands. I think the score is too modern and the convention too unusual for the opera public; and the people who know what they like are disappointed that it's not musical comedy with more tunes "you can take away with you". Pity.

It seems to day that *Sweet Aloes* will be done after all. There have been tremendous vicissitudes over leading lady. Everyone in London has been suggested & everyone in America. Joyce [Guthrie's agent] & I have veto. All the available ones we veto-ed and all the ones we wanted were unavailable. However, dainty Evelyn Laye has accepted & is coming from Hollywood at a perfectly staggering price. She's a risk – I think she may be good but may be just awful. Elliot will probably be offered the Aunt's part & be brought over. Needless to say I'm pressing it hard. It's being financed by Warner Brothers – AWFUL – however I don't think they will interfere much & my contract is very explicit and enables me to be very grand.

To Mrs Bretherton in Tunbridge Wells

Hotel New Weston, New York. Undated, January 1936

Call it a Day has been very smooth and plain sailing with the cast but tumult with the highly temperamental & vociferous designer who has had to cram innumerable English upper-class rooms onto a stage shaped like an ironing board. His ideas of England are a jumble of Tudor café, Olde Hunting Prints and Chippendale chairs – it's hard to convince them that we know about electric light and hot water; or that there is any kind of house between Chatsworth and the slums. Screams have rung out and angry notes have had to be answered.

I really think you and Gordon should make a trip to this amazing land – the home of Marmee and Dillinger, the Land of Liberty and Prohibition. It's worth the fare over and over and over again.

To Mrs Peggy Butler at Anaghmakerrig

Hotel New Weston, New York. 29 January 1936

In bed recovering from the strain of last night's "Opening" of *Call it a Day*, quite an effort both mentally & physically as it was all a bit anxious and also there was a great deal to do involving very long continuous hours on the job. *Sweet Aloes* rehearsals begin on Thursday. Warner Brothers, backer, is AMAZING. The Warner brothers themselves are, I believe, very quiet, nice respectable Jewish citizens of the U.S.A. with "lovely quiet wives" and "lovely homes in Bronxville" and "a lovely estate in Florida" – they are in the Motion Picture business to make money, which they spend largely in charity and social work. Sometimes they make a film for uplift – *Midsummer Night's Dream* (Rheinhardt) was a gesture in this direction. The New York office is off-Broadway and is about the size of Huntley & Palmer's biscuit factory. I deal with Mr Jake Wilke, about 50, German Jew from Wisconsin who spits into an ashtray and says "Pardon me" but is shrewd and kind and not (when one recovers from a supremely unprepossessing appearance & manner) uncongenial. He is the head of The Legitimate Department. His assistant is Mr Barney Klawans (pron. Clay Wens), also Jewish, about 45, heavy, slow & rather humourous. I like him. He is an ex-Front-of-House manager & knows about that end of the business, but *nothing* about getting a show on. I think it's going to be alright. Joyce [agent] & I have watertight contracts and can, I think, expect a pretty free hand. What Evelyn Laye will be like I don't know. She's frighteningly artificial and puts on an amazing act of Wee Girlie Prima Donna but I feel reasonably sure that once we get down to business she'll be sober, honest, cheerful and industrious.

To Mrs Norah Guthrie at Annaghmakerrig

Hotel New Weston, New York. 5 February 1936

Am finding it a wee bit of a tussle doing *Aloes* right immediately on top of *Call it a Day* with a new company, new staff, etc etc: necessitating a good deal of office work and "business" apart from the rehearsals. *Call it a Day* [now running] is too long & we have to keep on cabling Dodie Smith about cuts – she's an obstinate wee creature & the wires just hum with ceaseless long involved cables each of which necessitates long involved 'phone conversations with the Theater Guild, Gladys Cooper etc.

Evelyn Laye is a bit of a risk in *Aloes*. I'm liking her. She means very well & is working like a black. Elliot [Mason] has arrived. She had a desperately rough crossing & had had 'flu before sailing. But she stumped down the gangway on the crest of the wave. She is in great form and will give great vitality to the sour Aunt. She's staying here temporarily & we have a lot of meals together. Plans after this are completely vague. Shall hope to return with £200 or so saved on wages out here. Taxation is rather onerous as one pays income tax here and then again at home on same earnings. And of course we are living very expensively but I think it's nice for J. to have a complete holiday from h'keeping and cookery.

To Miss Bunty Worby at Annaghmakerrig
Hotel New Weston, New York. 14 February 1936

Here the main excitement is that poor dear Elliot fell down in the street y'day and has hurt her ankle quite badly. She just might have fractured the bone but it's more likely a torn ligament. Falls are almost inevitable, the ice on the streets is so hard it can only be removed by electric drills which cut it up in to blocks like granite.

Aloes rehearsals have been quite exacting. Am liking Evelyn Laye. She's a very common uneducated maid with a divine voice and extremely pretty magazine-cover face. She is brisk, business-like, and most prepared to be helped and guided; but her ideas are amazingly crude – charm equals smiling and blinking; anger equals shouting and stamping. And so on. She walks like a rheumatic old sailor. And what she likes is to have maid's talk about her inside – "I had a bit of steak yesterday, dear, I know I oughtn't to've but I did, and I could feel it all night – just here, etc etc."

In the late spring Lilian Baylis, on behalf of the Board of the Vic-Wells organization, invited Guthrie to return to the Old Vic Theatre as 'producer' – equivalent to a twenty-first-century 'artistic director'. He immediately started planning a season of Shakespeare while concluding contracts with commercial managements.

To Mrs Norah Guthrie and Mrs Peggy Butler at Annaghmakerrig
Royal Hotel, Weymouth. Undated, July 1936

I am going to produce the new Marie Tempest play [*Short Story*]. It's much as usual – only I think lighter and more witty & elegant than most. The author – a hideously fat, ugly and shy young man called Robert Morley – has been down here with me for 3 days and we have been working on the play in fits and starts and crevices of the rocks. It really is often very funny – a perfect vehicle for M.T. Am hopeful of getting Sybil Thorndike to play her girl-friend, also an excellent part, a very silly warm-hearted ex-Gaiety girl married to Lord Bucktrout (pronounced Boo-Tro), I think Sybil would be very very funny – and unexpected – in it. There's an excellent girl's part for which I'm trying hard to make them cast Ursula Jeans; 3 excellent men, not easy to cast & I fear we shall have to have dear old Willie Brown in one of them. Also a very very funny grand maid called Peacock for which I want to get Mayery Phipps Walker in pince-nez.

I expect old Maria T. will be no end of "a handful", but it will be rather interesting to have worked with her; it is her Jubilee Year (!) and I want to do something very showy and commercial before the Shakespeare venture. Plans for that are gradually shaping but nothing tangible can possibly happen till Feb. at earliest.

To Mrs Norah Guthrie at Annaghmakerrig

No address. 7 June 1936

I thought, while it was still quite fresh in my mind, I would write you about my visit to Bernard Shaw. I suppose he is one of the great Persons of Our Time – as great as Dean Swift or Dr Johnson. I went to see him in order to try and get permission to produce his new play *The Millionairess* at the Old Vic next season. I don't admire the play very much and only want it in order to secure the services of Edith Evans for whom he wrote the leading part.

My appointment was for 6.30 at 4, Whitehall Court – one of those blocks of flats near the National Liberal Club – dreary, dismal fronts and entrances but the rooms overlook the river – lovely view – and very airy and spacious. I was shown by a maid into a large drawing room and on a sofa near the fire sat Mrs Shaw. Unfortunately my impressions of the room and of Mrs Shaw are clouded by the fact that I was in a sweat of self-consciousness, of being aware that one was meeting A Great Man, of having to conduct a business negotiation of some importance to oneself but of little to him, of determining neither to be servile nor bumptious. She was in brown silk, I think, and spotted; had white hair and looked comfortable, pleasant and considerably less subdued than the wife of G.B.S. might be expected to look. We chatted for a few minutes pleasantly and a trifle laboriously about Edith – our mutual acquaintance. Then G.B.S. came in. He is 80 this year and would pass easily for 70. He wore a greenish rough tweed suit – trousers not knickerbockers.

He got to business at once about the play but was exactly like his writing, at once brisk but evasive; I think he means to let us have the play but would not commit himself and enjoyed mischievously dangling the prize before me and then whisking it crudely and ruthlessly away. He made great play with the fact that his last few pieces had been written to please himself but that *The Millionairess* was written to please the public – "My first pot-boiler since *Saint Joan*" – and that therefore he must sell it in the most advantageous market. He thought he would, however, allow the Old Vic to produce it provided we guaranteed a West End production. I said that if the play was a success at the Vic then every manager in London would come crawling on his belly to have the honour to present it but that if it was a failure, then, surely, he would not either expect or want a West End production. He hemmed and hawed at that; but Mrs Shaw backed me up quite heartily which makes me think we shall get the play in the end.[10]

They were interested that I had seen Katherine Cornell do *Saint Joan* in New York and Shaw did imitations of Madame Pitoëf and they had a tremendous wrangle about Sybil Thorndike's performance, Mrs Shaw insisting that she missed the climax which was in the trial scene and Shaw saying that anyone could play that scene, the crux of the play was the cathedral scene.

SHAW: I ought to know; I wrote it.
MRS: Well, you used to think the crisis was the trial scene.
SHAW: Well I don't know.
MRS: Well I did; and I do still.

It was very amusing and very charming; a little bit staged for the benefit of Young Visitor, but only a little bit.

---

10   The play was first produced in Vienna that year in German and in English in Melbourne in 1937. It did not go to the Old Vic at any time and the proposed production with Edith Evans was cancelled because of the outbreak of World War II.

To Mrs Norah Guthrie at Annaghmakerrig

Pencilled letter, no heading. 8 June 1936

Literally all the young things in London want to join the Co. [Old Vic] and the letters are overwhelming. Thursday, for instance, I did letters from 10-11; saw people at 5 minute intervals from 10-1; lunched with Larry Olivier to talk plans; interviews again 2.15–4. I saw 36 artists during the day. At five there was a sort of tea fight given to possible wealthy & distinguished supporters who had to be addressed about "our plans" – so tiring. That sort of semi-impromptu, semi-formal speaking is so much worse than a real "speech" – it was a hopeless hopeless affair, no one there who wasn't already interested or who had any real drive or push towards the £50,000 we require. The only thing is that Lord Lytton, who's the chairman of the Nat. Theatre Fund is very favourably inclined towards the Vic.

To Mrs Norah Guthrie at Annaghmakerrig

23 Old Buildings, Lincoln's Inn, London WC2. 7 July 1936

On Tuesday I went to Larry Olivier's for a couple of nights to work at *Hamlet*. Mrs Jill Olivier is "expecting" – in about ten minutes by the look of her – & they are living at her mother's house, a very pretty little old house & garden in that v. pretty & oddly countrified region between Maidenhead & Henley. I liked them both & had very satisfactory grapples with *Hamlet* with Larry – what a play!

To Mrs Norah Guthrie at Annaghmakerrig

23 Old Buildings, Lincoln's Inn, London WC2. Undated, August 1936

The European situation seems just as grave as can be. I would not, of course, do a hand's turn for the British Empire or King & Country or any of those, to me, meaningless symbols; but I would do a very great deal for Reasonable Liberty of Speech & Thought – and that is precisely what seems to be disappearing in every state;

One feels that the causes preached by Hitler & Mussolini are so pitifully small that they cannot for ever, or even for long, hold great masses of people together. Clearly the apparent solidarity in Germany & Italy is only a façade. Unfortunately one feels that they are ever so much more solid than our great, unwieldy, wealthy, ill-gotten Empire. And that the wildest utterances of the dictators are no more unreasonable and far less contemptibly smug than the habitual attitude and expressions of British Imperialism. And yet – and yet – the Union Jack, hated symbol that it is – may yet be the rallying point of the forces of liberty & moderation.

To Mrs Norah Guthrie at Annaghmakerrig

23 Old Buildings, Lincoln's Inn, London WC2. Undated, August 1936

Love's Labour's Lost is a heavenly play – and if I die tonight let it be recorded that I *loved* trying to do it – I don't think I have ever enjoyed a show more. We need more time – only now that it is too late to make the necessary changes & improvements do I see what I think is the true spirit of the play emerging. Something so gay and sweet and lively and above all true. It's that truth that we are missing – the show ought to have a certain amount of gaiety and I think it will be decorative in the right way – a mannered but not an effete elegance – but the psychology isn't right: we are only now beginning to unwrap the spirit of the thing from the cobwebs – the veils of gauze that time has put between itself and us … to say nothing of a rather corrupt text. Clearly the text shews signs of revision & equally I think there is a chunk missing – not a big chunk but it means one has to guess at the meaning of some strands in the skein. Molly [McArthur]'s design work has been very good. As always, most ingenious & inventive & humourous; and this time, as seldom, free from nearly all the slight cheapness and commonness that prevents her from just being as good as she is ingenious.

To Mrs Norah Guthrie at Annaghmakerrig

23 Old Buildings, Lincoln's Inn, London WC2. Undated, September 1936

Love's Labours Lost has had much praise but plays as yet to very poor business. Things have been extra complicated because that wretched Oliver Messel is terribly behind-hand with all his scenery & costume designs for *The Country Wife*. The sketches, when he does cough them up, are perfectly beautiful but we've been through agonies that the dressmakers cannot achieve them in time. We have a glittering cast headed by Edith Evans & Ruth Gordon, an American star (Chas. Loughton says she is the finest living comedian).

To Mrs Norah Guthrie at Annaghmakerrig
23 Old Buildings, Lincoln's Inn, London WC2. Undated, September 1936

L.L.Lost is doing a bit better – but that's not saying much. Those who come seem to love it; but few come!

Well, expect you have heard from Peggy herself by now. They [Peggy, Hubert & Julia Butler] arrived off the train at Euston [from *Dublin* en route for Yugoslavia] all 3 looking very well. Julia had begun to get a wee bit restless they said during the last half of the journey and had loved the boat – tramping around in her reins & making "social contacts". Judy took P & Julia straight off in the Rover to the Waldorf Hotel & Bunty, Joan [Hubert's sister] & I followed in a taxi with at least fifty thousand pieces of small luggage. I would have thought it so immensely simpler on a journey of that nature to have one good big trunk instead of innumerable oddments.

To Miss Bunty Worby at Annaghmakerrig
23 Old Buildings, Lincoln's Inn, London WC2. 29 August 1936

Well, *Short Story* rehearsals progress *very* slowly – with 3 really old people in the cast it slows things up greatly. They keep losing their places & are in every way inelastic. However I suppose we shall get it together somehow. Maria [Marie Tempest] is *quite* a tussle – very dictatorial and frequently cross – not just to me but to everyone – & poor old Willie Mathews yatters & chatters & wastes an *awful* lot of time. I try to be very pleasant & yet quite firm; but it isn't easy to be adequately firm without being a little cheeky to such venerable & distinguished persons. Yet if one isn't very firm she just rides roughshod. Sybil Thorndike is such a nice woman & will I think be very helpful and tactful. We work pretty short hours – as 2 hours at a stretch is as much as the Old Girl can manage – &, as it is, the last half hour or so before lunch becomes very teasing as she gets hungrier & hungrier so she gets more & more snappy & goes snapping & grunting about like a little old terrier. It's really very funny. She barks out at me, "What's the time, dear?" about every 3 minutes, & taps her foot &

looks vexed at every delay. Also she never will admit she's wrong – if a cue is missed (by her) she always pretends that someone else is to blame. "I couldn't hear – speak up, Sybil dear" – "Don't fidget, Willy, you're putting me out" – "Ursula dear, how can I get to the table if you … Tony, need she stand there?" – all barked out in a staccato basso profundo. She's about 2 feet high and as pretty as possible; & full of charm & pretty ways; but really I think she's a selfish, disagreeable, common, little old woman – but has great spirit – real "bel esprit".

To Mrs Norah Guthrie at Annaghmakerrig
Central Hotel, Glasgow, on tour with Marie Tempest in Short Story. *Undated, September 1936*

Just arrived here after night journey – shall be here probably till Saty. & will then either go direct to M'chester or else go to London for week-end & up to M'chester on Monday morning. All these jauntings are at management's expense & as I am being paid no extra fee for this supervision work [of Marie Tempest on tour] I have no conscience about suiting my convenience.

We left Edinboro' on Friday night & the weekend has been hectic with *Dance of Death* [Auden] rehearsals. It opens tonight. I fear it is no box-office proposition but I do think it's an interesting & vital experiment – it's ever so much better than the Sunday show – more gay & finished & ever so much more intelligible – & a far more appropriate cast – 10 real singers & 10 real dancers. Some of it is lovely to look at.

Now there is a possibility – but only a poss: it depends entirely on whether Miss Tempest is sufficiently safe to leave – that J & I could get over for a dash about 5 days – around Oct. 10. All depends on Maria. At present she is being rather detrimental to the play because she *won't* play her part as lightest of light comedy. She thinks she is the peak of a rather moving sex-triangle (so unsuitable at 75) & when the audience is all ready to roll about with laughter (& has been rolling about at all the other characters) silly old Maria comes on & does a lot of heavy acting (which she isn't very good at) & is the complete wet blanket at the party. When remonstrations occur she either gets very cross & shouts out that she supposes she knows something about the business after 50 years & who do the people pay to come to see anyhow; or else she does an enormous act of being shaken with sobs & supposing it's because she's growing too old – which, alas, is pitifully true. It all has to be very patiently & gently yet primly coped with – & I fear I'm not being very successful. However, there are still 3 more weeks!

It would be so much easier if one could have a real good rumpus & say what one thinks. But you can't be candid or have rows with people of 75 without being very cruel & impertinent; & I'm always afraid she'll have a little tiny stroke. The latter fear is really sentimentality: I feel sincerely convinced that she's as strong as a horse – & when she swoons & clutches at furniture & does Little Broken Butterfly it's *all* pose & an underhand manoeuvre for victory. Also, I will hand it to her, she has a *great* sense of humour; & not only bears no malice but likes the people who stand up to her & refuse to be trampled. But the fact remains that she is a cruel, ruthless & deceitful little bully.

To Mrs Norah Guthrie at Annaghmakerrig

Central Hotel, Glasgow. Undated, late September 1936

The play [*Short Story*] has again done colossal business – smashing records for a straight play in Scotland. They will have paid off the production, I hope, & have quite a nice profit before ever we open in London. I'm glad to say that I participate in this to the extent of 1% till prod. is paid off, thereafter 2%. Did I tell you that Maria received a Straight Talk on Thurs: as a result of which she has abandoned the idea that she is playing in a drama with Big Scenes & Strong Situations & is giving a comedy performance with immensely beneficial results. This means, I hope, that it will be poss. to get over [to Annaghmakerrig].

To Mrs Norah Guthrie at Annaghmakerrig

23 Old Buildings, Lincoln's Inn, London WC2. Undated, November 1936

Friday was one series of "Meetings" – the Old V. and S. Wells governors – dreary old generals with red old rheumy eyes like bloodhounds; a sprinkling of Good Women of upper-class and Considerable Means looking cool and tasteful in black crêpe "relieved" with touches of silver grey and doing a little act of women-being-just-as-good-as-men-on-a-committee; Lord Lytton looking quite incredibly feudal in the chair. I don't know what he's really like, but outwardly in his conduct of meetings he is the *perfect* advertisement for Breeding & the Ancien Régime. I think they're all nice good public-spirited people and a proportion of them would be good ballast on a board – they have a point of view, they have balance, tolerance (in some degree) but they are all over sixty; and in consequence have *no drive*; tend automatically to oppose innovation since they have little knowledge or interest in anything that has occurred in the last decade; and not one of them has any real acquaintance with the theatre. They don't know either the business conditions or the working conditions of how a play is produced. Yet they are all theatre lovers and full of Helpful Suggestions.

Then came the London Theatre Studio (Michel Saint Denis School) board meeting. A much more satisfactory affair & things are going on v. well. There has been quite a good response to the issue of shares. Anyway there's enough to go ahead with the conversion of the hall in Islington where the school will open in full glory next October. Meantime all classes are full to overflowing & there's a very cheerful, progressive air about the whole enterprise.

Well then, the weekend was spent at Hastings. The Left Theatre was by way of having a weekend school – or conference. The school was fairly painful. The speaker on Sat. was Llewellyn Rees, a very nice man & a great friend of Elliot's. He is an actor & works on all kinds of committees – e.g. he & Elliot are representatives of Equity (actors' trade union). Llewellyn made a speech on *The Russian Theatre*, rather too many statistical facts but not boring; but followed by the most unthinkably tedious & hopeless discussion. A very few "workers" (who talked the biggest rot of all) but nearly all the rest were communist intellectuals exactly like the comic drawings in *Punch*, so humiliating, men with little wispy beards and corduroy trousers, women also in trousers with thick thick glasses and long long prominent tusks & cigarettes hanging from their lower lips, just a sloppy, dreary lot of sausage-frying Bohemians.

These people were still drivelling away about Idle Rich like socialists of the Cobden epoch, and using terms like Freedom which they think is a corollary of Socialism. They won't admit that one cannot be both Free and Protected, and that any form of govt. must be in some measure a compromise between individual autonomy and complete state control in return for complete state protection. All the time their talk had a disgruntled whining air because Someone Else wasn't providing them with Amenities which they were too lazy & too uninventive to provide for themselves.

To Mrs Norah Guthrie at Annaghmakerrig

23 Old Buildings, Lincoln's Inn, London WC2. Undated, December 1936

Can't find anyone we want for *Othello* in Jan. so we're going to do *Hamlet* [with Laurence Olivier] then instead of at end of Season. I'm terribly excited about it; much the most stimulating & interesting of the books on the subject I'm finding is an essay by Dr Ernest Jones – a leading psycho-analyst – *fascinating*.

I've joined the London Library at £7.7.0 and am now a bit inclined to want the money back – it's all so ancient – Venerable Bedes behind the counter; Methuselah in "the desk"; & in the holy of holies where I was taken to be "introduced" after paying my sub. sate an aged aged aged mid-Victorian dandy with striped pantaloons and a button-hole and exquisite courtesy and a knighthood – a real Old Gentleman – but so old, older than the Pyramids. He is called, believe it or not, Sir Hagsberg Wright, and to think of him makes God feel rather parvenu. Perhaps it's been worth seven guineas to have a peep at Sir Hagsberg.

Guthrie's Old Vic production of *Hamlet* with Laurence Olivier and Vivien Leigh at Elsinore, 1937.

4

ELSINORE AND OTHER PALPABLE HITS

1937 turned out to be Guthrie's most important year in the theatre to date. He was now firmly re-established at the Old Vic, a position consolidated by the death of the theatre's co-founder, Lilian Baylis. He increased the company's sphere of activity by establishing a festival at the Buxton Opera House in Yorkshire with productions that would transfer to London, and vice versa: in the first year *Pygmalion*, *Ghosts* and *Measure for Measure*. More importantly for his career, he directed the production of *Hamlet* that went to Elsinore where his thoughts on playing Shakespeare on an open stage accidentally came to fruition, leading to a revolution in production design later exemplified at the Edinburgh Festival, at Stratford, Ontario, and at Minneapolis. He also directed Lehar's operetta *Paganini* for a commercial management and took part in Korda's film *Vessel of Wrath* during time off from the Old Vic. His sister Peggy and her husband Hubert Butler and their baby daughter Julia rented a flat in Hampstead.

To Mrs Norah Guthrie, Annaghmakerrig

23 Old Buildings, Lincoln's Inn, London WC2. 23 January 1937

> *Hamlet* [with Laurence Olivier] is doing excellent business – cheap seats jammed at every performance; 7/6d stalls well filled but not full except on Sats. It always "goes" splendidly – deep, riveted attention throughout the 4½ hours and a clamorous reception for Larry at the end. Such an interesting audience – masses and masses of "ces autres" – quite Poor People, my dear, in the quaintest clothes; and a greater proportion of men than women – a great many parties of young men,

people who look as though they might be public librarians or electrical engineers, secondary school type. In the West End there are usually 65 women to 35 men.

To Mrs Norah Guthrie, Annaghmakerrig

23 Old Buildings, Lincoln's Inn, London WC2. 30 January 1937

We have started rehearsals for *Twelfth Night* but in quite a leisurely way. Larry [Olivier] – with *Hamlet* entire at night – sleeps in the afternoon; & anyhow the *Hamlet* business is so good that we needn't hurry, so we're just rehearsing in the mornings.

To Mrs Norah Guthrie at Annaghmakerrig

23 Old Buildings, Lincoln's Inn, W.C2. 3 February 1937

I'm finding *Twelfth Night* terribly terribly heavy going & can get up no enthusiasm – & what is far more serious find myself completely without invention. Partly I think anti-climax after the effort of *Hamlet*, which was considerable; and partly that I'm stale on *XIIth Night*, it all seems old and boring & I hate Sir Toby – I think he & Falstaff are a couple of old beasts & have for me no charm at all – nor would have in "real" life, and all that roaring & screaming with laughter & "practical joking" that goes on is so teasing. I fancy I partly don't like it because I am myself a bit of a Malvolio. But also apart from its meaning it is hard work to prepare – that screaming and laughing seems immensely bleak at 10.30 A.M. in an empty theatre.

To Mrs Norah Guthrie, Annaghmakerrig

23 Old Buildings, Lincoln's Inn, London WC2. 7 February 1937

Yesterday Charles B. Cochrane [West End impresario] made me an offer to produce a Lehar operetta, *Paganini*, starring Richard Tauber – rather a thrill! I've always wanted to try my hand at a big musical. The book is utter BOSH – a fictitious & very silly episode in the life of Paganini but I fancy one would have a fairly free hand to make cuts & alterations, & anyway it's nothing but an excuse for melting top A's amid a welter of pwetty fwocks and calico clematis.

To Mrs Norah Guthrie, Annaghmakerrig

23 Old Buildings, Lincoln's Inn, London WC2. Good Friday, 1937

Rather exciting: we've been invited to do *Hamlet* at Elsinore in the open air at end of May or early June, in the courtyard of the castle. It's the first time that the castle has ever been allowed to be used for anything of the kind – we should be the guests of the Danish Govt. The King of D. would probably attend & it would all be very grand and gala and honourable – & I think Larry [Olivier] & Lilian [Baylis] & I should at least receive Danish peerages or Doctorates of Philosophy or anyway teeny little Nobel prizes. It's all a bit vague still & Larry has a film that may conflict, but I think it will probably come off – & seems rather fun.

To Mrs Norah Guthrie, Annaghmakerrig

23 Old Buildings, Lincoln's Inn, London WC2. 2 May 1937

Paganini is awful – but of course I've been seeing it through a haze of impending 'flu. I hate Richard Tauber [tenor] – he's a vulgar blatant little tike. The voice is divine, & he works hard & with rather endearing energy and absence of reserve, but he can't act *at all* – he merely goes through embarrassing motions of "showing off" and his singing is just an exploitation of one showy vulgar trick after another accompanied by really laughable grimacing. However the public will certainly take Aunt Becky's view and fall a victim to the luscious sexuality of those golden top notes! And I don't think there's much doubt of box-office success. Rehearsals are quite well advanced – I'm going to be quite firm about not rehearsing till I am quite better.

Awful about Guernica, but I think it must have been terribly harmful to Franco. Even rabidly capitalist & imperialist papers like the S. Times are greatly changing their tones about the insurgents.

To Mrs Norah Guthrie, Annaghmakerrig

23 Old Buildings, Lincoln's Inn, London WC2. 15 May 1937

By the time I got back [to *Paganini*] time was short and it was all far from ready. It will I think now be ready on time – but NOT good.

Tauber & Evelyn [Laye] act very badly and it would take Salvini & Rachel to convince one that it was anything but drivel. However I'm now quite enjoying trying to make it efficient drivel.

Coronation [King George VI]: glad you heard it all so well. Had quite a reasonable view of the procession as it passed up St James' Street, that is to say we were in about the 40th row from the front & I could just see the caps of the foot soldiers & the torsos of the cavalry! Actually I saw less because I had an intensely excited small boy on my shoulder – his papa was too short to be any help in hoisting him up. He saw splendidly & broadcast an extremely lively & wildly incorrect account of the goings-on – "'Uzzars – at least I think it's 'Uzzars – a carriage – Mr Baldwin – no! it's a woman, Queen Mary – no, it's Mrs Baldwin – no, it's one of them Sultans!" After leaving our place in the crowd armies of scouts were already at work clearing up the litter, which, incidentally, was INDESCRIBABLE – TONS of newspaper, orange peel, chocolate paper, to say nothing of tweed caps, mackintoshes, sandals, sticks, bags, etc etc.

To Mrs Norah Guthrie, Annaghmakerrig

23 Old Buildings, Lincoln's Inn, London WC2. Undated, late May 1937

Paganini is an immense success apparently – just what the public likes. Actually it's AWFUL. Common, silly, slow & dull, but LUSCIOUS. We took a "party" to the first night and it was quite fun. I enclose a suitably gracious letter from Charles B. Cochrane which would have been more suitable still if it had contained a cheque. Between now & Friday we have Hamlet rehearsals – such a joy after awful awful *Paganini* – Elsinore will be fun, I think, but NO REST.

To Mrs Norah Guthrie at Annaghmakerrig

Hotel Marienlyst, Helsingør, Denmark. Undated, June 1937

Miss Baylis is in her element, determined that we should enjoy the trip, and no less determined that we should be 'good' and give the foreigners a nice impression of the Old Vic. The Opening was to be an important occasion. Royalty was to be present; a special train was chartered to convey the royal party & the diplomatic corps from

Copenhagen and that night it rained as never before. It was out of the question to abandon the performance. Miss Baylis, Larry Olivier & I held a Council of War: the performance was to be at eight; at seven-thirty the rain was coming down in bellropes: we would give the performance in the ballroom of the hotel. There was no stage but we would play in the middle of the hall with the audience seated all around us as in a circus. Larry conducted a lightening rehearsal with the company improvising exits & entrances & rearranging business. George Chamberlain and I, assisted by the critics of Dagbladet, the Daily Telegraph and Paris Soir, arranged eight hundred and seventy basket chairs in circles round the ballroom. Miss Baylis put on her academic robes and kept things going with royalty & the ambassadors till we were ready.

Actors always thrive on emergency and the company did marvels. But *Hamlet* is a very long play. After two hours of improvisation the actors became exhausted and a little flustered. The finale was a shambles, but not quite in the way the author intended. Still, it had been quite a good evening; royalty looked pleased, ambassadors clapped white-gloved hands & the press next morning acclaimed a "sporting gesture". The impromptu and rather haphazard performance strengthens me in the conviction which has been growing with each production at the Vic that for Shakespeare the proscenium stage is unsatisfactory. I should never have suggested staging this rather important occasion as we did if I had not a strong hunch that it would work.

To Mrs Norah Guthrie, Annaghmakerrig

23 Old Buildings, Lincoln's Inn, London WC2. Undated, June 1937

Elsinore has been an incredible experience – just one crisis after another & all plugged full of amusing & queer episodes. I don't think the outdoor performances were good a bit – *Hamlet* is the very last play to survive open-air treatment – the poetry, the philosophy, the immense complex web of thought & feeling, just melted away & we seemed to be performing a big exciting melodrama punctuated by long dreary "talky bits". But the press was excellent – the Danes say it has had the best theatrical press in living memory, and for a week we have been front page news. A.E. Wilson in The Star has written that it was "certainly the most astonishing triumph over difficulties I have ever seen in the theatre". It's all so stupid, really – the performance wasn't nearly so good as at the Vic – but the *idea* of *Hamlet* at Elsinore seems to be what the editors think the public likes. Anyway, it's been the biggest advertisement the Old Vic ever had.

To Mrs Norah Guthrie at Annaghmakerrig

23 Old Buildings, Lincoln's Inn, London WC2. 20 August 1937

Buxton has been more than a handful. I'm a wee bit disappointed with *Pygmalion* – neither Diana [Wynyard] nor Robert Morley are good enough. *Measure for Measure* one can't tell about yet – I think it's pretty good but definitely not box office. Saw a full rehearsal of *Ghosts* on Friday and think it brilliant – really first class acting and production though I'm not mad about Molly [McArthur]'s set. She & Esmé [Church, director] were very anxious to get away from English mid-Victorian trappings & have gone into great research & trouble to get an authentic Norwegian interior of the period: but the result is not in my view entirely happy, it just looks as if Mrs Alving, instead of inhabiting theatrical digs in Huddersfield, has a Lady Betty's Tea Rooms on an arterial road full of quaint peasanty knick-knacks.

To Mrs Norah Guthrie at Annaghmakerrig

23 Old Buildings, Lincoln's Inn, London WC2. 22 September 1937

Well things have been simply humming, in fact they have hummed to such a tune that I retired to bed last night with a temperature of 101. I went to see Charles [Laughton] & Erich Pommer [director] about the film *Vessel of Wrath* – the dates seemed to be possible & they wanted me to make a test on Monday afternoon. I explained that I had to light *Pygmalion* on Monday afternoon so they made it morning & I was sent home to learn two scenes & to leave for Elstree at 8.30 next day. J. drove me & I was made up & dressed by 10.00 & acted my scenes and was considered to have done well & offered £400 for 10 days work + £50 for whoever should do my work at the Vic during those 10 days + any expenses I may incur in connection with the film. All highly satisfactory especially as I think the work is going to be rather fun &

Guthrie with Charles Laughton at the Old Vic, 1937.

interesting – the script isn't bad & I'm really fond of Charles & Elsa [Lanchester] & my part is fun – a missionary, very stern & narrow-minded & highly ridiculous but also very noble & conscientious. And I'm to look absurd but play it as truly & sincerely as I can.

To Mrs Norah Guthrie at Annaghmakerrig

23 Old Buildings, Lincoln's Inn, London WC2. 24 October 1937

Measure for Measure has been a complete & utter flop, the worst business the Vic has done for many years. Quite sad but useless to repine. I suppose it's very understandable that people should prefer to go to the familiar plays, & should resent a play that has neither "hero", "heroine" or "villain", but I'm afraid it also means that *Richard III* won't do well as Emlyn [Williams] is evidently not a "draw".

I finished the film [*Vessel of Wrath*] yesterday – but what a day! We rose at 5.45 A.M. and I got back between 9.30 & 10 P.M. having spent the day on a sequence when I am supposed to have a relapse from malaria, faint & get carried into bed. If I crashed to the floor once I crashed eighty times – amusing for the first fifty-six, then increasingly teasing until eventually the reason began to totter. That went on from about 9 till tea-time. We did the dragging to bed & that had to be done a million times too. Charles had to tuck me in & then Elsa & Bob Newton had to cover me up, take off my slippers, etc, while playing a very short quick scene in whispers – simple enough really but we were all so tired & became rather grisly. The bedclothes, unless handled exactly right made a noise (on the microphone) that drowned their whispering, and that caused endless repetition. Then I was heavy and Charles tired & we kept getting the wrong position on the bed – once we missed the bed altogether & both rolled on the floor laughing helplessly, but the total result was EXHAUSTING.

To Mrs Norah Guthrie at Annaghmakerrig
23 Old Buildings, Lincoln's Inn, London WC2. Undated, November 1937

Having a very busy time with *Richard III* – it's a huge undertaking – such a vast cast & many puzzling awkward scenes from a production point of view, & so many parts that are too small to pay anyone good money to play, demand experienced & firm playing – & just don't begin to do when tackled by our very young, very raw, students. Also Emlyn [Williams] isn't a big enough personality to hold the evening together – the performance has many interesting & clever "touches", but that's not enough.

To Mrs Norah Guthrie at Annaghmakerrig
The Old Vic, Waterloo Road, London. 3 November 1937

Richard III opened last night & did not go too badly. I'm not pleased with it; but it's not so bad as I feared & hasn't been badly received.

To Mrs Norah Guthrie at Annaghmakerrig
23 Old Buildings, Lincoln's Inn, London WC2. 21 November 1937

I am inclined to be starting a cold & staying warmly wrapped by the fire. We were to have gone to Peggy's for supper but are putting off the engagement the more so as visitors with heavy colds will not be much help to Miss [Julia Butler]. It's rather sad not seeing the Butler's flat but no doubt there'll be frequent opportunities. Do you think they have enough money? Annette [Prévost] rather amazed me by suggesting that perhaps they were awfully cramped for funds.

Robert Helpmann as Oberon in Guthrie's production of *A Midsummer Night's Dream* at the Old Vic, 1937.

I hadn't supposed so – as taxis at will, trunk calls, new clothes & long journeys never seem to present much difficulty.

We are going to open *A Midsummer Night's Dream* on Boxing Day. The [Oliver] Messel designs are going to be lovely I think. With the Mendelssohn music, full orchestra, ballet and all frills it's going to cost about £1,000 a week to run; & at Vic prices that means we've got to play to *huge* business to make ends meet. It's all rather alarming.

To Mrs Norah Guthrie at Annaghmakerrig

23 Old Buildings, Lincoln's Inn, London WC2. Undated, November 1937

Lilian's departure. We shall miss her *very* much. Actually her death was very merciful. She was in the theatre on the Wedy. – was ill that aft. – heart, but not considered very grave, & her doctor saw her that night & said she was much better. During the night she was worse & [Annette] Prévost stayed up with her; at 5 she was worse but not frantic & Prévost sent for the doctor; at 6.30 she went down to let him in and when they went upstairs together to the bedroom she was gone. The funeral is to-morrow & there is to be a big memorial service on Wedy. I can't describe the wires, the cables, the flowers, the quite extraordinary expressions of regret from the King & Queen down to the humblest gallery "patrons".

Week was just a real tussle – physical & spiritual. In addition to the Queen's Theatre show (*School for S.*) *Macbeth* at the Vic was altogether beyond a joke. I used to go down to the Queen's dress rehearsals and was twice there till 5 in the morning. During the week the men did 45 hours of overtime – George [Chamberlain, stage director] & the electricians did – believe it or not – 60 hours of overtime. From Friday to Monday they didn't go to bed at all.

Macbeth opened on Friday. Lord Lytton [Chairman] spoke a few words at the opening to a packed emotional house and then we all stood in silence for a moment & then the play began. Never can the three witches have opened to such a prologue. They're doing immense business; & Bronny Albery is transferring it to the New at Xmas on quite good terms – £100 per week to the Vic + 15% of the profits. *The Dream* opens on Boxing Day & we began rehearsals today with Ralph Richardson [as Bottom] heading the cast. *Ghosts* opens in Cambridge tonight & goes to Brighton next week. *School for Scandal* has, I am sorry to say, had distinctly "mixed" notices; rather a surprise I must confess as it seemed to go well; & is, I thought, very mild & very unrevolutionary, just gay & light with pretty dresses & scenery which, far from being the vehement obtrusive kind of thing that Agate [critic] suggests, errs perhaps in being rather too quietly in good taste!

To Mrs Norah Guthrie at Annaghmakerrig

23 Old Buildings, Lincoln's Inn, London WC2. Undated, late November 1937

Peggy's flat [in Hampstead] is so nice. The balcony & view over trees & heath are the making of it; but the rooms are nice shapes as well. As yet they're a little short of furniture but not to the point of hardship, not even of discomfort. Julia has grown & developed tremendously since I saw her. She was a teeny bit shy but only for a very short time, & is very sweet about showing her toys & answering enquiries.

Miss Baylis' obsequies have been the principal feature of the week. The funeral on Tuesday – memorial service at St Martin's-in-the Fields on Wedy. We assembled at the Vic at 10 – the personal staff, governors, old servants, etc. about 7 car loads and drove off in icy icy sleet to her church at Kennington. The church was packed, densely, suffocatingly, & this was supposed to be the very quiet intimate little service. The service was very "high" – practically Roman – incense, bowing bobbing priests in full regalia, bells ringing, candles flickering. Some people – Judy among them – hated the popery & formality, but I simply adored it. I saw for the first time the point of it all – how that symbolism is the nearest we can get to worship – one can commune in spirit with God for short moments on occasion "when the spirit moves us" but the spirit doesn't always move one at 11 A.M. on Sunday – & the mere repetition of prayers in the Evangelical manner is just as formal & unreal as the papistical gabblings without the elaborately thought-out, age-old, ritual & symbolism, linking one visually & aurally, rhythmically in thought, word & deed with the savage beating his tom-tom; the Indian at his totem-pole; the three witches at their cauldron.

This lasted over an hour with a very brief, very simple, very excellent address by the Bishop of Southwark. Then we went to Golder's Green for the burning – a very brief service here & I don't think any of us could take in or give out any more. The Bishop of Southwark had come accompanied by the mildest curate going who carried his great silver crozier. A very young reporter came to the Vic to have his report checked and had written "The Bishop arrived accompanied by a crook"!

The memorial service at St Martin's was quite wonderful. The opera orchestra played – I don't know what but very beautiful & dreamy; then we had a few prayers of a simple and quite unsectarian nature; then we sang "Jesus, lover of my soul"; then there was a little address by Father Andrew – Miss Bayliss' own priest & confessor (v. high Anglican); then we sang "Fight the good fight"; then a blessing was pronounced; then the opera chorus sang simply magnificently – a great shout of triumph & joy, something from Wagner; it was absolutely thrilling & moving to the last degree. The place was packed. A real Full House – which would have given her great joy – "Turning them away from the doors, dear!"

Guthrie's new production of *Hamlet*, with Alec Guinness, did not achieve the acclaim he felt it deserved so soon after the production with Laurence Olivier. During time off from the Old Vic he directed *Goodness How Sad!* by Robert Morley in the West End. With the outbreak of World War II in 1939 he took on the management of the Sadler's Wells Opera and Ballet companies as well as that of the Old Vic theatre company. London theatres closed, reopened and closed again with confusing consequences.

To Mrs Norah Guthrie at Annaghmakerrig

23 Old Buildings, Lincoln's Inn, London WC2. Undated, 1938

> *Coriolanus* opened last night at the Vic. A wretched press, un-understanding & common & v. damning from the box-office point of view. It's a fine play: but they can't see the point of it. Larry fair – picturesque but not many subtleties of character. Sybil delightfully vigorous – Lewis's production workmanlike but lacking in subtlety & handicapped by *awful* scenery & dresses!

To Mrs Norah Guthrie at Annaghmakerrig

Old Vic Theatre, London. 16 October 1938

> There has not been a minute all week what with *Hamlet* opening on the Tuesday & *Goodness How Sad!* opening next Tues. I've been at one place or t'other all day & every evening. The political situation is odd, isn't it? I don't think we're going to have war now; but I do think we're going to have a Fascist régime – heavily disguised of course under some noble-sounding title like National Brotherhood or Imperial Christian

Alec Guinness
as Hamlet
in Guthrie's
production at
the Old Vic,
1938.

Fellowship. But clearly democracy as philosophy just doesn't do at the present moment – no one can believe all that Rousseau stuff about man being born equal and free.

Hamlet isn't doing well. We clashed with Priestley's opening in the West End & we got office-boy notices, mostly favourable but usually three dreary little lines of illiterate & faint-hearted quality: "Hamlet is spoken with distinction & clarity by Allen Guinness." And no business is being done. I think the political situation is the chief factor; & of course having no big star personality at the head of the cast. Alec is much, much better than Larry – but Larry with his beautiful head and athletic sexy movements and bursts of fireworks are what the public wants – & most understandably – they don't know or want to know much about the play & character. They just want a show.

It's been a blow, I must admit. I have found it just awfully discouraging & disillusionizing. I know it is good – not, probably, by absolute standards – but comparatively; taking into account the money, the talent, the time, etc, it represents the very utmost effort. It's easily the best work I've done so far & may very well be the best I shall do – in this job as in all creative & semi-creative work experience tends to kill invention - & it's a blow to have it fall very flat.

I've been very sad about it all week. It's personally important & has been a first-class whack in the eye. It's been far more difficult for Alec to weather. The actor's position to success or failure is so terribly personal. The work of art is inseparable from himself. It's *him* "they" like or fail to like. And it's a very personal ordeal to have to tussle thro' that enormous physical effort to empty houses. Still, it's got great spirit & sense of proportion. And the houses, tho' empty, are immensely enthusiastic – & nearly all the people whose opinion we value have been sincerely & wholeheartedly praising of him.

The poor Old Vic is absolutely in Queer Street. The Westminster Bank rings us rampageously every day – but *literally*, *every* morning – to say What about the overdraft? And poor old Sir Reginald [Row, Hon. Treasurer] has to rush about Threadneedle Street in a suit of sackcloth, putting ashes on his poor old head, screaming Spare me! Spare me! Lord Lytton has to bow his Tudor neck under the heel of Col. Mitchell of the Carnegie Trust. Lady Gooch has flown the land: 33 Wetherby Gardens knows her no more: her house is become an house of lamentations: daws peck at her wig. Never mind! RESURGAM. And, if not, what the hell?

Goodness How Sad! has been rather fun – & has been a great distraction from the woes of the Victoria Hall. It's a little play – just a trifle – but has much charm.

To Mrs Norah Guthrie at Annaghmakerrig

23 Old Buildings, Lincoln's Inn, London WC2. Undated, late October 1938

Hamlet, I'm very glad to say, is picking up grandly – every perf. this week has more than doubled receipts at corresponding perf. last week. It goes awfully well & the "word of mouth" reports are evidently good & everyone is much more optimistic. *Goodness How Sad!* had an excellent press & seems likely to do well – goes to continual laughter & is charming though very slight.

Went on Wed. to opening of *St Martin's Lane.* The film is baddish but not as bad as I'd expected. Some of it looks nice & Charles [Laughton] is mostly pretty good. The opening was an incredible affair with troops making a Guard of Honour (tho' whose honour was being guarded we could not determine) & literally squads of police holding back jumping phalanxes of screaming women. Then inside the foyer we were televised – a hopeless sort of semi-impromptu affair with Elsa [Lanchester] "receiving" guests in front of the camera & making very forced & playful remarks to each in turn. I was to walk in with The Great Dane [Clemence Dane, author] herself but (very sensibly) she didn't turn up so there was a terrific hurroosh – Bobby Newton was pushed on looking like Robinson Crusoe as he's just grown a huge beard for some other picture – whether he was introduced as Miss Clemence Dane I don't know!

To Mrs Norah Guthrie at Annaghmakerrig

23 Old Buildings, Lincoln's Inn, London WC2. 9 March 1939

Business at the Vic has dropped to a deadly zero – & one really sees no reason why it should mend – which, apart from everyone's preoccupation with National Issues, considerably takes the heart out of preparations for the *Shrew.* Also makes it difficult to concentrate on plans for the future. It doesn't seem to matter much whether one is or isn't Manager of the Vic-Wells if civilization is about to explode into ten million fragments. Yet one knows that the only possible hope for sanity & a return to Normal Psychological conditions is by concentrating firmly upon the things that are nearest in whose fulfilment one can have some – even if not entire – belief.

To Mrs Norah Guthrie at Annaghmakerrig

23 Old Buildings, Lincoln's Inn, London WC2. Undated, March 1939

Man & Superman [Shaw; directed by Lewis Casson] is doing well – a *leetle* galling, it's doing really v.g. business, much better than *Hamlet*, but it just isn't a good show. *The Dream* is now cast & will go into rehearsal on Monday week. Next week for me won't be awfully busy as Esmé needs the company all the time for *Rivals*; I shall just have a few intermittent attacks on *Viceroy* just to keep it brushed up.

I have nearly decided to accept the management of the theatres [Old Vic and Sadler's Wells], if offered. I feel increasingly sure that it's the right step to take.

To Mrs Norah Guthrie at Annaghmakerrig
23 Old Buildings, Lincoln's Inn, London WC2. 29 March 1939

I have accepted the Vic-Wells Management. As soon as I see how things are shaping I shall try to come over to you. *Shrew* opened last night – the first critics all went elsewhere but such notices as there are favourable & there was much laughter. We & Liveseys gave a small party afterwards & Butlers were going to have come but in the end they marched out of the theatre & when run after by Judy said they'd changed their minds & didn't want to come after all.

To Mrs Norah Guthrie at Annaghmakerrig
Parkland House, Buxton. Undated, spring 1939

Well, I'm not making any plans for the moment. I still don't think there will be a war.[11] If there is, I shall wait & see what's going to happen to the Vic & Wells, transfer the organisation to the most suitable hands, and then volunteer wherever help is needed – unless the most helpful thing seems just to be getting on with one's work.

The town is far from full. This hotel alone has had endless bookings cancelled. In spite of everything we play to very good houses & much enthusiasm – people are glad to be "taken out" of themselves for a couple of hours. I still believe the German government will not attempt to force the issue – even if they won the war they would still have to face a reckoning with their new "ally". Equally I think that England and France will do everything to make a climb-down possible for Germany. I think that all these negotiations mean that a "formula" is being sought that will save

---

11   War was officially declared on 1 September 1939.

every nation's face – probably may lead to a complete (& long overdue) revision of the Versailles treaty.

Try not to worry – above all don't give way to feelings of impotent "fury" – that is silly as well as useless. Who or what are you furious with? It's none of it the fault of any one person or group of persons. It's the product of the stupidity, the greed & the misdirected energy of the whole human race, for which you and I & every one of us must bear the share of the guilt, &, if need be, take a share of the punishment.

To Mrs Norah Guthrie at Annaghmakerrig

Old Vic Theatre, London. 15 September 1939

All well here but we're in an absolute swirl & whirlpool of conflicting plans & carries-on, all involving ceaseless trunk calls here, there and everywhere; ceaseless wires; ceaseless important decisions that have to be taken; ceaseless filling of gaps. One thing: it's nice to be so busy – the perfect anodyne. One races round and round like a bluebottle all day & just sinks down like a log at night. The whole situation is most disquieting. One hears horrible rumours – lots of people think that Chamberlain & Sir Horace Wilson are still intriguing with Germany; & there's a strong feeling that it's just a race between us & Germany, not for who will "win" the war but who will first collapse internally! Such fun! No one believes anything they're told – all the news is doped; all the fine sentiments about fighting for Freedom are discredited by the obvious lies & manoeuvres & shuffles that are taking place "in ministerial circles".

Evacuation is chaos; my salary is now £7 p.w. instead of £20 but I feel profoundly thankful – because it may stop at any moment, since the Vic & Wells have NO reserves at all except weekly earnings which couldn't be more precarious – to have some occupation & to have a cause, in which I do believe, to fight for. All this may sound depressed. But my feeling is not exactly depression – more dizziness. One seems to be stationary but spinning – while scenes, grand pianos, St Paul's Cathedral, dead cats & meteorites hurtle through the air around us.

It's all such a waste – of life, of money, of effort: but what's the good of saying that?

To Mrs Norah Guthrie at Annaghmakerrig

Sadler's Wells Theatre, London. Undated, September 1939

Saw Hubert & P. y'day afternoon & – & P & I had lunch alone together today – a *very nice talk*, our happiest, most intimate meeting for ages – we were able to feel such deep confidence & affection & communion. It made me very happy. P. gives very good account of Aunt Sue. Judy went down to see Gordon & Nellie & they're all right too. Hubert & P. will be arriving with you [at Annaghmakerrig] very soon & will help you to make plans & give you lots of first hand news & views. Don't listen all the time to the radio – it's only depressing & anyway the news is heavily doped. The apprehension of horror is always worse than the actual events – all one's experience teaches that – waiting for an operation; the day before going to school; the week of tensions before war was declared which to me was infinitely worse than this week is being.

Air Raid sirens went off 6.45 y'day morning. I was awake, wakened Judy & we toddled down to our shelter – we'd left out warm clothes, gas masks, thermos, rugs etc – everyone quite calm & after we'd sat & strolled around for ages there was a general tendency to drift off to our different chambers & make tea, shave, etc: & at 9.5 the All Clear sounded. Our shelter is for the inhabitants of staircases 18-25 [Old Buildings] so we are all neighbours & have quite a party, & as the shelter is about 5 seconds walk from the staircase , just across the square to the chapel – we are lucky. And you needn't worry.

Theatres are not likely to open, & even if allowed won't do any business. Any activity in that line will be in the provinces. I intend to go on trying to place the Vic-Wells organisation in the service of any authority who can make good use of us. And if they do not require my services I shall find something else. But I feel it's quite daft to race around looking for work for which one is not trained when one's trained qualities might be useful.

To Mrs Norah Guthrie at Annaghmakerrig

23 Old Buildings, Lincoln's Inn, London WC2. 18 November 1939

We are, of course, in a ferment of hope that Germany is cracking up. Oh dear, one hardly dares to think how wonderful it would be if peace

The Sadler's Wells Theatre, London, 1940.

would come SOON. One goes every day to the Wells & tho' one is busy every second of every minute and every minute of every hour here seems to be very little to show. The Ballet are going to do a Season at the Wells (as well as the Opera) from Boxing Day & we've done all the budgeting for that and the preliminary contract letters. It's a budget of £700 a week mostly made up of odd teasing little items like "coke for the radiators" which has to be charged 3 parts to Opera & 4 parts to Ballet. All of which takes time & shows NO result whatever. I've also prepared an incredible and shaming "Letter" which is going to go to all Old Vic Associates – a band of 1200 of the most zealous supporters – telling them what we're up to & bidding them be of good cheer. I've just written as tho' I were a colonial bishop & they were district visitors racing in snowshoes to dying esquimeaux in igloos – quite shameless.

To Mrs Norah Guthrie at Annaghmakerrig

23 Old Buildings, Lincoln's Inn, London WC2. 23 November 1939

The blackout is really *crashing*. Darkness now descends about half past four – & you really can have no idea how dark it is & what a tussle it makes everything – & how dangerous. It's pure suicide to cross the road; & at any moment one may shoot to doom through an open coal-shute; & measure one's length over unsuspected sandbags. The result of course is that people are very reluctant to stir out – which looks as if it would be very daft reopening the Vic. No shortage of food yet – though bacon not always available & what there is is of poor quality: but prices are going up.

To Mrs Norah Guthrie at Annaghmakerrig

23 Old Buildings, Lincoln's Inn, London WC2. Undated, December 1939

I've been madly contending with all the broken plans & contracts & to keep people cheerful & sensible. The Company are staying in Buxton en bloc till end of week anyhow. We left [Buxton] at 6 this morning arriving here lunchtime as I had conference with heads of departments at Vic & Judy had to sort out flat for A.R.P.[12] We go back to Buxton probably on Thurs or Friday. Everyone is calm & there's a great deal of good neighbourliness going on in all directions. The first flush of good feeling won't last I dare say but it is none the less touching & beautiful in its spontaneity. Do not worry about our Safety – there is a Providence in the fall of a sparrow as Hamlet says. Neither Peggy nor I nor Hubert nor Judy are very physically brave & therefore unlikely to be physically rash! I feel perfectly calm & not particularly – in fact not at all – unhappy. I realize very consciously that one's future depends on regarding these outward events merely as the artistic material for the future.

To Mrs Norah Guthrie at Annaghmakerrig

23 Old Buildings, Lincoln's Inn, London WC2. Undated, December 1939

We had a v. nice weekend at Peacemeal. I walked over on Sunday morning to see Becky [former nanny] & had such a nice visit. Miles [husband] wasn't in – he's really always at the fire station – he's captain now of the Fire Brigade – head of 50 men.

Last night we gave a party at the Wells before the opening of the new Ashton-Lambert ballet [*Dante Sonata*]. It was what you might

---

12   Air Raid Precautions – an organization of voluntary workers who watched for enemy aircraft, advised householders on the effectiveness of their blackout and directed members of the public to air-raid shelters.

call a diplomatic party – people invited who have been or about to be asked to be helpful to the Ballet & a few distinguished or socially fluent others! The ballet is, I think, superb – a real masterpiece. Awfully tragic but *most* impressive. They go off on another long provincial tour on Monday. The London season has lost money; but unless bombs begin they ought easily to recoup it on tour.

To Mrs Peggy Butler at Annaghmakerrig

23 Old Buildings, Lincoln's Inn, London WC2. 29 December 1939

There seems to be a terrible feeling that we're settling in for years & years of war with a gradual lowering of standards of living, physical and spiritual, which is awfully depressing. Oh well, I suppose we must be thankful that the bombs haven't started to fall here – yet.

We only had a very short time [at Christmas] as the British Council held a carol concert (for which we lent the Sadler's Well Theatre) on the afternoon of Xmas eve and we did not reach Peacemeal [Bretherton home, Tunbridge Wells] till 9 that night and then had to leave right after lunch on Boxing Day for the Ballet opening. The carol concert was a very touching & sad affair – 30 nationalities were present – there was a little nativity play simply & beautifully done by Austrians; an English, a Czech & a Polish choir and two refugee soloists.

Gordon [Bretherton] was in good form we thought; but Nelly [Bretherton] terribly jumpy & restless & unable to settle to any occupation for more than a few seconds at a time, until on the morning of Boxing Day we made a presentation bouquet for Ninette de Valois to receive at night. It was rather a gorgeous affair & took two hours to construct. It was "built" on a foundation of laurel – three big sprays about 4 feet long upon which we laid a terrific composition of Honesty, a few hothouse lilies and dozens & dozens & dozens of chrysanthemums of all colours. The eventual result could only be raised from the ground by weight-lifting machinery and fairly *staggered* the dainty recipient when "handed up" at night! But it looked as tho' quite £3 had been spent instead of 30/-.

Aunt Sue came to a turkey luncheon and stayed to hear the Empire greetings on the wireless and the King-Emperor. A terrible terrible BBC Daddy-man to link it all together but some of the bits very good

I thought – a great Welsh mining choir howling out the Hallelujah chorus gloriously; very touching highland folk-singing from Glasgow; the Belfast contribution was slick but phoney I thought; & there were two brutes of male & female gender from Canada & Australia respectively. The Monarch's [George VI] effort I found very moving – I think it really wonderfully brave of him to risk world ridicule of that stutter. The contrast is very fascinating between Hitler whose vocal technique is really dazzling and poor Guelph: the spell-binder and the wretched inbred inhibited mamett forced, most unwillingly, to wave a sceptre over *us*!

All tour plans, which seemed nicely set, collapsed like a card house the week before Christmas. Now we plan to open the Vic at the end of Feb or early March 1940 – there's an emergency Governors' meeting next week – & I must begin once again planning a programme & collecting a company. I had to get out of a film contract which is a bore as the money was enormous & the magnates, naturally, are *not* pleased. One has to be like Bruce's spider & patiently, endlessly, begin again to patch up the broken web. I feel NO confidence that the Vic can pay its way – nothing is acceptable now but rowdy musicals – yet we cannot stay shut without grave loss of goodwill; losing our subsidy from the Parochial Funds (£2000 p.a.); & not keeping at the head of the queue for handouts from a Socialist government after the war.

The earnings of last autumn's tour will be spent before we open – cleaning, rehearsal, production & preliminary advertising will run up a bill of £1000 and thereafter we can lose about £400 a week, which there are no assets to meet. The Wells also is doing badly – we'd hoped to do well with ballet this week but the snow has blotted out the moonlight & left the streets in a fearful mess so that we're losing anything from £50 to £100 every night. I'm not seriously fussed about this tho'; the advance booking is heavy & I think we'll come out on the right side.

I shall try & get over soon but don't weigh too heavily on the Advent as things are so anxious & chaotic one can't come away leaving everything in a mess: even on days when one isn't actually tussling one is there to be responsible & to give – I hope – a feeling of confidence & authority – probably an illusion but I hope it's something even to make the effort.

5

BLITZ AND EVACUATION:
FROM DUNKIRK TO BURNLEY

During the 'phoney war' the future of all theatres was in question; many – including the Old Vic and Sadler's Wells – were sporadically closed without notice. During the Battle of Britain the Sadler's Wells Theatre was used as a refugee centre. In May 1940 the Sadler's Wells Ballet company set out for Europe on an ill-conceived British Council 'propaganda' tour, becoming caught in the German invasion of Holland, losing everything and returning in the vanguard of the Dunkirk evacuation. Lewis Casson and his wife Sybil Thorndike headed one of the companies designated to tour Wales and the north of England. Many performers were 'called up' to the forces so the companies were largely made up of older and very young personnel as well as those considered medically unfit for war service, plus some 'conscientious objectors' and a few exempted figures deemed 'essential' to the work. Guthrie, as Director of the entire Vic-Wells organization, was constantly travelling, often by night, to 'keep the shows on the road'. At the same time he became increasingly concerned about the future of Annaghmakerrig where his sister Peggy Butler was taking in paying guests.

To Mrs Norah Guthrie at Annaghmakerrig

23 Old Buildings, Lincoln's Inn, London WC2. 1 January 1940

> Isn't it simply alarming? Where have my forty years gone? They fly forgotten as a dream flies at the opening day. I think Sandy's [Uncle Sandy Guthrie] suggestion of letting Annagh-ma-kerrig furnished is 1/ impractical – who'd take it? 2/ Idiotic – what would *you* do while the tenants were in possession? I've written to tell him so!

Very busy – all departments humming. Opera & ballet both, thank goodness, doing well at the moment – ballet, in fact, made a clear profit of over £900 at Liverpool last week but it won't take long to lose it again!

To Mrs Norah Guthrie at Annaghmakerrig

23 Old Buildings, Lincoln's Inn, London WC2. 7 January 1940

I'm still struggling with no tangible result to find a wise plan for the Vic. A programme that will honourably maintain our policy without leading straight to financial ruin. Latest idea is a tour of *Trilby* with Ernest Milton as Svengali, Margaret Rawlings as Trilby, Alec [Guinness] as Little Billee. The dramatic version is excellent, I think; & now so dated as to be once more quite modish.

To Mrs Peggy Butler at Annaghmakerrig

23 Old Buildings, Lincoln's Inn, London WC2. 25 February 1940

It worries me no end that I am not taking my full share of responsibility for Annaghmakerrig; and not for being a support for Mrs G. The "burden" has fallen on you. I want you to know that I realise this. I want to state it in black and white because Hubert definitely implied to me the other day that my selfishness or/and my obtuseness was being resented. He spoke very bitterly and it was the tone more than the words that terrified me for the whole future of our relation. Show this letter to Hubert and discuss it together and let me have an equally plain answer. But you must be frank. I could not bear, darling, that there should be an unspoken resentment between us. If you feel that you have an unfair share of responsibility, too heavy a call on your time, *say so at once.* I will then re-arrange my life so as to be more free; tho' I fear that just now I shan't get permission to live out of England.

Now about money matters. We agreed that the economies so far arranged are only palliatives – they won't make ends meet. Nor do I think will paying guests tho' Hubert does think so. And anyway I'm quite agreed that it's worth trying to get them. If, after further discussion you all agree to go ahead vigorously with the pursuit, you will no doubt advertise in the paper – meantime, I'll find out whether

English people over military age would be allowed to go; if so, it would be worth putting advertisements in the English papers too. BUT even if this were to make ends meet, which is not my opinion, I think we ought to consider Mrs G's immediate comfort and peace of mind as being infinitely more important than the preservation intact of a certain sum of capital. The impression I got was that Hubert considered the sanctity of the capital dominantly important. While naturally we will try not to attack the capital, I feel strongly that to regard it as sacrosanct is wrong.

Reasons: 1/ Mrs G is too old drastically to change her way of life without real hardship. And I am convinced that drastic changes will make ends meet. 2/ Even if we preserve the capital intact by way of sacrifice (of which Mrs G as the oldest person will bear the brunt) I think there will soon be a capital levy. I quite admit that you and Hubert have had most of the dull coping to do and consequently are entitled to a stronger voice in council than I. I quite agree that the way Annaghmakerrig is being run is now quite *out of date*. I notice a distinct change in Mum this time, she's quite a bit older, tires more easily, is deafer, more forgetful, less alert. It was a terrible stab to find it so. But it's just got to be faced.

If you feel that I have been or am being selfish or unreasonable or un-understanding, say so. I'd rather anything in the world than that a bad situation should come between us all.

To Mrs Norah Guthrie at Annaghmakerrig

23 Old Buildings, Lincoln's Inn, London WC2. 28 February 1940

I think at last we're on the verge of a good plan for the Old Vic – it is to open after Easter with ballet 3 times a week & drama 4 times. The Ballet will pay its way on 3 shows if we use 2 pianos instead of orchestra. We have enough money to open. And I think I have a chance of £2,000 guarantee against loss on the season – £1,000 being the savings of the O.V. Association & £1,000 coming from an Australian heiress called Mrs Robinson. I spent an hour yesterday with Dr Mallon who is the Warden of Toynbee Hall & Governor of mainly all the semi-charitable cum cultural funds. He was tremendously helpful with advice and more practically by promising introductions to the

Carnegie Trust people and a dinner party at the H. of Commons to meet Herbert Morrison [as Leader of London County Council]. I came away feeling more encouraged than at any time since the war.

You know we've been working madly to save the military-aged ballet boys from being called up, because they literally are irreplaceable. If they go the Ballet finishes. General exemption has been refused but I hear now that there is every chance that each particular case will be considered on its merits by a "Hardship Committee". It is based on (1) Hardship for the boy since career can not be resumed; (2) Unemployment of 70 people if the Ballet is disbanded; (3) Loss to the community of a valuable amenity. I go on Wed. next with one of the dancers, Michael Soames. It will be interesting to see what will happen. I think our case is strong.

To Mrs Norah Guthrie at Annaghmakerrig

23 Old Buildings, Lincoln's Inn, London WC2. Undated, 1940

Michel Soames, one of the ballet dancers, has been given the postponement by the Hardship Committee. It's quite an amusing storicule, no adventure or anything, but interesting.

To Mrs Peggy Butler at Maidenhall

23 Old Buildings, Lincoln's Inn, London WC2. 4 March 1940

I hereby give notice that I do NOT wish money spent on the disposal of my "Remains". I don't want flowers. I don't want black worn. If my carcase can be useful I shall be happy to have it dissected by irreverent medical students and if, when they take out my false teeth (which are gold & should be sold) I look funny & make them laugh, I am *delighted*.

If only Mr Chamberlain [Prime Minister] weren't so old; his perky, satisfied timidity *don't* strike the right note.

To Mrs Norah Guthrie at Annaghmakerrig

23 Old Buildings, Lincoln's Inn, London WC2. 17 March 1940

A mêlée of arrangements to get going at the Vic – you see it involves not merely the Company but the entire staff from someone to stoke the furnace thro' all departments , stagehands, carpenters, wardrobe (male & female), painters, waitresses, programme girls, queue stool attendant, up to a catering manageress & house manager.

Meantime the Ballet has had an offer to go propaganding to Holland for a fortnight under the British Council; & is going to France for a month for the troops. This has meant preparing detailed estimates & programme plans at top speed – & the B. Council people are so tiresome & inefficient – fearfully grand & suave & polite but just incapable. Of course the gentlemen in striped trousers have never heard of anything so common as National Health Insurance & it does not occur to them that an orchestra which has never seen the score might possibly require to rehearse!

To Mrs Norah Guthrie at Annaghmakerrig

23 Old Buildings, Lincoln's Inn, London WC2. 4 May 1940

Business is completely awful – *Lear* [John Gielgud] is now losing heavily. For *The Tempest*, apart from a wee sprinkling for the first night, there is just no booking at all. But we must keep the people employed till the money runs out. Of course if air raids do develop on a big scale no doubt all theatres will have to close.

To Mrs Norah Guthrie at Annaghmakerrig

23 Old Buildings, Lincoln's Inn, London WC2. 11 May 1940

I have to be at the phone to answer the queries of distraught Ballet parents. They are being very good – only one hysterical Mama – for it's NOT NICE. We have heard that they're all together at The Hague & yesterday were quite all right. But of course, at the moment, removal by land, sea or air is out of the question. Naturally the phone never stops as there are 41 families & what is far more teasing, excited "fans" who ring up from impossible places like Swindon and say Oh the poor darlings aren't you just miserable about the poor sweets? They get short shrift from Miss E.M. Williams [Secretary] I can tell you.

Yesterday everyone really did think there might be trouble & the wires never stopped saying Take your gas mask so Williams stayed at the Wells to deal with the phone & Judy & I went to the Vic in case there was need to lead Rock of Ages in front of the safety-curtain.

Naturally there wasn't so much as a mouse stirring. When the raiders do come I shall be in a bath, or in a Certain Apt.

I am sorry about poor old Daddy B[utler]. It's really horrid. I hope for everyone's sake the end will come soon. Give my love & sympathy to Hubert. I hope the Britain-Eire trade agreement will give Bunty a market for her eggs – we'll get no Dutch ones now. Think you should talk to Eddy [Daley] again about pigs & see if there's no possibility.

You know one can't help a feeling of relief that there is *action* again. The killing & so on is ghastly – but not, I think, so hard to bear as the certainty that it must come. The expectation of either pleasure or pain seems always more concentrated, more felt, than the experience itself. When the time comes one is too busy for very much feeling. That anyway has always been my experience so far. And with things moving at this pace the end must come before very long.

To Mrs Norah Guthrie at Annaghmakerrig

Sadler's Wells Theatre, London. 14 May 1940

MANY HAPPY RETURNS OF THE DAY... what a world! The Ballet Company returned yesterday or rather this morning. Naturally the parents have been in a perfect *fever*. We've had fairly constant news of them & it's really been rather thrilling. Thursday night we knew they were dancing at Arnhem but motoring back to The Hague after the show. I'll write more when I've seen Ninette [de Valois].

[LATER] Friday 4 a.m. Arnhem invaded.

Friday 9 a.m. British Council in touch with B. Legation at The Hague on the phone "All S. Wells Ballet together & safe in The Hague."

Friday & Saty. Press reports of bombings, parachutes, etc.

Saty. night. Legation phones that they hope to get them away by boat.

Sunday morning. Legation phones that they are on a boat waiting to sail. Meantime pressmen ring up to say Reuter telegraphs that they are on a boat near Amsterdam. Legation phones that they are on a boat at the mouth of the North Sea Canal.

Monday tea-time we hear they are at Harwich.

Monday 9 p.m. Train due L'pool St. at 11. We all – Williams, Judy,

Bridges Adams (rep. B. Council) 20 pressmen and a multitude of tremendously excited Mums, Dads, Aunties and sympathisers.

At 1 a.m. the train still hadn't left Harwich – hundreds of refugees to be landed & passed thro' customs.

At 2 A.M. we all mustered at the barrier (not allowed on platform) – the station by now was completely silent & empty & of course eerily deadly dark.

Policemen arrived & detectives & an L.C.C. officer to herd the refugees [into] 4 great busses & 6 ambulances with white coated attendants like ghosts.

You could have heard a feather drop.

At twenty to three the train slowly crept in – no lights showing & not a sound – it just sort of rose out of the darkness. And then there got out the most exhausted, dirty, bleary, tatterdemalion crew. Everyone was herded into a great gymnasium attached to the station – a huge place & brightly lighted where kind elephantine police sorted them out. We had taxis waiting – & of course there were tremendous scenes of reunion tho' modified by the utter exhaustion of the travellers. They'd had no food since b'fast the day before – we didn't try to hear their story but just sorted them into cab-loads & sent them away to bed.

Scenery & dresses I fancy a total loss but heavily insured. That tangle remains to be sorted out. Business, naturally, has slumped heavily since the invasion – the Opera at Hull dropped from £287 to £75 on Friday night. Vic – *Lear* – figures much in proportion. Not funny: but what can one expect?

To Mrs Norah Guthrie at Annaghmakerrig

23 Old Buildings, Lincoln's Inn, London WC2. Undated, spring 1940

Cardiff has been awfully interesting – I've enjoyed it. Lewis [Casson] & I met at the barrier at Paddington at 8.30 on Saty. morning; got to Cardiff about midday & went straight to the HQ of the Council for the Encouragement of Music & Arts (our sponsors) – the local head was an upper class, well intentioned, haw-hawing Guardsman type – quite a poop but full of zeal; the Drama man who is to act as our agent was a diminutive white-haired minor prophet – about

45 & full of "go" with the most overdone, outrageously picturesque S. Wales intonations & Celtic turns of phrase & gift for repartee. Lewis & I, to our amazement, found our visit being regarded as practically a Royal one & luncheon almost a State Occasion. However, we soon rose above that & after lunch went off with the minor prophet (whose name is, believe it or not, Haydn Davies). This involved covering a large part of S. Wales by car with amazing calls on Mr Jones Gas and Mrs Evans Butcher and Mrs Price Post Office to extract keys & information [on availability of halls].

Eventually we went up the Rhonnda Valley which I was thrilled to see & found very much as one had pictured it – infinitely romantic in a squalid way. Thence over a wonderful mountain road to Aberdare & then back down another valley past Mountain Ash. They never stop having air raids but amazingly little damage seems to have been done. But I think the perpetual alarms are pretty wearing – there didn't seem the slightest evidence of panic but one did notice the topic recurring pretty constantly e.g. the waitress hustled us out of the hotel dining-room where we were inclined to linger over eggs & bacon & tea with "Come along now pleece, you'll excuse me won't you but I want to be getting home and before the old syreens start buzzing off." But sure enough at 2 in the morning "Woo-oo-oo" all over the town, "Woo-oo-oo" faintly from down the coast, fainter still from the valleys.

Lewis & I had agreed that we wouldn't get up – our rooms weren't on the top floor & there were 2 layers of curtains over the windows & anyway there was nowhere much to go except the lounge which wasn't really fortified. So I just lay abed and wondered for a few minutes if I heard planes & then went asleep again till the All Clear awoke me at three. I found that having planned definitely *not* to get up, *not* to do anything, I wasn't the least bit frightened. Of course last night really wasn't frightening, there was no gunfire & no bombs. But the sirens at first are quite haunting: and tho' last night I had no physical symptoms like quick breathing, trembling or sweating, I have caught myself all day *listening* for sounds, wondering if a starting car, a banging door, might just be …

We had another alarm at 9 just as I was dressing – I finished my toilette & went down to find everyone completely calm except an admiral's wife who was running about in a dressing-gown saying to

The Royal
Victoria Theatre,
Burnley,
Lancashire,
where Guthrie
was in charge
of the Old
Vic Theatre
Company and
the Sadler's
Wells Opera and
Ballet during
World War II.

the porter "I'd just got into the bath – I don't know what my hair can be like!" and laughing rather loudly. Lewis was out in the street scanning the sky – but that I simply could *not allow* and made him come in at once and have breakfast.

Did you hear the Vic "starring" on the 9 o'c News on Sat? Judy says they all did and that the Man on the Wireless gave us a great boost. The prospect in general is pretty gloomy isn't it? Just an interminable vista of dwindling stocks & disappearing amenities, or else the Inferno. I suppose God has a plan. And we are but dust on the knob of the least of the Pawns on the chessboard. But even that great reflection isn't frightfully *comfy*!

This reconnaissance resulted in fit-up tours of *Macbeth*, *Medea* and *Candida*, directed by Lewis Casson with Sybil Thorndike in the leads, later organized from the Royal Victoria Theatre, Burnley, Lancashire. Letters from Britain to Ireland were opened by the official censor and mentions of wartime activities scissored.

To Mrs Norah Guthrie at Annaghmakerrig

Sadler's Wells Theatre, London. Undated, early June 1940

The cumulative damage is rather fearful – each night another crop of wrecked buildings, fires, broken gas & water pipes, homeless refugees. Our first batch of refugees arrived here last Thursday – 89 at ½ hour's notice. We had mattresses, pillows & blankets & got them distributed quickly into the safe parts of the basement while others registered the numbers & particulars of the incomers (who are sent by the billeting officer). After an influx like this one of the symptoms is a series of distraught relatives who come & say "Have you a Mrs Hadby here?" – "No, we have Winnie Hadby" – a sort of gruesome game of Happy Families – only nobody by any chance *ever* collects a happy family.

We have our clothes & belongings in a dressing-room on the 1st floor & share another d. room with Williams, Prévost & Geo as a kitchen & larder. The lack of gas & hot water is very frustrating. Last night again at terribly short notice another 60 arrived but of course we could not refuse – there was a dreadful land-mine two nights ago near here making 500 homeless. They are too fussed & exhausted to be grateful for our attentions or to grumble, they're just utterly passive. We slosh out mattresses & slosh out stew & slosh up dirty cups & saucers.

In addition, Williams & I have never been busier in the office. We've got tours arranged for the Ballet and the Opera is, now almost for certain, going out in two detachments, one doing *Figaro* in Lancashire & the other *Fledermaus* for E.N.S.A.[13] in camps. I think we did 60 letters today in addition to refugee work.

The roof of 23 Old Buildings was set alight last night but fire was quenched before serious. Conditions in the tubes [subway] are, I believe, frantic. Everyone swaps experiences all the time – the ghastly bang at 2 a.m. … the incredible escape of the Rev. B. … what they've

13   Entertainments National Service Association

done to Bourne & Hollingsworth ... my dear, have you seen the Queen's Theatre? – a heap of rubble, my dear, & Marie Tempest still legible on one of the bills ...

I don't think I've made it clear, the misery of the refugees. One of the great problems is the lack of clothes – they have nothing but what they stand up in – & they arrive in a muck sweat after their terror & covered in brick dust & so on. The w.v.s.[14] run a half-hearted little clothing depôt but lady-volunteers aren't always present.

To Mrs Norah Guthrie at Annaghmakerrig

No heading. 13 June 1940

Without wishing to alarm you – & I know you won't be easily & stupidly alarmed – I don't think you should underestimate the possibility of Ireland being invaded. I think it almost certain that the Germans will try. You see, Eire might easily be a manageable proportion for troop-carrying, gun-carrying, tank-carrying planes. And it clearly is a vitally important strategic point to hold if they mean to invade England. And they clearly do mean to attempt that. I can't think that you at Annaghmakerrig are likely to be a battlefield. We're not, as far as I can see, on the road from anywhere to anywhere else of importance. And it, mercifully, could be a less suitable landing ground for planes! I do think, tho', that you should face the very real possibility of communications being totally disorganised for a considerable period & lay in wise stores of necessaries that will in such circumstances be unobtainable. Talk to Eddy about all this: he'll be awfully steady & sensible. And don't feel it's fancy & craven to *take precautions* and to *warn* the *neighbours* so that they aren't driven too roughly out of a Fool's Paradise. You will be a great old Rock of Strength I know; but it is easier to be that if ready for the worst & not pooh-poohing at the enemy à la Chamberlain et Cie.

We've left a case of clothes with Aunt Sue.

And having got that off my chest I must stop & go and haggle with the British Council over replacement of losses suffered by Ballet in Holland. My life at present is a round of haggling parties at committees – much more interesting than it sounds. I enjoy most of it.

---

14   Women's Voluntary Service

To Mrs Norah Guthrie at Annaghmakerrig

Sadler's Wells Theatre. 18 June 1940

> We've very busy here reorganising all companies [theatre-opera-ballet] on basic minimum salaries & percentages of the takings past a certain figure; so as to make it possible to carry on in face of reduced business. Everyone very nice & co-operative about it all. One feels it's dotty enough to go on. But as yet the alternative is even more dotty – closing down, putting all employees out of work & not having the entertainment available. Even now there are many, many people wanting our sort of entertainment – even last week over 2,000 people went to the Vic and more than double that came here.
>
> Lewis & Sybil's eldest son is missing. He was a Squadron Leader in the Fleet Air Arm. They were, true to themselves, wonderfully resolute & hopeful about him; but of course it's a ghastly, haunting anxiety & fear. In *The Tempest* Lewis plays Gonzago, one of the lords in the shipwrecked party. The king, in the play, keeps on lamenting, as you remember, "My son is lost, my son is drowned" – the night the news came Lewis weathered all that & got through his performance perfectly all right till it came to the moment at the end when Ferdinand & Miranda are discovered playing chess in the grotto & the father & son are reunited. Then he just broke down and wept on the stage.
>
> I think the Pilgrim Trust are now definitely prepared, with Ministry of Education, to finance a Vic tour. Failing that, I suppose we just continue fiddling gaily amid the flames. Provided the fiddling is of really high quality I can think of sillier occupations.

To Mrs Norah Guthrie at Annaghmakerrig

As from Peacemeal, Tunbridge Wells. 30 June 1940

> The Pilgrim Trust thing is now all set & details of plans getting started. At first we're sending Sybil & Lewis in *Noah* [André Obey]. No word, alas, of their son. The Wells had two big houses y'day, over 3,000 people between the two. After endless ding-dong we've made a cost settlement with the B. Council in compensation for our losses in Holland: £4,000. It's quite fair, I think; and far better for us in cash than in materials we can't immediately use.

To Mrs Norah Guthrie at Annaghmakerrig

As from Peacemeal, Tunbridge Wells. 25 August 1940

> Raids & raiders are of course the topic. I don't know whether the censor will allow this [he did not, name of neighbourhood cut] ... was bombed & machine-gunned (no loss of life) by a raider which, my dear, was brought down at [cut] ... I must say people are taking it all amazingly well. In a way I almost think it's being enjoyed. We had 3 alarms y'day – one for breakfast, one for tea & one for supper. Judy had the honour of being one of 4 of her 1ˢᵗ Aid Group to be chosen to give demonstrations to neighbouring detachment of Home Guard.
>
> Please share this with Peggy. I meant to write to her but find I don't know address – Clifden just seems a bit inadequate. Don't worry about air-raids. If the bang is sufficiently thorough it will further save the expense of the funeral since there'll be nothing to bury.

The Butlers, with three other families, the Fitz-Simons, Killens and Perrys, had taken a holiday property in the west of Ireland to avoid the anticipated German invasion of the east. Performances at the Old Vic and Sadler's Wells were given in the afternoons, members of the audience often sheltering from the Blitz in the theatres afterwards.

To Mrs Norah Guthrie at Annaghmakerrig

23 Old Buildings, Lincoln's Inn, London WC2. 1 September 1940

> So far audiences are still coming to the Wells. We shall go on next week unless compulsorily closed.

To Mrs Norah Guthrie at Annaghmakerrig

23 Old Buildings, Lincoln's Inn, London WC2. 8 September 1940

> The noisiest period was between 5 & 6 in the evening when every gun in London seemed to be shouting away – impressive orchestration. We stayed at the Wells till about 3 a.m. by which most of the people had evaporated – a few ancients were bedded down in the cellars & a certain sprinkling of orchestra & staff were also crumpling up on chairs with newspapers over their faces. Herbert Menges [conductor] was with us so he & Judy & I set off in a comparative lull but with

the entire landscape flickering in the lobster-coloured reflection of the flames. The dome of St Paul's stood up looking really terrific in silhouette …

To Mrs Norah Guthrie at Annaghmakerrig
Sadler's Wells Theatre. 12 September 1940

Last night we slept at the Wells as we had to be available to take refugees if required (none came), so Williams, George, Prevost, Judy & I all slept in the Band Room, a splendidly strong basement – also the Sergeyeffs (of whom more anon). The anti-aircraft barrage was tremendous – I don't know that it was any good, as far as I can gather just as many bombs were dropped but the psychological effect has been immense: at last something is being done and the bangs, instead of being purely terrorising and music, hundreds of gigantic watchdogs bark bark barking at the sky & quite drowning the hypnotising mosquito buzz of the raiders to which we have listened helplessly all the other nights.

The Sergeyeffs are Russian – he is the maître-de-ballet & teaches all day long up in the rehearsal room at the top of the building. He sits with a long stick, counting the beats & poking at the dancers with the stick. A tiny neat grey squirrel of a man with pince-nez – he might be any age between 45 & 70. He was connected with the Russian Imperial Ballet – pre-Diaghilev – & has some unique method of notation which makes him the sole repository in the world who knows the whole traditional choreography of the big classical ballets. To possess him is an enormous score for the Wells & means that we perform far the most accurate versions of all the Petipa ballets – *Giselle, Swan Lake, S. Princess, Coppélia* – rather fascinating, don't you think?

Madame Sergeyeff was in the Diaghilev corps-de-ballet – her life has been an affair of world tours – frowsty lodgings, frowstier dressing-rooms, bouquets, Sunday morning train-calls, eternal packing of suitcases – Moscow, Kiev, Breslau, Copenhagen, Milan. When the Diaghilev organisation broke up Ninette flew over to Paris & nobbled Sergeyeff for the Wells. They have had their little flat in Gordon Street & come every day to the top room at the Wells, he to teach & she to act as his interpreter – she speaks two words of incredibly queer English, he speaks none – he teaches in a mixture of Russian & German with Italian musical terms – lento, piu mosso, dolce dolce dolce & a wealth of tiny experienced nett gestures.

Two nights ago their little flat was bombed – now they're back in their suitcases & a bundle made of a silk bedspread. Moscow, Kiev, Breslau, Copenhagen & Milan are no longer attainable. There are no Sunday train calls to anywhere. There is no more ballet at Sadler's Wells. They are our first refugees. Last night, in return for the hospitality of the theatre, they gave us a party – they brought in sausage-rolls & fearsome little "pastries" from Lyons – there were 4 bottle of beer, a bottle of sherry & a bottle of Cointreau bought years ago in Paris, saved from the wreckage. We were all dressed for the night, i.e. scarves, oldest clothes, the Venue was the Sergeyeffs' temporary home, the Conductor's Room at the Wells which is about the size of a grave, contains a wooden shelf & two kitchen chairs but is very safe – ground floor, reinforced walls, window boarded up, which gives it the look of a fortress. All this accompanied by the *Roar*, the incredible volleys of our watchdogs outside. Eventually, & not without ceremony, we broached the Cointreau – Madame proposed the toast of the Royal Air Force and we had one of those emotional moments amid gaiety that are so "Russian" in the theatre.

I forgot to tell you before, our sitting room & kitchen windows [at Lincoln's Inn] are broken & a large part of the hall ceiling is down & the entire flat is silvered o'er with a fine impalpable ash from the terrible fires on Holborn. Poor Puss-cat was terrified & hid for some hours but emerged at last & has been sent to Hampstead to the villa of the mother-in-law of Dr Russell Thomas who runs the First Aid post; she has a bright bed-sitter to herself, is eating well, likes Mrs Bennett her hostess & rings up every day ...

To Mrs Norah Guthrie at Annaghmakerrig

Sadler's Wells Theatre. 19 September 1940

Just a line to say we're alright. The nights are still incredibly noisy & I believe to go thro' the streets is very very dangerous mainly because of bits & pieces from our own barrage. Everyone just goes to ground & stays there. Here our little colony disposes itself in the basement like rabbits in a warren – Williams, George, Prevost, Judy & myself are here always; the Sergeyeffs are in at nights; & we have a [stage] staff of

6 who do alternate day & night shifts headed by Harry Catch the old flyman & Bill Lavender the foreman stagehand.

To Mrs Norah Guthrie at Annaghmakerrig

Sadler's Wells Theatre. 24 September 1940

Thousands trek into the suburbs & the West End each night to sleep but that in itself is a tussle. The authorities are "coping" but you can't accommodate thousands at a wave of a wand. Of course it all *ought* to have been foreseen & tackled in advance but the people who scream this out forget that the greatest obstacle to this is not authoritarian slackness but public apathy & stupidity. People wouldn't (& won't) evacuate their children; they wouldn't make safe places in their basements; they wouldn't (& haven't) made sensible coverings of earth over their Anderson Shelters.

To Mrs Norah Guthrie at Annaghmakerrig

Sadler's Wells Theatre. 3 October 1940

Working terribly hard over tours & terribly handicapped by difficulties of communication. The phone is just dotty: you never can get the right number; the posts take a week to reply even to local letters. Too fussing & frustrating when we're trying to cast 3 companies simultaneously. No further refugees [in theatre] & our 160 are gradually beginning to drain off – some to the country, some to rooms, some to relatives. You'll have read it's the suburbs are now catching it most. One mustn't mention names but one of the suburbs S. of the Vic where a lot of our stage-hands live has had a fearful going-at. None of our boys or families are hurt but many are homeless. We have Puss-cat [Lizzie] here now. Her hostess in Hampstead has gone to the country. She's settled in wonderfully easily & runs about the dressing-rooms quite gaily & is already earning her keep by scaring away the mice.

To Mrs Norah Guthrie at Annaghmakerrig

Sadler's Wells Theatre. 8 October 1940

I am rehearsing *Figaro* & enjoying that very much: it's a complete escape & I am very lucky to be able to hide in it *entirely* for hours at a time.

To Mrs Peggy Butler at Annaghmakerrig

Chorley, Cheshire. 20 October 1940

This morning we left Judy for Manchester to buy artificial flowers for *Traviata*, I to Chorley to see the Vic Co. On arrival I was whisked into a car by Jo Hodgkinson, our advance agent, & we visited Bury, Preston, Blackburn, Accrington & Burnley seeing halls, checking booking plans, interviewing the Secretary of this & the Committee of that, arranging motor transport for opera scenery, etc etc. Gave us a far better idea of the touring conditions than any number of letters. We got back to Chorley around 7 & I saw them play *She Stoops* in a perfectly gigantic cinema to an audience who sat in interested but utterly unamused reverence – I don't think any of them had ever seen a play before, only films. Then, after much talk with the Company who were eager to hear about London & tell about their own experiences & adventures, I fetched up at Ernie's exceedingly squalid pub where we had supper & talked plans.

We would be more efficient out of London now. As yet I see no systematic driving to cope with the shelter situation there. They are not digging deep shelters; there is no systematic evacuation. I intend seeing the Town Clerk [of Islington] tomorrow & explaining that we are not prepared indefinitely to staff the [Sadler's Wells Theatre] building as a relief centre. Now that we have all our Companies working I intend to concentrate on our evacuation plans.

Guthrie had asked the Old Vic advance man, Jo Hodgkinson, to seek a theatre 'out of bombing range' to which the entire Vic-Wells organization could relocate. J.H. Linscott, manager of the 1800-seat Royal Victoria Theatre in Burnley, Lancashire, responded; in mid November 1940 the Old Vic Theatre with the Sadler's Wells Opera and Ballet companies were evacuated there. Seasons of drama, opera and ballet were given regularly, with Burnley the centre from which tours circulated: at times as many as four companies (opera, ballet and two theatre productions) were simultaneously on the road.

To Mrs Norah Guthrie at Annaghmakerrig

In the train. 26 October 1940

> I'm now heading for Manchester to discuss plans with the heads of the
> Opera Co. at Burnley where they open tonight. We've practically arranged
> with the manager of the Burnley theatre to give an 8 week season there
> beginning Jan. 26th & the details of that has to be worked out.
>
> If we go to Burnley our removal will be an immense affair as I
> suppose a certain amount of furniture, crockery & co. will need to be
> transported – apart from files & some reserve of dresses, canvas, electric
> equipment, etc.

To Mrs Norah Guthrie at Annaghmakerrig

Sadler's Wells Theatre. 4 November 1940

> The story of our impending departure is out & I've had newspaper
> people phoning & calling all day. Judy & Prévost took several cases
> North [to Burnley] as an advance guard. We had a melancholy time on
> Saty. afternoon sorting the flat. The roof leaks, there is a lot of plaster
> down. No raid at all last night. The first unmolested night for 56 nights.
>
> I'm afraid Ailish [Fitz-Simon] will be very worried about Simon.
> Egypt & Palestine aren't nice places just now. How nice it would be if
> one could feel the tiniest little bit of confidence in any of our generals.
> But the very youngest is 80 and they all think in terms of Fuzzies &
> Wops. I'm so tired of hearing that the Egyptian desert defeated
> Napoleon. Napoleon – poor dear – didn't have a motor-car & like Mr
> Chamberlain had never been in an aeroplane.
>
> It's rather exciting moving to Burnley. To be on the eve of The
> Removal & not have the slightest conception of what one is moving
> to – whether a house or a flat; I have almost no mental picture of the
> town as my visits have all been hasty rushes between the station & the
> theatre. All the uncertainty is rather fun. I suppose the Vicar will call.

To Mrs Norah Guthrie at Annaghmakerrig

Sadler's Wells Theatre. 14 November 1940

> The flat is all packed up & all the furniture we are taking is on the stage
> here awaiting collection by a great van that will go North – we hope

– on Monday. Packing the theatre up is a much more formidable undertaking & there's endless fiddle-de-dee over rates, gas, electricity and all the rest of it, most of which I am just blatantly handing over to our lawyer to cope with, he's as sharp as ten needles and infinitely better able to deal with it all than I am, and blow the expense.

Poor old Sergeyeff is very ill – pneumonia. He's in hospital & wee madam creeps about looking terribly anxious & haggard. I think they think he will pull through but it will be a long time before he is able to travel. When he's fit we've arranged that they shall go to Margey Le Lacheur at Looe in Cornwall who has two rooms and she is prepared to take them at nominal rate. Alas the delay is likely to mean that she is unable to preserve the rooms from clutches of billeting officers, both military and civil as that being a safe area people are literally standing on one another's heads. Meantime our [Opera & Ballet] leaving here means that Madame Sergeyeff has to turn out. I've given her twenty five pounds of Larry's hundred so she'll be able to manage for the next while. Poor things, the abnormality of everything does so emphasise their isolation.

To Mrs Norah Guthrie at Annaghmakerrig

Mackworth Hotel, Swansea. Undated, mid November 1940

Just leaving here en-route for Manchester & thence Burnley. Judy travels up today with the Ballet company & endless luggage including Pussy in her villa [basket] & Pussy Lloyd in their villa. Such an interesting day y'day. We had a "conference" in the morning, Sybil & Lewis & I & the district organiser for the Council of Social Service – really to discuss the results of this tour & to rough out future plans. We're to have another meeting on Monday week to meet more reps. & trade union leaders – it means my coming down from Keswick (!) where the Opera will be but it's important & worth it.

After lunch we went out to Cross Hands where the evening perf. was to be. Cross Hands is a mining village but far away in the country so that it's really a rural community. The hall is large & handsome & very well equipped – they all are: Miners' Welfare funds. The Company was met by a "Reception Committee" of locals who took them off to billets. The whole living arrangements in all these towns are being very diff. – you have no idea of the crowdedness of everywhere – there isn't a village up these valleys that isn't full of evacuated Londoners. I assisted the Stage Management to arrange handsome but perilous rostrums for the Chorus (we do *Macbeth* with a male and female Narrator) & the whole covered in black serge. Then at 4 we all reassembled for tea in the Minor Hall – the whole Coy. and about 60 or 70 locals, the committee, some clergymen & prominent persons: oh you know.

The performance began was distinguishedly staged & lit – highly professional. Sybil is now too old for Lady Macbeth but not so as to seriously matter – she looked very fine & her sleepwalking is immense. Lewis does intelligently as Macbeth but the trouble is that Macbeth shouldn't look like a stocky little naval commander as Lewis does! The rest of the Company very good and the whole thing had great pace & drive & style & was immensely pleasing to Cross Hands.

To Mrs Norah Guthrie at Annaghmakerrig

Victoria Theatre, Burnley, Lancs. 18 November 1940

Well here we are! At the moment we're ensconced in very comfy "digs". I got in from Swansea at 10 having travelled for 12 hours. Judy didn't get here at all – a long saga – but turned up today. So far I've only caught a glimpse from a passing bus from what I think is our mansion. It looked quite nice & J., after being there most of today, is really pleased with it. Burnley – such friendly, homely people. One sees that in "little" places (compared with London); life is lived at considerably lower pressure & slower tempo – with many advantages. The workmen who are doing the house & the office are so friendly & chit-chatty in a simple countrified way & it's all more neighbourly & more leisurely.

The Opera is at Bury tonight & is already sold out; already sold out at Keswick for the latter part of the week; already sold out at Kendal for the whole of the following week. Our office is charming. A quaintly decayed slum building plumb in the centre of the town but off the main street & perched amazingly above a roaring mountain torrent – rather like one of those riverside shacks in Ballybay.

Sybil Thorndike, Lewis Casson, Ann Casson, Douglas Campbell (a conscientious objector) and others on tour in wartime with *Candida*, *Macbeth* and *Medea*.

To Mrs Norah Guthrie at Annaghmakerrig

Victoria Theatre, Burnley, Lancs. 21 November 1940

A picture of Burnley. Grey stone houses – hardly any brick or red colouring – slate roofs & endless steep little streets of identical rows; unpromisingly squat & uniform without but Oh so cosy within – with frequently very nice bits of old furniture, & much more roomy & comfortable than the exterior promises. Ever so many great barracks of mills, very solid & prosperous looking & madly busy now - & forests of chimneys all smoking - & everything piles up & down steep hills with unexpected fascinating rushing torrents dashing downwards to the [River] Brun which appears every now & then in the centre of the town between tunnels where it dives here under Woolworth's, there under the G.P.O. Altho' a big town – 90,000 people – it's compact & very soon one climbs up onto wonderful wild craggy moors. Our house will do – it has many good qualities but absolutely no charm. It's a decent, sensible lower middle class villa – nothing about Burnley aspires higher than lower middle class.

The office on the other hand is less respectable, probably far less sensible, also more amusing. You come out of the stage door of the theatre onto a sort of wide platform with a railing along one side & a row of slummy little houses on the other. From the platform a steep flight of stairs leads down 20 feet to street level; from it too there is a thrilling view of factory chimneys, mills, etc. Inside, the wee house has 2 rooms on each of 3 floors – just what we need – so far no snags have appeared, at least nothing nearly serious enough to explain why we have been allowed to rent it for 12/- a week.

To Mrs Norah Guthrie at Annaghmakerrig
Victoria Theatre, Burnley, Lancs. 22 November 1940

We lunched in the new house today (177 Manchester Road, Burnley) – only a picnic lunch but it was quite pleasant with a nice coal fire & sun coming in at the windie. The blackout is a little holding up our entry as it just isn't enough to hang curtains & hope for the best – that way lies a 50/- fine, also the only curtains we have are a rather scratch lot of oddments from the theatres so a Little Woman & her little machine have to be collected, rods rigged up, etc. Poor Pussy is overjoyed with the coal fires & soft chairs.

We are so pleased with our office. It's awfully snug & central & just wonderful to have a telephone that works: but a call to London to poor old George (who is left behind to clear up at the Wells) never got through at all. One of the amenities here is a first rate public library.

Sad account in P's letter of old daddy Butler. Poor old man, he sounds so restless & ill at ease.

Postcard to Mrs Norah Guthrie at Annaghmakerrig
Victoria Theatre, Burnley. 9 December 1940

Booking for our Season here opened to-day & they've sold nearly £400 – isn't that quite something?

To Mrs Norah Guthrie at Annaghmakerrig
177 Manchester Road, Burnley. 9 December 1940

So maddening: permit has come but I can't get a travel pass [to Ireland] till after Xmas; then I can't leave here because there's so much on that I really must not delegate, & the permit expires Jan 15! There's a Governors' Meeting Jan 10 in London that I have to attend & *The Beggars' Opera* opens here Jan 16 & I must be present. I shall immediately apply for an extension.

The Guthries' temporary home on the corner of Manchester Road, Burnley.

It's amazing to hear of Dublin with its lighted shops & trains & butter & eggs, dog shows, etc. Mind you, I see Dev's point about the bases. I'm sure it makes you rage. But I think he's right.[15]

Last weekend George & I went up to Ulverston to see the Opera Co. – they're always having ructions. We borrowed a car (George contrived it – I can't imagine how) & drove thro' the most divine wild Pennine country. Saw the matinée & had endless confabs till 2 a.m. Drove next morning to Lancaster, had further confabs till after lunch when we drove back by another even more wonderful route. On Monday we had to go to Blackpool (Ballet), this time by bus, stopping en route to keep several appointments in Manchester. Long confabs with Ninette [de Valois] & Ballet heads till all hours & I was off again to Lancaster to take a rehearsal of *Figaro* for the new Suzanna – as I'd sacked a particularly teasing soprano at Ulverston. Blackpool is amazing & I suppose I mayn't enlarge [censor] but it's packed with people & not trippers either.

I think we've made very satisfactory arrangements with the Director of Education. There will be 400 seats available at 6d a head in the gallery for school parties every Tuesday matinée. I think we're going to manage that they have special classes about the plays (*XII*

<hr>

15   Eamon de Valéra, Taoiseach (Prime Minister) of neutral Ireland, refused to allow the Royal Navy the use of certain ports.

Night, Macbeth & *Trilby*) before they see them; & after they've seen them a special class when they can either write essays or draw pictures giving their impressions. I will offer prizes for the best of these & we'll have an exhibition in the Public Library.

On Friday Sir Reginald (Row; Hon. Treas. Sadler's Wells) wired announcing himself – couldn't have been less convenient really but he's such an old dear & obviously wanted to come. Sir R. is dreadfully pale & I don't think he'll last long.

When my passport came back from the permit office in L'pool it had a wee note inside it saying "Very best wishes to yourself & all at the Old Vic & Sadler's Wells – E.J. Reynolds, your interpreter at Elsinore" – wasn't that rather fun? And so glad to hear he's not in Elsinore now.

Postcard to Mrs Norah Guthrie at Annaghmakerrig
Rochdale P.O. en route for Oldham. 19 December 1940

Didn't explain that I'm rehearsing *Die Fledermaus* in Oldham – had intended staying there but can find no rooms.

To Mrs Norah Guthrie at Annaghmakerrig
177 Manchester Road, Burnley. 27 December 1940

Madame Butterfly is rehearsing in Manchester with orchestra augmented from the Hallé & will be broadcast. A difficulty arose with *Macbeth* on tour when the set got stuck in Llanelly and could not be got out!

The Guthries were now established in a Victorian terrace house built of local limestone grit. Hubert Butler's translation of *The Cherry Orchard* was one of the plays revived by the Old Vic on tour, with changes of cast since the London production. Hubert Butler's father died at Maidenhall in April.

To Mrs Norah Guthrie at Annaghmakerrig
177 Manchester Road, Burnley. 5 January 1941

Mysterious bombs on Eire. None of the published "explanations" make any sense. I still think they were mistakes of lost [German] airmen who thought Dublin was a town in England.

It's immensely cold & a light powdering of snow lies on roofs and ground. Burnley looks quite beautiful under the dark skies. It's exactly the sort of landscape I most admire & would like to paint it if I knew how. Chimneys & railway tracks & canal winding between dark throbbing factories; black forbidding tabernacles – all bounded by these glorious wild moors.

It's so odd to be isolated here. Actually that doesn't mean isolated at all because we're quite a colony with endless comings and goings – in the last two weeks, apart from the residential staff & visitors from the companies, we've had in the house Maggie Furse, Ninette de Valois, Sir Reginald Row & Fred Cooke. But it doesn't alter the fact that one is entirely severed from ordinary connections & routine – & it's rather fun to be so. Being in the centre of the Spider's Web involves a lot of social work, missionary, hospital, rescue & prevention.

To Mrs Norah Guthrie at Annaghmakerrig 177 Manchester Road, Burnley. 2 February 1941

I shall be most of next week at Huddersfield with the Opera as I think I would tidy up *The Beggars' Opera* a good deal before they take it into London.

To Mrs Norah Guthrie at Annaghmakerrig
177 Manchester Road, Burnley. 11 February 1941

Esmé's Co. opened here last night in *Trilby*, which was well liked. They've been going for nearly 30 weeks. After a fortnight's rest they go into rehearsal with *The Merchant of Venice* for very tiny primitive stages in the mining areas of Northumberland & Durham. Meanwhile, Sybil & Lewis are away into North Wales. In May we hope to open the new [James] Forsyth play for a v. brief season in London, then join all forces for a big prod of *King John*, opening here, playing a few weeks in Lancs. & the NW & then to S. Wales, & that will get them to November – IF we ever get that length.

To Mrs Norah Guthrie at Annaghmakerrig
Norfolk Hotel, Strand, London WC2. 26 February 1941

I darted down here on Monday afternoon. I'm begging really from
c.e.m.a. & Carnegie to get them to pay for an orchestra for Ballet –
reduced since blitz to two pianos. Also hoping to get increased subsidy
for Opera. It means a lot of interviews, committees, delay, red tape &
probably ultimate disappointment. But nothing venture, nothing win.

To Mrs Norah Guthrie at Annaghmakerrig
177 Manchester Road, Burnley. 1 March 1941

I started this y'day afternoon as I had a five hours spell of *firewatching*
& thought it would be a great opportunity for letters. But not at all.
It proved to be a most sociable occasion. Geo & I are part of the
Watchers contingent at our store – not at the theatre – & there we
share the duties with two big [cotton] mills co-watchers, Mr Smith
the boilerman at one of the mills & Mr Shackleton the warehouse
foreman at the other.

To Mrs Norah Guthrie at Annaghmakerrig
Theatre Royal, Glasgow. 8 March 1941

By a nice coincidence Elliot [Mason] is here with the Emlyn Williams
play [*The Corn is Green*]. Have seen quite a number of old friends &
went to lunch with the Buchanans – Meg much the same as ever,
getting stouter.

Opera bookings are very good indeed, over £3,000 for the season.
Long queues at the booking office all day & great enthusiasm at
curtain fall. Important that Glasgow & Edinboro' should be strong
holders for the future if we make a good impression. No more now –
the radio is blaring *Fledermaus* – how I detest that work.

To Hubert Butler at Annaghmakerrig
177 Manchester Road, Burnley. 13 April 1941

Just a little line to tell you our affectionate thoughts are with you. You
could not, I know, have wished your father to live on & yet not really
live; yet The End, the full stop, cannot but be solemn and sad. One

twitters and tweets from a nearby bush in a true fervour of wanting to assist. All one can do is write this futile wee note between whose lines you will, I know, see a real affection and sympathy in this crisis trying to make itself articulate.

This is Easter Sunday – I've only just had Mrs G's note about your father's death – the day of resurrection. I think it must be rather cheerful and cheering that at the end of an epoch in your own life, and at such a crux in the world's affairs, the earth is bursting with new life. I always remember with pleasure the primroses and daffodils at poor old James Dane's lonely and rather meagre burial. Affectionately, T.

To Mrs Norah Guthrie at Annaghmakerrig

Hotel Regina, Bath. Good Friday, 1941

Today being Good Friday there is no performance & most of the [ballet] Company are taking the day in the country. This hotel is full of ancient well-off evacuees. It's still very warm and clean but the food is pretty Spartan. I expect you're very short of tea. What a queer world! I grumble a good deal about my journeys and dreary work etc: but really feel most determined not to give up and not to judge myself on result but on the attempt and not to mind if the result is nothing. This isn't easy as the theatre teaches one to judge too much in terms of the pleasure given & the success attained.

To Mrs Norah Guthrie at Annaghmakerrig

177 Manchester Road, Burnley. 27 April 1941

I had an interesting time away. Bath on Thursday to see Ninette about future plans; thence on Friday to the Vic School, evacuated to a farm near Moreton-in-the-Marsh, a ridiculous journey, it would have taken an hour & a half by car but it took me (by train) from 7.10 a.m. to 3.15 p.m. Very interesting when eventually I did arrive – it's lovely country & a lovely old stone farmhouse. Greta Douglas who is running it has done a wonderful job. We took it unfurnished – but completely empty – & just left Greta to cope, with instructions to keep inside a very small budget. Each student has to bring a camp bed; their own rugs, sheets, blankets; knife, fork, spoon & mug; & no more clothing than they can carry in a suitcase.

Greta has organised the classes; & the whole domestic economy. Food, as you can imagine, is no end of a problem as nearest shops are 3 miles off & without a car the transport of groceries for 38 people is a problem – they solve it on horseback! After each blitz in the midlands 1000 or 2000 extra people arrive in to the district before food supplies can be re-organised. At the coldest spell of winter they were without coal. All the difficulties have been surmounted & a real community established. In addition they've got a big garden prepared & planted with veg.

In the evening the students did a performance for my benefit – songs & dancing & "turns". I'm taking two of the girls away to train as electricians under our own two "real" electricians as you now can't get them for love or money, all under 60 being engaged in government service. The girls are delighted (at present!) &, if they can tussle, will fill a very gaping chasm in the organisation.

To Mrs Norah Guthrie at Annaghmakerrig

177 Manchester Road, Burnley. 11 May 1941

I'm madly busy rehearsing *K. John* which is a great change & relaxation & relief – though toiling at the office makes simultaneous demands which cannot entirely be ignored. Nor can the bombs – the Opera Co had an incredible time in Hull last week – I was over there on Friday & tho' I cannot give any details of damage the coup d'oeil was like Sodom & Gomorrah after *their* blitz. Today comes the word that the Vic has been "badly hit". As we get no communication of any kind with the South, George has gone down to see what's to do. I only hope & pray T. Wells is alright.

On days like this, full of news of calamity & violence, one longs to abandon responsibility. But really that's only a mood, and largely created by the difficulty of everything. One longs for the responsibility of a small job in the army or munitions or something: & then one tries to rationalise & glorify that longing, which is really a longing to run away from a particular & private battle.

To Mrs Norah Guthrie at Annaghmakerrig

177 Manchester Road, Burnley. 6.30 am. Undated, probably May 1941

Am down in the office fire-watching – a bore – one sleeps on a mattress on the floor and it really could be much worse but it's a tease when it comes at a busy time. The Guinness weekend has been very nice but very short. Alec as a seaman is always on the move and there seems no reason for Merula not to go to the various relations who want her, and every economic reason for going; but everlasting visiting isn't good & is unsettling for the little boy. He (Matthew) is adorable & as good as gold. Doesn't talk yet and doesn't quite walk but is as quick & intelligent & lively as can be.

Alec is writing his autobiography – at least his childhood. Such a tragic, unloved, un-cared for little illegitimate son. It's interesting how the inability to accept present conditions is normal, & the isolation-in-a-crowd imposed by life in the Forces is drawing the sensitive people into their pasts, or into a dream-world of pretence or to the bottle. The sensitive Alec Guinnesses are "difficult" and very often inefficient. As always, the ideal is the Happy Mean – but how attain it? How even recognise it?

I go to Bolton today to join the opera, with whom I shall be for a fortnight. We're making new scenery & dresses for *Traviata* & a little rearranging of the production. Bolton isn't far from here, 20 miles or so, so I shall be back & forth; but next week it means going to Oxford; & from there I shall go on to S. Wales to see the Cassons. I think we have our spring plans fixed for one of the Vic companies – they'll do *The Merchant*, *The Witch* (Masefield) and Shaw's *The Simpleton of the Unexpected Isles*. But neither Esmé nor I are very happy about Sybil in *Candida* – she's years too old, and since she & Lewis either don't or won't see this, it's a bit awkward. One is so fond of them, and one has reason to be grateful to them and it's never nice for an actor or actress to have to face up to fact that the time for heroes & heroines is *past*.

James Forsyth is in N. Ireland with the army & I've told him that if he likes to suggest himself you'd have him for a short leave – 24 hours or something when he wouldn't have time to go home. He's a very interesting Scots boy who has written what I think is a most remarkable play. He has most interesting qualities of character, I think, & though he's very shy & quiet & has no great fund of small talk, I'm sure he wouldn't be a burdensome guest. I don't really suppose he'll turn up, but if he should you don't need to worry at all about entertaining him. He'll be happy to read & write in quiet surroundings, to wander about, to be given nice meals (the change between army food & rations will itself be a real holiday) & be allowed to tell you about his wife & wonderful wonderful wonderful baby son.

To Mrs Peggy Butler at Maidenhall

No address. 15 June 1941

I'm worried about Aunt Sue. Was at Tunbridge Wells 2 nights ago & spent an hour with her. She isn't progressing well. The shingles I gather have given place to what is labelled neuritis but the effect is just as nasty. She looks just any age – 100 – tired and spiritless – & she seems to have terribly lost buoyancy & the capacity to look forward. What I want your advice on is: 1/ How much of this shall I tell Mrs G? So far I've written truthfully but a little guardedly but I think she ought to know that I don't think Aunt Sue will get over to A'kerrig again. 2/ In that case Mrs G'll want to go over to England. I'd do the journey with her & save as much fatigue & fuss as possible.

To Mrs Guthrie at Annaghmakerrig

Peacemeal, Tunbridge Wells. 6 July 1940

K. John opens tomorrow in London – no booking – Shakespeare, or anyway the less familiar plays, must I suppose seem pretty remote in present circumstances. We think of reviving *The Cherry Orchard* with Athene in her old part; if this comes off it will begin about August 25. I wonder if Hubert owns his own rights or did he sell them to Dean's? I'll ring up Dean anyway & find out.

To Mrs Norah Guthrie at Annagmakerrig

Peacemeal, Tunbridge Wells. 10 August 1941

What a nice 10 days [at Annaghmakerrig] – all too short. Every moment of it was a pleasure & a blessed rest & change.

Now I'll tell you about our journey. We sat for over an hour at Newbliss [station]. Arrived over an hour and a half late at Belfast to find that all English boats had already sailed & nothing going till the Monday night! So there was nothing at all to be done but find a room for the night – felt too dispirited to ring Migsie. Had a very dreary rationed supper & went straight to bed. Next day we got an unbelievable Romanist excursion train to Dublin arriving (after an amusingly suffocating packed 4½ hours) about 2. We lunched (amazing contrast in fare between Belfast & Dublin, flowing with sugar, cream, butter etc) & proceeded to Dun Laoghaire harbour which was packed for bank holiday. But we were very graciously accommodated on two camp beds in the drawing-room of the Salthill Hotel – a magnificent apartment with 6 huge windows overlooking the bay. We bathed & had an amusing walk round the coast, finishing up *marvelling* at the lights, the cars with headlamps and a military band concert in a fairy-lighted bandstand on the mole. It was like another world. Very agreeable: but the more I think of it the more cynical & shameful & contemptible seems Eire's attitude to the present state of the world. I can't see a single redeeming argument except cynical expediency & looking after No. 1.

Simon [Fitz-Simon] was in the train at Holyhead & we had quite a reunion crowned with cups of lukewarm tea in the Refreshment Room, Chester! We got to Burnley about 9 on Monday night: to find everyone well & everything going very well. There's a big boom in theatrical business at the moment. The Ballet has played a three week season in London without a single empty seat; the Opera at one of the big midland towns drew £2,000 last week, & even poor old *King John*, which is obviously no box-office smasher, is doing very well.

Just back from a call on Mum Scaife, she'd written me to Burnley about Xopher who has been desperately ill – infected desert sores incurred in Libya – he's a captain with some regiment of mixed origin. Latest cables report progress but he's been at death's door. Mrs Scaife is a wonderful old thing, I have to like & admire her very much despite overwhelming volubility!

To Hubert Butler at Maidenhall

In the train but 'permanently' at 177 Manchester Road, Burnley. 10 September 1941

I've been meaning for days to give you some impression of your *Cherry Orchard* but life is such a mêlée of impossibly long journeys with hectic days between. I think it's "a success" – the press is mostly v.g. & the box office receipts flow steadily. It was ready in the sense that everything was in its place. The grouping was for the most part

THE OLD VIC THEATRE presents ITS GREAT LONDON PRODUCTION
of the FAMOUS RUSSIAN COMEDY,

"THE CHERRY ORCHARD"

By CHEKOV.   Translated by HUBERT BUTLER.

Characters in the order of their appearance:

Dunyasha (maid)	DOROTHY BAIRD
Lopahin (merchant)	JAMES DALE
Epihodov (clerk to the estate)	JAMES GIBSON
Firs (old footman)	O. B. CLARENCE
Mme. Ranevska (owner of the cherry orchard)	ATHENE SEYLER
Anya (her daughter)	OLIVE LAYTON
Varya (her adopted daughter)	ROSALIND ATKINSON
Gaev (brother of Mme. Ranevska)	NICHOLAS HANNEN
Charlotta (governess)	LUCY GRIFFITHS
Semyonov-Pischik (neighbouring landowner)	FRANK PETLEY
Yasha (young footman)	ALAN BLAIR
Trofimov (a student)	DAVID MARKHAM
Tramp	CHARLES BARRETT
Guests	RENEE BOURNE WEBB, DINAH MALONE, JEAN FRASER, DONALD ROSS, D. VAUGHAN ROBERTS

The action of the play takes place in Mme. Ranevska's home in Russia.
There will be three intervals during the play.
The Play produced by TYRONE GUTHRIE.
Scenery by FREDERICK CROOKE.   Costumes by SOPHIE HARRIS.
Wigs by " BERT."   Furniture by The Old Times Furnishing Co., Ltd.
Men's Costumes by B. J. Simmons Co., Ltd.

For the Governors of The Old Vic:

Business Manager ... HENRY CROCKER   Carpenter ... FREDERICK JORDAN
Stage Director .... MICHAEL NORTHEN   Electrician .. MARJORIE CRICHTON
Stage Manager ..... JESSICA MORTON

" THE CHERRY ORCHARD."

This Play, like any great work of art, has a meaning more universal than its story; it is, in fact, a parable. Those to whom this is apparent will please forgive the explanation and need read no further.

The sale of the Cherry Orchard symbolises any old order giving way to new; and though all change carries with it an element of sadness, without it there cannot be the joy of new beginning.   Just as all life carries within itself the element of death, so without death there can be no regeneration.   If Winter comes can Spring be far behind?—TYRONE GUTHRIE.

These Performances are given with the goodwill and assistance of C.E.M.A. (Council for the Encouragement of Music and the Arts).   C.E.M.A.'s policy is " The Best for the Most."

A page from the programme of a wartime tour of Chekov's *The Cherry Orchard*, translated by Hubert Butler and directed by Guthrie, 1941.

expressive, ditto the tempo, the rise & fall of each act, timing of the individual lines & business. But the rehearsals were too short for the actors to find much richness & subtlety & instinctive liaison with their characters. In this respect the previous production was better, tho' the team-work & the balance of casting is better in this. Athene [Seyler]'s performance has deepened & mellowed & amplified very beautifully – she still misses the kind of qualities you might describe by words like "melody" and "fragrance" and "romance" and "beauty" even, but the effect is to me very light and attractive and poignant. [James] Dale's Lopakin is a far better performance than [Charles] Laughton's mannerisms, and the acting is technically far more proficient. But he has not Laughton's almost hypnotic ability to rivet the attention and attack the unconscious.

A scene from *The Cherry Orchard* in Burnley.

I can find no way of managing the end. It seems to me that Tchekov's construction here is seriously at fault. The play I think ends when the general exit is made. There should be a pause here showing the house (the central symbol of the piece) empty, dead, awaiting dissolution and rebirth; then curtain. As it is, one has that pause; then Yepihodov executes a short variety act; then another pause; then Firs does his turn; then another pause; then curtain. The exigencies both of logic (naturalism) & mood dictate the pauses – you just can't eliminate them; but it gives the whole thing far too long a "dying fall" in my opinion and I always detect the play's grip on the audience relaxing in those pauses.

I think it is a good play for now. The theme of the old order giving way to new is topical; its treatment so gentle as to be a wonderfully welcome contrast to the roughness of the world at large and the boisterous vulgarity of most current entertainment.

Thank you for your letter about England-Eire. I appreciate very much that you wrote it. I'm utterly unconvinced by any of your arguments. Tho' I accept penitently the rebuke for generalising after 10 days' visit to Eire. But, contrariwise, my ten days *did* include 3 ½ hours penned in a railway coach containing about 120 excursionists

– R.C.s from Belfast – and *did* we hear some nice little cynical bits of brutality about isolationism! And if I mayn't express opinions about Eire's present attitudes after 10 days I don't think you are entitled either to views about England under present conditions. And you'll agree it would be a dull world if we ALL spoke only when fully entitled to an opinion.

Guthrie's mother had been applying for permits (i.e. wartime passports) without success for herself and her companion Bunty Worby to visit her ailing sister Susan Power in Tunbridge Wells. Guthrie received a permit that allowed him permanent access to the Irish Free State. In London the New Theatre had been made available to the Old Vic Company by Bronson Albery for visits between blitzes with only a few performances cancelled due to air-raid warnings. The Old Vic Theatre had been damaged by bombs, demonstrating the wisdom of evacuation to Burnley.

To Mrs Norah Guthrie at Annaghmakerrig

177 Manchester Road, Burnley. 12 September 1941

Oh dear your permits! I wish I could do something about it. It's hateful we can't meet oftener, hateful Peggy's so cut off by petrol situation; hateful that you & Aunt Sue can't meet. But in most ways these are hateful times & looked at fairly we have, as a family, suffered wonderfully little so far.

The Opera Co is here this week & we have done a lot of satisfactory planning & discussing. They're doing a terrific week's business [*Traviata*] … literally hundreds turned away from gallery each night. *Cherry O* is doing very nicely in London which is satisfactory & will I hope produce a little supplementary revenue for Hubert and P.

News – better, don't you think? We are led to believe that Russia will certainly hold the Germans thro' the winter; & the Atlantic situation seems to be in better order. Oh wouldn't be wonderful if this was the last winter! Thank you very much for the bacon which was absolutely delicious and a most welcome extra. With the Opera here we've done quite a bit of mild entertaining of a seemingly diplomatic nature and it has come in quite wonderfully handy. I am still hopeful about your passport: & if I were you I would step over if you get it, unless horrid raids have already begun.

To Mrs Norah Guthrie at Annaghmakerrig

177 Manchester Road, Burnley. 18 September 1941

Fred Valk, the new Shylock, an *immense* success here. Very, very striking & impressive – a massive mittel-Europa vehemently romantic style of acting that should be quite a valuable influence on our more naturalistic & more gentlemanly style! Anyway, he's supremely to the taste of Burnley, which is flocking & applauding to the echo.

Tony Quayle & his General were up in Yorkshire last week, inspecting. Tony hopped over on Thurs. from Huddersfield for the night – great fun. We gave a party after the show in his honour – just the Old Hands: Esmé, Geo, Williams, Sybil, Lewis, & didn't retire, alas, till 3 A.M.

To Mrs Norah Guthrie at Annaghmakerrig

Burnley. No date, September 1941

The Opera Co. (after a triumphant packed week here – a real gala) goes by motor coach to Whitehaven. And we're deeply embedded in plans for next Jan-Feb-March so you see the grass doesn't grow round the feet. But it all – for the moment – seems to be more systematized & less hand to mouth & far less harassing that it has been. When one thinks of our life this time last year it is indeed peace! Oh dear, then one thinks of Russian villages; of Alec Guinness climbing frozen rigging …

Judy is getting on seriously with her play [*Queen Bee*] which really shapes most interestingly – Act 1 is rough-finished; Act 2 well under weigh; and Act 3 clearly planned.

Such a much more cheerful letter from Aunt Sue – sending a pair of beautifully made string gloves for Guinness and admitting that she feels more like herself – altogether more encouraging. And your [travel] permits? It has been unsettling & teasing, but don't give up hope and don't worry about the journey. Wire the very second you have news and we can make plans.

To Hubert Butler at Annaghmakerrig

Norfolk Hotel, Strand, London. 26 September 1941

We're extending the tour of the *Ch. Orchard* from 6 to 11 weeks. There's been a great hullabaloo with the Welsh Co. (Sybil & Lewis) as the

S. Wells electrician who was with them has collapsed with a bad duodenal ulcer (poor chap) without warning & I've been scouring London for an electrician. By the grace of God one of the *Cherry O.* understudies – a young man just invalided out of the army – has a little electrical experience & was game to push his hand into the hole in the dyke. I'd had the foresight to train a couple of girls but they're already working with other of our troupes.

I suppose we must just consider ourselves fortunate that neither Annaghmakerrig, Maiden Hall, Crossways nor 177 Manchester Road is part of the Scorched Earth Policy.

To Mrs Norah Guthrie at Annaghmakerrig

177 Manchester Road, Burnley. 28 September 1941

You'll be grieved to hear that Lizzie is no more. A strange woman called about 5 on Thursday & told Judy there was a cat lying on the step of a house two or three doors up that was like the cat she'd seen on our windowsill. Judy raced up & there was poor wee Puss stretched stiff & stark. We think she must have been struck by a car & that either the motorist or a passer-by set her body on the step. We shall both miss poor Lizzie very much. The symbolism of burial is potent – buried grief, buried treasure; back to earth; the decaying body down in to earth; the spirit soaring upward.

I read the New Statesman & The Spectator from cover to cover in the train y'day & thought both expressed a state nearer to panic than we have yet been. We were all, of course, too relieved, too optimistic, when the Russians showed themselves capable of resistance. In one's own reaction to the war I fancy I see what it feels like to be old – one gets more & more tired of the effort of adaptation to new things. It doesn't matter if changes are better or for the worse.

To Mrs Norah Guthrie at Annaghmakerrig

177 Manchester Road, Burnley. 2 October 1941

Cherry O is at Brighton & doing better bus. than they've had there for months. Brighton of course is terribly hit by present conditions & it's barred to visitors & most of the wealthy are in Torquay, Buxton or Windermere!

I'm preparing a long memorandum (Lord knows who'll read it) on the Function of the Theatre in the post-war community. I think it's wise to get it written down even though most of it will be completely out of date long before one can do anything practical about it. Ivor Brown [*The Observer* theatre critic] is coming next week & will help.

To Mrs Norah Guthrie [staying at] Maidenhall

177 Manchester Road, Burnley. 7 October 1941

We had quite a nice little semi-business, semi-pleasure, visit to Huddersfield on Friday night – saw *The Barber of Seville* & invaluable & needful talk with Joan Cross dotting up many matters of organisation, staff, artists, etc.

Please thank Hubert for his letter. Tell him I'll send Deane a note about royalties, which will continue on same basis. Unless something ghastly occurs Hubert should receive some more dainty wee cheques.

To Mrs Norah Guthrie at Annaghmakerrig

177 Manchester Road, Burnley. 29 December 1941

We went to church on Sunday – a nerve-wracking experience, as the organ elicited to break down & wartime organist, a little lame lady, was reduced to a harmonium which the choir (also very wartime, tiny boys & ancient males & a sprinkling of veteran contraltos) couldn't hear, with the result that they kept neither to tune nor to time. They had planned to sing quite a complicated elaborate musical service with introits, canticles, choral responses etc etc etc & *sing it they did*, from incompetent beginning to bitter end. It wasn't even funny! After which we prepared for The Party. Considering we were such a very mixed bag it passed off very well, except for Joan Cross who most uncharacteristically elected to behave like a Prima Donna, held the floor with egocentric anecdotes, behaved with gracious condescension to the poorer guests & conveyed, none too subtly, that we all ought to be grateful for her radiant presence. However fortunately she left early, poor dear, to catch a night train to Merthyr Tidfyl to sing a Christmas *Messiah*.

To Mrs Peggy Butler at Maidenhall

177 Manchester Road, Burnley. 31 December 1941

Ring out the old ... & never was the old year less regretted – I should think *never* the whole world over. I suppose some countries have been gladder to see other years go – Ireland the famine year, England the years of the black death – but nowhere can poor 1941 be regretted. We greet the new year by rising at 5.30 to take train for Cassons at Portmadoc. Not far as the crow flies but a journey of 8½ hours of which one spends 3¾ on junction platforms. We're going for 2 nights, to talk plans & "have a nice time". They are so nice & the place so charming that I shall be surprised if it ain't enjoyable.

Things are in quite a whirl of preparation here. The Opera Co. – 65 of them – and the Drama Co. (*Witch* and *Merchant*) occupying the Mechanics Institute, the Co-Op Hall, the Church Assembly & St Anne's Parish Room – to say nothing of "upstairs" at Pollard's (the music shop) – & there's an absolute maelstrom of darning, washing of lace cuffs, ironing of curls, etc etc, & the offices are like Bank Holiday at the Zoo. Everything gets more & more impossible as there's *no-one* to *do* anything. The wig-maker who is now an air-raid warden writes that his leave is stopped so he will therefore not be able to come north as arranged; no substitute is available & the little women round all corners have been called up.

6 WARTIME OBSTRUCTIONS AND OPPORTUNITIES

If the residency of the Old Vic Theatre and the Sadler's Wells Opera and Ballet companies in Burnley, Lancashire, with wartime shortages of personnel and materials, was the most overworked and exhausting period of Guthrie's career, it was later recalled in the autobiographies of several celebrated actors, singers and dancers as the time when he showed his greatest sense of leadership: his rallying cry in moments of difficulty and frustration, 'Rise above!', was often quoted.

To Mrs Norah Guthrie at Annaghmakerrig
Norfolk Hotel, London. 12 January 1942

> I meant to write y'day from Burnley but was involved all day in various events connected with the companies. *The Merchant* [with Jean Forbes-Robertson & Frederick Valk] and *Witch* [by H. Wiers, translated from the Norwegian by John Masefield] left at midday for York & there were quite a lot of skuffles and plans as two wardrobe women remain in Burnley to finish the *Witch* dresses which are behind time – but it doesn't open till Thursday & *The Merchant* (which plays Mon. Tues. Wed.) will D.V. be ready & complete. Then there was a dress rehearsal of *Rigoletto* which opens tonight. I'm down now for the opening of the new ballet *Comus* [Purcell/Helpmann] which they've asked me to light. I saw a full rehearsal immediately on arrival and we light first thing tomorrow morning. I'll be South till Saty. for various committees & meetings and will try to see Miss Aunt [Sue Power].

Guthrie with Vivien Leigh and
Laurence Olivier of the Old Vic
Theatre Company.

Have I written since we heard from Sybil about Judy's play? She's jumping to do it, my dear, and Judy is to see Binkie Beaumont [impresario] about it this week. If Binkie will put it on, that's much the best management for it and will give it the best possible chance. Personally I think he'll do it; as, quite apart from the merit it may or may not have it's so inexpensive (1 set & very few characters) that the financial risk is small & Dame Sybil Thorndike a good insurance.

To Mrs Norah Guthrie at Annaghmakerrig
177 Manchester Road, Burnley, 'actually from London'. 16 January 1942

I'm having quite a satisfactory week here and plan to leave at 8.15 tomorrow morning for Burnley with a little black kitty which I'm expecting Vivien Leigh to bring me here at any moment! I had supper with her and Ursula [Jeans], Larry [Olivier], Bobby [Helpmann] and others after the ballet and she promised we could have it then. The ballet was a great success – being ballet the enthusiasm was boundless & out of all proportion the work might have.

Where in the old days a ballet first night would mean literally cartloads of hothouse bouquets, the other night the Ballerina was handed one exiguous spray of daffodils and two carnations and couldn't have been more pleased if the Crown Jewels had been sent! I feel pretty guilty about our drama co. at York who are having Hell's Delight getting *The Witch* on, & are receiving no support of any kind from George [Chamberlain, administrator] & me. Still, one can't be in two places at once. They opened last night having been up the whole of Wedy. night after the performance of *The Merchant*. Not too funny.

Rigoletto on Monday at Burnley evidently passed off very well – very good contrasting descriptions of the occasion from Judy & George: agreeing that it was exactly what the populace of Burnley wished for & had considerable merit as well. Cassons re-open *Medea* on Monday at Tenby; and *Cherry Orchard* rehearses in Burnley next week and re-opens there Monday week with Athene [Seyler] still heading the cast.

To Mrs Norah Guthrie at Annaghmakerrig
177 Manchester Road, Burnley. 18 January 1942

I don't think I have ever felt so driven & tired. There seems so much more to be done than can ever be possible, though infinitely better than London as regards communications – even from here it's difficult to keep things running at a distance – there are so many little queues, little arrangements that need to be personally settled between the artists & the office. I've found *Fledermaus* a great tax: I had to do it, there was no-one else available, and the work I absolutely abominate so there wasn't even the compensation of doing something "worth while". The journeys by bus – leaving before it was light & not getting back till 9 or 10 at night – so cold & so long – I don't normally mind that kind of thing at all, but this time, whether it's advancing middle-age or whether it's just plain fatigue, it rather wore me down. The Sunday night was the very bad raid on Manchester only 7 miles away [from rehearsal at Oldham]. We didn't finish rehearsal till after the last bus so I'd to stay at Oldham & the gunfire made sleep – even for me – intermittent. A dress rehearsal at 10 next morning of the gay champagne revels with the chorus blear-eyed from sleeplessness & blue with cold, was a quite gruesome affair.

Judy came over to Oldham y'day & we bore the rather dreary Opening of *Fledermaus* together – it always succeeds; & was, I think, well taken despite a leading lady who suggested not a sprightly Viennese soubrette but a good-natured & extremely myopic daughter of the vicar who was very kindly deputising at the eleventh hour.

To Mrs Norah Guthrie at Annaghmakerrig
Peacemeal, Tunbridge Wells. 31 January 1942

We're again in trouble with Opera – two absolutely indispensable singers have been refused further [military] deferment. Joan [Cross] & I spent y'day scurrying from this one to that one mobilizing support & Sir Reggie [Row] & I hope for an interview next week with the Ministry of Labour. If we fail, then I think the Opera will have to pack up.

Saw John G[ielgud]'s *Macbeth* in M'chestr. No good. A really poor Co. – very wartime – John himself ill suited & all worst mannerisms well to the fore. Given [Gwen Ffrangcon] Davies' very interesting as Lady M & Leon Quartermaine good as Banquo – the rest is silence. The scenery far too pictorial & elaborate and not in the least suitable (to our way of thinking) to the play. All blue – quite good for Maeterlinck but I don't think Macbeth should look like illustrations of Maeterlinck by Dulac.

To Hubert and Peggy Butler at Maidenhall
Peacemeal, Tunbridge Wells. 1 February 1942

Nellie [Judith's mother] has become alarmingly routinée & the "upset" of our visit made it really questionable whether it's a pleasure or no. The rationing agitates her – she can't bear Judy contributing our food to the general stock, which is idiotic since our coupons for this week won't be any good for next week; and, what is saddest, seems to have lost all interest in things outside her own immediate ken. This is quite painful for J. who would like to be asked about Burnley, her play etc etc but instead has to simply press the information at Nellie. Gordon [Judith's father], on the other hand, is full of interest.

Binkie Beaumont doesn't want to do Judy's play which is a bore as that firm would have been much the best "auspice" under which to appear. Quite a tactful and unhumiliating letter of regret, but none the less a refusal. It's already off to another management, but I fear Binkie's criticism of too little plot, despite excellent characters & dialogue, is fair enough and may damn it for the present when the audiences require jerking out of themselves rather forcibly by broad laughter or emotional punches in the solar plexus (wherever that may be).

The Cherry Orchard went gratifyingly well at Burnley. We had a valuable week of rehearsals, putting in a new Trofimov & Yasha and generally polishing up. I was afraid the provincials would find it meandering and tedious & rather remote in class & feeling. After all, the Burnley "aristocracy" exactly share Lopakin's views about the bungalows and I thought the weavers would find the subject-matter altogether out of their ken. But not at all. There were delightful laughs in the *right* places – not just at Russian quaintness. It is, of course, a piece that is quite half played by the audience – if they don't laugh at the fun then the serious, pathetic & lyric bits don't fall into contrasting & complementary place in the pattern and the whole thing becomes formless & monotonous.

I never, Hubert, thanked you for p.c. granting permission for renewal of *Orchard* tour, nor for polite regrets that I had never been troubled to go & swear to Commissioner of Oaths. Latter was quite a trouble but also rather enjoyable – the Commissioner was so "Dickensy" the oath so farcical and Mrs Pöe returned the 2/- I had to expend with almost incredible mixture of modern speed and olde-worlde courtesy.

Our wee kitten [Lizzie] is a bright spot – both are entranced by its pretty ways and play with it by the hour.

To Mrs Norah Guthrie at Annaghmakerrig

As from 177 Manchester Road, Burnley. Undated, March 1942

Have been greatly on the move, Cambridge, London & now Durham whence I returned last night. *The Magic Flute* was an enormous tussle, but worth it. It's a heavenly work & the performance is "worthy" by any standard, & a blooming marvel considering present difficulties.

Went over to Durham to see the Cassons about plans, & y'day morning spent an hour in the cathedral: it wasn't nearly long enough but did just give one a first wonderful glimpse. I don't think I have ever seen anything that so completely bowls one over. The absolutely staggering combination of enormous massive strength with delicacy of invention & rich fantastic spontaneous imagination. The first impression is a thrilling experience.

Our poor kitty has been very ill, for two days like to die. Cat 'flu, the vet says. Its wee eyes & ears have run with sticky evil discharges, it tasted nor crumb nor drop for days & wasted away to a perfect little skeleton almost too weak to stand, that still pathetically purred when petted. Today, however, it is really better, eating heartily & beginning to take an interest in life again. They have such amazing power of recuperation that I expect it'll be normal again very soon.

Have quite a little bout of broadcasting in view. Next Sunday I'm "Narrator" in something or other after the news, on the 14th April I "introduce" Sybil & Lewis in *Medea* & on the 19th April I do a new short play by Laurence Houseman. So, if your battery still works, listen then.

Alec Guinness is on the S. Coast now, learning to be an officer, under Roger Furse [stage designer] who already is one, & Alec has primly to salute him!

To Mrs Peggy Butler at Maidenhall

177 Manchester Road, Burnley. 19 March 1942

Loved the photograph of Julia which awaited my return y'day. It's a real pleasure to look at & to have. The fussy jumper will "date" outrageously and annoy Julia herself in the years to come. And then it will come round again & be to her grandchildren the most charming feature of the picture. Tell Joe [Hone] we were going from here to Durham & we suddenly saw a Bomber Aeroplane sitting in a field, so huge that a man standing beside the wings looked no bigger than a starling standing beside a house. And while we were there it started up and flew over our heads so low you could almost have given it a poke with an umbrella.

I have had a great deal of pleasure from re-reading Grimm's Household Tales. I hope you let Julia & Joe have them. I think they are a very important part of education, dealing, like the Old Testament myths, in a symbolic way with the ideas that lie below consciousness. They are full of frightful & ferocious incidents but I cannot think these are harmful like the calculated literary horrors of Hans Andersen &

the snobbish obvious morality of Perrault. Andersen is a great artist but I would have thought a most pernicious companion for small children. My favourite book (for a while) was by Miss Amy Le Feuvre about A Cripple whose big idea was to steal away into a church and play the organ. It was "put away" on the top shelf as being mawkish. Mawkish it was, but I think now more honestly and less detrimentally mawkish than Jack Challoner & healthy boys' fiction of that ilk.

I did too much a week ago at Cambridge & am now enjoying the pangs of rheumatism in my "good" knee. After a week of Rising Above it, I have made it much worse and am today reduced to bed & calling the Dr & have both knees stiff as biscuits & as creaky as rusty gates. I have not told your Mama about it & please don't you. *The Cherry Orchard* finishes up this Saty. at Henley – in the potteries. It is sold out there, or practically, for the whole week in advance. We believe that they think it is a gay spectacular Muscovite counterpart to *Lilac Time*.

The thing I long for most, more than for an egg or jam or a banana (for these one misses more as symbols of the general confusion & retrogression than for themselves) is leisure. I want so very much to have a long morning reading something unconnected with practical life, to have days & days with no appointments & no journeys. Even if one didn't feel Naughty & a Shirker (& I should feel this) the atmosphere here is one of stress & strain & urgency. I can't react to it as buoyantly and resourcefully as I sincerely believe one ought. I keep wanting to Steal Away on my crutch to Church & play the most frightfully sweet Voluntaries, the most luscious Easter Hymns, the most cringing Nunc Dimittis, in the twi twi twilight. But No! Jack Challoner's[16] bugle calls; the helmeted ghost of Miss Bayliss[17] waves me to the battlements.

To Mrs Peggy Butler at Maidenhall

177 Manchester Road, Burnley. 7 June 1942

Friday and Saturday were immensely hot and we had all meals out in our really amazingly bleak patch which on those days was quite a Paradise of smutty privet with busses for bird-song, good-natured Mrs Whittaker [landlady] peeping slyly through her net curtains and saying

---

16   Children's author.
17   Co-founder of the Old Vic.

with infinite aged espièglerie "it's as good as a play" and Mr Smith the greengrocer suddenly looking over the wall and saying "Joost to complete the loonch" as he placed an orange into Judy's hand. It couldn't have been more gracious and gratifying if the King-Emperor had placed his Orb in her palm. The news about *Mutiny* [working title of *Queen Bee*] is rather dashing as Ruth [agent] cables from N.Y. that as she can't cast the chief part suitably she will have to let her option lapse. This we feel is only a polite way of saying her enthusiasm has rather cooled off. Still, Sybil is as mad as ever but isn't free for a long time to come. Naturally Great Authoress is a trifle crestfallen – the more so as both New York and London had both seemed as good as settled.

The war news is certainly more reassuring than for three years tho' the Observer today is very grave about shipping losses. The O. is such an infinitely better paper now than the Sunday Times – so much more liberal in political outlook and so much better served by literary and artistic reviewers. I don't know if you can ever get to the pictures in Kilkenny but if *Citizen Kane* ever turns up you must on no account miss it even if it means great inconvenience and expense. It is revolutionary from a technical aspect, but what is much more important, it's about something, the content is not unworthy of Ibsen, and it moves at a pace and assumes grown-up mentality of its audience. Needless to say it's a crashing flop with the box-office.

The Guthries were again using their flat in Lincoln's Inn, repaired following blast damage, for visits to London from Burnley. The New Theatre in the West End was being used for some Old Vic and Sadler's Wells productions. Severe material hardships in Britain, experienced mainly through food and fuel shortages, made the conspicuously different lifestyle in the Irish Free State appear excessively easy and wasteful.

To Mrs Peggy Butler at Maidenhall
23 Old Buildings, Lincoln's Inn, WC2. 17 July 1942

Your letters bring a wonderful aroma of peace and normality, with accounts of Gymkhanas and lordly grumbles at a mere 14 pounds of jam sugar. A month or two ago it used to annoy me a little, but now – for no reason that I can discern – it gives great pleasure, like reading Trollope. It's all a stage, I suppose, in war psychosis.

I am having a nice little lull today & tomorrow preparatory to wrestling with *Othello* which opens next Wed, at the New, Mon & Tues will be a hurly-burly of lighting, setting & rehearsal. Much depends on this Season – if it isn't on the bull's eye many teasing problems arise: so we are meeting them halfway, and anyway I have forestalled some of them with *networks* of plans. Most of my energy goes in contingency planning. Have had a good old week of conferences & committees & hope I have launched a PLAN that may get a move on the whole framework of State subsidised theatre. No doubt the plan will be modified & mauled & watered down & smoothed out by a series of committees till it's quite inoffensive to all (& consequently fully acceptable to nobody) but I think the launching was rather more auspicious than I'd hoped. [J.Maynard] Keynes was I think rather "taken" with it & he'll be a powerful ally.

To Mrs Norah Guthrie at Annaghmakerrig

George Hotel, Huddersfield. 23 August 1942

Arrived here just in time to race to the theatre to see *Jacob's Ladder* (thank heaven being satisfactorily performed to a full house) & have long confab. with the Business Manager [local theatre], Stage Manger & Clemence Dane [author] till 1 a.m. Leave for Bradford at 7.50 A.M. for a full rehearsal of *Bohème* (for which I must do some prep. tonight) at 10. On Friday I go to L'pool with George & meet Brownie [James Brown, Old Vic general-manager] there & we three are empowered to come to terms with the Directors of the L'pool Rep. about a joint Season there beginning Nov.9 for 3 months, to be extended if successful. I think at last the way is clear & Brownie agreeable to taking most of the administrative direction off my hands. If so, that will be an absolutely huge relief & will be, I think, a much more efficient plan. I have coped adequately (but only just adequately, & that's not good enough) with the business & admin. side but at disproportionate expenditure of nervous energy. I think I can be better value if able to concentrate more on the artistic direction; & Brownie, tho' a bit too old – he must be 60-65 – is going to be hugely helpful. There are dangers, that he's over cautious, & misses opportunities by shilly-shally & a poor ability to distinguish the essential from the trivial.

To Mrs Norah Guthrie at Annaghmakerrig

177 Manchester Road, Burnley. 6 September 1942

Liverpool is en-train. Judy has been over & has looked exhaustingly at flats. We shall keep Lincoln's Inn, but hope to find a sittingroom, bedroom, spare room & kitchen in L'pool as a H.Q. will be needed & a certain amount of "entertaining" is almost a necessity. Meanwhile, all sorts of things have been happening in the other Cos. Bernard Miles (Iago) has been madly tiresome in a number of different ways & we're "reporting" him to Equity. More serious, there has been a burst water-main under the New Theatre (supposed to be result of disturbance of soil due to bombing) with the result that the theatre was flooded to stage level – stalls & pit submerged in evil-smelling water!! It was unusable for one performance & for nearly a fortnight now we've been open, but only upstairs.

Hardly had I set foot here on Friday night when the manager of the Jacob's Ladder Co. rang to say that Lewis [Casson] had just made a speech in acknowledging applause from a packed house & had apologised for the noise made during the perf. by the Stage Staff. Result – the Stage Staff all behaved like insulted Prima Donnas – screamed & fainted & declared they had never, no never, in all their bloody lives been so affronted, & marched out in a body never never never to darken these doors again! So then the theatre manager – not unnaturally, since staff now is quite unprocurable – began to squeal like a hog in a gate; in fact, there was a Kettle of Fish. Lewis was, I think, very much to blame – he shouldn't have complained publicly. But he gets into rages when he'd say anything to anybody. Anyway, by last night, "peace" was reigning again – the staff with much pouting & head-tossing was on duty & Lewis made an apology that was about as gracious as a smack in the eye with a wet fish.

To Mrs Norah Guthrie at Annaghmakerrig

c/o Town Clerk, Wigan. 10 September 1942

Eventually we decided on a top flat in a doctor's house in Rodney St which is L'pool's Harley St. It's a little more expensive than we wished & not as interesting or individual as the others we saw but has certain advantages, 1/ Newly painted & plastered; 2/ Nice Dr. & wife as landlords & lower neighbours; 3/ Moneyed – which means the house will be kept warm & dry; 4/ Very central locality – most important in view of late hours & almost certain stoppage of all transport.; 5/ The extra money spent on rent will soon be recoverable in fares saved & meals at home.

Bohème opens [Burnley] on Thursday. I'm quite pleased with the rehearsals & have enjoyed them – so I think has the Co. My knee mildly troublesome again – not alarming or bad enough to keep me awake at night, but grumbling. Do hope Bunty's boils are better.

To Mrs Norah Guthrie at Annaghmakerrig

23 Old Buildings, Lincoln's Inn, London WC2. 27 September 1942

Bohème plays to packed houses. It is nice to look at, but only so-so in acting & singing – resources now just aren't available. The Australian girl who plays Mimi is going to be good – you may have thought her shrill & thin on the wireless (did you listen?) but that's a distortion which seems to happen to all the *big* high voices – the transmission takes all the "body" out of the top notes – actually she floats effortlessly & powerfully to top C and D with lovely clear full easy tone and it has the carrying quality that sends it bang through all orchestral & choral climaxes like a beam of light.

To Mrs Norah Guthrie at Annaghmakerrig

Grand Hotel, Stoke-on-Trent. Undated, September 1942

I'm here for two days discussing future plans with the Shakespeare Company [Stratford-upon-Avon], go back to London tomorrow afternoon. This is "the provinces" with a vengeance – I have never seen anything quite so dowdy – not especially poor, there's obviously plenty of money knocking about, but an absolute minimum of style or cosmopolitanism. The mental & spiritual horizon seems quite astonishingly bound by the Five Towns. Beaux Arts, however, as represented by the Old Vic are being extremely well patronised – the houses are packed, & tho' the come-back is not very lively, it's hugely attentive & warm at the end.

The news is terribly thrilling – what a ghastly hell upon earth Stalingrad must be, but what heroism. If only we were doing more to help. I think everyone feels shame that the Russians are left so long holding the baby but no doubt there are reasons – & plans. One tries not to allow oneself to be too hopeful; hopes have so often been terribly dashed; but this time … this time …

To Mrs Peggy Butler at Maidenhall

23 Old Buildings, Lincoln's Inn, London, WC2. Undated, October 1942

Judy will go north with me & straight on to Burnley to pack up & send the stuff south. We're very short of everything at Old Buildings.

To Mrs Peggy Butler at Maidenhall

23 Old Buildings, Lincoln's Inn, London, WC2. 9 November 1942

L'pool opened on Wedy. – a full house, with Lord Mayors abounding in curtain rings, & they've done a good week's business. Went to Burnley for w/e to pack up the house, rather sad; we have, all things considered, been happy there. One thing our circumstances have brought well home to one: an awareness of the transitoriness of human affairs; & the folly of attaching oneself too closely to possessions; a good look at a bombed house puts house-pride right where it belongs!

Gone are the days when you could take a lot of hand luggage – we staggered down y'day with a suitcase apiece & a bundle & the cat (in basket) & it really was a cope arriving at Euston in the blackout, no taxi or sign of a taxi, a packed bus, twenty-five minute wait at the bus stop & (understandably) *black looks* when one fights one's way aboard like a heavy-laden but extremely unlighted Xmas tree!

To Mrs Norah Guthrie visiting Maidenhall

The Playhouse, Liverpool. 13 November 1942

Isn't the news madly thrilling? [Allied Victory at El Alamein] We're to have the church bells rung on Sunday in celebration. I expect some of them will be broadcast; listen to them & think of us hearing them peal out for the first time in three years.

To Mrs Norah Guthrie visiting Maidenhall

Liverpool Playhouse. 30 November 1942

Merry Wives opens here tonight. And rehearsals for *6 Characters* begin tomorrow. Opera opened new prod. of *Figaro* at Cambridge last Friday with immense éclat. It's evidently very good, which is exciting. I think the Opera is now at last on the up-grade artistically without a doubt. Financially things are O.K. Between them opera and ballet in the last 2 years have paid off the *whole* enormous debt on Sadler's Wells. We're so spoilt now that we think it a bad week if Opera doesn't show a profit of £500 despite the fact that since the first blitz tour we've more than trebled the size of the Co.

I expect you all listened to Churchill last night. [Allied offensive, Tunisia]

To Mrs Norah Guthrie at Annaghmakerrig

Victoria Theatre, Burnley. 6 December 1942

This will be absolutely & positively our last weekend here. The house is already practically stripped. We'll be *really* sorry to see the last of it. Rehearsals for *6 Characters* quite interesting. Fourteen years since we did it at Cambridge! And Flora [Robson] & Robert Donat now international celebrities in celluloid. It's going to baffle the Liverpool audience utterly – they're very provincial – & also shock the Pants off them. At the other end of the [social] scale, ugly, waterfront seamy-side Hogarthian goings-on. The blacked out streets at night are illuminated by the hoarse mating cries of the sex-starved seamen & American soldiers & the answering squeals & shrieks of excited females – largely Irish. None of the girls from the theatre can go home alone. It's quite Dickensian & quaint, with the gaunt ruins & acres of rubbish to prevent one from feeling too amused & cosy.

To Mrs Norah Guthrie at Annaghmakerrig

Liverpool [on Old Vic letterhead]. 17 December 1942

Six Characters opened on Monday & contrary to all expectations went brilliantly – lots of laughter & marvellous "frissons" – almost screams – at the suitable points. V. gratifying; & wonderful & quite intelligent press. One paper headlined "Mr.Guthrie's Triumph", which, after my apprehensions, was flattering. All the stuff has arrived from Burnley & the flat looks like Gomorrah "after".

To Julia Butler (age 7) at Maidenhall

The Playhouse, Liverpool. 11 January 1943

My Dearest Julia, Thank you first of all for your very nice Christmas card – it was awfully nicely painted. We have hung it up and it looks very handsome. Then thank *you* for your letter thanking me for my present. I didn't know you could write so well.

The other day our kitty got onto the roof and couldn't get down again and cried and cried for help so I had to climb up a long ladder and fetch it. It was terribly pleased to see me and purred and climbed onto my shoulders to be carried down the ladder. But when it got near the bottom it just jumped off and ran away. Not very nice. Quite different to you and me, how grateful we are to one another and write nice letters to say so!

I think Joe would love this town because it's full of aeroplanes and ships and sailors from all over the world. Thick pink sailors from England and Norway, thin grey sailors from America, shivering sailors from hot parts of Asia looking very miserable poor things, and lots of smiling smirking Chinks. Love from Uncle T.

To Mrs Norah Guthrie at Annaghmakerrig

No address. 4 March 1943

Merchant of V, I regret to say is a failure & very poorly thought of & has done us quite a lot of harm – a pity. But no use grieving. We've taken a lease on the London Playhouse at Charing Cross & open *Abraham Lincoln* [John Drinkwater] there on April 12. Meantime Liverpool goes on well. Our real difficulty is lack of a "star" or two to head our casts & advertise to the public.

Judy's work [munitions factory] isn't physically exacting. She sits and there's a sunny window nearby. It involves a lot of work with scissors which is exacting on the hands. And of course the hours plus housework makes a considerable tie – really no free time.

We have all been terribly cut up to hear that Jimmy Hoyle [actor] was killed on Monday – we think in the big Berlin raid. He and his wife [Lorna] spent Friday evening with us – he had 3 days leave – and they were so happy together, & so young & promising. The waste of it all is just crashingly obsessingly black. There is a wee girl – not yet 2 – my godchild. It's a funny thing, I've always *felt* that Jimmy wouldn't survive. I think he felt sure himself. As I was travelling to London from Liverpool on Wednesday I found myself wondering if Lorna would wire me if she heard bad news of Jimmy, and if so how it would be phrased. I went straight from the train to the theatre & the stage doorman handed me a wire from her that answered both questions conclusively. Oh dear.

We had a noisy night last night. We lay in a bed that shook, not with our trembling but the general vibration, and when one heard planes overhead all I could think of was that there were young men in them like Jimmy with their lives before them & people [in Germany] who'd miss them & grieve for them if they didn't get home.

Such waste. Such waste.

I've got to dash out to Golder's Green & see *She Stoops to Conquer* – a prospect which I couldn't regard with more disfavour.

To Mrs Norah Guthrie at Annaghmakerrig
No address. 11 March 1943

Life is a turmoil of work. Trying to strengthen the *Lincoln* cast; trying to cast *The Russians* [Konstantin Simonov] – casting now is just despairing work, there's *no one* about; trying to make sense of Liverpool & Bristol repertory plans for summer – oh and a hundred dozen other things, each one trifling but summing up to an exhausting total with almost nothing to show for it but frustration at the end.

To Mrs Norah Guthrie at Annaghmakerrig
No address. 13 April 1943

Lincoln opens tonight. There is no booking. We need a success just now – badly. Our stock, after long absence from London & the failure of *The Merchant*, is at a low ebb.

To Mrs Norah Guthrie at Annaghmakerrig

Liverpool. 27 April 1943

Today I have a lot of talks & arrangements with Miss Carpenter, the manager here; with the Corpn. Parks Cttee (for whom we're doing 2 weeks open air prod. of *Love's Labours*); & John Moody who is producing here. And in the evening 100 of the L'pool Film Socy. are coming to *The Seagull* & staying for a discussion afterwards which I have to lead. I then catch the midnight train in order to be in time for rehearsals of *Traviata* which is to have a brush-up before going into London Season. We have a new tenor called Peter Pears[18] who is a distinct acquisition. Meantime casting goes on for *The Russians* which will go into rehearsal next week.

No producer for Judy's play. We had hoped that Murray Macdonald was going to be given leave from Army to do it but at the last moment his leave was cancelled. And we have no backstop. There are no backstops these days. The cast is excellent – Sybil of course, and Jean Forbes-Robertson as the daughter; an excellent actor called Ronald Simpson as Widge; Laurence Harvey as the Butler. We have a distinctly possible Irish girl in view for Bridie. The title is now *Queen Bee*: do you like that?

To Mrs Peggy Butler at Maidenhall

23 Old Buildings, Lincoln's Inn, London, WC2. 13 May 1943

Just a line in haste. You probably heard Aunt Sue fell climbing into bed off some contrivance or footstool or something or other – she didn't injure herself organically but it's been a *bad shock*.

Terribly terribly busy and rather low. One of our best ex-students killed in Africa, & the dear old fireman at Sadler's Wells heard just now that his son is missing after Dortmund raid ... the apple of his eye & just made an officer, the poor old man just broke down & cried like a child ... Judy's play quite promising in rehearsal and cast gratifyingly interested.

---

18   Peter Pears sang Alfredo in *La Traviata*.

To Mrs Norah Guthrie at Annaghmakerrig.

Norfolk Hotel, London. 20 May 1943

Judy's in Bristol with *Queen Bee* so I've come here for a few nights as I really haven't the strength or time to cope with even skeleton meals or skeleton bedmaking. I'm in full swing of *Russians* rehearsal & quite enjoying it. A good cast & everyone working with a will. Afraid I oughtn't to go to Bristol for Monday's dress rehearsal of *Q.B.* – mustn't spare the time away from my own opus – but Williams & I are going down to First Night & George will be there over w/e to hold the hand of the palpitating authoress – & they'll wire me if they feel my presence urgently required on the Monday. Gordon's definitely going to the 1st night, Nellie possibly. Latter won't decide & shies like a horse when the topic is raised; but I think in the end she will go.

Went to see Becky [Miles, former nanny, widowed] who's in a deplorable state – utterly to pieces. Her one wish & cry is to get over to Ireland – home. I'm now inclined to think she should get over if she can get a resident permit.

To Mrs Norah Guthrie at Annaghmakerrig

Norfolk Hotel, London. 28 May 1943

I had a calm but despairing letter from J. on Saty. saying the production [*Queen Bee*] was v. unsatisfactory & she & Sybil thought I'd better go down to Bristol for the Monday d. rehearsal & try & cope rather than wait for 1st night. Well I went down on Sunday & saw a rehearsal that night in costume & on the set & thought it all pretty terrible. The producer [Hugh Miller] has directed it as a story play & not as a psychological play. And of course there practically is no story. All pretty grim, & really too late to grapple.

The 1st night I had to miss (couldn't be away longer from business) but Williams went down and says it passed off – tho' the Dame was v. fussed & v. exhausted & didn't do well. Williams thought the Bridie crashingly bad – I think she is bad but not so crashingly as Williams. Judy returns tonight – it's been a pretty teasing experience for her but I think she has stood up to it very philosophically & well.

To Mrs Norah Guthrie at Annaghmakerrig

London, no address. 11 June 1943

> *The Russians*: it's been a big undertaking. Large cast; difficult sets; innumerable props (meals on the stage, battles both "off" and "on") & endless effects – aeroplanes, rifle fire, artillery, machine guns, fire, snow, wet clothes – just a first class cope because of course *everything* is hard to get, from star actors to hairpins. Well, we opened last night with a Gala "Do" to endow an Old Vic bed in the hospital arising from the ruins of Stalingrad, with the Ambassador & suite, wires from Moscow, Movietone News in the Foyer, Adolphe Menjou [actor] in a box. It was received with immense gusto & storms of cheering but I can't feel this indicated much, as the house, tho' packed, was a political rather than a theatrical one. Still, it did go well; & I was more than relieved because I'd been feeling very low about it & I'd been the one who, rather against everyone's advice, insisted on our doing the play. We have had the "close assistance" of the [Soviet] Embassy which has meant that two dreary young men have come and sat like images at rehearsal & nattered & nittered in broken English about totally unimportant trifles like the exact size of collar badges. They are full of suspicion – I really think they believed that instead of putting the play on as a sincere gesture of allied goodwill it was a deeply laid plot to discredit them.
>
> *Queen Bee* is doing very well in Liverpool.

To Mrs Norah Guthrie at Annaghmakerrig

London, no address. 17 June 1943

> Went to Crossways y'day for tea & supper. Aunt Sue not in wonderful form. But she is not depressed. She dozes endlessly & dreams, I think, rather happy little dreams which get confused with actuality.
>
> I saw Becky by apt. at Crossways. I had her permit application form for travel to Ireland & filled it in for her. I think she'll be O.K. She's fearfully gummidgy – just no spirit at all - & most irritatingly sorry for herself to such a pitch that it leaves no room for one to be sorry for her. I was resolutely brisk & just paid no heed whatsoever to the snivels & snuffles. I don't know whether it's the wisest & kindest line or not. But she wants over, & the formalities have got to be gone through, & there's no use grumbling about it. I may have difficulty & delay over my

permit having been over so recently. D.V. – but don't count on this – she & I will be over in the middle of July. She for good, I for a fortnight.

To Mrs Norah Guthrie at Annaghmakerrig

London, no address. 15 August 1943

Abraham Lincoln is shaping quite well. I *hope* it will draw on tour. I think it's far likelier to do so with a provincial residential audience than with the present West End audience which is almost entirely either very sophisticated "playgoers" or war-workers on the spree – of whom the first category find *Lincoln* vieux-jeu & the second too serious.

To Mrs Norah Guthrie at Annaghmakerrig

Liverpool Playhouse. 12 October 1943

I try to come up to see as many as possible of the dress rehearsals & openings of new plays & to give all hands the impression that they are not an isolated unit of guerrillas in the far-flung "provinces" but regarded as of great value and importance by "the office".

Last week was very social – I never stopped having lunch with this one and a drink with that one for discussions of plans. Last night we took Kenneth [Rae] to the ballet & on to supper & on Fri we went to *Love for Love* [Congreve] & had John [Gielgud] out to supper. The two occasions could not have been more of a contrast, &, I'm sorry to say, the meeting with John was the pleasanter and "happier" of the two. He's loving the success of *Love for Love* & was at his very best – gay and forthcoming and charming – his horizon is completely & alarmingly bounded by the theatre but inside that limitation he is delightful – full of enthusiasms, idealisms, intelligence & humour. But the world outside – the world of factories & banks, of suburban trains, of collieries, of piggeries, slaughter-houses & workhouses – his lacking of knowledge & his lack of interest, of desire to know, are truly marvellous. Kenneth, on the other hand, is a poor case. His pre-war world has utterly crumbled; Mrs Rae well up in the 80s; the young people of the family scattered to the four winds, & physically & mentally too occupied to have much time for Knowles Bank [country house] – a Knowles Bank moreover that is servantless, that is almost impossible of access & when you do get there rather chilly & infinitely depressing. The Wiltons & the Chatsworths & the places where he stayed are no longer delicious pleasure domes but remote icy vaults, laborious anachronisms. I think Kenneth will bob up again – this is only a very bad phase – he has too much spirit & philosophy to be permanently downed.

To Julia Butler at Maidenhall

Visiting Annaghmakerrig. Undated, December 1943

Thank you very much indeed for your lovely calendar. We all like it *very* much & it is up on the Study mantelpiece. I had a difference of opinion with Christopher [Fitz-Simon, 9] about the bird that is sitting in the hayshed. Christopher says it's a hen. I say it's a crow. Who is right?

Chrissie [Morgan, parlour-maid] left yesterday and everybody cried. But we are very busy thinking how nice it will be for Chrissie to have a house of her own; and Gretta [Mullen] who is reigning here in her stead, is a very nice-looking girl and seems to be taking on well. She had the greatest drilling by Miss Chrissie in all her duties, and big cook Susan [Murray] is being very nice to her and helping all she can. We pretended it was Christmas last Sunday & had an Xmas Dinner with turkey & pudden and holly on the mantelpiece. And the maids all came in & we drank to Chrissie & Jack (and everybody cried again); & to Susan for being so wonderful; & to Gretta to welcome her to Annaghmakerrig – all in brown sherry & Christopher had a wee dreg out of the bottom of my glass & Nicky just had a smell.

Do you and Joe know your parts in the play yet?[19] If not you must hurry up and learn them. All the children here have their parts off by heart and rehearsals go on every day after tea. Did you know that there are parts this year for Joan and Lora [Daley]?

Please will you tell your Mummy that the honey arrived in good order. Unfortunately, tho' we would have been allowed to take it last week there is a new order forbidding export. However, we may be able to get it by Underground thro' Clonmackin.[20] Now I must go out – we are sawing wood for the fires like anything. With love, from Uncle T.

19   *The Stolen Princess* by Ailish Fitz-Simon performed at Annaghmakerrig on 26 December 1943 with Julia Butler, Joe Hone, Jennifer Cullen, Pamela Cullen, Lora Daley, Joan Daley, Nicky Fitz-Simon & Christopher Fitz-Simon.

20   Chrissie Morgan's home, where the front door was in the Free State and the back door in Northern Ireland.

To Mrs Norah Guthrie at Annaghmakerrig

23 Old Buildings, Lincoln's Inn, London WC2. 4 December 1943

Raquin rehearsals from 10 to 4, greatly delayed by Flora [Robson] being away all week with flu & in addition an awful lot cropping up in the office. I was in each day from 9 to 9.30 and then again after rehearsal. The two kinds of work & too many things to focus on is extremely wearing. I find the kind of concentration needed at rehearsal & the kind of concentration needed in administration are very different; & the two don't happily mix.

There is a very important plan boiling up with C.E.M.A., just what one would have hoped in a dream might happen. Alas, it needs great energy & drive behind it which I ought to supply.

We went on Thurs to hear a preliminary playback of *Matrimonial News* [new production of radio play]. By no means in the bull's eye. The production (by me) is not satisfactory, but alas it's too late. Flora's performance is good but doesn't record well – too subtle, & a little too fast. My fault. Sybil [Thorndike] is tremendous – real tigress – & awfully funny. She & Lewis [Casson] came with us to hear it & we all rolled about with amusement at The Dame.

It was sickening you couldn't get to Chrissie's wedding.

To Mrs Norah Guthrie at Annaghmakerrig

23 Old Buildings, Lincoln's Inn, London, WC2. 27 January 1944

We are having a holiday today. Judy has taken the day off from the factory and will make up the time one morning. On Saturday the *Hamlet* set will be ready [Old Vic at the New Theatre] – an elaborate affair of built platforms, pillars and staircases made of salvaged timber from the Vic. Without these stairs and things we can't get much forrarder & are knocking off today and will work on Sunday instead.

I feel very strongly that Eugene [Maguire, Annaghmakerrig gardener] should get the same rise as the rest of staff. To begin with, the rise is intended to offset the rise in the cost of living. Next it reflects supply and demand – at present labour is in short supply, consequently its price is high and continually rising. Though it has nothing to do with *your* price scale I mention as a matter of interest that charwomen in London get up to 5/- an *hour*, 2/6 is usual; our stage carpenters get as much as £14 per week; that we are paying £6 per week to unskilled, unintelligent nonentities to walk on and understudy small parts. Third, returning to Eugene, he is very much more intelligent and capable than Brian [McGoldrick] and Seamus [McGorman]. Finally, if he isn't treated fairly he will leave.

It would be the greatest mistake in the world for you to fret and fume about spending a little capital. If you were living in selfish extravagance you might have a qualm or two of conscience. But you're not. I think it is your plain duty to spend on the material wellbeing of your staff regardless of whether the money is income or capital. If you want to employ an intelligent conscious skilful man like Eugene you must be prepared to reward him.

If you are worrying about spending capital, remember this: capital is not only money but land. By keeping the garden in good cultivation you are increasing a capital asset. On no account WORRY. Money should be a material cushion between its possessor and material ills. To turn the cushion into a burden is just plumb dotty!

To Julia Butler at Maidenhall

23 Old Buildings, Lincoln's Inn, London WC2. 27 January 1944

I was very pleased with the photo of Joe [Hone] and yourself. I hear that you have a new pony and that he is a great success. Also new puppies. How nice. But I'd rather have kittens than puppies. I expect our Myrtle will have kittens sometime. At present she doesn't seem to be a very motherly type. She's more of a Sports Girl. She's very intelligent & when she wants to open the door she speaks to it first and then jumps at the handle and clasps it. She has joined the Lincoln's Inn Cats' Club & goes down every morning to the Club Smoking Room which is an underground Boiler Room – very warm & snug.

To Mrs Peggy Butler at Maidenhall

23 Old Buildings, Lincoln's Inn, London WC2. 27 January 1944

Just a line to enclose with Julia's. We're going through the throes of a first class internal crisis at the Old Vic with resignations being offered right, left & centre; recriminations being bandied in dignified letters & rather less dignified "Scenes"... I, personally, am not involved; it's mostly anti-Brownie &, consequently, by contrast, my stock is rather high – for the moment. I think most of the trouble will blow over & is a symptom of fatigue & nervous exhaustion more than anything else. *Hamlet* rehearsals [with Robert Helpmann at New Theatre] are in full swing & it's an enormous unspeakable relief to be able to go away for some hours of each day into a world that is sufficiently real & elaborate & interesting as to occupy one's imagination fully & yet removes one from the drab "real" world of real battles, real murders, real sudden death, real drabness, scarcity, monotony & *weariness. Hamlet* is full not only of thought, feeling, intuition, intimations of a greater mysterious hinterland above, below & behind consciousness, but of the sensuous richness & pleasure we are all missing just now. It's heavenly to be able to shut a door on Roll out the Barrel, on all American products, on the whole rawness of the New World, on ENSA & UNRRA & GHQ & CEMA – the whole drab wartime Abracadabra of initials[21] (initials because the proper names are so horribly pompous & so invincibly dull); on coupons & points & bone-salvage – the whole apparatus of scarcity – the material famine as ENSA & USA are symbols of spiritual famine, & to live in a world that is prodigally, lavishly supplied with a coinage that buys something one really wishes to possess.

You seem to be involved also in your share of squabbles & civil wars.[22] I suppose if one lived alone on a desert island one would manage to quarrel with the stones on the beach, the stars in the sky; it's an expression of inner unrest. If one were at complete peace with oneself there'd be no need to attack others or even to repel their attacks (which would not be made if they did not sense aggression) but then if one were at complete peace with oneself one would be dead.

I personally feel very much heartened in the last week or so because I've had an idea for a play.[23] Maybe it'll be no good but I think it's more mature than anything I've written before. I think it really has

21   Entertainments National Service Association; United Nations Relief & Rehabilitation Association; General Head Quarters; Council for the Encouragement of Music & the Arts.

22   Domestic difficulties connected with the settling-in process at Maidenhall with family, governesses and neighbours.

23   Guthrie's newly envisaged play would become *Top of the Ladder*, produced at the St James' Theatre, London, in 1950; it addressed themes formerly treated in early radio dramas.

some idea behind it. It seems to sum up what I've been collecting in tiny bits for ages. The idea isn't so tinkling and trumpery as my ideas mostly are – though for that matter the idea may be small enough; but not if I can invest it with the feeling, the mysterious "over and above" that it seems to me is knocking about. Technically it arises from *Matrimonial News* but it has, I hope, ever so much more to say. I'm afraid I'll have to write it for the wireless which is a bore because it's so ephemeral & so ill paid. When will the leisure come to get it written?

Hubert Butler wrote of his concern regarding the injustice of the British government's (temporary, as it turned out) travel ban between Britain and the Irish Free State, imposed on 13 March 1944. The opposing views of Guthrie and Butler on Irish neutrality appeared to have the making of an ideological rift. Meanwhile, London was subjected to raids of V2 rocket bombs. Becky Miles (*née* Daley), Guthrie's former nanny, returned to Annaghmakerrig following the death of her husband in Tunbridge Wells.

To Mrs Norah Guthrie at Annaghmakerrig
23 Old Buildings, Lincoln's Inn, London WC2. 6 February 1944

Hamlet at the New. The company is inevitably a bit wartime; some of the "extra" men have to be seen to be believed. Simon [Fitz-Simon, coaching stage soldiers] is a shining exception and is doing very well though I think he must be wondering at the queer company he has got himself into. Bobby [Helpmann] is small & fragile & rather too much the "delicate & tender prince"; but chock full of intelligence. Owing to the Ballet Boom [he] is as big a star as Pavlova. On the whole the leading parts will be pretty adequately done, Ophelia particularly – a girl called Pamela Brown. It will be an interesting & amusing First Night as the profession and critics and pundits are lying in wait to pounce – "a little male dancer as Hamlet: another Old Vic stunt" & so on. We could have sold the house out twenty times over with ease.
 How is Becky getting on? Give her a special message from us. Have you and she had any talks about old times? I feel you'd both enjoy it; she is a splendid raconteuse & fully relishes an audience that can appreciate the gift.

To Mrs Norah Guthrie at Annaghmakerrig

23 Old Buildings, Lincoln's Inn, London WC2. 13 February 1944

Hamlet was launched last Friday so one breathes not only more freely but with a little more leisure. Bobby was paralysed with nerves and did not in consequence give the best performance in the world or half as good an attempt as at rehearsal. He was vocally weak & fell back on a lot of tricks and external manifestations – gasps and gestures; there was too much movement, far too many and too long pauses – holding a long pause demands more weight & authority than he commands; and the technique of timing & spacing pauses is very different when there is no orchestra as in ballet. Also, in ballet he is the oldest and FAR the largest personality; this gives everything he does in ballet a drive and authority. Up against some of the actors in the cast he seems very much smaller physically & very much less commanding – the whole personality dwindles. Nevertheless he "got by"; the press is not enthusiastic but does not heavily damn.

The [air raid] alert went most dramatically at the moment in the play scene when the King calls for lights; & the King's big soliloquy was drowned in a tornado of gunfire. The actor, Basil Sydney, did not bat an eyelid nor seem to lose concentration for a second & not a soul in the audience even shuffled – pretty creditable to all concerned.

Simon did very well, most reliable & conscientious & a great improvement on the really awful riff-raff that is all that is available for humble walk-on work at present. It is humiliating and disappointing beyond measure to be such a drag on the market at the moment. If he were a navvy, an electrician, a miner or any kind of manual worker he would get a well paid job in five minutes, but to say you have been a professional soldier, a colonel, and an officer and a gent, cuts no ice at all. Then there is a large plan with C.E.M.A. which really requires maximum drive and concentration. It's really a whacking opportunity to establish the Vic as a State Theatre on a big scale. I can't organise except on the spur of the moment; I can rap out orders & get people to carry them out happily & enthusiastically even; but without the immediate objective and the pressure of an audience find it the greatest task to organise a campaign. Lewis Casson is MOST helpful from the C.E.M.A. end (he is their Drama Director), has a great feeling about the Vic & is, I think, very fond of me personally and a great fighter of my battles with his committee, but he is over sixty and his ideas are often very old-fashioned. The absence of youth from civilian life is simply obsessing; nothing but tired, harassed people over forty-three or youngsters who are so physically unfit that they haven't the stamina to fight battles.

Do not worry about us when you read or hear about raids. Nights just now are amazingly noisy but we really are not frightened at all. It's less a question of bravery than adaptability.

To Mrs Peggy Butler at Maidenhall
23 Old Buildings, Lincoln's Inn, London WC2. 19 February 1944

The play [*Top of the Ladder*] is beginning to take shape. I am in a phase when it is easy and pleasant to write – the nicest phase of all when one just writes down the scenes that are waiting to be expressed with none of the boring difficulty of placing in logical context or right proportion, when there is no need to bother about consistency or intelligibility. I've been given (by Bobby Helpmann) a very beautiful book on L da Vinci; it brings very vividly before the eye the enormous amount of drudgery and donkey work that goes to the making of a work of art. The vision in the heart, product of all the senses – eyes, ears, feeling, taste and what-not – only gets expressed in tangible form by a process of painful adaptation, most of it tedious to a degree. Aunt Sue's view of the Glory of Craftsmanship is, I fear, solely the view of the gilded amateur who treats "art" as a pleasant relaxation from the important business of "life". To the real craftsman the craft is not glorious or inglorious but entirely instinctive and made so by the most tedious repetition of certain movements and processes, physical and psychic. Without this automatic reaction – that makes the hand of the painter or the pianist, or the memory of the writer, move in a certain way – the technical transformation of an idea into a tangible work of art could never take place.

To Mrs Norah Guthrie at Annaghmakerrig
23 Old Buildings, Lincoln's Inn, London WC2. 6 March 1944

Plans are forming but slowly in face of great difficulties. Larry [Olivier] and Ralph [Richardson] are willing to work with us for a long period. A trial trip of a year and, if successful, longer; with all sorts of interesting tie-ups with films. We have applied for their release from Fleet Air Arm.

Brownie [James Brown] has resigned. Things have been getting increasingly difficult for some time. He had a crashing row with Joan Cross who resigned on the head of it but has been persuaded to stay. That shook him. Then he and I have fought inch by inch for this Drama plan which he considers wildly extravagant and I don't deny it will be expensive but there is a difference between expense and the fact that he doesn't see this is a radical diff. between us. He is a most endearing & loveable creature but hopelessly conservative in outlook.

To Hubert Butler at Maidenhall
23 Old Buildings. Lincoln's Inn, London WC2. St Patrick's Day, 1944

Awfully nice to get your letter … tho' I hope by now you are all feeling calmer & rumours less agitating.[24] Naturally your angle on it all must be a good deal more hectic than ours. The whole affair while not exactly being "played down" in the British press, is naturally only a comparatively unimportant item. Most people one speaks to aren't even awfully interested, & I don't see why they should be. Russia, Anzio, Cassino, the bombs, the pre-eminence of [the] second front all dominate. I'm afraid it may mean that you are awfully cut off. Suppose there is a risk of all sorts of shortages and increased discomforts. I can imagine too a growing and horrible feeling of claustrophobia. It's ghastly. Pray God it won't last long.

No news. I'm in a swirl of plans which would be important if one could feel anything important. But Events do really make personal concerns appear in a devastating true and insignificant proportion! A healthy theatre is an important long-term amenity – it's just that at this particular moment it seems utterly trivial.

To Mrs Norah Guthrie at Annaghmakerrig
23 Old Buildings, Lincoln's Inn, London WC2. Good Friday, 1944

We went down to Salisbury where Murray Macdonald is running a garrison theatre. We sent *Thérèse Raquin* [with Flora Robson] there. The play went awfully well, broke all records for the theatre, and the rather unsophisticated audience of troops were evidently and

---

24   Britain banned travel to and from the Irish Free State following US allegations that Ireland's neutrality favoured Axis.

gratifyingly thrilled. Do you know it is twenty six – TWENTY SIX – years since I was in Salisbury? It really is wonderfully beautiful. The cathedral has such a splendid air of coming out exactly as the designer intended. We went to Sunday Matins; a large congregation, mostly in uniform; but some vintage cathedral townswomen in vintage toques from *Barchester Towers*.

To Mrs Peggy Butler at Maidenhall

23 Old Buildings, Lincoln's Inn, London WC2. 23 April 1944

Myrtle produced four kittens on Friday afternoon – one tabby like herself and three little blacks. Two of the latter we have had taken away by the R.S.P.C.A. Their lethal service still exists and a nice young lady called, gave maternity advice and left with the two poorest kitties in a basket. I couldn't help thinking they were Jewish babies in Poland; but that, I suppose, is neurotic and a very towny anthropomorphic view of animal life.

Raquin opened [Lyric, Hammersmith] last Tuesday and has rather failed to please the critics. Judy has had a blow this week. Her [munitions] factory has to work an hour later at night. Their production has to be greater and they can't get more workers.

Now, with a delicious plot, Larry [Olivier], Ralph [Richardson] and The Prince's [Theatre] have fallen into our lap [at the Old Vic]; and, just for good measure, Sybil [Thorndike] has been able, with a lot of (also unscrupulous) fiddling, to rearrange contracts and join the party too. It's all been most frenzying and wearisome as almost every other day the whole edifice has seemed like to topple. Even now there will be ten million alarums as, undoubtedly, the big commercial interests will be out for our blood. The opening trio will be *Richard III* with Larry as the humpback, Ralph as Clarence and the Dame as Margaret of Anjou. *Dandy Dick* if we can get Morland Graham as the Dean.[25] And finally that trifling little offering *Peer Gynt* with Ralph as Peer, Larry as the Button Moulder and Dame as old Mum; to say nothing of an orchestra of five-and-twenty and a good sized chorus of singers – where we shall find them God alone knows.

---

25   They couldn't, substituting Shaw's *Arms and the Man* with Richardson as Bluntschli, Olivier as Sergius Saranoff and Thorndike as Catherine Petkoff.

To Mrs Peggy Butler at Maidenhall

23 Old Buildings, Lincoln's Inn, London WC2. 30 April 1944

I will try and observe the strictest political attitude in all my letters even at some cost of spontaneity. I think your feelings in this matter [Ireland's neutrality] are too sensitive – no, I don't, or if I do – well your feelings have a right to be respected; and where one cannot say all, maybe it's best to say a minimum. My attitude to Neutrality is, as you must know, charged with conflict (in myself, I mean) coloured by the press and the attitude of those one meets, and undoubtedly disfigured by jealousy. My attitude to you is entirely independent of outside events. I love you because we have so many things in common – experiences, traits of heredity and influences of environment. I love you because you are yourself – your good points are many and strong but I don't know that I love them any more than things in you which reasons tells me are not your good points but your bad. Temporarily our environment is utterly different but this difference is so trivial compared to what binds us together. You may not always have from me that "good opinion" which you say is important to you; but you will always and in absolutely any circumstance have what I hope you value far more – my deepest, truest love.

As one grows older one changes within as without. I have only the haziest idea of how either my character or my appearance are changing. But I suspect from the looking-glass on the one hand and the attitude of other people to me on the other that I am developing into rather a sharp and possibly formidable customer ... these last few years have not been very softening.

To Mrs Norah Guthrie at Annaghmakerrig

23 Old Buildings, Lincoln's Inn, London WC2. 11 May 1944

We wait and wait for a Certain Event ['D-day' invasion of France] with dreadful expectancy. As the next months promise to be uncommonly exacting and as I am feeling pretty run-down I thought it would be wise to see [Dr] Bevan & just have an overhaul. He was most reassuring – says, Yes, I am run down & has prescribed a weekly heat treatment of ultra violet rays & given me a strong tonic – but the point is that he says, tho' tired, like everybody else, I am really in good order.

Although overworked, Guthrie accepted an invitation from the Prince's Theatre in the West End to direct a commercial production of *The Last of Mrs Cheyney* by Frederick Lonsdale on condition that the management make the stage available for certain periods to the Ballet and Opera while the Sadler's Wells Theatre was under repair, an arrangement that worked well.

To Mrs Norah Guthrie at Annaghmakerrig

23 Old Buildings, Lincoln's Inn, London WC2. 21 May 1944

> *The Last of Mrs Cheyney* is coming along alright and I really would be enjoying it were it not such an interruption to the more important work of the Old Vic. It's nice to let others have all the contending coupons [for clothes], staff, lodgings, arrangements – Blackpool in Whitsun Week so you can imagine the cope – scenery which won't be delivered in time, properties which can't be got and so on. Meantime Old Vic plans are coming along well though the expense of it all is simply shattering and rather gives George and me the willies when we are feeling tired and low.

To Mrs Judith Guthrie at 23 Old Buildings, Lincoln's Inn, London WC2

Annaghmakerrig. Undated, June 1944

> Got here last night after longish bus & train trek from Maiden Hall. The place looking too lovely with beech green at its freshest, may trees nearly out, hybrid rhododendria nearly over, ponticums in bud showing colour, sweet aloes hugely increased, in full bloom. Miss Mary Louise Davis [Migsie, visiting] in thunderous form – when America or Russia are mentioned she pops out, like a cuckoo from a clock, an enraged man-eating cuckoo, and STRIKES THIRTEEN.
>
> Was glad to have gone to MH, I think Peggy would have been a little wounded if I hadn't. The journey is awfully nice, the arrival at Waterford [steamship from Fishguard] is simply enchanting as one winds for 1½ hours up a simply exquisite estuary, quite quite narrow with beauty, Beauty, BEAUTY all the way. And then to crown all, the quaintest, daintiest of Old World grass-grown XVIII century quays to arrive at. Maiden Hall is very charming and they seem to have it in v.g. order. Garden looking really well cared for; staff in fairly good control. Sister has Great Taste & has made it both pretty & serviceable.

The Joe [Hone] business is bad.[26] Theft. I think they are coping well and wisely; & I thought Hubert being awfully wise and good about it – controlling Peggy who is apt to be in A State over it all – most understandably – & taking a very firm line over the old Hones. Julia arrived for w/e on Friday evg. with Miss Una Farrington & her parents with whom she boards in Dublin. Nice people but I saw little of them as I had to leave right after b'fast on Saty.

The lake [Annaghmakerrig] is way down – quite a wide shore all round with quantities of kingcups.

To Mrs Norah Guthrie at Annaghmakerrig

23 Old Buildings, Lincoln's Inn, London WC2. 25 June 1944

Just got back from Liverpool. Last night was the end of the Season there and it seemed suitable to be present. Now the Company packs up; not all are returning so farewells had to be said and the thanks of the management conveyed. Now they have three weeks hols and then three weeks rehearsal reopening the new Season with Ibsen's *John Gabriel Borkman* – a great masterpiece. Peter Glenville will be producing.

Judy is revising & slightly re-writing her play [*Queen Bee*] as another management has expressed a desire to read it and Dame [Sybil Thorndike] is still keen as mustard, though not free for some time.

To Mrs Norah Guthrie at Annaghmakerrig

23 Old Buildings, Lincoln's Inn, London WC2. 9 July 1944

It's rather thrilling to feel that we are now at a stage that it is not only possible but desirable and necessary to think of a future that involves young talent and the absorption of new people – not desperately trying to hold on and to make the tired old stagers do rather more than they can or should.

The Doodlebugs. Neither Judy nor I find them [VI rockets] as alarming as live bombs for the reason that one knows they are just automatons and cannot change their mind nor exert their reason. They are very noisy – a sound like a very large sky-motorbike chugging along at immense speed, and at night they leave an incandescent trail

---

26   Young Joe Hone had been caught pilfering from the village store. See his memoir *Wicked Little Joe* (Dublin 2009).

of fire behind them – rather beautiful. When the engine stops they fall and when they fall they explode. So it's rather like musical-chairs: you wait for the music to stop and then if you're late you're OUT. It's rather humiliating when they come right overhead how you can't help hoping the engine will go on just a leetle bit further.

To Mrs Norah Guthrie at Annaghmakerrig

23 Old Buildings, Lincoln's Inn, London WC2. 31 July 1944

My main work next week is going to be an attempt to infuse some new blood into the governors of the Old Vic and Sadler's Wells. We had a meeting last week and after it was over George [Chamberlain, administrator] and [Evelyn, secretary] Williams and I decided we really dare not wait till the war is over before trying to get a move on. They are all – or almost all – so TERRIBLY TERRIBLY OLD. The meetings are just like the Old Maids of Lee – poor old Lord Lytton with his hand to his deaf ear, someone else with a crutch, Lady Gooch practically falling to pieces, poor old thing, while you look at her. They are no more capable of steering the ship through stormy waters than of flying to the moon; and that puts too much responsibility on the staff. So I shall go to Sir Reggie [Row] and Lord Lytton who will I think agree that the time has come. Though it's no business of ours, Geo and I have prepared a list of people we think should be asked onto the Board and a Night of the Long Knives must be had and some of the old guard liquidated. It won't be hard as many of them like Canon Scott-Lidgett haven't attended for years and can have no possible objection to being sacked.

To Mrs Norah Guthrie at Annaghmakerrig

23 Old Buildings, Lincoln's Inn, London WC2. 5 August 1944

The Theatre Co. – travels to Manchester for dress rehearsal tomorrow & opening of *Arms and the Man* on Monday – have immense booking. Incidentally, we estimate Shaw's share of the business we do in Manchester at seven hundred and fifty pounds and I suppose in the same week there cannot be less than twenty or thirty performances of his going on in different parts of the world. They are filming *Caesar and Cleopatra* on a scale that will certainly ensure him every penny of half a million. He was nothing more than a hack journalist and a vestryman of St Pancras' parish. To have survived that degree of public indifference without becoming bitter takes qualities of the very highest; and then to swing to the dizziest boughs of the tree of worldly success and not lose your head. It is ironical that now at ninety he is, I suppose, the most revered contemporary in the world, and rich beyond the dreams of Midas.

As in the last war manners have changed quite a bit & become much more democratic & informal. This is partly, I think, due to the influx of women into public jobs – you wouldn't expect a man conductor on a bus to call you dear or duck when he gives you a ticket but the women do & it's rather pleasant. The trains are so crowded that first class has been abolished on suburban trains and might just as well be abolished on long-distance ones as well.

To Mrs Norah Guthrie at Annaghmakerrig

23 Old Buildings, Lincoln's Inn, London WC2. 20 August 1944

The doodles are quite a tease but we have had nothing near since this time last week. The dirt and dust are still very vexatious – piles of glass and ruined furniture heaped outside every staircase and still not cleared away because of labour shortage.

I've rehearsed *Peer Gynt* all week except for a dash to L'pool to see the opening of the Season – *John Gabriel Borkman*, a gloomy masterpiece of Ibsen excellently performed to a packed house. Peter Glenville's production was *so* good. His appointment was a bit of a gamble because he's never produced before but he is a talented and clever young man and a good critic. He is also handling the Company well.

To Mrs Norah Guthrie at Annaghmakerrig

23 Old Buildings, Lincoln's Inn, London WC2. 3 September 1944

Peer Gynt [Old Vic at the New Theatre] passed off with what I suppose you would call Eclat. The business is phenomenal and the press almost all very laudatory. I wasn't too pleased with it myself. Ralph [Richardson] gave an efficient but very uninspired performance and I find the production lumbering and pretentious. I don't know how otherwise to manage the play, but there it is.

Firth Shephard definitely wants to buy *Queen Bee* and Judy has asked for – and without difficulty received – a month's leave from the munitions factory to finish revising the text. It won't be produced yet awhile and anyway Damey must stay with *Peer Gynt*. *Peer* has taken four hundred pounds in four performances (which is phenomenal).

To Mrs Norah Guthrie at Annaghmakerrig

23 Old Buildings, Lincoln's Inn, London WC2. 17 September 1944

Richard III opened on Wednesday with vast Eclat. I didn't myself enjoy it very much. Larry gives a really wonderful performance but the play and the production have longueurs. But I am tired and blasé these days and well nigh impossible to please. Anyway it is a spanking success and we are playing to full houses of every performance of all three plays. Now it remains to bring the old Opera up to the level of prestige of the plays and the Ballet. I think this we shall do. Meantime so many other things will happen. That's the worst of trying to drive this Troika. As soon as Opera and Ballet are going along nicely the Dramatic horse kicks up its heels.

To Mrs Norah Guthrie at Annaghmakerrig

Shaftesbury Hotel, Liverpool. 6 November 1944

Judy came up on Sat. & is here for week – attending rehearsals [Andreyev's *He Who Gets Slapped*]. Play going quite well I think. Also have quite a lot of confabbing to fit in. For instance, Ninette [de Valois] comes up to see me on Wed. night. And on Sat. & Sun. we have an important conference on opera & poss. alliance with new Covent Gdn. syndicate. Joan Cross will be singing here at a big concert on Sat. One of the C.G. directors will also be here as he's a director of the L'pool Philharmonic so Professor Dent & Willie Walton are coming up here to join us. I think it's all pretty important really for future of Brit. Opera. It means quite a lot of "prep" as Ninette, Joan and I have to prepare a united front & agree our "case"; & Dent & I are preparing a long memorandum on opera which has entailed endless work.

The hotel here is v. comfortable, not at all grand, it's very much a "commercial" but these sort of places are now far more congenial than the swagger hotels. The latter are staffed by female riff-raff (mostly

Sybil Thorndike and Ralph Richardson in Guthrie's production of Ibsen's *Peer Gynt*, Old Vic
Company, 1944.

from Eire) with unexampled inefficiency & discourtesy. Whereas
places like this still have a nucleus of old – very old – retainers with
some loyalty to the establishment & affection for its management &
good name. Cups of tea appear at odd hours & hot soup when the
kitchen has closed & so forth … very helpful in these days, as in most
places you can't get anything at all after 7 which is awfully teasing
if you arrive after travelling all day: or very tired & hungry after a
day's work. Still, when one reads & hears of life in France, Belgium,
Holland, Spain, Italy, Greece & so on – when one *imagines* what life
must be like in the German cities – well, I suppose we can be devoutly,
deeply thankful.

To Mrs Peggy Butler at Maidenhall

Shaftesbury Hotel, Liverpool. 6 November 1944

I'm intending to reach A'kerrig about Nov 28 and to stay till early Jan. Isn't it lovely? I'm as thrilled as tho' it were indeed Christmas hols & I thirteen instead of 44 ½ ! The grand London season being successfully launched it seemed wise just to take a real holiday & try & get back some vitality & enthusiasm for the welter of plans & decisions that are already beginning to surge up. V. interesting – & lovely – to feel that one can begin to think in terms of expanding resources & terms other than survival in desperate emergency. But tiring. And one is so tired not on the surface, but in the spirit. I have developed an 'anxiety' neurosis that is less, I think, due to temperament than to having had for five years to cope with quite a lot of responsibility in v. teasing circumstances. Mind you, I do realise the whole world is tired. Everyone has had to make adjustments to a world revolution. We haven't had to put up with half the privation & danger of any of the European countries.

Tell you an interesting thing: I have now for the first time begun to dream about air raids. I don't normally remember my dreams. But since lately I have wakened to remember that in my dream bombs were falling (with realistic sound effects) & that I was crouching for shelter under the legs of that aspidistra tripod that stood in the angle of the stairs at Belmont. The experience did not seem to be frightening – just that one had an uneasy feeling that it was silly to be so near the window. Strange, isn't it?

A distinct note of moving on to new initiatives creeps into the letters before the end of the war. The Guthries re-established themselves permanently in their flat in London, Guthrie supervised productions for a second Old Vic Company, produced Benjamin Britten's major opera *Peter Grimes*, and, the war over, accepted an engagement in the state that was about to become Israel.

To Mrs Norah Guthrie at Annaghmakerrig

23 Old Buildings, Lincoln's Inn, London WC2. 1 January 1945

> It was a lovely, lovely six weeks [at Annaghmakerrig]. The complete rest & change of rhythm & occupation has done me a whole heap of good and everyone remarks HOW WELL I look. There is a most grimly noticeable change in the atmosphere the moment one gets back to England, a strain that is noticeably absent in Belfast as well as in Eire – principally because in Northern Ireland and Eire there are plenty of able-bodied young people available for ordinary occupations whereas here it is a real rarity to see such creatures. I found things going on here quite well. *School for Scandal* is a very creditable show at L'pool and has had its run extended from four to six weeks. The Opera at the Prince's hasn't played to such full houses as was hoped but business in general is greatly down in the south of England due to enemy action.
>
> Oh – I heard a most exciting tenor in Belfast. James Johnston. It seems to me that it's a much better voice than any of the tenors over here – great power and quality and splendid breath control. He is a butcher, aged thirty-nine. He thinks he would be quite prepared to consider an offer if we were prepared to make one. I'll ask Madam [Joan Cross] about it.[27]

---

27   James Johnston subsequently sang leading tenor roles in *Carmen*, *Il Trovatore*, *Rigoletto*, *Faust* and many other operas over a decade at Sadler's Wells and Covent Garden.

Sir Reggie Row didn't seem to me to be so bad as I had expected from all accounts. He is perfectly lucid and by no means as physically helpless as he was a couple of weeks ago. But, poor old man, he is longing to go – he foresees no interesting or lucid future for himself and rails against the doctor for keeping him alive.

To Mrs Norah Guthrie at Annaghmakerrig

23 Old Buildings, Lincoln's Inn, London WC2. 21 January 1945

We are preoccupied today by the fact of Sir Reggie's departure. He died very early this morning. The sister-in-law rang for Judy to go over at four; he had had another stroke and was taken by ambulance to hospital and died very soon after – mercifully.

Negotiations with Covent Garden are in the air and are going to be interesting and worrying; before my holiday I should have found them ONLY worrying, now I feel able to take them in the stride.

To Mrs Norah Guthrie at Annaghmakerrig

23 Old Buildings, Lincoln's Inn, London WC2. 20 March 1945

Have been today to County Hall with Lord Lytton to see Lord Littleton and councillors about theatre site on S. bank of the Thames – nothing conclusive, just a preliminary wave of ostrich plumes and sparkle of ancient tiaras with a view to possibly, just maybe – well perhaps – coming down to something so common as brass tacks in a dim future. Personally I'm by no means enamoured by the site and anyway there'll be no building of pleasure domes – even semi-Sacred Domes like a National Theatre – for yeahs and yeahs and yeahs.

Back to L'pool on Thursday morning to grapple with *The Alchemist* [Ben Jonson] which is a magnificent, but magnificent, play.

To Mrs Norah Guthrie at Annaghmakerrig

The Playhouse, Liverpool. 11 April 1945

Killevan Parish Sale of Work sounds quite a "do" – tho' one can't help feeling raising funds to convert the benighted Heathen from their happy natural squalor in mid-Africa & turn them into good little Ulster Protestants is a most fantastic notion as well as rather arrogant. If you do decide to come over this summer & do get a passport your plan will be to fly right thro' to Croydon & then be met in state by a car. The rail & boat journey is now far too crowded for you even to consider.

Owing to an outbreak of mumps in the company our rehearsals have been very delayed as the Ophelia in *Hamlet* [playing at night] was off and also her understudy. *Alchemist*, the play we're doing, is so difficult we couldn't afford to miss any rehearsal so we have had to close the theatre for a week and open it next Monday week instead of next Wed. It is, I think, a great masterpiece of comedy to which we shall not do justice but which may, all the same, revive a more than duty bound interest in the play. It's by Ben Jonson, a contemporary, more or less, of Shakespeare, & was first produced in 1610.

This morning was so bright & lovely I had to be out in it so took a long & most interesting tour of the slums behind the docks. Such terrible terrible squalour – a frightful indictment of urban life one thinks at first; then one remembers the way people live in the country – Susan Atty or even those intensely respectable Steensons [Aghabog farmers] & one has to admit that the slums are more crowded but that the disadvantage is counterpoised by considerable amenities. The "Beauty" of the country I do not regard as a factor at all. Most country people are unaware of it; & further, it's only a convention – & I think a rather silly one – that the country is beautiful & the city ugly.

Judy was up for Easter, arrived Thurs night & left Tues at 8 A.M. No word yet of her factory stopping war production. I think the Russians denouncing their pact with Japan is the best news in ages. The Germans can't go on much longer. But the food & administrative situation in Europe is apparently so terrible that the end of the war is more of a formality than an event of acute significance.

Am reading with great enjoyment Lennox Robinson's auto-biography – I think you & Hubert & Peggy would enjoy it. It's called *Curtain Up!* & is less pro-ey than that tiresome title suggests. Hubert's name is mentioned, by the way, in connection with all the wonder-boys whom Lennox collected as librarians.

To Mrs Norah Guthrie at Annaghmakerrig

23 Old Buildings, Lincoln's Inn, London WC2 (on Sadler's Wells letterhead). 29 April 1945

It's simply lovely having the blackout relaxed, not that at this time of year it makes a very great practical difference, it's just the symbolism, the feeling that the night sky is no longer to be dreaded. I expect you, as we, are listening pretty constantly to the Wire in case the rumours and rushings are really true and that Himmler is indeed suing for peace.

The Benjamin Britten opera [*Peter Grimes*] goes into rehearsal on the stage next week – they have been working at the music for some time now; we are all much excited about it; it is planned to reopen the Wells with it on June 7. I think the whole future of the Opera Company hangs to some considerable extent on the standard of performance reached in this work, composed as it is for our Company; and hangs too on the public reception if it. But that is, I think, of less importance than we must succeed or fail to establish the reputation of the Co. in the eyes and ears of the connoisseurs.

Judy has had another flurry of cables from America on *Queen Bee*. It lies now with Firth Shephard to decide whether to see, as he is now the legal owner of the copyright. Judy goes to lunch tomorrow with Ruth Gordon's husband Captain Garson Kanin of the U.S.A. Intelligence Corps. – and the intelligence corps is the right department for that shrewd little funniosity who is a celebrated film director when not manning the silver-fox-holes in Claridge's Hotel where the U.S.A. Intelligence Corps. is roughing it just now.

To Mrs Norah Guthrie at Annaghmakerrig

23 Old Buildings, Lincoln's Inn, London WC2 (on Sadler's Wells letterhead). 11 May 1945

Well – peace. One really cannot grasp it yet. One's reason accepts the fact but the implications can only make themselves felt by degrees and one has grown so accustomed to the fact of war that the sub-conscious realisation that it is over will be slow. Aeroplanes keep on passing over London – more than we ever used to get – now they are flying food to Europe and repatriated prisoners home again. That is a thrill; and that is something that one CAN take in instantly and thankfully.

Am having an anxious and difficult time over Covent Carden plans. I think the upshot will be the establishment of a National Ballet, and, more problematically by far, a National Opera; but the elimination to I think a rather sad extent of the identity and esprit-de-corps of Sadler's Wells. I think our governors are being terribly supine and poor-spirited about the whole affair – of course it is hardly to be wondered at as the majority are now a very war-weary galaxy of Distinguished Dotards.

It looks as if J. would really be able to stop the factory very very soon. Her application for release is already in the hands of Min. of Lab.; and, if the papers are to be believed at all, married women with domestic responsibilities are very high on the list for demobilisation.

Sybil & Lewis have got their John home safe & sound, he was flown home on v Day itself from Lübeck.

The post-war reorganization of the British theatre resulted in Guthrie feeling that he should move on. He resigned as Administrator of the Old Vic and Sadler's Wells companies. The Sadler's Wells Opera was eventually retitled as English National Opera. The Sadler's Wells Ballet became the Royal Ballet. The Old Vic Theatre Company was reconfigured in 1945 under a triumvirate consisting of Laurence Olivier, Ralph Richardson and the director John Burrell. Guthrie did not believe this arrangement would work – it did not – but he was happy to participate as guest director for *Cyrano de Bergerac* while responding to offers from the US, the first being for *He Who Gets Slapped* (Leonid Andreyev adapted by Judith Guthrie) for the Theatre Guild of New York. He encouraged his mother and Bunty Worby to obtain travel permits to visit Aunt Sue in Tunbridge Wells.

To Mrs Norah Guthrie at Annaghmakerrig

9 St Martin's Court [temporary Old Vic office], London WC2. 30 May 1945

J. is awfully enjoying her freedom – it's almost worth having been in gaol to have the experience of being let out!

I have a good offer to go to New York this autumn from the Theatre Guild – not quite definite yet & of course one might not get an exit permit. What I hope is to be able to finish up here in early autumn & have a spell with you before the next phase.

To Mrs Norah Guthrie at Annaghmakerrig

23 Old Buildings, Lincoln's Inn, London WC2. 10 June 1945

> *Peter Grimes* last Thursday went off pretty well. The house was absolutely jammed; and "everybody" was there – it was all very grand and ambassadorial below; all the musical pundits in the circle; and a suitable demonstrative assembly in the gods. I think, on the whole, the pundits were impressed. The work has received immensely respectful press notices & was an event of really important quality and quite rightly in my very prejudiced opinion that it was a slap-up effort for the sixth year of war and a fairly hefty come-back for The Wells. The less expert and sophisticated members of the audience, and especially the elderly but not particularly professional ones, obviously were disappointed not to have more juicy passages in a familiar idiom. It would be quite untrue to say that the work lacks melody but the melody is not of the kind made familiar by Mozart nor again of the kind made still more familiar by Verdi; nor has it the obvious straight-to-the-pit-of-the-stomach appeal of the Puccini works.
>
> The chief fault of the performance, in my opinion, was that not enough of the words were made clear. This will improve. The singers were nervous; the music is wildly difficult with the result that for a few performances too much concentration will have to be devoted to following the beat, too little to putting across the text.
>
> It was, I found, a fearfully tiring evening. One was so agitated by the strife backstage – the atmosphere behind the scenes was EXACTLY like the cheapest satire on operatic life, with people "not on speaking terms" brushing past one another in wide skirts and narrow passages; then George and I had the great anxiety of wondering whether the very very "scratch" end-of-armageddon nonagenarian staff would manage the various front-of-house duties adequately. Anyway, all was well; tho' George and I were obsessed by a sudden panic that "vibration" (caused by I know not what) would bring the great glass chandelier crashing down upon their Excellencies in the stalls. It was, of course, taken down when the raids began and only hoisted up a few days ago.
>
> Anyway it was all Such An Effort – as one had to be "about" looking pleased and serene and sure of success, with gracious greetings

to friends, Romans and countrymen. These sort of occasions are so much easier to deal with – as indeed is any emergency – when one has definite duties and occupations. As it was I had nothing to do except grin like a Cheshire cat which I did to the point of Lockjaw, with the stomach *churning*, while inwardly I bled: from the crash of the chandelier, played every instruments in the orchestra, sang every top note with Madam, shrieked every chorus – even in eight parts and cross-rhythm – checked every ticket, balanced every cup of coffee, tested every fire-appliance, pulled the curtain up and down, wiped every lavatory seat, shifted every single piece of scenery and every single prop, put on and took off every costume and every wig – but all in feverish imagination with that gay serene spontaneous grin FIXED. A terrible, terrible evening. Far worse than the raids.

The great thing, however, is that it passed off. Even George who is arch-pessimist had to admit it was a real success as an evening. The catering takings were a hundred pounds.

So we locked up the safe and tottered in a state of physical and psychic collapse to one of those ill-judged post-first-night parties which Ralph Hawkes (the music publisher and a bandit of the deepest dye) was "kindly" giving to the company and influential guests at the Savoy.

To Mrs Peggy Butler at Maidenhall
9 St Martin's Court, [temporary office of Old Vic Theatre Company] London WC2. 5 September 1945

Your Mama is the Belle of Tunbridge Wells & laying about her socially. She is the wonder and envy & pretty nearly the death of her war-weary contemporaries. But I think the whole visit is being a great success. She managed the journey so well that I think Aunt Sue need not feel the parting is necessarily the last. She's very frail and shaky; the arrival of Yer Ma nearly killed her and was much too much. But she really is better now; but just awfully old ... no longer really wishful to do anything; & of course perpetually moaning about her awful aches & pains which we all think exist almost wholly in her fantasy – but of course imagined pains are not necessarily less painful than physical pains – one can never know.

I'm appreciably less biz & it's dwindling all the time as I hand over – very pleasant. Nothing final or definite about America – I'm being an Artist & a Dreamer who doesn't understand about horrid dull things like calendars & pennies & puffer-trains but dwells on the mountain tops contemplating Bewtee. Tony Quayle is staying with us & will take over flat when we're in N.Y. Such a nice chap.

To Mrs Norah Guthrie at Annaghmakerrig

23 Old Buildings, Lincoln's Inn, London WC2. 21 October 1945

Well we're still here. No word of sailing yet. We have to wait to hear from the Cunard Co who will ring up when the Silver Oak will depart. I went down to T. Wells on Thursday and saw Aunt Sue. I lunched at Crossways and then went on for a cup of tea at Peacemeal with Nelly. Then I came back and we went to the Old Vic first night of *Oedipus* and *The Critic* after which George and Prévost came back here to their supper and T. Quayle came in from *The Rivals* and we talked very pleasantly till all hours, and George and Prévost gave us very sweet little parting gifts of jewellery – gold links if you please for me (not really Me at all but I shall value them all the same) and a very pretty unusual chrysophase brooch for J. with which she is very pleased. On Friday I had my knee done – quite successful and very little "reaction".

To Mrs Norah Guthrie at Annaghmakerrig

Hotel New Weston, 23 West 53rd Street, New York City. 12 November 1945

We are enjoying the food and general luxury extremely. The Theatre Guild sent a vase of orchids so we really felt like someone on the films. The War exists merely as a tiresome distraction occurring far far off and one sees that that is really all it means to many of the people here – they have *no* conception of what has happened and is happening. I'm afraid the food is almost indecently a pleasure. Parcels are going to be quite a possibility – parcels of food and fine things, I mean, for our English friends.

Last night we went to see the piece called *The Glass Menagerie* which is the great hit of the season – quite a charming little play with some terribly boring pretentious symbolism which this baby-race enjoys; the play would be nothing without the performance of Laurette Taylor who gives the best performance of its kind I have ever seen: the most magical command of an audience that I have ever witnessed except with the aid of song – Gracie Fields and Harry Lauder, for instance, do the same thing but thro' singing, which is much easier. It was Ruth Gordon who sent us to this and sent a note to Laurette Taylor to expect us so that the red carpet was unrolled & we were led round to see Madame at the end in company with Sam Goldwyn. It was rather a lark to see these two American legends come to life together. Ruth's idea is that we should all try to get Miss Taylor interested in *Queen Bee*, for which she would be perfection.

To Mrs Norah Guthrie at Annaghmakerrig

Hotel New Weston, 23 West 53rd Street, New York City. 23 November 1945

We are sending off an immense number of [food] parcels. You and P are not going to do so well as the people on the English side of the channel because they need the fine things more and have had to do without more for longer.

To Miss Susan Power, Crossways, Tunbridge Wells.

Hotel New Weston, 23 West 53rd Street, New York City. 23 November 1945

We have been here already over three weeks but it feels like three years. The work has been rather delayed by difficulty in casting the play [*He Who Gets Slapped*]. The luxury & abundance of all physical necessities and comforts is enormous and rather shocking when one thinks of Europe. It makes us continually jealous on behalf of all of you who could do so nicely with a little codling. Judy has already sent off fifty parcels and will keep it up, the only limit is that we cannot spend too recklessly as we have to pay income tax here before we leave and then again at home on the residue which means I think that we shall keep just over a quarter of what we earn. We are both very well paid, it just means that we can't ship off quite the amount of fine things we long to do.

During their American visit the Guthries spent time with Robertson Davies, a Canadian writer and newspaper owner who had worked in the theatre in London and who would later become influential on Guthrie's Canadian career.

To Mrs Norah Guthrie at Annaghmakerrig

c/o Robertson Davies, Peterborough, Ontario. 31 December 1945

> Peterborough, Ontario, is quite nice. It would be a bit daunting to be told one had to live here for ever. It is awfully provincial and small-town. It's about the size of T. Wells, but Oh! the difference. It's odd what a queer difference it makes in the back of one's mind when a place has no past.
>
> There is something immensely fascinating about Canada. Less so here in Ontario which is too like a more provincial Scotland or Ulster with most of the least congenial characteristics of each well to the fore. But Quebec has the great superficial charm of Catholic Eire – gracious manners and an apparent appreciation of other things than the "sensible" values of Ulster & Ontario. But underneath this charm is the sinister machinery of the R.C. church in power – with its censorship and bigotry and petty tyranny.

To Mrs Norah Guthrie at Annaghmakerrig

Theatre Guild, 23 West 53rd Street, New York City. 9 January 1946

> I think we really shall begin rehearsals [for *He Who Gets Slapped*] next Monday – & open in Newhaven or possibly Princeton 3½ weeks later; & then play Boston, Philly & Baltimore before opening on Broadway.

To Mrs Norah Guthrie at Annaghmakerrig

Theatre Guild, 23 West 53rd Street, New York City. 13 January 1946

> The leading part is going to be played by John Abbott who was with us at the Vic in several shows – notably the King in *Hamlet* at Elsinore. Dame May Whitty [English actress] goes off any minute back to Hollywood & we are moving into her suite which has what is known as a tea pantry – that really means a sort of Petit Trianon kitchen which will enable us to get small meals for ourselves which will be much pleasanter, as well as cheaper, than being dependent on "Room Service" or going out to restaurants.
>
> Ty Power was at Terry [Director, Theatre Guild] Helburne's party last night with his very pretty wife, a French actress called Annabella. He is extremely nice looking, moderate height, dark, with small good

A scene from Guthrie's production of Andreyev's *He Who Gets Slapped* in a version by Judith Guthrie, New York, 1946.

features & a very pleasant agreeable expression. He and I met with effusion as Cousins & then found we felt very awkward and had nothing to say to one another – parted after about three seconds and didn't meet again all evening!

To Mrs Norah Guthrie at Annaghmakerrig

Theatre Guild, 23 West 53 Street, New York City. 20 January 1946

Last night we went as guests of the management to *Pygmalion* with Gertie Laurence & Raymond Massey. It's had a smashing success but I'm sorry to say we all thought it quite poor & the success simply & solely due to old Mr Shaw who, being less familiar here seems funnier than he does to us – people just rolled about at all the old jokes, NOT too well cracked by the cast at a deadly slow tempo, and when Gertie reached the Not Bloody Likely curtain you really would have thought you were in the Union Hall, Newbliss, judging from the unsophisticated squeals and shrieks and delighted shocked *surprise*!

We had John Burrell and Laurence Evans of the Old Vic to dinner – they are over for a flying visit to sort out the many offers the Vic has had to come over and do a season. The Old Vic want me to direct Ralph [Richardson] in *Cyrano de Bergerac* in mid July.

To Mrs Norah Guthrie at Annaghmakerrig
Theatre Guild, 23 West 53rd Street, New York City. 3 February 1946

We had a truly devastating run-through of the play on Friday afternoon before the Guild directors. John Abbott lost his head & gave a truly dreary & deplorable performance and the whole affair was just as bad as it could be. Naturally the Guild people were rather perturbed about Abbott whose work they do not know and were for getting in touch with someone else to replace him. I dissuaded them from this but unless he improves very greatly between now and next Fri when we open in Princeton we shall probably have to do something drastic.

In about half an hour Charles Laughton and Elsa Lanchester are coming in for a drink – they've just arrived from Hollywood – and then we are going to dine with Stella Adler (who plays the Lion Tamer in the play) and her husband Harold Clurman. We both like Miss Adler quite a bit and Clurman is easily one of the best producers over here.

To Mrs Norah Guthrie at Annaghmakerrig
Princeton Inn, New Jersey. 9 February 1946

The opening last night [*He Who Gets Slapped*] passed off reasonably well though the play wasn't what I consider really ready for the public. But the American system makes a really adequate opening quite impossible in a show as large and complicated as this. Owing to the *prohibitive* Trades Union rates one doesn't get any scenery, furniture, lights, properties & effects till the last moment. Naturally this "throws" the actors who have hitherto rehearsed with kitchen chairs only. However they all made valiant efforts to cope – & anyway Princeton doesn't matter much. The Boston opening night is a far more serious matter.

This is a pretty place. Quite a tiny town centred about & created around the college. The college buildings are a rather sadly uninventive copy of Oxford & Cambridge in shiny smart pale grey stone which makes it all look a little like a big "set" for a film. The little town is like Welwyn Garden City only Einstein lives here instead of Bernard Shaw. The hotel is charmingly "colonial" architecture, beautiful tasteful décors, madly expensive but the Guild pays!

I've had several rows with our leading young lady, an extremely cheeky pert piece from Texas called Miss Beatrice Pearson. I lost my temper with her – a thing I have only done once before at rehearsal – & she is at present lying down in a state of hysterics. Do her good! We were rehearsing the curtain-call & Miss P lined up but instead of standing "at the ready" stood reading a newspaper. I know this was just bravado – I think she resents not having a solo call, I only allow an ensemble call – so I advanced on her suddenly & tore the newspaper from her astonished grasp. After a stricken & deliciously electric silence Miss said – and I admired her control – "I don't think that was very polite, Mr Guthrie." And I replied in a sub-zero voice, "In the matter of politeness I give what I get. We're rehearsing now; you can read the newspaper when the rehearsal has been dismissed – not before." Tableau.

To Mrs Norah Guthrie at Annaghmakerrig
Hotel Touraine, Boston. 11 February 1946

Well here we are in the next stage of our Rake's Progress. The Boston opening last night was important & went none too well. A ¾ full house; they listened attentively & clapped politely. There was neither laughter nor enthusiasm. The press today is respectful but implies that the evening, tho' worthy, was a bore. I think it was!

The Guild are now panicking & stampeding & wishing to make all sorts of changes in the cast. Most of these I approve. But, as always in America, there is a tendency to *rush* at things in a frenzy, to get wildly excited about little, to be too enthusiastic, too full of praise & blame, to lose all sense of proportion. The chief actors are sending for their agents from N.Y.

This is an immense town full of Irish people; & much of it old, gracious & beautiful.

To Mrs Norah Guthrie at Annaghmakerrig
Hotel Touraine, Boston. 18 February 1946

Yesterday the Business Manager was told to tell me that five of the small part people must be sacked as the expenses were so heavy; so I got onto our agents in N.Y. and told them to tell the Guild that if these people were sacked I should leave too, so at five o'clock tonight I had the Guild in force on the telephone and butter wouldn't melt in their mouths. The Co. are all behaving very well and rallying round with excellent discipline – J. & I are MADLY, but MADLY popular, which is always very gratifying! – but of course we shine with a sort of antiphonal glory because the Guild is being so silly & unwise, & we, to the actors, signify something that fights for their interest against Big Biz.

To Mrs Norah Guthrie at Annaghmakerrig

Baltimore (no address). 26 February 1946

Well here we are now at Baltimore. It's a handsome town & we are in such a pleasant small hotel. There is a wonderful Art Collection in which we spent a very happy couple of hours – a really splendid collection of Italian primitives & lots of interesting minor works that one doesn't meet in the greatest & most famous collections – early Corots & some wonderful Daumier drawings.

To Mrs Norah Guthrie at Annaghmakerrig

The Willard Hotel, Washington D.C. 5 March 1946

Here we are in Washington after ten years. It has changed and grown enormously, tho' the actual centre of the town looks much the same. But there are vast block on block on block of new govt. & admin. buildings – like stone matchboxes: each one full of its clerical ants.

The opening of the play here last night was marred by the illness of John Abbott. It may be no more than a slight flu + great fatigue & strain that ails him: but there are aching joints that make the Dr. wonder a little if it might not be rheumatic fever so he's still in bed & taking sulphur pills & won't, I fear, play for another night or two. The understudy did most creditably to get through the words & business all correctly; but as a performance it doesn't live at all. The papers praise the performance but neither understand nor care for the play. I have sent my agent to see the Theatre Guild to tell them I feel this: that I will, if they wish & if they give me an entirely free hand, stay & do what I can until the N.Y. opening. But that I am quite unhappy about the whole thing and would prefer to leave now that the contract is fulfilled. It's a pity. But we aren't either of us at all depressed. The whole trip has been so interesting & fascinating.

By mutual agreement Guthrie stayed on, but the play was not a success on Broadway. Guthrie was invited to return to the New York Theatre Guild the following year to direct *The Merchant of Venice* but declined, ostensibly due to other engagements but he did not wish to undertake his first US Shakespeare production with the actors suggested.

To Mrs Norah Guthrie at Annaghmakerrig
The Willard Hotel, Washington D.C. 11 March 1946

> [Washington] is a spaciously planned & beautiful town but *terribly* in need of a past. There are colossally large rich memorials to Lincoln, Jefferson & so on – all handsome but express their homage in such loud moneyed terms. I dare say time will cure that. The beautiful monuments will grow more beautiful & glow, like a great painting, with the appreciation of the centuries; the ugly ones, like most, will become quaint & endearing.
>
> The play is not in good shape. Denis King [replacement lead] is, in our opinion, crushingly miscast. An operatic, "effective", mature performance that entirely upsets the balance of the ensemble. It means the whole thing has no solidity or cohesion. He's working quite well to adapt himself but I'm sure it's not going to do. It's a bore, too, having to go on and on rehearsing & tinkering. I'm sick of it. We're due to open [on Broadway] March 19 and we shall catch the first possible boat after that. This last week feels like exam-week – week before the end of term!

To Mrs Norah Guthrie at Annaghmakerrig
23 Old Buildings, Lincoln's Inn, London WC2. 2 May 1946

> To Memorial Service at W'minster Abbey for [John Maynard] Keynes [Economist & Old Vic Board Member]. The Prime Minister was there & there was quite an impressive array of politics, arts & letters, assembled to pay tribute. The service was very short but very beautiful. The choir sang quite wonderfully well & prelates read from Ecclesiasticus "Let us now praise famous men" & from Pilgrim's Progress and we all sang "The k. of l. my shepherd is", "O God our help" and Parry's Jerusalem. His old parents were there aged 94 and little Lydia looking very sad and old, and very dignified.

Everyone has been flatteringly and hearteningly glad to see us back [from the U.S.] – all the nice people and shopkeepers as all the theatre colleagues. When I attended the Arts Council Drama Cttee., of which I'm a member, I was made a formal little speech by the chairman which was blush-making. I'm finding that I have to spend a *lot* of time answering the telephone & answering letters & am missing the aid of Miss E.M. Williams very much.

To Mrs Judith Guthrie at 23 Old Buildings, Lincoln's Inn, London WC2

Annaghmakerrig. 19 July 1946

I miss you a lot. And from the practical point of view require you badly to revise the play [*Top of the Ladder*]. I know it FAR too well and am finding it hard to change.

To Mrs Norah Guthrie at Annaghmakerrig

23 Old Buildings, Lincoln's Inn, London WC2. Undated, August 1946

We have Migsie [Davis] here now, you know. Getting on very well, I think, and really enjoying the change [from Belfast] and feeling that all her old friends are really pleased to see her. Yesterday we looked at the rather sensational bomb damage in this region. Started out via the Temple and thence by tram along the embankment to Westminster Bridge where we took ship for Greenwich – a not over-crowded Queen Boadicea – Queen Boadicea had been through both Dunkirk and the landing in Normandy as the crew were proud to relate – such a tiny little boat too. Interesting to see what a smashing the London docks had taken. D'you remember that fine old hotel at the Pier with a big verandah? – gone, flat, disappeared without a trace. On Migsie's first evening here we went to see Alec Guinness in *Vicious Circle*, a play translated from the French [Sartre: *Huis Clos*], and out to supper with Alec, so at least her visit has been filled with event and I think she's quite enjoying the stir-about.

Cyrano has started. I think it should be all right. Most of the cast seem quite suitable; but except for Cyrano de Bergerac himself (Ralph Richardson) the parts are small and rather unrewarding. Roxane is a girl called Margaret Leighton who has been with the Vic for three seasons now. A nice girl – very tall and slim and fair and graceful.

Beau Hannen not well cast as Raguenes the pastrycook but there is nothing else for him to play and no one in the Co. so much more suitable that one had any excuse for passing him over; but he is far too much the gent and not a natural comedian.

To Mrs Norah Guthrie at Annaghmakerrig

23 Old Buildings, Lincoln's Inn, London WC2. 15 August 1946

The bread rationing has come as The Last Straw and there is a great deal of unconscious resistance. If it had come in the war and everyone had felt it was one more reason to fight for freedom and against the Nazis... but as it is the general feeling is that England is about the worst off country, except for the defeated wickeds, and that IT'S NOT FAIR. Understandable.

To Mrs Norah Guthrie at Annaghmakerrig

23 Old Buildings, Lincoln's Inn, London WC2. 19 August 1946

Habimah [Theatre, Tel Aviv] have wired suggesting that I do *Noah* by Obey which is good and seems a wise idea – I've agreed that. Their other suggestion was a play called *Elizabeth the Queen* by a Frenchman I've never heard of about the Loves of the Virgin Queen and I think the idea of doing this IN HEBREW with some dark-eyed, voluptuous grande-dame impersonating the v.q. is a thoroughly poor one! I've countered with a couple of mittel European highbrow melodramas that give lots of scope for the stylised emotional antics at which they excel. We shall reach agreement about programme soon. The next thing will be visas – and I really think you have NO cause to worry, if it's dangerous His Majesty won't give us permission to go there and get mixed up in Incidents. On the whole I think that if allowed to go it would be very wrong not to do so. The offer to have a British director for their theatre just now speaks rather well for them, I think, and it would be horrid not to reciprocate the little gesture.

We plan to go for a few days to the Mavors at Bearsden outside Glasgow. Ought to be nice and I can do some useful work with Osborne ['James Bridie'] on the play he has promised for Edinboro' next year on Mary Q of s and John Knox.

To Mrs Norah Guthrie at Annaghmakerrig

23 Old Buildings, Lincoln's Inn, London WC2. Undated, September 1946

Cyrano must take an entirely back seat in the Vic programme for several weeks. The company goes today to Manchester to open the new Priestley play – it's called *The Inspector Calls* [sic] and opinions on its quality are mixed. Then they all return and grapple with the dress-rehearsal and opening of *Lear*. Then the Priestley opens in London – and not until after that shall we settle down to a final two and a half weeks slog at *Cyrano*. It's claptrap, but Oh so well managed.

Last night we went to *The Rape of Lucretia*, the new Ben Britten work at Sadler's Wells but presented by Glyndebourne. A full house, but on the whole the biz is poorish. I'm pretty sure it's an important piece of work and will be heard of – and even performed – a hundred years from now. Very small but exquisite orchestra, no chorus, moving "difficult" story and no obvious juicy fruity hunks of hot strawberry jam as in Puccini. After the performance we went round and had a very heart-warming reception from the theatre staff and then went back unexpectedly to a birthday party chez Madame Cross – her birthday party at her house in St John's Wood.

To Mrs Peggy Butler at Maidenhall

23 Old Buildings, Lincoln's Inn, London WC2. 26 October 1946

I think *Cyrano* has been A Great Success – it's booked up entirely for weeks ahead; but I don't think it's a very good play – certainly not in the English version. It's a light opera libretto. And, tho' the French has immensely ingenious rhymes which give it brilliance and wit, this is lost in translation and one is left with a quite gay and brisk but extremely unimportant piece of fustian romantic costume drama.

Ralph [Richardson] has many good qualities for the part – chiefly that of being a sufficiently large personality to fill an evening (all the other parts are entirely trifling) but he lacks wit. He manages some of the rhetoric with a fine manly sweep. But where the core of the play should be like a sharp rapier he makes it like a good old garden shovel. His swagger is the swagger of a police sergeant, not the hero of a romantic drama. The scenery (Tanya Moiseiwitsch) is lovely. We have gone all out to build five solid Tableaux in the romantic-naturalistic style of the nineties and I think the result is very stylish. All in all it's a professionally competent job – but in no way a valuable contribution to ART.

We aim to leave for Tel Aviv about Dec 15 but the agency who deal with the journey (in broken English and with that terrible mixture of Yiddish fawnings and hand-lickings suddenly interrupted by shrill bullying) simply couldn't be vaguer and more unsatisfactory about the whole biz and I fancy that now they have got our passports that is all they want and at this very moment a "Mr and Mrs Guthrie" with emeralds welded into their dentures are crossing the Pyrenees as Tourists from Poland!

Sophocles' *King Oedipus* was finally selected for the Habima rather than any of the previous suggestions. The Guthries left for what was still Palestine (not yet Israel) on 27 December 1946.

To Mrs Norah Guthrie at Annaghmakerrig
Armon Palace Hotel, Tel Aviv, Palestine. 29 December 1946

We left in the dark & bitter cold on Xmas eve from the air place near Victoria & were at Heath Row (somewhere near Uxbridge) by 8 & in the air by 8.30. Two nice young stewards covered in medal ribbons served breakfast as soon as it was ready. At 4 we reached Malta & came circling down for refuelling & tea. One dozed. And in a twinkling – literally – the lights of Cairo were sparkling like myriads of stars. We were met here by rather a nice disreputable little old rogue of an interpreter sent by Peltours. He helped us do the Security Office (horrible looking soldiers in tarbooshes & breeches who would beat one to a jelly as soon as look at you). We were shepherded by our kind old dog into a glittering auto. At last we reached Shepherd's Hotel – Shepherd's, my dear! – it's FRIGHTFUL. Enormous, and contrives to be at once, and each in the highest degree, glittering and shabby. And then it was midnight and bells started to ring Christmas in! It seemed like a dream that that morning we had left our own beds in the cold of an English winter, and that you were preparing to celebrate the Day in a Dickensy Protestant manner – that Santa Claus was driving his reindeer!

We were into the air again at 11.30, this time a tiny aerial tin lizzie driven by a handsome Oriental. I can't tell you how wonderfully beautiful the desert looked from the air – a soft pearly pink sea that softly met a pink & pearly sky, with clouds so much whiter, softer, wetter, more chaste than western clouds can ever look. It was real enchantment. And after an hour and a half which seemed no more than a moment we were over the coast of Palestine. Then we circled down over orange groves and those sort of juniper-cum-cypress trees that always appear in representations of Gethsemane – and coming right bang out of the emptiness of the desert one powerfully realised something of what caused the Children of Israel to feel that this was the Promised Land, the land of milk and honey.

At Lydda we were met by a Deputation – several members of the Habima and the Asst. Commissioner of the district with a huge bouquet of roses in cellophane. Once more we whizzed in a grand car, this time from Lydda to Tel Aviv, about ½ an hour's drive mostly through groves of oranges with the fruit hanging like great globes of gold on the trees. The Asst. Commissioner, educated at the London School of Economics, is one of those terribly aggressive but clever bores – he squirted out information in perfect English but with the most devastating caricature of a Jewish accent – statistics, summaries of white papers about historical, geological, architectural, archaeological, meteorological and religious lecturettes till one could have shrieked for mercy. I'm glad to say the Habima members were no less teased, &, tho' not a word was said, not a glance exchanged, it was an instantaneous bond.

The hotel is delightful – bang on the sea with a really charming staff. The theatre – in use but not quite finished – is large, modern & very fine. The company are very prepared to be friendly in a nice & most hospitable way. I have been allotted one of the actresses called Fanny Lubitsch to be my interpreter – small, forty-ish, bookish, trained as a dancer, talks perfect English as well as Russian (she is originally from Russia), Hebrew, German, French and Italian. We have had a reading of the play & start rehearsal tomorrow. I have also had a long & v. satisfactory conference with the designer, a man of 45-50 called Sebba – such a nice person & a v.g. painter of excellent taste. Have also had a press conference with gracious speeches & replies over

התיאטרון הלאומי
הבימה

.ZION Hall, Jerusalem   אולם "ציון", ירושלים

PREMIERE   הצגת בכורה

ביום חמישי, י אדר תש"ז   THURSDAY 27.2.47

אידפוס
המלך:

מאת סופוקלס   סופוקלס
ההצגה - מ"ירון גאסר   שאול טשרניחובסקי
תב"ד ה - 5ss א"א

OEDIPUS THE KING
BY SOPHOCLES   Hebrew version by SAUL CHERNICHOVSKY

Produced by TYRONE GUTHRIE

התחלה בשעה 9 בערב

HABIMAH

Poster for Guthrie's production
of *Oedipus the King* at the
Habima Theater, Tel Aviv, 1946.

coffee & brandy; and tomorrow at 9 A.M. we are to call on the mayor!
The Habima evidently intend that we see the country thoroughly.

One of the very endearing & admirable things is the enormous
consciousness of being part of an important political experiment &
a great desire to prove it a success. Everyone makes (and of course
they are in honour bound to) very light of the terrorism & expresses
real regret about it. Since we left the airport, which is closely guarded
by R.A.F., we have seen practically no sign of British occupation; &
Tel Aviv shows absolutely no outward sign whatsoever of unrest or
abnormality. It is the queerest mixture of Europe & Asia – one had
expected to find it more sort of American – but that is not so at all. It's
a sort of mixture of Welwyn Garden City & the Mile End Road in a
setting of palms, bougainvillea & "modernistic" (but rather attractive)
architecture.

To Mrs Norah Guthrie at Annaghmakerrig

Armon Palace Hotel, Tel Aviv, Palestine. 9 January 1947

You ask can Judy go about alone. The answer is, *Yes, of course.* Curfew
doesn't exist in this part of the town just now – indeed I don't think in

any part of Tel Aviv. But you couldn't guess from general appearance that there was anything amiss. I simply cannot sufficiently stress the fact that the overwhelming impression of the place is of thriving, cumfy petit-bourgeois domesticity.

I am going to tell you about My Day - & really it's going to be almost as trivial as Mrs Roosevelt's. Breakfast in the dining-room – waiters most friendly, chatty & sociable – the atmosphere is more that of a seaside boarding-house than a grand hotel. B'fast: huge glasses of perfect fresh orange juice, 2 eggs & bacon, toast & coffee – how I wish they could share it in England.[28] Also at breakfast was the designer, Sebba, who often comes here for meals (he's a lonely wee soul & has a small flat tout-seul) so after b'fast we joined him for a little chat, then he and I walked up in the sunshine to the theatre – about a mile – & I rehearsed with the chorus (8) of old men, aided by my interpreter Miss Fania Lubitsch. She is one of their leading actresses but is, I think, being tentatively prepared to be a producer. We rehearsed for about 2 hours quite profitably, then Fania & I had an interview with the theatre musician who rejoices in the name of Fordhouse Ben-Cissi & is obviously a crank of the first water. He talks with huge excitement – *molto* allegro – about little while his eyes rove excitedly and brilliantly all over the room and he pulls at a curly Meerschaum pipe like Bismarck's. He has a bald crown but then two huge grey bushes of wiry grey horse-hair above the ears like a very hastily contrived character-wig – no, the whole affair suggests less the art of the Friseur than that of the Topiarist. He obviously thought very poorly of the fact that I didn't intend *Oedipus* to be a sort of Richard Strauss Music Drama with a big Wagnerian score playing off-stage all the time; but when he saw that I simply wasn't touching the idea with a barge-pole he abandoned it with great good humour, struck a few frightfully dreary modal chords on an out-of-tune upright, suddenly lost all interest and wandered off still talking excitedly about little and casting glittering glances at inkpots and the catch on the window and imaginary spots on the oilcloth. All very like an overacted English repertory performance of Tchekhov.

Well, that's all except for one very sad bit of news. A very nice letter from Elliot's niece Caroline MacKinley to say that on Christmas Day,

28   Food rationing was still in force in Britain.

just as they were making ready Xmas Dinner for 14, Elliot [Mason] took a stroke. They got her to bed at once but on Boxing Day she lost the use of all her right side & lost the power of speech. All is as right as it can be in the very sad circumstances but I suppose even if she makes a very considerable recovery her life henceforth will be very severely circumscribed.

Continued on January 12

Well here we are round again to the Sabbath & we are just back from a most intensely interesting day to visit one of the big communal settlements in the country about 30 miles south of here, not far from Gaza. The settlement is quite thrilling: it has been going 13 years – that is to say that 13 years ago the place where it now is was a bare, sandy & rocky hillside. Now it's beautifully irrigated & is a self-sufficient, communally-owned & run settlement of 1,300 people. They began in tents. Now there are many charming houses; a flourishing farm; smithy; carpenter's shop; jam factory; and a small factory for making drugs from peppermint & foxglove. Also a beautiful convalescent home: the matron of this was our Cicerone – Mrs Leah Berlin – an impressive serene old party of 63, originally from Russia. Of course we were intended to be impressed – the visit was definitely to "make propaganda" – confessedly so – but it is an achievement of which they are right to be enormously proud.

I think perhaps the arrangements for the children were what impressed me most. The children don't live with their parents at all – tho' the parents can of course see them as often as they want. They go right away into the "Baby Houses" where the mothers feed them but where they are under a predominantly medical régime. Then at 18 months they go in groups of 5 into little houses of their own – tiny little houses with suitably sized little tiny furniture. Each group of 5 has its own full-time nurse tho' the parents put their own children to bed and can be with them when they want; there is no attempt to cut them off, just an attempt to let the children lead their own, not their parents', lives. Then at 5 they go into the Kindergarten which is organised in groups of 20. Then from 6 – 16 they are in the school which is 200 strong. And from 12 they begin to work – at first only I hour a day, working up to 4 hours. At 16 they have a completely free year. At the end of that time they are free to choose whether they will return to the settlement or not. No one owns any private property. The selling of produce, advertising and all that, for all these settlements (and there are hundreds) is done by a single co-operative agency which charges 7½ % & whose profits are shared among the members. The whole thing seems to me a very very impressive & important experiment in living, combining most of the advantages of Russian communism plus far more freedom.

Oedipus goes on all right. I'm liking the Co. & I think they're liking me; & the language, though undeniably a difficulty, is not by any means insuperable. Fania is immensely intelligent & brisk as an interpreter & splendidly keen & quick. We like her, but find her quite a little tartar – would just as soon be on her right side.

Continued on January 17

Well, to resume. The actors. Madame Hania Rovina plays Jocasta & is definitely the star of the troupe. She looks about 45 – very beautiful – with lovely wide-set blue eyes & crisp dark hair going becomingly grey. She is very tall by local standards (actually only about 5'7") slim & elegantly built with very nice hands & feet – looks like A LADY – & acts a v. ladylike figure in quiet clothes, flat shoes & no make-up. She is a very gifted tragic actress by any standards, also sings beautifully & still appears in certain pieces as a Young Girl & skips about in a manner that is quite reasonably convincing & not the least embarrassing or undigni! Oedipus is played by a man called Finckel – a domesticated sweet-natured stout thing from Germany. He has a big, stout good-natured wife with kidney trouble & a great bouncing fair schoolgirl daughter of 12 who ADORES her Daddy too much – & a little shrewd dowdy old mum who reads Kant & the Talmud & knows about Bi-metalism while she works a knitting-machine with one hand & cooks a hash with the other. Finckel has, as an actor, much ready, rather too slick, technique but a real warmth of emotion. He's only 40, but looks more; & is really far too fat & soft & tumfy for Oedipus & immediately turns Primitive Passions – Incest, Parricide & Witchcraft – into cosy parochial tea-&-toasted-crumpet affairs. But he will be alright – he works with great will & a lot of common sense and intelligence. Next comes Meskin, who plays Creon. He is a great hefty lumbering ex-Red Army soldier with a terrific great rumbling bass voice. I think he's the best artist of the men – slow, serious, simple with a moving manly peasant dignity – barring devastatingly flat un-princely feet – like two great flatirons fixed to the end of his legs – he is perfect for Creon. Tiresias is a man called Amytai – an oriental-looking creature with snow-white hair but I don't think he's more than 39 or 40. He has little personality of his own but has a feeling for movement & rhythm & a strange light voice; he accepts a lot of "Svengali" from me and makes it his own. There is a darling little old man called Beetouov who plays the v.g. part of the old Shepherd. He's 70 & literally as broad as he's long and in a very simple way full of feeling & talent.

Continued on January 28

We had a v. nice day on Saty. It was radiant weather. After b'fast Sebba (designer) & Fania (interpreter) called and we discussed the organisation & timetable of last rehearsals, dress fittings, lighting etc. Then about 11 a party of Young People called to take us to see Jaffa. They were from a club to whom I had "spoken" & this was a little hospitable pay-back. Jaffa & Tel Aviv adjoin in point of Locality, they are London & Croydon, Dublin & Dun Laoghaire. But between the two there is an absolute minimum of coming and going, maximum of difference in race, religion, architecture & way of life. Jaffa is an Arab town, Tel Aviv wholly Jewish. Jaffa is old, T.A. brand new. Of course J. is wonderfully "picturesque", with mosques through whose open doors one cd. see alluring, cool, cloistered courts with robed figures lying face down in prayer. There was a wonderful market with rugs, earthenware & jars in great heaps & profusion of lemons & oranges with hanging baskets of lavender, rosemary, hyssop & many other dried herbs. We wandered about for an hour or so – the area of the city is v. small, not much bigger than Monaghan though I suppose there are at least twelve times as many people.

Continued on January 29

I'm writing this while waiting for Sebba who is coming to discuss lighting. We had our first run thro' of the play today – not bad. Most of them were in their dresses for the first time. Owing to the curfew [following a terrorist incident] we have lost a full day's work & are behind in our schedule but I think we have enough time in hand not to worry. The dresses are *lovely* – a tribute to Sebba's good taste, good sense & real knowledge of his art. Everything scales down from Oedipus who wears a great cloak of red that is mid way between terra-cotta & dark coral, a very subtle colour that is made to seem powerful by the extremely clever gradations of colour in everything else. The set is soft pale sandstone colour; the chorus is in all shades of grey from lilac to pink to bluish – each different, but very similar, to the set. Jocasta is in the colour of corn before it's ripe but after it's stopped being green with a white cloak in soft light woollen stuff. Tiresias is dead white. The servants are in palest grey – sort of ivory colour – & Creon is in grey-blue – the coldest and darkest dress. The whole effect is just what I hoped for – very classical but very light and springlike: the absolute antithesis of the common notion of Greek drag – heliotrope and black velvet with silver gimp "key pattern" on the hems!

Continued on 3 February by Mrs Judith Guthrie at the Habima Theater

Well, a line from me this time as Master Boy is in dress rehearsal week and probably won't get time even for a P.C. *Oedipus* progresses v. well, I am most impressed with all I have seen of it – Tony's work is very good, ditto the designer's. The designer, Sebba, is a maddening admirable fanatic with the single-mindedness & egotism of a child or near genius, he is alternately in ecstacy or despair which is exhausting for his colleagues and he has no idea at all of compromise or co-operation but has a first rate talent & his work on *Oedipus* is really distinguished. I am sitting on the roof of the theatre which provides the classiest sunbathing imaginable, also the classiest view: to the west blue sea & white roofs mixed with ilex, olives, eucalyptus & palm trees & to the east rising ground with more ilexes fading in the distance to Bible-illustration mountains.

There is no description of the opening of *Oedipus* in Tel Aviv – the Guthries left the following day; the production later transferred with immense acclaim to New York. There followed several freelance engagements. Guthrie was invited to join a United Nations deputation to Poland to advise on cultural recovery. The Guthries were considering inviting Colonel 'Simon' Fitz-Simon to take charge of the Annaghmakerrig estate as a retirement position, Mrs Guthrie and her farm steward Eddy Daley now being advanced in years.

To Mrs Norah Guthrie at Annaghmakerrig

23 Old Buildings, Lincoln's Inn, London WC2. 8 March 1947

I've been asked to join the board of directors – I think we are called Trustees – of the English Opera Group which is Joan Cross and Eric Crozier and Ben Britten and their Co. They gave a party at Ben's yesterday, just the singers and the board and a few of the prominently interested people. I also gather from Ben that I am about to be asked to direct *Peter Grimes* at the Garden. The offer hasn't been made yet; but the manager, David Webster, one of my least favourite boys, was at the party and was in such a fervour of nods and becks and wreathed smiles that there's obviously something in the wind. I don't think, if offered, I shall accept. I'm not just in a faint to be associated with Covent Garden at the moment and anyway to revive Grimes after its initial and most successful opening at the Wells [1945] feels to me rather like warming up cold pudding. However, we'll wait and see what the offer amounts to – if the set-up is very good and the fee very large I'll toy with the notion!

Elliot [Mason] is improving a great deal but still not well enough to have visitors.

To Mrs Norah Guthrie at Annaghmakerrig

23 Old Buildings, Lincoln's Inn, London WC2. 23 March 1947

Helpmann and Benthall would like me to do *He Who Gets Slapped* at the Duchess Theatre.

Stratford was perfect – we boated on the Avon – and largely IN the Avon – all day yesterday getting back just in time to dress ourselves a bit more grandly for the play at night. We saw *The Merchant*, a delightful production by Michael Benthall with designs by Sophie Fedorovitch. The next night was the opening of a new production of *Pericles*. It's very very seldom given so we were all agog. But alas, the production by Nugent Monck, who is seventy three, was more lackadaisical and antique and feeble than words can say; the designs appeared – and indeed I suspect were – a hash-up from memory of an old production circa 1910. The company, with no firm direction, were all everyhow, and the evening was depressing in the extreme. The reception, however, was excellent – it was just what the Stratford ladies and visiting foreigners and American schoolteachers wanted – nice straightforward Shakespeare, dear, nothing horrid and modern about it, none of this silly psychology or whatever they call it. The press likewise are pleased and say it was swift-moving and interesting which is just exactly what it wasn't. So there you are. We all – the six or seven pro's present – were at one in thinking it *the bottom*.

After the performance there was a party on the terrace overlooking the river – really heavenly. I think I will most certainly do a play at Stratters next year.

To Mrs Peggy Butler at Maidenhall

23 Old Buildings, Lincoln's Inn, London WC2. Undated, summer 1947

Amazing goings-on at the Duchess Theatre. The play [*He Who Gets Slapped*] was whisked off far too soon, say it's supporters; and J. was present at the final performance and says that never anywhere has she heard such a reception – the welkin, as they say, RANG, and the Co. took curtain after curtain after curtain with great style and dignity – then Helpmann stepped forward and said "I would like to say two things: first, thank you very much indeed for such a cordial reception; secondly, although I am a member of the board of management which has presented this play I am entirely opposed to its withdrawal which was done without my consent and without my being given previous information of the intention of the Board." Sensation and renewed uproar in court!

I'm supposed to leave for Poland from St James' St (seems such an odd taking-off place) at nine o'clock on Tues. I gather we have no function other than to be *agreeable* and to say How *nice*, how *clever*, how *interesting*; coming as we do from the land of Shakespeare's birth we find it all so *interesting*, so *clever* and so very *nice*. My passport is now in order and I hope I shall get the currency arrangements straight on Monday. It seems to me it would save so much fussation and bother if we could all decide to adopt a uniform decimal coinage and since silly old money is of no intrinsic value I can't see why it should be insuperably hard to arrange. Russia of course would want some separate and fancy arrangement. But there!

Judy and I have talked about the Fitz-Simon business. We both agree it would be wise to go ahead and open the ball; but essential to make it clear at an early stage that we all feel it is a trial trip and we must all see how it works and not feel at this stage committed for life – in their interest just as much as ours.

To Mrs Norah Guthrie at Annaghmakerrig

23 Old Buildings, Lincoln's Inn, London WC2. 8 August 1947

Poland was all immensely interesting and the recovery very gallant and wonderful. Their treatment by Germans simply unthinkably terrible but it's no use going on about how frightful the Germans are – that's just childish, one can't hold one community to blame and another guiltless – humanity must share the blame; but the Poles, as so often before, have had more than their share of the punishment.

Plans all most confused – everyone nervous about economic situation and theatre business at present simply terrible. There are going to be fewer commodities than ever, and fewer films. My only fixed plan at present moment is *Peter Grimes* at Covent Garden at a huge fee. It opens early November and Tanya Moiseiwitsch does the décor. She and I are working on that now – we heard the whole thing on records at Boosey & Hawkes' the day before yesterday and will go to Aldeburgh for a few days at end of month to get an idea of what it all looks like – also, and more important, I want to try and get Ben to make some alterations. This won't be easy as musical form is fixed and alteration is not like scraping out a word of text and putting in some others but involves more elaborate changes in entire orchestral score – still, I think there are things that ought to be done and think I can probably persuade him.

I've been approached about going to Finland; also America; also Australia – awfully attracted to latter but feel it's too far away for just now. Finland is more suitable – if the offer finally gets clinched and money satisfactory I might do that, it would only be for a few weeks.

To Mrs Peggy Butler at Maidenhall

23 Old Buildings, Lincoln's Inn, London WC2. 14 August 1947

I don't think I liked the Poles very much; ten days as a tourist hardly entitles one to an opinion but one naturally has an immediate reaction which, based as it is on Instinct, is apt to be righter than revised opinions based on Second Thoughts; but whether they are congenial or uncongenial one can't but bow down in deepest admiration before the courage and gaiety with which they are setting-to and trying to get going again.

Economic outlook here jolly bleak. The Labour Govt. may have made some bad mistakes. And Mr Atlee [Prime Minister] certainly not inspiring as a figure-head however valuable he may be behind the scenes on committees; but my goodness I think the [Conservative] opposition are making a poor showing – with lip-service paid to national solidarity and then turning every issue into a feeble party bicker; and old Mr Churchill, who ought to realise that he is not just a Conservative politician but a great Symbolic Figure already secure in a niche with Pericles and Lord Chatham and Richelieu, getting up and booming and roaring just in a rude way as though it were all a game.

To Mrs Peggy Butler at Maidenhall

23 Old Buildings, Lincoln's Inn, London WC2. 28 September 1947

About your necklace: I asked Binkie Beaumont about it, as being the shrewdest person I know or am ever likely to meet, where the question of buying and selling are concerned. He said that his mother was the best person he knew to deal with the matter. She is married to a man who has something to do with wholesale diamonds and loves taking pretty jewels to be valued. Anyway Mum was away when I saw Binkie; and then he was away in Portingal when I went to Poland, and away somewhere else when I got back, but I haven't forgotten and will cope.

As far as I can see *Peter Grimes* is going to be the usual operatic "picnic" – we shall rarely have the more than a small proportion of the needed people at rehearsal as they will all be bellowing out *Hiawatha* at Merthyr Tydfil or travelling from Thurso to Truro to give out Stainer's *Crucifiggers*.

To Mrs Peggy Butler at Maidenhall

23 Old Buildings, Lincoln's Inn, London WC2. Octobert 1947

Binkie Beaumont is now back and shall have your gems for sale.

Peter Grimes at the Garden is being rather interesting, but not very satisfactory. We have never yet had a complete cast to rehearse and shall hardly do so more than once before the opening. It's difficult to see how this can be avoided, the economic conditions of opera being what they are. Fortunately *Grimes* depends more upon chorus than on individuals; and the C.G. chorus is simply first-class – nearly all young people under a nailingly good stout little tartar from Leeds called Douglas Robinson. I'm afraid I can't but rather enjoy seeing the management at Covent Garden, who rather elbowed Sadler's Wells out of the position for national subsidy, steadily bogging down in a series of difficulties largely caused by inexperience – it's very agreeable to be in the position of saying I TOLD YOU SO and then to be able to refrain from saying so in a silence far FAR *FAR* louder than the loudest yell!

To Mrs Norah Guthrie at Annaghmakerrig
23 Old Buildings, Lincoln's Inn, London WC2. 2 November 1947

Peter Grimes would be a joy if only there were more time. I like and admire the work more and more. There is every – but every – possibility of equipment: vast stage, splendid lighting apparatus; the scenery has turned out exactly as we had envisaged and could look fine. But all is frustrated by lack of time. They have undertaken FAR FAR more than is wise. *Grimes*, new settings for *Rigoletto*, new people into the casts of *Trovatore*, *Turandot* and other operas, and two full new ballet productions. Staff and chorus are already overtired and one can do nothing about any of it, except by careful planning make the most of the limited time available. This means that everything has to be done the quickest – i.e. the easiest and simplest, not necessarily the best – way. Of course it imposes an economy of means which can be positively a good thing artistically. But it's NOT the way to get the best result. Rehearsal should be a process of trial and error and should occur in an atmosphere of calm experiment, not in a frenzy of exhaustion and clock-watching.

In fact, I am not really busy at all – one only rehearses for three hours each day; then, as the clock strikes a whistle blows and everyone rushes off to their next appointment – it doesn't matter where the rehearsal has got to, even if the prima-donna is in the middle of the highest flight at the sound of the whistle there is one mad rush from the stage and invading hordes start setting up another scene. It just means that we are producing a factory-made product, not a work of art. Helter-skelter from the assembly line there will roll not a Rolls Royce but a rather gimcrack, ramshackly little Ford.

Went to see Elliot yesterday. She is decidedly better; but the whole condition FAR FAR from satisfactory. It is a vicious circle – if she exerts herself at all her blood pressure rises and that, of course, makes her liable for another stroke. And with that energetic and generous nature, to live without exertion is not life at all.

To Mrs Peggy Butler at Maidenhall
23 Old Buildings, Lincoln's Inn, London WC2. 8 November 1947

Grimes passed off rather well. It was a tremendously foggy night and by the end of the evening you could hardly see the stage through the pea soup, but till half-time the fog had a most delightfully "softening" effect upon the harsh electrical candles and it really looked very beautiful; the singers made a goodish showing too. There was much hysterical shrieking and yelling at the end from the Britten fans but, allowing for this, I think the recep. was more than cordial and well above normal Covent Garden standard.

8   EDINBURGH'S LIBERATING LOCATION

Within a year of directing *Oedipus* in Tel Aviv, Guthrie was directing the same play in very different surroundings at the Swedish Theatre in Helsinki where post-war consumer shortages reflected the harsh climate. At Annaghmakerrig plans were in train for Colonel 'Simon' Fitz-Simon to come as estate manager – Mrs Guthrie now being eighty – installed with his family in the apartment that Peggy and Hubert Butler had occupied in the early 1940s. Susan Power – 'Aunt Sue' – died at her home in Tunbridge Wells.

To Mrs Norah Guthrie at Annaghmakerrig
Svenska Teatern i Helsingfors. 16 January 1948

> It's all being most interesting, especially in contrast with Tel Aviv last year. The blue skies there, the grey ones here; the flowers & sunshine versus these piles of snow; the abundance of food there & the really formidable scarcity here; the vivacity & forthcoming manners of the Jews, their dark, tragic, haunted eyes, their fanatical devotion to ideas, their torrents of too-ready emotion seem almost like a dream compared to these people. There are two peoples [in Finland] as in Ireland; two races; two languages. Everything from place names (Helsinki – Finnish; Helsingfors – Swedish) street names, menus in restaurants, are duplicated. Finland was formerly a Swedish colony so the Swedish element in the pop. tends to be the grander & more cultivated element; the Finns are the Slavonic aborigines. It's really not dissimilar to the Scottish & Celtic elements with us except that Ireland does not have an enormous Celtic neighbour overshadowing, faintly menacing, ready at any moment to gobble. The Swedes are

fair, tall, gravely courteous and rather dull. The Finns are shorter and square – quite quite square – great square heavy merry faces with shrewd little pig's eyes.

The theatre is wholly Swedish but its policy is to provide an indigenous Swedo-Finnish expression – not just be a province of Sweden. My interpreter & assistant is Mrs Wrede (pronounced Vrady), a tall, brisk & very able woman of about 43. I saw her production of *Hamlet* a couple of nights ago and was very much impressed – nothing either flash or provincial about it. The company too was quite impressive – nothing like the dazzling & eccentric talents of Habima. Oedipus is a man called Schurmann (pronounced Show-man), about 40, tall, fair, distinctly noble & prepossessing to look at with quite a capacity for declamation. I don't find his attack on the part – so far – very interesting or exciting but he's obviously quite prepared to be "guided". The chorus – who are supposed to be Old Men of Thebes – are all splendid-looking fair young Vikings of twenty – two of them are international footballers – they'd look simply gorgeous stripped to the buff and doing P.T. but for this I'd rather have the crotchety, fanatical, labyrinthine but poignantly sensitive Jews.

As at Tel Aviv one is going to be mildly "lionised" in a very provincial way – so far the Jews do it better. Their forthcoming, rather vulgar, manners are easier to deal with than the stiff bows, ponderous pleasantry & grave formality. And of course these dreadful pittery-pattery occasions float more happily in the Tel Aviv atmosphere of sunshine, bougainvillea, roses, cream-puffs & abundant cognac rather than in these stifling Arctic interiors with great big snow-booted Ibsen character-parts and not quite enough of salt fish or red cabbage!!

To Mrs Judith Guthrie at 23 Old Buildings, Lincoln's Inn, London
Svenska Teatern i Helsingfors. 18 January 1948

We rehearse from 11.30 with a break for a snack at 1.00 – oh such much more Spartan snacks than the creamy puffs and kaffeeklatchens at the Habima, just some hard black rye biscuits and a cup of black coffee-substitute – then rehearse 1.30 to 3. Then theoretically the rest of the time is my own. But I am working with a Miss Nyberg v. hard on literal translation of text, and being rather heavily entertained.

The Svenska Teatern, Helsingfors, 1949.

Miss Nyberg (pronounced Kneebare) is a great big chunky teacher. I don't think it has crossed her mind for one instant that the play has a meaning beyond its story, nor the words a meaning beyond their literal philological one – a word, to her, can have synonyms, but that's all, no reverberations. And yet she's a thoroughly, thoroughly nice dear thing – as honourable and truthful and reliable as ever she can be.

Although the text is much easier for me to manage than the Hebrew (once one gets the hang of the language it's really quite like ours) communication with the Co. is more diff. partly because fewer of them speak English, partly because they're not nearly so quick and intuitive. I like Mrs Gerda Wrede increasingly and greatly respect her ability. So far I haven't given away any of the things you packed except the tin of chocolate for Mrs Wrede, which was very very acceptable.

Last night I was asked to dinner by old Rönngren [Nicken Rönngren, theatre director]. It was a real formal Swedish dinner party. I'll tell you first about the flat – charming. Dark frowsty continental wall-paper in heavy red-cabbage shades and several dimensions – you could pick off crusty lumps. A mass of actors' and actresses photos with gushing messages scrawled across them in great sprawling artiste calligraphy. Very good old heavy furniture of the 1850s. He's a bachelor and lives alone with a sweet old housekeeper of about 75 who was adoring the party and coping very happily in a great white cap with streamers – the kind maids wore in 1900. There was a Plan of the table laid out in the hall so that we could study it as we took off our snowshoes. Then, after standing about making the teeniest of talk for far far too long we formed the Procession with ladies allocated to suitable gentlemen and terrible little stiff bows and arch curtseys and then Set Off to the dining room – viz. across the threshold of the Parlour. You don't drink until the host drinks, who raises his glass and says "Skoll" very fervently – then everyone, holding their glass, says "Skoll" and that's that. The tedium.

Walking at night is so beautiful. The light on the snow and the silence. Having virtually no autos or trams may be inconvenient but it has advantages. At night there's nothing to be heard – no footfalls, you see, except the bells of the horses that pull the sleighs.

P.S. Railway engines running on wood, not coal; almost no trains & busses; empty shelves in shops.

To Mrs Norah Guthrie at Annaghmakerrig

Klaus Kurki Hotell, Helsingfors, Finland. 28 January 1948

Rehearsals go on quite well; it's not going to be as interesting as the Habima production because the people aren't nearly so gifted; but I don't think it'll be bad. And I think they are enjoying the rehearsals and finding it stimulating to work with someone new despite linguistic diffs. Fewer of these speak or understand English than in Tel Aviv and the interpreter, tho' very nice & thoroughly able, isn't quite such a good linguist nor so sharp a little lady as Miss Fania Lubitsch.

To Mrs Judith Guthrie at 23 Old Buildings, Lincoln's Inn, London

Klaus Kurki Hotell, Helsingfors, Finland. Undated, 1948

We are working quite hard and the play is taking shape – all except the Tiresias scene which is being deadly slow. Tiresias is a man called Slangus (isn't it an amusing name?) a hefty thickset type of about 50. I think he's a v.g. actor but won't have the magic of Amytai at Habimah. In the latter part of the scene he shows real grip and imagination but in the first part where Amytai was so weird and fascinating he is just a great lumbering lump of dullness and can't – or won't – see it my way. I have tried flattery, tried bullying, tried Long Talks – it all produces good-natured square nods of incomprehension and pleasant obstinacy. He is, apparently, a thorn in every producer's side – so slow but unquestionably gifted and imaginative. Schaumann (Oedipus) will be alright. He hasn't half the intelligence of Finckel but he will look a lot better. Kreon is a good actor, but miscast; he's one of those sturdy old women who have come as a man in one of Dame Nature's silly mistakes; he'd be excellent as Chorus Leader. Jocasta, Gerda Rysselyn (pronounced Reesaleen) will be rather good, I think. She is in reality the Empress of Bourgeoises and talks for hours about the price of eggs and what she had for lunch and looks terribly thick in her coat and skirt but when she gets into blue robes and a rather good blue wig she'll look v. well and she has a sort of cow's instinct for acting and a rich thickly maternal personality – everyone likes her and so do I, she's hugely pleasant and kind and when Meanings and Symbols and Philosophy and That are explained to her she takes a respectfully self-important interest rather like Evelyn Laye! The boy-beauty Chorus works with the most winning zeal and a modicum of talent and will be good and be thought, I think very "new". The Messenger is the very nicest fellow rather like Shamus McGorman and so keen that if I suggested that it might be rather effective if he dipped his clothes in benzene and then set fire to them and ran on in flames he would only think it thrilling to try.

To Mrs Norah Guthrie at Annaghmakerrig
Svenska Teatern i Helsingfors. 2 February 1948

Have you had any further discussion with Eddy [Daley] about Simon [Fitz-Simon] coming? Are you making any arrangements about Fitz-Simon cooking stove? or are you leaving it to them to deal with in summer? But shouldn't it be being got on with?

To Mrs Judith Guthrie at 23 Old Buildings, Lincoln's Inn, London
Svenska Teatern i Helsingfors. 7 February 1948

I've had quite a high time here, as on Thursday after rehearsal I went with Ronngren (who I now call Nicken) and Mrs Wrede (whom I now call Gerda, pronounced Yerda) to Borgo, a wee place about 25 miles to the East of here to attend the Runebergsfest. Runeberg was a poet who lived at Borgo and is much beloved – he has become a sort of symbol of Finnish culture and every Feb 5 (his birthday) there is a "do" in his honour, like Burns Nicht in Scotland Gerda was reciting *Vart Land* (Finnish version of God Save plus Rule Britannia plus All That by John of Gaunt plus Land of Hope and Glory plus Tipperary plus There'll Always Be An …). On arrival we partook – at the Royal Hotel – of a collation. After our collation we again put on all our outdoor wrappings (*such* a bore, overcoat, scarf, hat, overshoes, but quite needful) and walked round to the Runeberg house. The custom is for the invited guests and grander people to meet at the house for coffee and "Runeberg cakes" (it's practically Holy Communion) and thence to witness the Torchlight Procession and then to proceed together to the Soirée. There were swarms of guests – almost all in Full Evening Dress with the men in crosses and orders and it all looked like a party in an Ibsen play – great square, chunky dowdy things. It was all rather sweetly provincial – nearly everyone obviously unaccustomed to social occasions, eyeing one another and the room like children, half in pleasure, half in fear, but very determined to miss nothing that was afoot.

The house is lived in and "kept" (at the State's expense) by Miss Ida Stromborg – a relative – aged about 76, blind from cataract, twisted like Sycorax by arthritis, fanatically – but monomaniacally – devoted to The Memory. She was a weird and rather noble little figure "receiving" us all in a fur cape, touching us with dry twisted little hands as cold as death, like the hands of a dead marmoset, looking past one with her blue-filmed eyes into what sights. Hardly had one settled to coffee and cakes and the smallest talk with a Lutheran clergyman, an authoress with the head of a bulldog, and A Great Grandson, that word flew round that The Procession was approaching. Gerda and I booted and went on to the balcony and later into the street. It was *lovely* and hugely touching, the torches winding up thro' the snow with the Town Band playing, flags proudly carried, the Fire Brigade, and so on; and the eyes of all the children shone with solemn excitement at the beauty of it all.

Came the Soirée. The local amateur orchestra doing splendidly in some of the slower and simpler movements of Haydn and Schubert. Then Gerda spoke Vart Land and you could have heard a feather drop. She spoke it very simply and very very quietly with no attempt whatever at dramatic emphasis. Then the Borgo Sangerbroder (Song Brothers) – about 20 men under a gorgeous wee Bertie Scott – excellent. Then the Great Grandson lectured for a solid hour. I was bored naturally, as his "delivery" was monotonous to a degree and one could only understand one word in several thousand, but I gather he bored the pants off one and all.

To Mrs Judith Guthrie at 23 Old Buildings, Lincoln's Inn, London
Svenska Teatern i Helsingfors. 11 February 1948

I lit the [*Oedipus*] set yesterday & it looks very good: very simple but spacious. Had a v. grand lunch with an old man called Amos Andersen – he's 70, a "self-made" multi-multi millionaire – he owns 2 newspapers and I don't know how many paper mills & timber works. He is also converted to the Roman Faith and is wildly dévote – has a grand flat above one of his newspaper offices & above that a private oratory. He's a bachelor and very fond of entertaining large crowds of guests – they are received in the flat, given a great deal of schnapps and then reel upstairs to the oratory where they sit in a drunken stupor while a musical hireling plays sacred music on the organ. It's rather sad, isn't it, & very "self made"! He's a tiny little stumpy peasanty old man rather like Cardinal Logue, talks incessantly in rather capable English about nothing – facts facts facts, prices, how far it is from x to y, what was the date of z.

Then in the evening *another* party – for dinner with Schaumann who plays Oedipus. He's a nice man with a very charming & handsome wife who is a professional dietician & two nice wee boys of 8 & 7. It was a very pleasant occasion, entirely friendly, and unpretentious tho' a great deal of culinary effort had been made by the Dietician & to some good effect.

To Mrs Judith Guthrie at 23 Old Buildings, Lincoln's Inn, London
No address or date. Svenska Teatern. February 1948

I'm not spending anything approaching my allowance. I get 2,000 marks a day and I don't think I spend on an average more than 450. As I can't take any of it out of the country and as absolutely everything is rationed (except meat) I think I shall have to give it to Charity. Of course the sum won't really be large – even a million marks is nothing out of the way – but I think it will probably be the equivalent of £40. I might give it to the theatre school to help a poor student.

To Mrs Norah Guthrie at Annaghmakerrig

Klaus Kurki Hotell, Helsingfors. 16 February 1948

Well I dare say you may have heard from Judy [in London] that our opening night is postponed owing to illness of leading man (Schaumann). We now open tomorrow week. I am having a less exacting time owing to the postponement. We have no rehearsal tomorrow but I have promised to give a poetry reading at a school and on Friday am going to Abö – the next biggest city after Helsingfors – to speak to Anglo-Finnish Society. I'm glad you are coming over [to England] to see Aunt Sue. Partly because I know what pleasure a SHORT visit will give; & partly because you & I will meet then & I wouldn't otherwise have got seeing you till after *Traviata* and then only briefly as *Beggar's Opera* follows hard upon the heels of *Trav.*

Back in London Guthrie was busy with ongoing commitments at Covent Garden Opera, the New English Opera Group, the Edinburgh Festival and writing a series of light-hearted talks on local events for BBC Radio in Manchester and Glasgow. His mother was reported as having had two 'falls'.

To Mrs Norah Guthrie at Annaghmakerrig

23 Old Buildings, Lincoln's Inn, London WC2. Undated, 'Bank Monday', 1948

Truly *Traviata* [Covent Garden] is being quite a cope. The choral rehearsals are necessarily strenuous as the management of about eighty people *against time* cannot but be exhausting but at the same time rather exciting and if we had a bit more time the ensemble scenes wouldn't be at all bad. But this new tenor! [Kenneth Neate] Oh dear, words fail! He's quite a nice fellow, an Australian ex-police ex-airman of about thirty-two – very handsome and acceptable to look at, but Oh! Such a stupid thing; with no capacity whatsoever for impersonation or feeling; and, in my opinion, a quite terrible terrible singer – a high, loud, expressionless dry bleat comes forth, and he's musically inaccurate as well. He drives the conductor as crazy as he does me. He has a v.v.g. opinion of himself and argues and talks big about both the singing and the acting in a way which is very hard to bear. But one simply can't give him the dreadful speaking-to that he sorely requires without depriving him of the confidence he needs if he's to get through at all. It isn't quite the young man's fault. He's been playing big roles, like Don José in *Carmen*, for nearly two years – very very badly and to the great detriment of the company as a whole, but he has sort of got away with it and hasn't ever received a flogging from the press that he would get if the critics of opera began to know their business.

We have seen Miss Williams [Old Vic secretary] who came to her supper last Sunday week as she and I had to compose an article on the Old Vic which I am to record, and record will be sent to Australia by British Council as part of the "promotion campaign" of the Olivier visit, which has assumed all the proportions of a Royal Progress – did you hear of the Departure from Euston with mounted police called out to control the hysterical mobs? After them the Royal Guelphs' [King George VI & Queen Elizabeth] tour of the Antipodes will be rather flat – it's bad showmanship that George and Lizzie did not go first! Then Tanya [Moiseiwitsch] supped last Sunday as she and I had been at Ben Britten's, listening to a play-through of some of the opera arrangements [*The Beggars Opera*], simply thrilling, but v.v. modern and will cause a good deal of lifting of eyebrows, and, to my mind a far righter approach to the spirit of the text than the dainty Chelsea China approach of the Lyric, Hammersmith, twenty years ago.

To Mrs Norah Guthrie at Annaghmakerrig

Queen's Hotel, Manchester. 11 April 1948

Have run off the first of my talks this evening. I wrote the second one this afternoon – on the Brass Band Contest – which I fire off next Wed. in Glasgow. The Band Contest was delightful.

I don't know if Judy has written to you but there was a great scare at Peacemeal last week as not only did Gordon have another "turn" but Nellie was very near to collapse with nervous exhaustion. She won't allow Judy to go there and do things for her which is very distressing but Martin says if that's the way she feels it's better for J. not to press the point. Nellie is now in bed and having quite a lot of sedative stuff.

Traviata passed off with suitable éclat on its first performance. There are no notices in the Sunday papers but that only means that opera slips between the two stools of musical and dramatic criticism. The Times notice was favourable but wholly imperceptive and boring. It is very good to look at; but on the whole it has been a worrying, depressing and unsatisfactory business – not, in artistic result, worth the nervous energy expended. I was very exhausted by it and am finding this complete change of rhythm very restful and helpful.

To Mrs Peggy Butler at Maidenhall
23 Old Buildings, Lincoln's Inn, London WC2. 17 April 1948

Got back y'day from trip to Lancs and Scotland – really very enjoyable. In Edinboro' saw big halls and wee halls, halls ancient & modern, halls secular and halls holy, halls upstairs and halls in cellars, lecture halls and beer halls, 'cos the piece [*Ane Satire on the Thrie Estaites* by David Lyndsay], never played since the XIV century, is absolutely unplayable on a proscenium stage but seems to offer fascinating opportunities to put into practice some of the theories which, through the years, I've been longing to test. The minute I got inside the [Presbyterian] Assembly Hall I knew we were home. The Scottish Kirk, with its austere reputation, might have been expected to take a dim view of mountebanks tumbling and painted women strutting before men, but no difficulties raised.

Traviata was a great big tease. It is a huge success but that is for no better reason than that two of the principals and not particularly adequate artists are FOREIGN; and the décor is very pretty. But it's bad and the whole thing was a disappointment and a worry. However, it's now over, thank goodness, and one prepared for *The Beggar's Opera* in Ben Britten's exciting new arrangement. There are great compensations in the fact that time is an ever-rolling stream. This was forcibly borne in on one by returning to Glasgow after so long an interval and meeting old colleagues – many of them for the first time in twenty years – and seeing the bright eyes blear, and the bright hair grey – or fallen, and the slim figures bowed and bow-windowed. It

A scene from
Guthrie's production
of Benjamin Britten's
version of *The
Beggar's Opera* with
Peter Pears and
Nancy Evans.

was truly interesting and impressive to see how the "good" people had
mellowed and matured; and the "bad" ones grown wizened and sour –
of course this is no more than to say that everyone's characteristics are
but deepened with the passage of time and settlement of habit, one's
own included, so that one's own reaction to the same stimuli becomes
more automatic and unfaltering.

To Mrs Norah Guthrie at Annaghmakerrig

23 Old Buildings, Lincoln's Inn, London WC2. 17 April 1948

Got back yesterday morning having travelled overnight (but in
state in a 1st class sleeper) from Edinboro'. Had quite pleasant and
satisfactory, but rather too rushed, time in Scotland, mostly seeing

people in connection with piece for the E. Festival. *Beggar's Opera* now well on tapis – went yesterday to a sort of preliminary read-through – though I don't fully start with them till Monday week. *Traviata* is apparently a great popular success because it and the lady who plays Marguerite [Elizabeth Schwarzkopf] are pretty and acceptable in an easy charming way – but it's NOT good. Singers in Britten opera will be v.v.g. but of course being primarily singers the acting in many cases will leave much to be desired.

Talked theatrical haute politique with Llwellyn Rees (Head of Drama at Arts Council). We settled the future governance of the British Theatre at one this morning! Tomorrow we go to Windsor to see H.M. the King of England review the Boy Sprouts – it is the last of my B.B.C. assignments – I think a poor one as I don't think there'll be much to comment on and clearly it's unsuitable to poke even the mildest fun at poor, stammering gawky shy Guelph. He battles gamely against his infirmities and wickedly ironic casting in rôle of Monarch.

To Mrs Norah Guthrie at Annaghmakerrig
23 Old Buildings, Lincoln's Inn, London WC2. 2 May 1948

Hope you've had a nice visit from Simon [Fitz-Simon] & got things moving promisingly.

B. Op. is going well, I think; and I'm enjoying it very very much, Ben's work I find truly brilliant & find him a delightful collaborator. We've been rehearsing at a hall up in St John's Wood & it's been a pleasure going each morning early across Regent's Park. I get an 18B bus from the foot of Gray's Inn Rd. to N. end of Harley St. & then walk straight across the Park. The lilacs, laburnums & above all the tulips are just glorious.

Dreadful state of events in Palestine. We believe & hope the Habimah people are in America [with *Oedipus*]; but it's a ghastly business & truly crashing for moderate wise idealistic Zionists like our Dr. friends the Kriegers. How's Bob [Burns, Annaghmakerrig chauffeur] going on and was the subscription equal to squaring up his Dr's bills or is he still in debt? Think you ought to find out if you haven't already done so; & then maybe we should have a final whip around of the family.

To Mrs Peggy Butler at Maidenhall

23 Old Buildings, Lincoln's Inn, London WC2. 16 May 1948

Here's a cheque for £25.0.0. for necklace as I know you want to pay for the car. I haven't sold the jools. I hope you won't be angry, but I think it's so foolish to sell that thing for so little just to meet a current emergency. If you like, you can think that I have bought the necklace; &, if later, I sell it for a better price I will *consider* sharing with you any additional swag! Am enjoying *Beggar's Opera* more than anything I've done for years – perhaps anything I've ever done – & am very pleased with results but still feel that public won't be nearly as thrilled as I!

To Mrs Judith Guthrie at Lincoln's Inn, London

Annaghmakerrig. 29 July 1948

Arrived at 11.30 at Clones off the Belfast-Bundoran *Express* – does not stop at Smithboro'! All well here. Domestic arrangements might be much worse & Bunty is being v. sensible & nice – but does treat the wee maids, who are just children, as tho' they were a squad of Prisoners Doing Time for violent offenses. The Fitch [Fitz-Simon] part of the house is going to work well. I think. It really only amounts to putting in a sink & a v. nice looking small cooker; but minor arrangements of rugs & pictures has kept Mrs G in a ferment – I think almost wholly pleasurable & she loves "showing" it all. The garden is inclined to be running a bit downhill but not, I think, lastingly & formidably so. Strawberries a total failure; rasps. scarce & poor. The hens are in the doldrums. But I think Simon, if he "takes on" at all, will be able to make great improvements in all these respects.

Now I am going to weed carrots; & then to bathe [in the lake].

To Mrs Judith Guthrie at Lincoln's Inn, London

c/o Edinburgh Festival. 3 August 1948

We've had quite a good first day at the play [*Thrie Estaites*]. Douglas Campbell v.g. as Wantonesse. Solace & Placebo also good. King rather weak but will just do. Molly Urquhart terrible – but frightful – as Sensualitie.

I'm glad you wrote to Mama about Aunt Sue. I think she takes it in that Aunt Sue is far thro'; but she keeps asking if Sue does this or does that & when I explain why she doesn't she says, very sadly, "Ah, no, I suppose not."

To Mrs Norah Guthrie at Annaghmakerrig

c/o Edinburgh Festival. Undated, August 1948

The Thrie Estaites is an entertainment in 2 parts. The main character is allegorical, called King Humnanitie. He's surrounded by a group of Young Sparks under whose influence he admits to his court Dame Sensualitie and her attendant damsels. The virtues – Veritie, Chastitie & Gude Counsel – are banished; the Vices – Flatterie, Falsehood & Deceit – are made welcome. Humanitie is all set for a grand spree when Divine Correction arrives & calls him to account. In the second part there is some hard-hitting stuff at the expense of Ecclesiarchs and the play ends with the spectacle of a Public Hanging. The three Vices are strung up and the cast troops gaily off to Paradise leaving the bodies dangling. The stage is a try-out on my part, a first sketch for an Elizabethan stage I've long hoped, somehow & somewhere, to establish.

To Mrs Peggy Butler at Maidenhall

7 Stone Buildings, Lincoln's Inn, London WC2. 21 September 1948

Aunt Sue is slowly dwindling and her lucid periods now occur more seldom & last for but a few minutes. It's frightful for your Ma but I think her presence is helpful. And I know she'd hate not to be there. Judy was down y'day & I am going tomorrow. Today Katie Gielgud is going – indeed there are inclined to be almost too many sympathetic lady callers – it helps to pass the time, I suppose, and makes a slight gruesome bustle.

Thinking over the Kilkenny [Agricultural & Horse] Show: it does seem to me weird that you should be training Julia to be a Somerville & Ross heroine, which you neither of you admire. I was trained to be a British Officer and you to be a suburban Tennis Girl – which our parents did not admire either, & which didn't suit either of us a bit. Of course I realise that it's a nice point how far parents are to impose their own beliefs on children as opposed to current local conventions.

Of course I do see that a physical and psychic ordeal like The Jumping has its wholesome side, but the same can be said of putting red hot skewers thro' the nostrils of young gels in Central Africa. In both cases one wishes the ordeal had a more desirable practical intention.

I don't think I'm making enough allowance for the pleasure/ love/excitement/tenderness excited in young gels by HORSES. It's a manifestation of the Demon s∗x – but I don't know what is the analogous symbol in the lives of boys at same stage of development – the Railway Engine/Aeroplane/bow & arrow/Cunarder? I think those are for younger boys & correspond more to Dolls/Playing Houses/Tiny tea sets, etc, for girls. Enough!

To Mrs Peggy Butler at Maidenhall

Crossways, Tunbridge Wells. Undated, following Aunt Sue's funeral, September 1948

Just a line to say that yer Ma is being very brave and good. The funeral was less "trying" than might have been, but also quite uninspiring & unspiritual – a dreary cleric laid on by the crematorium (Kent County Council!) who rattled reverently but mechanically (like a piano playing Bach) thro' a dehydrated service of committal so worded as to *offend nobody*. The whole biz. took about 6 minutes! Then we went and sat on a pretty teak seat in the Garden of Remembrance & I thought I saw specks of ash on every leaf. It's a frightful place in the very best suburban taste.

Please don't take too high a line about the "low triviality" of dividing the furniture! This low triviality is precisely what we require at the moment to counteract the blank anti-climax. Mrs G is *thoroughly enjoying* being Mrs Wonderful with label and string. And it's got to be done. And, I think, it's more suitable to be heavily thankful for a fourth share in a dead aunt's comfy villa than to be too refined to participate. This is NOT meant as a rebuke in the least – I know all you were thinking of was not to be grabbing like Madame d'Amboise before the body was stiff.

Peter [cousin Norah Kesteven] is hugely helpful, gentle & nice with Mrs G but not a bit too lovey-dovey, and thoughtfully sensible & efficient in all practical affairs. Bunty [Worby] – as ever in a crisis – has been at her very A1 nicest throughout. Mrs G writing, I think, fully about the will & furniture arrangements & that. I just wanted to let you know that things here might be worse.

To Mrs Judith Guthrie at Lincoln's Inn, London

Annaghmakerrig. 12 October 1948

We [Guthrie, his mother and Bunty Worby] got over very easily & well & were met at Collinstown [Dublin airport] by Simon & proceeded here getting in about 5.30. We were most warmly welcomed; there was raging hot water & a cosy supper at Fitches'. They have made their rooms so nice. Old Mrs Killen [Ailish Fitz-Simon's mother] is staying – sadly shaky & feeble & elegantly mournful. She drips and drips like a graceful elegiac tap. Mama is very pleased to be back. She is endlessly occupied with very little & feels truly busy. I think she *will* have a reaction to the shock. And I hope Simon will make things move a trifle more briskly on the farm.

Forsyth [playwright] has asked to borrow £100 & I've sent him a cheque. I do think his *Villon* good but can't visualise it at all.

To Mrs Norah Guthrie at Annaghmakerrig

Edinburgh, c/o Osborne Mavor ['James Bridie'] & Park Hotel, Preston. Undated, December 1948

I think my Edinburgh lectures passed off alright – *very* nice & highly intelligent students of both sexes & many nationalities. Some of them asked me out for a drink with them one evening which was pleasant & flattering & I think they were interested & stimulated by a new & more practical angle on the topic of DRAMA which is apt to be presented as something quite removed from the theatre or acting or contact between people.

I had a lot of dealing with the Festival people, all most friendly if a little inconclusive. Finally it was left to Osborne ['James Bridie'] & me to settle the programme. *Knox* is off. Osborne grieved but very nice & realistic. I want to do a ballad opera called *The Highland Fair* which he thinks a crashing idea & he wants to do Ramsay's *The Gentle Shepherd* which is charming and sweet but will, I think, be pale and ineffectual in performance.

Sandy [Guthrie, maternal uncle] was in quite good form. He is older & incredibly stuck in a rut but he enjoyed our visit I think. I think the slight change of tempo was good for him and not too much. Wendy [Sandy's adopted daughter] is a pathetic figure & I don't think she and Sandy get on too well. We both thought them inclined to be "on one another's nerves". She talks with high nervous tension and in an amazingly affairé, self-important, consequential manner about little – of course it's all self-defence against *feeling* unimportant. I felt dreadfully sorry for her, but simply can't like her.

To Mrs Judith Guthrie at Lincoln's Inn, London

Park Hotel, Preston, Lancs. 16 December 1948

I am already quite tired of my lecture tour & shan't want to do another except in case of sheer financial need. But it's a bore & a rather fraudulent bore at that. So I shall regard it as a lesson learned & not do it again. This hotel is a costly padded penitentiary – I'm cutting short my stay & shall go from Blackpool this aft. to Crewe in order to shorten the long journey to B'water.

Guthrie did undertake further lecture tours when the Irish Farmhouse Preserves project in Newbliss collapsed in the late 1960s and he felt in honour bound to pay its debts.

To Mrs Norah Guthrie at Annaghmakerrig

23 Old Buildings, Lincoln's Inn, London WC2. 20 December 1948

Got back last evening from lecture tour to find J. still teased with a heavy cold but greatly "assisted" in housework by the ceaseless antics of the 3 liveliest and naughtiest kitties imaginable. Their particular joy is to co-operate in tipping over the wastepaper basket and rolling about the floor in it. The result is that the whole place looks perennially as if a rowdy drunken carnival had just occurred.

My lecture tour was quite "interesting" – I felt a bore getting up and yapping to people who would have been just as interested – probably more so – if the topic had been Politics, Economics, Science, Missions to Deep Sea Fishermen, Diamond Cutting, Potato Culture, Cookery, or anything. They just wanted A Lecture.

I'm plunging at 10 tomorrow in casting *L'Avare* [Old Vic at New Theatre]. It's the first "straight" play I've cast since the war – isn't it odd? I find myself quite a back number as regards who's available but the Arts Council can do a lot of the donkey work. Saw Neddie [Reginald] Wooley's designs for scenes and dresses this morning – quite nice.

The Rural Electrification Scheme was now reaching Co. Monaghan. 'Simon' Fitz-Simon, taking on the management of the Annaghmakerrig estate, was appointed chair of the local electricity committee. Guthrie visited Australia briefly on the invitation to advise on professional theatre; he had no stage engagements. He directed *Carmen* at Sadler's Wells, returning to Helsingfors for *The Taming of the Shrew* accompanied by Judy. He directed *L'Avare* for the Old Vic, *Henry VIII* for the Shakespeare Memorial Theatre and *Falstaff* for Covent Garden. The Guthries were temporarily housed at No. 7 Stone Buildings, Lincoln's Inn, pending repairs to 23 Old Buildings. Arrangements were made to share Aunt Sue's furniture with Peggy Butler.

To Mrs Norah Guthrie at Annaghmakerrig

7 Stone Buildings, Lincoln's Inn, London WC2. 5 January 1949

> *L'Avare* [Molière; Old Vic at the New Theatre] goes ahead & is, I hope, shaping well. We open in Whitby & shall travel there on Sat week. I've been asked to do *Henry VIII* at Stratford in June & have accepted; have also been asked to do a play for the Old Vic & have provisionally accepted for after New Year (1950!). The new Director of the Vic, Hugh Hunt, came to his supper last night to talk over his plans. He's nice & I was quite flattered he should want to come. I begin to fill the role of Doyen – & rather fancy myself in it!

To Mrs Norah Guthrie at Annaghmakerrig

7 Stone Buildings, Lincoln's Inn, London WC2. 9 January 1949

> *L'Avare* goes alright. The cast is young & keen – most of them not quite up to their parts – the sort of acting required depends far more on experienced trickery than on freshness & genuineness of feeling. I may go for a night to Edinboro' as I think we're going to do *The Gentle Shepherd* [Alan Ramsay] in a very intimate sort of drawing-room performance – frightfully classy XVIII century. Professional actors with the audience not sitting in rows but clustered in arm-chairs with drinks & sandwiches – late at night so that they can come after the opera, concerts & so on. I want to try to find a lovely XVIII century room & have it done by candle-light with Raeburns looking down from the walls – another piece of Scotland, in short, not Caledonia stern & wild in tartan & claymore but the Athens of the North.

To Mrs Norah Guthrie at Annaghmakerrig

7 Stone Buildings, Lincoln's Inn, London WC2. 29 January 1949

> *Carmen* rehearsals are now in full swing & I'm enjoying it very much & know the Co are too. The atmosphere & "morale" are so much pleasanter & better that at The Garden. And tho' the voices are not as large their quality is not inferior & there's a tendency for the mentality & education to be better. The huge voices are rarely matched by giant intellect!

To Mrs Peggy Butler at Maidenhall

7 Stone Buildings, Lincoln's Inn, London WC2. 29 January 1949

> I miss Aunt Sue very much. But am glad she is gone – her last year or so of decline was sad and life had ceased to be anything but a lonely and weary business. I plan to cross Glasgow-Belfast Feb. 24. Feb 25/26 I am judging at Feis in Derry. Then to A'kerrig for a few days till about March 2. May have to go to Edinburgh/Glasgow en route for Stratford where I must be on March 4 to meet Tanya Moiseiwitsch on her return from U.S.A. to discuss *Henry VIII*.
>
> I'm loving *Carmen* – it's just my cup of tea. Partly the large No. of people to deal with, partly that one acts unconsciously to the excitement of the music. But I think it is rather good for one – like an hour or two under a sun lamp on Blackpool pier.

To Mrs Norah Guthrie at Annaghmakerrig

7 Stone Buildings, Lincoln's Inn, London WC2. 6 February 1949

> Just a line before I leave for the Wells to light Acts I + II of *Carmen*, well ahead of time. I'm enjoying it immensely & so I think are all concerned.
>
> I was THRILLED to hear of tractor. Up Simon! On the whole has Eddy accepted the innovation nicely? Foreboding & glum coolness were right in character – any other attitude would in Eddy be light & frivolous. I do hope all turns out well. The news about electricity hardly less exciting tho' I'm sure there will be many a slip twixt the current and the bulb. Again it's up Simon. All very nice that he is chairman of the local electric board & makes a beginning in that sort of local leadership that will make his life more interesting and useful.

To Mrs Norah Guthrie at Annaghmakerrig

23 Old Buildings, Lincoln's Inn, London WC2. 20 February 1949

Carmen has been hugely, but HUGELY, enjoyable but I was exhausted. Hope Becky goes on well. Give her my & J's love.

To Mrs Peggy Butler at Maidenhall

Shakespeare Memorial Theatre, Stratford-upon-Avon, England. 12 June 1949

As you see, Duntnall's bill is £229 [carriage of effects from Aunt Sue's house]. Would you think it fair if you paid £100 of this and the whole of the transport from A'kerrig to Maiden Hall? Hope you are pleased with your share of the swag. The great bookcase an unqualified success, I think, in dining-room. The study at the moment is like a lunatic dentist's waiting-room with a tiny lodging-house table in the centre & 14 chairs of all sizes, epochs, shapes & hues around the walls.

To Mrs Norah Guthrie at Annaghmakerrig

Shakespeare Memorial Theatre, Stratford-upon-Avon, England. 22 June 1949

Here the weather has been perfect. And our boating really has been ideal. *Henry VIII* goes well. A nice young keen company – large crowds of them, about 36 young men & 10 girls & next week 15 "extra" gentlemen arrive (airmen, I think, from a nearby camp) to be Men-at-Arms, Bishops' Attendants etc etc.

You will be sad, as we all were, to hear that Elliot Mason died last Monday. No details, just the bare news from her niece. Of course on all rational grounds one can only be thankful that she is free from a wearisome dependence. But all the same it's a blow.

Gerda Wrede came y'day for the afternoon to discuss programme for Finland & we decided on *The Shrew*. She returns next week as a guest of the British Council "Course" for foreign actors & producers, so we shall see something of her which is nice as she's a delightful brisk person.

To Mrs Norah Guthrie at Annaghmakerrig

c/o Miss Franklyn, 22 Forbes Road, Edinboro'. 15 August 1949

All goes well here tho' I'm conducting Right Royal Battles with City Chambers who are late on all their commitments in respect of staging,

Guthrie's production of *The Taming of the Shrew* at the Svenska Teatern, Helsingfors, 1949.

electrical work, etc [for *The Gentle Shepherd*]. I stormed the Lord Provost this afternoon & had the various Heads of Depts summoned & firmly worded in my presence – much, as you can imagine, to their gratification & delight! I should think I may expect to be stabbed in a dark alley – but meantime if I ask to have the stage paved with gold it will be done by breakfast-time tomorrow & edged with pearls. The joke is going to be on the other foot if *The G. Shep* turns out to be a complete flop. I don't think it will be a flop. It's the silliest feeblest wee story but some charming verse for those that have the Scots; &, for those that haven't, there are nice looking young people in pretty dresses, two darling old Scots character men and, at about 3 minute intervals, some nice tunes well sung; & the whole thing ought to last about an hour & forty minutes.

To Mrs Norah Guthrie at Annaghmakerrig

Svenska Teatern, Helsingfors. 9 September 1949

We arrived here last Monday at II after really heavenly boat journey from Stockholm. Days have flown preparing literal trans. of *Shrew*; a day at Gerda & Walle's cottage in the pine woods on a lake; going to the theatre in order to cast the play.

To Mrs Norah Guthrie at Annaghmakerrig

Svenska Teatern, Helsingfors. 15 September 1949

The Shrew begins to make progress. It is anything but my favourite play – a lyrical, artificial comedy – the sort of thing Molière was to do so much, oh so much, better about 50 years later. Even so there's a good deal of fun to be got out of it for the audience; & it's a very good exercise in dexterity for the actors – but no great feeling or imagination required. It's all just a question of skill and neatness like a balancing act. The Company is so nice & a pleasant good feeling about the whole theatre.

Y'day we were taken to a grand Reception at the Foreign Office to meet an English parliamentary delegation. *Couldn't* have thought the British parliamentarians more undistinguished in every way – their looks, dress, accent, conversation were all drearily dowdily deadly. The delegation is headed by an individual called Lord Lucas, a smirking particle if ever there was one, with low-bred churlish manners – he had seen *Henry VIII* at Stratford and loaded me with the foulest toad-like vapourings of an over flattering kind.

To Mrs Norah Guthrie at Annaghmakerrig

Svenska Teatern, Helsingfors. 5 October 1949

We had the first of the 2 sets up y'day & lit & rehearsed in it & I think it looks v. well – & to local eyes "unusual". Oddly enough it's a snow scene – & though they have so much snow they have never had a snow scene on the stage & they find it very "unlike" what is the accepted idea of "Shakespearian" & I think were rather pleased.

To Mrs Peggy Butler at Maidenhall

Svenska Teatern, Helsingfors. 16 October 1949

I really think that my main item of news is that last night we went to a Dinner Party and the dinner was eaten off a black velvet tablecloth – did you ever! – with a stripe down the middle of dog's mess brown velvet bordered with steel passementerie. I think it was the ugliest and least hygienic thing I've ever seen. We sat round in a garish light like mutes eating off a rich pall. There was a bowl of white, white, corpse white "chrysanths" in the centre. Judy was thrown into such a panic that she threw a laden spoon of salad-dressing right onto it, missing her plate.

It has been Social Week in the biggest way. Another weird & wonderful entertainment was given by Amos Andersen, a multi-ulti-super-hyper millionaire who began life on a tiny farm. We were conducted thro' room after room whose walls were covered with pictures – some v.g., some terrible, all valuable – & in the centre of each room a cheap little office desk and some sub-Windsor chairs. To show the pictures, all the gold & crystal chandeliers were blazing. It looked like a post-war version of Poe's *Mystery of the Red Death*.

We had ascended by lift and been received by a pale floor-walker and handed our coats to uniformed attendants whom one recognised as coming from Restaurant Royale (which Amos owns) – the hall is lined with Gobelins except that one wall is panelled with black velvet against which stands a gleaming white marble life-sized female nude. We then mounted wide shallow polished wood stairs to a cosy bachelor den the size of two tennis courts in green morocco with a lot of expensive smoking equipment, beautiful rugs, crimson leather "albums", an old master or two and masses of photographs of good-looking young actors and actresses. Then, as the guests began to arrive, we moved through a Biedermayer drawing-room of unparalleled cheerlessness to a blue damask chamber, or an old rose and gold walnut chamber, or an apple-green and satin and mahogany chamber, each more suffocatingly rich, more hideously vulgar and more haunted by loneliness than the last.

Upstairs, in the attic really, is a large chamber, part Music Room, part Chapelle Ardente. It has a mediaeval stained glass window (lit from behind by electricity) a hanging sacred-hearty sort of lamp in red glass, lighted candles on a sort of altar with a priceless mediaeval missal and some very sacred paintings and statuary, and a pewter bowl whose purpose I could only guess. There was a scent of incense and an invisible gramophone was playing a record of the Sistine choir knocking off a little numero of Palestrina. On the stairs, Prof Kalinia, who speaks no English and looks like a wicked nervy old grey hen, whispered to Judy, "C'est une atmosphère tout-à-fait spéciale!" and gave a lewd wink. I sat in a perfect tingle of pleasurable horror, picturing Amos, stuffed and rouged, lying on the refectory table (I'm sure there for the purpose) in full evening dress with tiny gleaming boots sticking out of the masses of white arum and asparagus fern.

To Mrs Norah Guthrie at Annaghmakerrig

Peacemeal, Tunbridge Wells. 25 October 1949

Gordon [Bretherton] had a cold, nothing more serious, when on Wed. he collapsed. Martin wired to Judy to come at once & we flew on earliest possible plane [from Helsingfors, the play having opened successfully] & arrived, after frightfully bumpy trip in the storm – on Sun. evg. G. has not suffered any real pain so I do not think had any idea that he was in so grave a way. When we arrived he was quite quite deeply unconscious & so low that the sister said we'd better get Nellie up at once – so up she came and we spent a sad three hours watching the flame get slowly lower lower lower till at last it went out. No pain, no struggle, it was very like Aunt Sue's end. By the end of it all Nellie was a tiny little crone of 100.

Don't want you to think of us as plunged in daily, hourly, momentary crêpe. But of course bereavement is a sort of amputation. It doesn't end when the lost limb goes into pickle. There remain bleeding stumps and dangling nerves and the ever present danger of infection.

To Mrs Norah Guthrie at Annaghmakerrig

7 Stone Buildings, Lincoln's Inn, London WC2. 20 November 1949

Falstaff [Covent Garden Opera House] has been a great consolation. I'm loving it but do find opera rehearsals are a far greater tax on nervous energy than a "straight" play. I think, without realising it, one is continually excited by the music so that when it stops one finds oneself absolutely whacked. But the stimulus is delightful and enriching; it is satisfactory getting to know some of these masterpieces inside out & upside down.

1950 was a year of much variation. Following rejections from a number of managements, Laurence Olivier decided to produce Guthrie's expressionistic play *Top of the Ladder* at the St James' Theatre, London, with Guthrie directing. The production was admired for its technical expertise and the distinguished playing; the public reaction was mostly of bewilderment. Guthrie's modern-dress production of *Hamlet* for Ronald Ibbs at the Gate Theatre in Dublin was completely booked out for its limited run.

To Mrs Judith Guthrie at Lincoln's Inn, London
Annaghmakerrig. 9 April 1950

> *Top of the Ladder*: excited letter from [John] Mills to say Larry [Olivier] loves & adores & wants to put it on. Goody-goody. Would you, to save expense, also because you must be the table-arrangy-lady, get on to Larry & see if he wants to see me while I'm in tahn – viz Mon 23 – Thurs 27 A.M. only. We must start thinking of cast.
>
> Going to Dublin tomorrow to see Carl Bonn [designer, *Hamlet*]. I have cut hedge between garden & orchard.

To Mrs Judith Guthrie at Lincoln's Inn, London
Lohengrin, Torca Hill, Dalkey, Co. Dublin. 7 May 1950

> Sitting out in [Ronald] Ibbs' garden which is about 6" square but commands what must be one of the loveliest views in the world. They do *Lady from Edinburgh* [by Aimée Stuart & L. Arthur Rose] for 2 weeks & then *Hamlet*, opening May 29. I rather resent the general confusion & loss of time involved in putting off *Hamlet* – not Ibbs' fault – just the all-pervading, slack, slightly corrupt incompetence of this city. For all that it has immense charm; & one does see – just – that punctuality & reliability & so on are only "Beta" virtues.
>
> John Casson has flown over to discuss Festival [of Britain] casting for Belfast & Liverpool. He's at Christopher's.

To Mrs Judith Guthrie at Lincoln's Inn, London
Lohengrin, Torca Hill, Dalkey, Co. Dublin. Undated, May 1950

> Ibbs is a v. good actor – his Hamlet won't be bad at all. He is a very clever English character actor who married a witty, intelligent Irish girl called Maureen Halligan. For ten years or so they ran their own

company, sometimes in Ireland, sometimes in the United States. They managed to "tick over" financially. The actors are a handful of seasoned old touring pros accustomed to quelling the Irish populace from Dundalk to Kenmare but since *Hamlet* demands a large cast the group is augmented with some young people of different degrees of talent. There is a good Horatio from Godfrey Quigley and Coralie Carmichael makes of Gertrude a clinging, gauntly feverish neurotic, rather hauntingly impressive. She is a nice, sad, faded provincial tragédienne.

To Mrs Judith Guthrie at Lincoln's Inn, London
c/o Citizens Theatre, Glasgow. 3 July 1950

Started on *The Atom Doctor* [by Eric Linklater] & have roughed out Act I. It reads very well; but v. prosaic. But think there'll be laughs. [Duncan] Macrae will be good.

To Mrs Judith Guthrie at Lincoln's Inn, London
c/o Citizens Theatre, Glasgow. Undated, July 1950

I have a free morning – quite glad of a rest after 3 successive Dresses of *Atom Dr.* – with which I am thoroughly bored. It's a thin, ponderous, verbose, mechanical romp. Linklater is a clever, well-read but timid Scots dullard – who has behaved beautifully throughout – hats right off to gentle, Christian good manners. But the whole thing has the joie-de-vivre of a Sunday League service on a wet Sabbath on the shingle at Peterhead. Macrae is spectral. It may easily make hundreds of thousands of pounds all over the world.

To Mrs Judith Guthrie at Lincoln's Inn, London
Caledonian Hotel, Edinburgh. 31 July 1950

Saw Roger Ramsdell [designer]. He made no hooey at all about *Top/Ladder*, didn't make slightest pretence of understanding it at all. So I read it aloud! Of course after that the poor thing had to pretend to understand it better, & even to like it a little! All "the office" think it's frightful & lunacy of Larry to be doing it. The cast looks most promising: Esmé [Church] & Miles [Malleson] definite, Rachel

Kempson probably for Kate & Mary Kerridge for Kath; Allison Legatt to be approached for Mother.

Edinburgh is lousy with Americans – good biz for dollars – some of them look rather nice – but there are lots of pudgy pink Lady-men in rimless eye-wear & softening Henry Heath chapeaux, and great strong bony clubwomen like rouged dogfishes.

To Mrs Judith Guthrie at Lincoln's Inn, London
Lyceum Theatre, Edinburgh. Undated, August 1950

Osborne's play [*The Queen's Comedy* by 'James Bridie'] went really well on Monday. Think the play splendid but also a bit charady in spots. Walter Fitzgerald v.g. as Jupiter. I was quite anxious about it, & tho' I think it is wonderful stuff I was doubtful about its popularity. However, it went splendidly – lots of laughter & deathly hush when the ghosts come on at the end & for Jupiter's great closing speech. Then a tumult of applause.

Linklater piece opens tomorrow night. It's very thin, boring, mechanical stuff but has, I think, great elements of popularity. We'll see.

To Mrs Guthrie at Annaghmakerrig
23 Old Buildings, Lincoln's Inn, London WC2. 13 September 1950

Top of Ladder goes well. I am very happy with all the cast. I don't think it will be anything but well acted. It opens Oct 11.

No letters about the production of *Top of the Ladder* survive; it was 'respectfully' received. Guthrie later wrote that authors should not direct their own work. John Mills was universally praised in the leading role. A company to represent Northern Ireland was created to bring three plays to London for the Festival of Britain sponsored by the Council for the Encouragement of Music and the Arts – George Shiels' *The Passing Day* (1936), John D. Stewart's *Danger, Men Working* (contemporary) and *The Sham Prince* by Charles Shadwell (1719, adapted by Jack Loudan), with Guthrie directing all three. The company rehearsed in three sessions daily in Belfast.

To Mrs Judith Guthrie at Lincoln's Inn, London

c/o Council for the Encouragement of Music & the Arts, Belfast. 12 February 1951

> We made a most promising start this A.M. on *Passing Day*. Think the Co. will be good; & whole spirit of the proceedings very congenial. We have a delightful room to work in above a pub with big windows & a bright coal fire.

To Mrs Judith Guthrie at Lincoln's Inn, London

c/o C.E.M.A., Belfast. 24 February 1951

> I'm thinking the Shiels play v.v.g., most funny, and the funnier & more satiric I think the more pathetic do the characters seem. I wonder why Ireland is so sin-conscious? It's partly the weather, of course; but there must be other causes as well. The weather in Kerry has little relation to the bleak blackness of Ballymena. But Ballymena is no more sin-conscious than Tralee.

To Mrs Judith Guthrie at Lincoln's Inn, London

c/o C.E.M.A., Belfast. 5 March 1951

> I am really very pleased with the Co. in Belfast. Whatever may be thought of the play (& I like it very much) the acting in *Passing Day* must, I think, be well thought of. Tomelty really impressive in the big part, & two or three other first-rate perfs. You'll HATE Miss Bee Duffel – & indeed I don't care for her much myself – but she is a most talented small being.

To Mrs Judith Guthrie at Lincoln's Inn, London

Annaghmakerrig; as from C.E.M.A., Belfast. 10 March 1951

> *Passing Day* is really very well acted. *Sham Prince* is only just in the very early stages – it's the riskiest of the three but I think will have a certain charm & novelty & will go if the company is popular. Will you beat up any N of I friends & make them go to the 1st Night – March 20, Lyric Hammersmith. We had Dame Dehra Parker [Education Minister] & the Prime Minister [Basil Brooke} to a rehearsal on Thurs. night. They sat it out & did their stuff to the Co. very suitably.

Sir Basil is a member of the Upper Orders & it has advantages. I never stop giving chatty wees to *Ulster Magazine* & things – 3-minute recordings of extreme banality & blatant advertisement.

To Mrs Norah Guthrie at Annaghmakerrig
23 Old Buildings, Lincoln's Inn, London, WC2. 25 March 1951

Our first Ulster play [*The Passing Day*] has been a decided success. Not the play so much as the acting. They have really made an excellent impression; and I shall be disappointed if the acting of the second play [*The Sham Prince* by Thomas Shadwell] isn't equally praised as they all have very different parts – new faces, new wigs, new voices; & ones who were unsympathetic in the first play have opportunity for nice cosy plummy sentimental peepy-weepy moments in the second. The business is decidedly promising & I think the whole venture has made a fortunate start. The Co. is all very happy & pleased; & suitably sceptical about the value of press notices. One doesn't come from Belfast to be bowled over by praise from London, but surely Joe Tomelty must be privately chuffed at the Observer's "magnificent performance of Mr Tomelty"!

The Old Vic Theatre, under an unsteady 'Triumvirate' of directors, Glen Byam Shaw, George Devine and Michel St Denis – the latter also in charge of the Young Vic and the School – was on the verge of collapse. Serious differences on matters of policy and administration were not helped by the confrontational attitude of the chairman, Lord Esher. All three resigned, expecting that public opinion would see them reinstated. Hugh Hunt, the Artistic Director, was left in a parlous position.

To Mrs Norah Guthrie at Annaghmakerrig
23 Old Buildings, Lincoln's Inn, London WC2. 2 June 1951

You'll be surprised at the address. And indeed am I. I'll try to explain. Late on Monday night (I'd arrived in Liverpool that day at lunchtime to make Fest. of Britain arrangements) Hugh Hunt rang up from London to say would I be available if the Old Vic asked me to come & "help in the crisis". I said Yes I would. Rang off; & did some earnest thinking. At breakfast Hugh rang again to say would I be free if he sent Stephen

Arlen (general manager, young, energetic, capable, was a colonel at 26; I personally don't like him very much) to see me at once. I said Yes; & re-arranged the day. By now I had decided what I thought.

Stephen arrives off the morning express with "Proposals" from Hugh that he & I are to be joint directors. I said No. That I considered joint direction had been the cause of the recent breakdown; that if the Governors cared to ask me I would accept Absolute Powers to deal with the situation, get the machine running again (or *not*, as the case might be); and then, after an agreed period, clear out. If the Governors did not wish this, alright; no one need feel any embarrassment whatever; I said all this to Arlen & wrote it as well in a note to Hugh which he could, if he pleased, read to the Governors. Arlen departs on the afternoon train.

Came the dawn. George Chamberlain (Stage Manager) gets on the telephone saying that there is an emergency meeting of the Governors that afternoon. At tea-time Brownie [James Browne, a Governor] rings up on behalf of the Governors asking my permission to write an immediate press statement to the effect that Mr Wonderful was coming in to Save the Day. Brownie was clearly in what is known as A State; and speaking in high excited tones. I said Certainly Not. For one thing I couldn't possibly accept any responsibility till I have seen the Governors; for another I was under contract to the L'pool Corporation & must sue for release.

– When can you see the Governors?

– Tomorrow at 2.30.

Meantime Judy has arrived from London and I have booked rooms for a week in a Jewish "Guesthouse" in New Brighton with a chintzy bedroom overlooking the sea. Telephone goes all evening with one person or another saying Oh Oh Oh the crisis is very serious; but the high-sterics have simply passed the bounds & all sense of proportion has been lost. Next day we go to London, leaving the guesthouse almost before daybreak. Geo. meets one at Euston – very calm, normal, sensible – a really reliable pillar.

Meeting at the New Theatre. Present: Brownie, in the chair; Lady Violet Bonham Carter; Hamish Hamilton (publisher); Capt Evelyn Broadwood (piano manufacturer and a perfect fool); John Moodie (representing Arts Council). All are white to the lips and biting their handkerchiefs. They are only too ready to bestow on me *absolute powers* – & would gladly add the crown jewels, the chairmanship of Imperial Chemicals and the Throne of Peru. Letters are dispatched to Liverpool beseeching the Corporation to release their Adored One. Lord Esher (Chairman of the Govs) should have signed their letter but has retired to country smitten of a sickness – I think he's bitten too many handkerchiefs; Geo thinks he has already Fled the Land or destroyed himself in a loosebox!

I can't seriously think Liverpool can refuse to release me. After that, I simply don't know. A more temperate atmosphere is the first essential. I don't think anyone's going to be any bother. All are too relieved to have someone willing to cope. Even if I make some bad blunders things can't be worse. Also I think I shall have quite a tide of goodwill behind me. It's really a far easier task over 1939. Financial situation easier; I'm not flying in over the heads of a lot of older people; & the Old Vic is a much more manageable & compact proposition than the Vic plus Wells.

To Mrs Norah Guthrie at Annaghmakerrig
23 Old Buildings, Lincoln's Inn, London WC2. 15 June 1951

Everyone at the Vic, or lately at the Vic, has been very helpful & nice to me personally, and made the dot-up as little painful & embarrassing as could be. Rightly or wrongly I've backed Hugh Hunt; & Michel and party are *out* – or rather have not been begged to withdraw their resignations. Now we're at work on preparations for next season. It all has to be done rather too fast, which is harassing. The designs for 1st production must be in the workshops by July 20 at latest. One can't settle a designer until a play is chosen. No use choosing a play till the Leading Actors are fixed. That is inevitably a long tricky period of negotiation. A. will only come if we do *Macbeth*; B. will only come if A. does not do *Macbeth*; C. refuses to tour. Fortunately there are quite a number of suitable gentlemen who are much interested; & I think we're on the verge of clinching the two best.[29] Then designers have to be set to work. Then the smaller part people have to be engaged.

---

29   Donald Wolfit for *Tamburlaine the Great* and *The Clandestine Marriage*; André Morel for *Timon of Athens*.

At the same time there are the rather tricky decisions incident upon the resignations. I am finding Hugh Hunt most helpful & wise & capable. I think that alliance will work alright. All the frou-frou in the press; the letters of congratulation & so on makes a lot of work too; and has to be "handled" with what one hopes to be tact. However, the general impression seems to be one of great goodwill which is very heartening and should help to float next season and if that goes off reasonably well, then, in the course of a v. short time everyone's sense of proportion will be restored and the whole shemozzle be quickly forgotten.

In most ways I would greatly prefer not to have all the cope. But I don't think the s.o.s. could possibly have been ignored and of course one can't help being pleasantly flattered at being the person turned to. But I suppose that applies to any worthwhile activity. And this, I am convinced, is worth putting the back into. The tempest is now spent and everyone has started looking ahead.

The much-publicized routing of the Old Vic Triumvirate was ill-taken in many quarters. The critic Irving Wardle referred to 'the wretched irony that it should be Tyrone Guthrie at his most bitchy-autocratic who put the boot in'.

To Mrs Norah Guthrie at Annaghmakerrig
23 Old Buildings, Lincoln's Inn, London WC2. 14 October 1951

We are going out to tea today with sweet Canon Stevens of Southwark who is also a Governor of the Old Vic. He's a gentle and extremely silly little old person who doesn't attempt to understand any of the proceedings and who just comes to meeting after meeting because he has been appointed as its representative on the Board by the City & Parochial Foundation – a wealthy mediaeval charity which has some long *long* gone connection with the diocese in which the Vic is situate.

VERY bored with the gen. election. I simply can't understand or take the very tiniest interest in the political parties – all promise the earth in very similar terms and all, one knows, are equally incapable of fulfilling their promises. I shall vote Labour, but with no conviction.

To Mrs Peggy Butler at Maidenhall

Old Vic Theatre, London. 29 November 1951

Did I tell you how shocked I was by the Provost of Trinity [College, Dublin]? I "spoke" there at a meeting a few weeks back & the P was in the chair (also gave a recep. beforehand), he was either quite drunk or completely doting or both … moppings & mowings & inability to stand properly or concentrate or get the names of the speakers sorted out – a really grievous exhibition of senile decay. He should retire.

OEDIPUS AND THE CHORUS

Drawing by Grant McDonald of Guthrie's production of the Yeats version of Sophocles' *King Oedipus*, designed by Tanya Moiseiwitsch, at the second Stratford Festival, Ontario, 1954.

AMERICANA, CANADANA & ACHIEVEMENT OF THE IDEAL SPACE

In a year dominated by his renewed Artistic Directorship of the Old Vic Theatre, which involved much rehearsal and travel in England for Shakespeare's *Timon of Athens* and *Henry VIII* and Marlowe's *Tamburlaine the Great*, Guthrie fulfilled previously arranged engagements with the Metropolitan Opera in New York (for *Carmen*) and the Edinburgh Festival (for *The Highland Fair*). He received a flattering invitation from a committee in Canada to produce a Shakespearian Festival at Stratford, Ontario. At Annaghmakerrig his mother was clearly in the final phase of her life.

To Mrs Judith Guthrie at Lincoln's Inn, London

24 East 49th Street, New York. 3 January 1952

> *Carmen* [Metropolitan Opera, New York]. Have had my first rehearsals today and am rather pleased with results. Had 2 hours with chorus men – Torreador song – & the opening Scena. Really not bad & the men – mostly Germans & Italians – nice & keen. Escamillo excellent, French-American called Mark Guarrera has much dash & bel air. Then I had 2 hours with Risë Stevens & Richard Tucker. Former distinctly handsome – she sings splendidly & at least appreciates that acting is required. Tucker is a very short squat recruit from the textile trade with a great important head & good bright eyes, no neck at all and short fat legs tapering to tiny feet. He really looks *terrible* but the voice is so lovely that I can see they're right to have him. Rudi [Rudolf Bing, General Manager] sells me unashamedly as "the greatest director in Europe" & everyone is bowing & scraping.

To Mrs Judith Guthrie at Lincoln's Inn, London

c/o Kanin, Faraway Meadows, Sandy Hook, Connecticut. 2 February 1952

> Came here with Ruth [Gordon] and Garson [Kanin]. Well, *Carmen*, Grand Succès, rave notices in the cheap papers, more dignified (&

ignorant) but laudatory in the grand papers; cheers at the end & much extravagant gush – fortunately got away before too much of that went on. Rudi very pleased – he rang up here last night specially to say so which I though both polite and friendly and wage-earning. In the end it looked distinctly well, esp. the last act. Risë Stevens did a good job, looked awfully well, acted moderately well & sang loudly & accurately. Richard Tucker acted very poorly till it came to the final scene of melodrama, then he let fly with minimum technique but remembered his drill which was contrived to keep him behind large pieces of furniture; he sang really beautifully. Anyway the whole episode has wound up in an animated fizz of success & Yours Truly very popular around the Met!

I've been to Yale this aft. to lecture to the Drama Dept. about Ye Olde Vycce.

To Mrs Peggy Butler at Maidenhall

23 Old Buildings, Lincoln's Inn, London WC2. 19 April 1952

I leave tomorrow at the first blush of dawn for – Wolverhampton! Thence to Glasgow, Aberdeen, Edinboro' & Newcastle judging finals of Amateur Drama Comp. We've been to Tunbridge Wells this aft. Nellie *not* well – being foul to poor Martin & longing for The End, very sad & I don't think anything whatever can be done. It's sad how women – & I think this applies far less to males, who have to venture into the market place – cannot relinquish the reins. Nellie clings with tooth and claws to the Rule of her House when she's quite incapable of almost any decision, however tiny (we had a perfect crise-des-nerfs this afternoon about whether tea should be drunk in the house or in the garden with plans changed again and again, Nelly grey in the face with anxiety and neither Martin, Judy nor I saying a word).

To Mrs Norah Guthrie at Annaghmakerrig

Adelphi Hotel, Liverpool. 20 April 1952

Nellie isn't in good order & seems to get no pleasure out of anything except, intermittently, the garden. Martin is, I think, behaving very well & patiently; & is being of real use in the rôle of Elderly Spinster

Daughter era 1860 – that is to say he fetches her books & spectacles & makes small talk but doesn't lift a hand to cook or clean or deal with any of the "business", e.g. money affairs, paying bills etc – of course he wouldn't be allowed to. He leads a weird life, rises late, retires early, takes tea with old ladies, goes for tiny walks to "buy the evening paper" or to "see the view from Calverley Park". A life that one would only think supportable with the comfort of Secret Drinking or Betting or Opium. Yet he is a charming companion – humorous, sympathetic & absolutely no fool.

Poor James Forsyth's play[30] has taken a terrible beating from the newspaper scribes. One or two have had some good words to say for it, but most have simply written it off as Pompous & Long Winded. He has taken all this very well; but of course, quite apart from the economic problem raised for an author by failure to be popular, one simply can't indefinitely go on Rising Above misunderstanding and total lack of appreciation. James' attitude is one of quiet, polite but intense superiority, which isn't helpful to him on either the worldly or the spiritual plane, but seems to me all but impossible for him to avoid.

To Mrs Judith Guthrie at Lincoln's Inn, London

Glasgow (no address). 26 April 1952

Enjoying *Timon* very much. It's easier to understand when prepared & acted. Don't think André Morel has a big enough personality or enough brain to make a go of it. He will look large & noble & *maybe* will do. He's thoroughly pleasant & *wants to be told* what it's all about.

To Mrs Judith Guthrie at Lincoln's Inn, London

Glasgow (no address). 6 May 1952

Timon v. interesting. Fear André altogether too unimportant for a great rôle – the personality doesn't gain but dwindles when confronted with really large scope for expansion.

---

30   *The Other Heart*, Old Vic Theatre.

To Mrs Peggy Butler at Maidenhall

Edinburgh (no address). 9 May 1952

Timon distinctly beginning to shape. I think it is most interesting but don't expect it to be popular. Its theme is the Deceitfulness of Riches. It is bitingly satirical & has none of the ingredients of popular romance – no heroine, the only women are two whores, very tiny parts; no hero, Timon is a figure of pity and scorn; a lot of "difficult" philosophy and very little "story".

Parallel with *Timon* I've been working away at the organisation of *Highland Fair* [17c. 'Opera by Mr. Mitchell']. The dresses and set are now agreed & the plans for making all settled – rather complicated as the dresses are being partly made in London, partly in Glasgow and partly here in Edinboro' – the tartans have been specially designed and are now a-weaving near Lanark – think they'll be very lovely – one in scarlet & puce, t'other in yellow, orange & brown. The cast too is taking a lot of organising as in addition to actors we need a chorus of singers, 3 pipers & the 4 most brilliant Highland dancers extant. I am most excited about it – think it's going to be a rare combination of the original & the popular – an almost impossible combination.

Off tomorrow to Liverpool where they're playing *Top of the Ladder*: a most "respectful", almost warm, press; & I hear it's well done. Then on Mon. I have to go over to Newcastle for the rest of that week of rehearsal before *Timon* opens.

To Mrs Peggy Butler at Maidenhall

Annaghmakerrig. 1 July 1952

This will amplify what I said on the telephone this evening. Mrs G has been as you know, pretty poorly; suddenly up & then suddenly down. Marc [Dr Killen of Monaghan] has been twice and has twice given her what Bunty says is a very thorough and careful examination. He finds nothing seriously amiss except the fact that she is 85. Bunty & I have both agreed that, tho' you do fully realise this, it ought to be said quite categorically; so that you are, as the silly phrase goes, "prepared". Marc has told me he doesn't for a moment advise me to cancel going to Canada; that, I hope, will comfort you and help you to feel that there is not an "emergency".

To Mrs Peggy Butler at Maidenhall

Annaghmakerrig. Undated, July 1952

> All well here. Mrs G is really in v.g. form now. She is equal to only to the teeniest exertions of either mind or body. But I think she is happy & content and doesn't seem to find time hanging heavy at all.
>
> Nellie is evidently in v. poor case. Judy is taking out a season ticket and plans to spend most of her time there. But the great difficulty is not to pounce in and organise & arrange things in a rational way rather than in the way which is wished.
>
> I shall try to be here most of autumn & winter. Have refused various American offers and will try & do a minimum of outside work and arrange Literary Activities to occupy myself and more immediately mercenary to boil the pot. I shall have to do a production, if I get an offer, sometime in the winter, i.e. be away about 6 weeks. Off to Glasgow/Edinboro' on Thurs for a month [*The Highland Fair*].

To Mrs Judith Guthrie at Lincoln's Inn, London

Glasgow (no address). Undated, probably August 1952

> I left all quite well at A'kerrig. Mama is equal to only the tiniest exertions for only the tiniest periods of time. But her day is adequately filled – at least while Migsie [Davis] is there to play with her. But one feels the horizon has narrowed a good deal even from its narrow limits of last year.

To Mrs Judith Guthrie at Lincoln's Inn, London

Annaghmakerrig. Undated, spring 1953

> Took Mama up the garden today in wheelchair & lovely weather. It was much enjoyed. Mrs Killen evidently near the *end* but not necessarily at the end. Simon & Ailish both look like grey-faced centenarians.

Several brief trips to Canada resulted in the Shakespearian Festival at Stratford, Ontario, presented on an open stage designed by Tanya Moiseiwitsch in an immense marquee: the 'ideal space' that Guthrie had been hoping for since *Hamlet* at Elsinore in 1937. The initial plays were *Richard III* and *All's Well That Ends Well*.

To Mrs Norah Guthrie

Stratford Shakespearian Festival, Ontario. 7 June 1953

All is going well, we have now rehearsed a week & made good progress. I am very pleased with the Canadian contingent – most of them are rather too young and inexperienced but that is balanced by rude health and great keenness. Alec [Guinness as Richard III] being splendid & so nice to one and all. So far there have been no social hitches or contretemps whatsoever. There'd been (before we arrived) a frightful financial panic, the Cttee nearly abandoned the whole project. Well, now they haven't raised more than two-thirds of the estimated outgoings. But the *bookings* are excellent & from all over the continent.

The Site is really thrilling. The amphitheatre is now scooped out, terraced & completely concreted & looks really beautiful. The stage has been prefabricated and we are rehearsing on it, set up in an enormous shed. When the tent is up the stage can be moved in and re-erected in a day. The tent itself is due within a week; it's being made in Chicago. It will be a vast bun-shaped marquee – a square with rounded corners supported on two main masts.

We had to reorganise the supers, as, not knowing them very well by sight we had arranged for the big muscular young footballers to appear as decrepit aldermen and all the aldermen-types to fight the battle in *Richard III!* I think Alec is going to be most remarkable as Richard; & the young Canadians, on the whole, shaping up very well. *All's Well that Ends Well* will not, I think, be popular, but *we're loving it!* – it's far too unconventional & odd for the public – a 'heroine' who sticks at nothing to get her man; a 'hero' who behaves shockingly though the reasons are implicit if anyone cares to use their reason (but Reasoning is not a faculty which audiences are accustomed to exercise & therefore content just to 'feel' along the most conventional lines) – and a Comic who turns out to be pathetic.

To Mrs Peggy Butler at Maidenhall

Stratford Shakespearian Festival, Ontario. 13 June 1953

There's plenty wrong with the shows but I think they do bear evidence of very careful and serious preparation and won't be either slovenly or vulgar. The public reaction will be most interesting. A high proportion

Drawing by Grant
McDonald of Alec
Guinness as Richard III
at the Festival Theater,
Stratford, Ontario, 1953.

of each audience will never have seen a play. Their only ideas of
Dramatic Art are derived from radio & the movies. Also in new
countries where the population is largely immigrant and non-English
speaking the vocabulary is almost incredibly limited and dull. Speech
is for many limited to "Hi" = "How do you do?"; "S'long" = Goodbye;
"o.k." signifying agreement.

What are these people going to make of the Shakespearian
vocabulary & syntax and Shakespeare's treatment of mythology (*All's
Well*) and English history (*Richard*) which is not at all that of the
comic strip? One knows it's a mistake to confound unsophistication
with ignorance or to mistake illiteracy for stupidity. But even so ...
Well, we shall know more by next Wednesday.

I could go on and on about Canada and its newness which in so
many respects is raw & rough & ugly but in so many many more is
touching and wonderful. One sees that the community, exactly like
the individual, has to develop from inarticulate helpless infancy to

some sort of maturity. It's a paradox of our epoch that the juvenile communities (U.S.A., Canada, Australia) are enormously, vulgarly rich, which, just as in the case of individuals, makes growing up so much more tricky – too many noisy mechanical toys for the little boys, too much dressing up and Alice-Nellyism for the little gels. And then the older communities – Britain, France & Co – being so hard-up, are apt to turn themselves into jealous, sour, snapping, nagging, handing out unconstructive advice; furious at being left behind and yet unable, because of poverty & failing energy, to Keep Up. And it *is* frightfully irritating, whether for the Individual or the Group, to see one's own mistakes being made over again by a younger generation. It is maddening, for example, to see Toronto making exactly the same mistakes (for exactly similar reasons) in town-planning & organisation as ruined the European cities at their period of rapid expansion 100 years ago.

I think I am enjoying very much, and know I am very much interested in, learning to be an Older Person. I realise that it has to be learnt in just the same way as babies have to learn to walk and not to 'go' in their diapers. Against lack of energy and deep grooves of habit one has to oppose Experience and Philosophy, and in fact learning to live is really learning to die.

To Mrs Peggy Butler at Maidenhall

Stratford Shakespearean Festival, Ontario. 28 June 1953

The tent at the moment is nearly, but not quite, UP (it's lunchtime) the entire population of Stratford, having been at church, is out to watch. The tentmaster and a crew of about 40 men & 2 tractors have been at work all night. The stage is finished & looks beautiful. The auditorium is connected & wired for lights. The 1,400 seats, rather pretty wee birchwood chairs, will be installed this week by night shifts. The dressing rooms are ready enough for night shifts to finish the work – water for basins, showers & aunts is available; partitions are in place. It seems inconceivable that it's less than a year since the whole idea originated; & what Tanya & I were thinking out in model form in Balsa wood in the A'kerrig study last November is now In Situ and will be acted on in tonight's rehearsal.

To Mrs Peggy Butler at Maidenhall

Stratford Shakespearian Festival, Ontario. 18 July 1953

Well, the plays have been a solid, emphatic, unqualified, *success*. It really has been a great big smashing realisation of the most optimistic hopes. Since the opening I've been largely occupied with helping with plans for the future – quite tricky & extremely interesting. The weather is pretty hot & tent, both for players & audience, is SPIFLICATING. However, all are surviving.

The Service of Dedication last Sunday really was very thrilling & moving. It was packed – almost entirely by locals. The choir sang splendidly – so did the congregation – they howled familiar & good hymns with great vigour & conviction. I presented the Stratford [England] flag very dignifiedly! Monsignor Egan was unavoidably absent owing to a throat infection. However. The leading Presbyterian gave the address & was the only blot on a really spanking occasion – too long, utterly cliché.

To Mrs Norah Guthrie at Annaghmakerrig

Stratford Shakespearian Festival, Ontario. 20 July 1953

This will be nearly my last letter from here. I filmed for 13 hours on Sunday from midday to 1 A.M. and then the following day until 12.30 A.M. Of course one isn't actually acting all that time; but on the qui vive & most of the time in the broiling heat of the Canadian summer plus film arc lamps. An exhausting wearisome toil but I do get paid the equivalent of £150. The film is to be a "Documentary" on the theme of the Stratford Festival. On Sunday we're doing a fictitious representation of A Rehearsal; & y'day a re-enactment of my first meeting (a year ago) with the committee.

The success of the festival is absolutely amazing. Last week over 10,000 people saw the perfs. The coverage in the press is immense and the praise simply extravagant. My main preoccupation now is to help them to *use* the success. The committee members are all very very tired and inclined to sit back and fan themselves and bask like amateurs in their triumph. But I am yapping like a cross old sheepdog at their heels and trying to drum them thro' the gate of next year's Festival. The Gov. General is now here In State & I have had a confab with him in his private Pullman (the perfect way to travel) and have tried to plant little seeds.

Our party last Sat night passed off with almost too much éclat – the last guests got tea & toast & boiled eggs at 5.30 A.M. and did the washing up! It was a ghastly bore really and not the ideal prelude to 13 hours of filming – but just had to be done.

The Shakespearian Festival at Stratford, Ontario, was completely sold out so plans were immediately put in train not only to continue annually but also to design a permanent building encompassing Guthrie's precepts for an 'open stage' suitable for 'classical' plays. Many young Canadian actors who did well in the earliest Stratford seasons later rose to prominence on the international stage and in motion pictures, among them Lorne Greene, Christopher Plummer and William Shatner. In 1954 Guthrie returned to Stratford, Ontario, as Artistic Director, directing *King Oedipus* and *The Taming of the Shrew* himself.

To Mrs Judith Guthrie at Lincoln's Inn, London
Stratford, Ontario. 12 November 1953

I had a nice drive with Seamus [McGorman] from AK to Shannon. Flight was O.K. but tiring & I plumped immediately in Montreal into a whirl of calls & arrangements for next year. Left next A.M. for Toronto, had press conf. Enquiries for you from Rose McDonald & Herb Whittaker & then a long interview with Lorne Greene.

To Mrs Norah Guthrie at Annaghmakerrig
Stratford Shakespearian Festival, Ontario. 19 May 1954

Started *Shrew* today, distinctly satisfactory. Apart from the stars [James Mason, Douglas Campbell] this year's Co. includes all the best of last year's with one or two improvements. We have had a regular right royal welcome back to Stratford – total strangers shrill out "welcome back!" from doorways, windows & balconies; & Judy was 2½ hours over shopping which should have taken 25 mins. because of all the chats & greetings. My play [*Top of the Ladder*] did v.g. biz in Toronto but was not well thought of – far too farcical & rough – however, since my royalties amount to $509 one is not inclined to object.

Drawing by Grant McDonald
of James Mason as Angelo
in *Measure for Measure*
at the Festival Theater,
Stratford, Ontario, 1954.

To Mrs Norah Guthrie at Annaghmakerrig

Stratford Shakespearian Festival, Ontario. 21 May 1954

> James Mason is being very nice – great attention to duty & quiet
> suitable behaviour in face of dreadful staring & sort of passive mobbing,
> & as one of the world's leading Gentleman Beauties he attracts quite
> a different sort of interest from Guinness who is merely talented &
> whose impersonations on the screen don't make him recognisable in
> the street. With Mason, if he goes into a shop a crowd collects outside
> at once. "It can't be!"

To Mrs Norah Guthrie at Annaghmakerrig

Stratford Shakespearian Festival. 23 May 1954

> This year, at all events so far, we are definitely not so pressed. Having
> the tent [for rehearsal] makes conditions of work so much easier;
> then, most of the company were here last year so we're more of a team
> & more used to one another's ways which in an imperceptible way
> saves endless time and a lot of bother.

To Mrs Norah Guthrie at Annaghmakerrig
Hotel Palliser, Calgary, Alberta, Canada. 10 July 1954

> Had a most touching & really affectionate send-off from, first, the
> Governors at Stratford (dinner & presentation of 2 Hudson Bay
> blankets) and then the Co. on the stage at the end of perf. Speeches,
> bowls of "punch" and presentation of jewellery to Judy and Tanya and
> really choke-making "Tributes" to Yours Truly which I know were
> meant sincerely, and no blarney.

1955 was one of Guthrie's most busily nomadic years, flying to and from Stratford,
Ontario, where plans for the permanent open-stage theatre were rapidly
advancing, directing *The Merchant of Venice* there and overseeing a production of
Julius Caesar, advising on the *Oedipus* film, directing Sean O'Casey's latest play
The Bishop's Bonfire in Dublin and a radio version of *Peer Gynt*, also in Dublin,
directing Thornton Wilder's *A Life in the Sun* at Edinburgh, a revival of Wilder's *The
Matchmaker* in New York and a transfer of the Old Vic production of *Tamburlaine*
in Toronto and New York, plus a new production of *Six Characters in Search of an
Author*, also in New York.

To Mrs Peggy Butler at Maidenhall
Annaghmakerrig. Undated, early 1955

> Just finished typing draft of *Six Characters* [for Phoenix Theatre,
> New York]. Mama is only fairly well. Gets very easily & very much
> exhausted. Fear there is absolutely nothing to be done. Distempering
> of hall starting to-day. Great turnings-out of all furniture, stair-carpet
> up, & so on. Think Mrs G quite prepared to enjoy it; Bunty making
> rather heavy weather tho' trying quite hard to behave. She has become
> almost unbelievably "set in her ways". Specimen dialogue:
>
> > BUNTY: (Placing vase, or chair, or picture or any damn thing)
> >   This goes here.
> > TG: You mean it has always gone there.
> > BUNTY: (Like a weasel) Same thing.
>
> She is incapable of, & insusceptible to, logical explanation: if she
> were of a fanciful, dreamy, imaginative turn of mind this would be

easier to bear. In a very terre-à-terre common-sense mentality it is very irritating indeed. She is a VERY GOOD SOUL – I know that; but knowing it is one thing; feeling it is another. As with good Miss Prevost I find one has to spend rather too much time and energy dwelling on the GOODNESS and rising above small things that inflame the passions!

To Mrs Peggy Butler at Maidenhall

4 Dartmouth Road, Dublin. Undated, early 1955

Been reading the play [*The Bishop's Bonfire*] again. More than ever impressed.

To Mrs Peggy Butler at Maidenhall

c/o Radio Eireann, GPO, Dublin. Undated, 1955

All going well here. Master Cyril Cusack [Peer Gynt] is a charmer of the first water but as slippery as an eel & had managed to forget to acquaint Radio Eireann of the fact that he had three days filming to do in England during the next fortnight. The little R.E. person, who wants to please all the people all the time, was for accepting this; but I was very firm & said either he goes or I go – so Cyril is OUT, and one of the R.E. rep. is essaying the rôle of Peer – a dear boy but not really equipped with nearly enough of anything except an enduring willingness to do his best even if it kills him. This means that we rehearse morning & evening with the Co. (in which there is a great deal of excellent talent) & I rehearse from after lunch till 5 with Mr Christopher Peer Gynt Curran. It's rather more of a sweat than one bargained for but I'm quite enjoying it. I have also vaguely accepted to go to a Cusack party in Dalkey – in spite of events narrated above we're *dear* friends.

[Later:] Writing this while waiting before a final try-over of one or two things in connection with *Peer Gynt*. Alas, the young gentleman who plays P.G. is inadequate & it's a very "star" rôle so the effect is pretty tepid. Rise above. Quite enjoying it & being One of the Boys in R.E. Went to a party at Cusack's last night – Hilton [Edwards] & Michael [MacLíammóir], Connie Cummings, Wendy Hiller & Yours Truly. Quite fun.

To Mrs Peggy Butler at Maidenhall

4 Dartmouth Road, Dublin. Undated, February 1955

> Antony Quayle flew over to Dublin & we had a *very* nice evening together [discussing *Tamburlaine* for Toronto and New York]. Dinner at the Gresham at the expense of the Governors of Stratford-upon-Avon. O'Casey coming on; but we are rather behindhand & it'll be a battle to be ready. Old Paul Farrell (Canon) terribly slow learning his words. Harry Hutchinson v. much better.

There were protests outside the Gaiety Theatre, Dublin, on the opening night of *The Bishop's Bonfire* from ultra-conservative groups such as the Legion of Mary, who saw Sean O'Casey as a 'communist' and 'anti-Irish' (he was neither). The play received 'mixed' reviews and enjoyed excellent business.

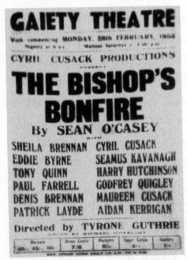

Poster for *The Bishop's Bonfire* by Sean O'Casey with Cyril Cusack Productions at the Gaiety Theatre, Dublin, 1955.

To Mrs Peggy Butler at Maidenhall

159 Ballantyne Avenue, Stratford, Ontario. April 1955

In my opinion O'Casey was not just writing about Ireland; & the fidelity (or non-fidelity) to current Irish "moeurs" is of comparative unimportance. He is writing, as he has done all his life, a tract against Authority, be that authority clerical, political, social or domestic. That is a theme of universal application. The Irish setting is incidental & largely symbolical (or do I mean allegorical? Not quite sure of the difference.) It is just Irish vanity, self-absorbtion, inferiority complex, that makes the "anti-Irish" stuff seem so important. Of course the silliness & fuss at the opening spotlighted all that & obscured the meaning of the play. It really seems to me such a spoilt-child attitude that "foreigners" should be expected to understand Ireland and reviled for not attempting to understand. No one is expected to "understand" America or Canada or England or France.

To Mrs Norah Guthrie at Annaghmakerrig

159 Ballantyne Avenue, Stratford, Ontario. Undated, spring 1955

> My first job is to sort out the walk-on people [for the third
> Shakespearian Festival]. We have 30 vacancies and several hundred
> applications. Tom [Browne, stage director] & I will have auditions here
> and in Toronto next week and will risk taking a few we haven't seen
> (exc. in photographs) from Halifax, Winnipeg and other places far off.

To Mrs Norah Guthrie at Annaghmakerrig

159 Ballantyne Avenue, Stratford, Ontario. 20 April 1955

> To N.Y. to see Thornton [Wilder, for *The Matchmaker*]. Stayed at
> the Algonquin & we were on the go from morning to night for two
> gloriously interesting but utterly exhausting days. Was able to clear
> up satisfactorily a lot of worrying technical points with Thornton
> (we were getting to crosser & crosser purposes by letter) but I am not
> entirely happy about whole business set-up but feel in honour bound
> to go ahead. It now looks as if there would be a separate production in
> America so all we shall do is get it up for 3 weeks in Edinboro'.

To Mrs Norah Guthrie at Annaghmakerrig

Stratford Shakespearian Festival. 15 May 1955

> Rehearsals [*The Merchant of Venice* and *Julius Caesar*] start tomorrow
> and this year we are even readier than in either of the previous seasons
> as regards tent, stage, equipment of all kinds. Booking also is excellent
> – I forget the simply astronomical sum in dollars, but between 25 & 30
> per cent of the whole season's capacity is sold already. So, unless the
> performances are really awful, the financial position seems assured.
> The stage this year has been built in a different kind of material – a
> mahogany ply. It's a lovely gold colour like cedar, really most beautiful,
> with a lovely grain and is most reasonable in price.

During the 1950s Hubert Butler organized an annual debate in Kilkenny with
distinguished speakers, broadcast on Radio Eireann. Guthrie took a somewhat
supercilious view of such events as an example of an insular attitude to
'controversial' topics, taking the stance of a sophisticated non-national against

Butler's expressed view of himself as an 'Irish country scholar'. An article by Butler in the *Irish Times* quoting the first Lord Charlemont (1728–99), liberal Irish patriot and patron of the arts, provoked the following:

To Hubert Butler at Maidenhall

Stratford Shakespearian Festival, Ontario. Undated, 29 May 1955

> You feel – & your life proves the sincerity of the feeling, which one must therefore admire and respect – that it is the duty of those who profess themselves "Irishmen" to live in, to work for, to serve (in the phrase of Lord Charlemont) an entity called Ireland. I feel that for me – I'm not trying (& I know you're not) to postulate a moral or political principle – it is less important to be a citizen of Ireland than a member of the human race; I want to serve my fellow creatures wherever opportunity presents itself.
>
> These two contrasted attitudes arise partly from contrasts in our own two temperaments; but more, I believe, from economic causes. You can do the work which you have chosen, in Ireland. I can't. Any young Irishman or Irishwoman (Julia is a case in point) of "artistic" bent, who wishes to live by one of the fine or applied arts, MUST go abroad. The same applies to the vast majority of those who want a career in industry or any of the "technological" occupations. You can stay in Ireland if you want to be a farmer; or a Dr.; or a Dentist; an undertaker; a grocer – if, in short you want to minister to primary needs. Even in these occupations (as I know you'll agree) one is all the better for having been out & about a bit. I am fully aware that to live in Ireland you make a commendable "sacrifice" – articles, broadcasts, books, ideas all command larger fees and a wider audience outside Ireland. None the less, you *can* work at home without unbearably cramping your style. You, and farmers' eldest sons, are in a fortunate and quite small minority.
>
> Lord Charlemont was a great man, a great patriot, but I think you ought to remember that Charlemont lived in an epoch when the journey from Dublin to London was longer, more hazardous and far further beyond ordinary people's means than is now the journey to New York, Melbourne or any other part of the world. In Charlemont's day a great measure of Isolationism was forced upon

everyone except a handful of Roving Spirits or else of wealthy and leisured noblemen. The fact that Ireland was an island was practically, as well as symbolically and sentimentally, significant.

The whole conception of Patriotism must be adjusted to the pace and facility of air travel, of communication by walkie-talkie and so on. In my view this makes Nationalism just utterly silly. Of course I realise that no one can really feel strongly about any aggregation so huge & vague as "Humanity". We must retain local loyalties, affections, responsibilities; *just* national ones are now on the wrong scale. National traditions do still exist, and I think it is the business of people like us to try to "sublimate" these into useful servants of a supra-national political order. Much as I share your admiration for Lord C. I think it is extremely misleading to apply quotations from him without re-orientating the terms to suit contemporary conditions.

Do write & tell about the Nationality Debate. P. sent cutting with summary (very bald & dull) of the speeches; but of course that's not the point. Did it serve the wished end? It has always interested and amused me very much that you find the Ulster Protestants so uncongenial. I remember it way back in the Coleraine/Carnegie days. I wonder why this is? You like to cherish the illusion of an IRISH stock, some of which is fortuitously Protestant, some Papish, but all of which is the product of the one green mystical wee western momma, the Island that Loves to be Visited!!

To Mrs Norah Guthrie at Annaghmakerrig

Stratford Shakespearean Festival, Ontario. Undated, June 1955

Tanya has been all day in the tent with the stage management. They have been working out the position of every prop (banners, shields, swords, flags, etc) in *J. Caesar*. It's complicated, there are 30 or 40 banners & it's necessary to know where each is at any moment so that it's available for its next appearance – they don't always reappear at the same place where they last made an exit. Our 30 "extras" join the Company tomorrow & the battle scenes in *Caesar* will be their man concern. So it's needful that all that is planned ahead.

The next 3 weeks involve an absolute network of arrangements as, in addition to rehearsal, all the fittings (dresses, hats, shoes, wigs) for "extras" have to be fitted for 35 principals in such a way that rehearsals are not unduly disrupted. In addition, we are now "News" in quite a big way which means we have refused I don't know how many offers from Canadian or U.S. television and cinema and radio "News" people; but have had to accept 3 T.V. programmes – one "important" one for U.S. with an estimated viewing audience of 20 million people which means (as its sponsors never stop pointing out) the equivalent of ten thousand capacity performances, i.e. the equivalent of a "run" of 30 years! But of course that is only in quantitative terms – the distinction between quality and quantity is one which most Americans find really hard to grasp and they have a strong instinctive idea that quantity is what really matters, quality is just something genteel and "fancy" and vaguely contemptible! Anyway, the result is that next Sunday will be almost entirely devoted to a filmed 3-minute excerpt from *Caesar* (the most we could allow). I was also expected to do a 3½ minute "scripted" interview on opening night, involving a mini-script by heart. I stuck at that, said I had too much else to do; that I would do it next Sunday or not at all. Great commotion! And I don't know what they've finally decided and really don't care. The Yankee T.V. people think that if they only pay enough we'll literally anything – & simply DON'T UNDERSTAND that we are more interested in the quality of the stage performance than in their 20,000,000 "viewers".

To Mrs Norah Guthrie at Annaghmakerrig

Stratford Shakespearean Festival, Ontario. 26 June 1955

Dress rehearsal of *Caesar* last night went well. I think most of it is excellent especially the difficult last 20 minutes when nearly all the noble Romans commit suicide – all most impressively & movingly managed. We're plagued by the T.V. programme – 25 minutes of "live" pick-up with 4 cameras at the entrance, 2 in the auditorium, 2 backstage and 1 on a swan's nest (literally!) in the lake! It's all just one more thing to cope with and involves as much equipment as a circus, 4 HUGE vans encamped at the Stage Door and all cameras connected by a veritable spider's web of cable to a sort of Mother Church in a baby tent like a pierrot's hat! Everyone says it's such wonderful publicity.

Interior of the original tent theatre at Stratford, Ontario, 1953.

To Mrs Norah Guthrie at Annaghmakerrig

Stratford Shakespearean Festival, Ontario. 1 July 1955

Caesar wasn't quite in the bull's eye – it's a fine production, I think; but the actors were v. nervous on the opening night & will do better in a while. *Oedipus* [revival] wasn't quite bull's eye either in my opinion tho' it's had *wonderful* notices, but I thought [Douglas] Campbell, thro' anxiety, rather pressed and boomed and overacted, but all the same he does give a most impressive showing. *Merchant of V* just went like a dream from beginning to end – the audience just loved it and you could hear and see and feel them loving it. I don't know that I've ever known a more enjoyed and intelligently appreciative performance. Somehow on Wedy. everything came off just as one would wish.

Thornton [Wilder] arrives tonight – that ball of fire! – and we have to buckle to and think of his play at Edinboro'. Also a *Tamburlaine-Oedipus* New York deal is going thro' and I must prepare cast and salary list for that and see the artists and start all the satisfactory but troublesome arrangements in connection with scenery & dresses.

To Mrs Norah Guthrie at Annaghmakerrig
Stratford Shakespearean Festival, Ontario. 7 July 1955

> Thornton's visit was delightful but very absorbing of both time &
> energy. He left on Tues early morning & I went down with him to
> Toronto as I had to record some stuff for a T.V. programme which
> they are preparing for autumn. Had a Royal Progress on the train
> with Perfect Strangers coming up right left & centre to say how
> greatly they had enjoyed the plays & how sorry to hear I wasn't
> returning next season.
>
> Rode back on The Special. The Toronto Evening Telegram hires a
> special train every Tues. which conveys the Telegram party (composed
> of readers of the paper) up to Stratford – they pay so much which
> includes return trip, a meal at Stratford and tickets for the play, & it's
> a wild success. They leave at 4.30 and don't get back to Toronto till
> 2.30 next morning. It's mainly teachers & elderly couples & students
> – people who haven't got own cars & who have to do it the cheapest
> way. The Special itself is most imposing – 11 coaches & a perfectly
> enormous engine - & nearly 600 souls aboard all agog to dash thro'
> thick and thin. We sail into Stratford slap bang on time and there are
> fleets of busses waiting to take pink voile teachers to meat teas in the
> basement of Knox Church.

To Mrs Norah Guthrie at Annaghmakerrig
Locust Theatre, Philadelphia. 21 October 1955

> Buzzing round like a mad thing between *Matchmaker*, *6 Characters* &
> the *Oedipus* film (fabulous money and I can't think how it can fit in,
> but that's their worry, not ours) and, of cahss, *Tambers*.

To Mrs Judith Guthrie at Annaghmakerrig
Locust Theatre, Philadelphia. 27 October 1955

> Writing this on the stage amid a bedlam of stage hands each of whom
> is smoking a cigar, has an emerald ring, a sapphire tie-clip and a ruby
> wristlet & is rougher than an orang-utang but OH so ready to weep
> at a Fairy Tale – rather endearing. Have been promised $250 to write
> a 2,000 word profile of Thornton for the N.Y. Times magazine. The

Ruth Gordon in
Guthrie's production
of Thornton Wilder's
The Matchmaker
at the Edinburgh
Festival, 1955,
following a New
York run.

management seems to be making a huge effort to promote *M'maker* – the cast are all going to do the hat-shop act on the Ed Sullivan Show which has a constant Sunday evg. audience of 40 million precious human souls. Did I tell you that Ninettte [de Valois] is in the same hotel as I am. We had a very nice reunion & are going to *Matchmaker* together tomorrow.

To Mrs Judith Guthrie at Annaghmakerrig
Locust Theatre, Philadelphia. 31 October 1955

Notices here v.g. and biz, which opened to no booking at all, now v.g. Have written my article on Thornton. Read it to Ruth [Gordon, leading lady] & Garson [Kanin] who acted ecstatic like I were Lytton Strachey and Plutarch rolled into a single improbable whole.

A.M. to Quaker Meeting – very impressive so long as we all sat mute; considerably less so when the Lord moved just one and then another Pink Faced Elderly Business Man to make silly little goody-goody Rotary speeches.

Considerable contractual problems resulted in Guthrie threatening to sue the producer, David Merrick; these were solved by a delayed transfer to Broadway and a cast change.

To Mrs Judith Guthrie at Annaghmakerrig
c/o Kanin, New York. 13 November 1955

Loring Smith makes a big diff. to *Matchmaker* cast & last Friday's perf. went with a real dash. Business in Philadelphia was splendid, let's hope Boston will be O.K.

To Mrs Norah Guthrie at Annaghmakerrig
Hotel Van Renesselaer, New York. 1 December 1955

Matchmaker is being exposed this week to "previews". The house is sold en-bloc to various charities who then resell the tickets to friends & well-wishers. This means a full house but an audience so dull, so unco-operative, so lethargic that the performance breaks itself to pieces like a wave on a rock.

6 Characters being most interesting & exciting to prepare but very hard work & I'm beginning to wonder if I really ought to have attempted to squeeze it in before *Tamburlaine*. Don't know WHAT an audience will make of it. Dresses are v.g. period 1922. However, too late now for regrets so we may as well enjoy what's enjoyable & Rise Above some not very excessive fatigue.

Tony Quayle [lead in *Tamburlaine*] arrives in Thursday which will be v. nice & will fly up to Toronto with us next Sunday morning. We have an apt. in Toronto with friends. Tonight is the opening of *Matchmaker* after very trying week of previews.

To Mrs Norah Guthrie at Annaghmakerrig

Hotel Van Renesselaer, New York. 7 December 1955

> Well, The *M'maker* passed off with immense verve. The audience really loved the evening & it was fun to see the rich & wildly over-sophisticated First N. audience. People who see *everything* & go *everywhere* just holding their sides at little Miss Gordon's antics & adoring simple fun like changing hats and hiding in cupboards. Hard at work on *6 Characters* which has a "public" preview tonight – a great mistake in my opinion as it's not quite ready.

To Mrs Norah Guthrie at Annaghmakerrig

c/o Stratford Shakespearian Festival, Ontario. 10 December 1955

> Last night's preview of *6 Characters* [in New York] went distinctly well & all feel rather encouraged. *M'maker* a huge success & likely to run for lucrative ages. Good biz. I get 2%.

Candide, 1956, with Irra Petina as the Old Lady and Barbara Cook as Cunegonde. Guthrie described his production of Lilian Hellman and Leonard Bernstein's musical in New York as one of his greatest flops.

10 **TRANSATLANTIC ENCOUNTERS**

Guthrie was making frequent transatlantic trips between 1956 and 1960. The Stratford Festival *Oedipus* (Yeats-Sophocles) was filmed. *Candide* (Voltaire-Hellman-Bernstein) in New York was a notable flop. Other productions were *La Traviata* (Puccini) and *The First Gentleman* (Ginsbury) in New York, *Twelfth Night* (Shakespeare) at Stratford, Ontario, *Maria Stuart* (Schiller) and *The Makropoulos Secret* (Čapek) in New York, *Tamburlaine* (Marlowe) in Toronto and New York, *The Bonefire* (McLarnon) in Belfast and Edinburgh, *All's Well That Ends Well* (Shakespeare) at Stratford-upon-Avon, *The Tenth Man* (Chayefsky) in New York, *The Pirates of Penzance* and *HMS Pinafore* at Stratford, Ontario, and in New York, *Love and Libel* (Robertson Davies) and *Gideon* (Chayefsky); and another trip to Israel, this time for *The Merchant of Venice*.

To Mrs Norah Guthrie at Annaghmakerrig
Hotel Van Rensselaer, New York. 8 May 1956

> The film [*Oedipus*] was a HUGE cope & left no energy for anything else. We just managed to finish by the skin of our teeth & everyone thinks it was remarkable of us to do it in the time. Quality of the work remains to be seen. It was most interesting.

To Mrs Norah Guthrie at Annaghmakerrig
Hotel Van Rensselaer, New York. 16 May 1956

> Last 3 days have been spent hearing singers for *Candide*, one after another endlessly all day – very tiring & rather embarrassing &

difficult business. Each night we've had some social or semi-social "official" plan: e.g. to see *Matchmaker* with calls afterwards on All Hands followed by supper with Ruth & Garson. It is hoped to nurse it thro' the summer with all royalty holders foregoing their shares in order to reap a final golden harvest in the Fall.

To Mrs Norah Guthrie at Annaghmakerrig
c/o Lilian Hellman, Vineland Haven, Martha's Vineyard, Mass. 20 May 1956

Well here we are in the Vineyard and it's *enchanting*. An island off Cape Cod about 45 mins in a very grand quick ferry boat. The island was named Martha's Vineyard because the Pilgrim Fathers found wild grapes on it. I'm due at Lilian's at 3 where all the posse will be assembled – Lilian & Leonard Bernstein & a nice man called Dick Wilbur, a Prof. of English at Wellesley who will write the verse for the songs. We are all to dine with L. & then we shall cycle back – rather fun.

To Mrs Norah Guthrie at Annaghmakerrig
c/o Lilian Hellman, Vineland Haven, Martha's Vineyard, Mass. 29 May 1956

The news of the film is good. The idea now is that I go out to the coast for 3 days next week to supervise the cutting.

I think Miss Hellman, who is writing the "book" for the Candide musical, may have one hand tied behind her back because we've all agreed that we would choose singers to do justice to the score rather than actors who could handle the text.

To Mrs Peggy Butler at Maidenhall
c/o Heinman, 730 N. Rodeo Drive, Beverley Hills, California. 3 June 1956

Mr Heinman [Lola Kipnis' uncle] who is a handsome 78 but only admits to 72, is beginning to get a little senile – forgets things very badly; can't concentrate for more than a v. short time and has very bad headaches due to hardening of the arteries. His relation with Lola is very touching & amusing; he treats L, who is a fragile 58, as tho' he were a naughty rough boy of 16, but with immense affection. The problem of how to cope with him is difficult. There's an adopted nephew & his wife nearby.

The reason for my visit is to superintend the cutting of the *Oedipus* film & we went at it all yesterday. I really think it promises to be a strange & interesting film – not at all on the beaten way of commercial screen but interesting all the same in a high-toned amateur way! I lunch today with one of the Moguls of Paramount who is like to offer me the direction of *Matchmaker* which Paramount has bought (250,000 dollars, most of which goes to Thornton). Even if offered I shall decline the honour. Judy, meantime, is staying on at the Vineyard and we shall meet in N.Y. Thurs.

There's a good deal to do in N.Y. (*Candide* mostly). Shan't attempt to give my impression of L.A. here – very unfavourable!

Mrs Norah Guthrie died at Annaghmakerrig on 6 July 1956. Guthrie inherited the house and lands; there were difficulties subsequently with his sister Peggy Butler about his disposal of this inheritance. The only known surviving letter from Guthrie about his mother's death is to his friend Christopher Scaife acknowledging a message of sympathy.

To Christopher Scaife at Paternina, Arezzo, Tuscany
Annaghmakerrig. Undated, July 1956

A merciful, even beautiful end. Grief is largely self-indulgence. All the same the parting is terribly painful and almost overwhelmingly mysterious and solemn. Really relief and happiness that she is at rest and no longer BLIND outweighs any feelings of sadness and loneliness.

To Mrs Peggy Butler, staying at Annaghmakerrig
c/o 34 Buccleuch Place, Edinburgh. 3 September 1956

Have you had a letter from Wylie's [solicitor] with approx. £1,000.0.0 being our share from Aunt Sue's estate? A nice windfall. Am NOT alluding to your last letter seems to me we can only get further and further at X purposes; after your letter I thought carefully: if I *were* aware of such bitter jealousy? And truly I am not. I'm convinced that the forces operating are not under conscious control – e. g. I don't consciously feel about Hubert in the very least as you say in your letter that I do. But if the feelings attributed do exist they are not on conscious level and therefore not under conscious control. You know that if I were to raise the slightest cheep about your and Hubert's affairs it would be resented (which I understand) and called "my paranoia for organising other people for their own good".

To Mrs Peggy Butler at Maidenhall

Martin Beck Theater, New York. Undated, December 1956

Candide – from the start the great risk has been that the thing would seem wildly pretentious. And that is just what it did seem. An artistic and financial disaster from which I learned almost nothing at all about anything but it has been fun to be associated with a group so brilliantly and variously talented. Only Bernstein's allusive score emerged with credit. None of Lilian's good qualities, even great qualities, as a writer showed to advantage. My direction skipped along with the effortless grace of a freight train heavy-laden on a steep gradient. As a result even the score was thrown out of key, Rossini and Cole Porter seemed to have been rearranging Götterdämmerung. I feel sorry for our lady producer, she and her backers lost a great deal of money, she proved a gallant loser.

To Cousin Norah Kesteven at Seal Chart, Kent

23 Old Buildings, Lincoln's Inn, WC2. 26 January 1957

After a lot of rather anxious switches we have decided to give up this flat. It's a wrench, partic. for Judy, and it looks as if we'll be away now for six months anyway and then want to be at A'kerrig for a full year continuously, so that cheap though it is, to keep it on hardly seems warranted. I leave tomorrow at midnight for U.S.A. J. is staying to pack up & will follow in about a week.

Letter from Bunty y'day to say the Kelly girls [long time cook & housemaid at Annaghmakerrig] want to leave & go to B'ham factories at £7.0.0 per week, no row or unpleasantness, just the lure of gold – you can't blame them. But of course that sort of thing multiplied by tens of thousands makes rather hollow the cries of patriotism uttered by I.R.A.

To Mrs Peggy Butler at Maidenhall

c/o Oliver Smith, 70 Willow, Brooklyn Heights, New York. 15 February 1957

Inventory from Adams, Auctioneers, of A'kerrig furniture has arrived. Guess you'll have your copy too. I shall send it to Murphy, Solicitor, with instructions to pay your half out of the Estate. Right?

Metropolitan Opera *Traviata* is now, THANK GOODNESS, in its final stages and my responsibility is virtually over. It's been a frustrating, maddening, depressing battle against time. The stupidity, conservatism & cunning of Italian singers! Tebaldi is a great – & I mean just that – *great* singer. A real Artist, a God-sent, neat, huge, flexible, *moving* voice. She's a large, handsome, thoroughly pleasant, great peasant. It's like having Biddy McGrotty – divinely gifted, experienced, world-famous, very very rich, quite unspoilt and utterly SIMPLE. She has as much idea of acting as a potato.

The scenery and dresses (Oliver Smith & Raef Gérard respectively) are very handsome and wildly expensive, but there is (for really very valid reasons) NO TIME to get anything together. The whole thing is a toil of expensive confusion, which is nearly, but not completely, something, but really a costly NOTHING. There remain 2 rehearsals with full orchestra, which are so expensive they cannot possibly be interrupted. The public simply won't notice the things that irk me. They will only be aware of Verdi's great masterpiece and the goddess qualities of Madame T.

Norman's *First Gentleman*[31] starts immediately. On paper a good cast has been assembled and handsome, practical designs.

To Mrs Peggy Butler at Maidenhall

Hotel Statler, Boston, Mass. 7 April 1957

Just got in here 4 p.m. having left Phila at 9 a.m. We open the *First Gent* in N.Y. April 24, then Geo. & Annette [from Old Vic] join us for a few days and we all proceed to Stratford in first week of May. All going remarkably well here – an awfully nice, capable co-operative

---

31   *The First Gentleman*, a play on the Prince Regent by Norman Ginsbury, with Walter Slezak, Belasco Theater, New York.

company. Play NOT on the bullseye, mostly due to Walter Slezak not having sufficient command of the language; but really due to extreme Englishness of the idiom and allusion which we are trying to deal with. It's been very trying for Norman; but he is behaving very reasonably and well. I don't see how it can possibly run the summer unless it's a smash-bang success and that doesn't seem the least likely.

Would you like some curtain material for your birthday?

To Mrs Peggy Butler

Hotel Statler, Boston, Mass. 18 April 1957

After *endless* tinkering *First Gent* now goes very well and has done v.g. biz here in Boston, even in Holy Week in a very R.C. city. But I don't think Walter Slezak good enough as Prinny. It was a bad day's work when I persuaded the producers to persuade him that he was the man. He looks wonderful, exactly like the Laurence portrait, and he's a v.g., if limited, actor, but he just hasn't the command of the English tongue to get round long florid phrases and make them sound, as they are, witty. On his lips they just sound wordy and clumsy because the rhythm is subtly, disastrously, *wrong*. Everywhere the critics have hailed the magnificent performance of Mr Slezak doing wonders with a stodgy verbose English play. An ironic situation. Think it will sink quietly but respectably in N.Y. and, for Norman, that's a serious financial disappointment. He will, of course, be no worse off, but this has, through the last lean years, always been the ray of hope. Sad.

To Mrs Peggy Butler at Maidenhall

c/o Alex Cohen, 40 West 55th Street, New York City. 26 April 1957

Will be my last letter from U.S.A. We're due in Stratford May 4. Norman's piece opened last night & went quite well, but the press today (I hear, have not seen any) is very tepid; so it's unlikely to do any biz. Pity. But all did their best & you can't do more. Plans at Stratford are well advanced on the building of the theatre, keeping, so far, up to schedule. I'll try to send you some pictures of it when we get there. We hear we have a house in a Workers' Arrondissement with terrible wallpaper but all essentials in working order.

Walter Slezak as the mad King George III in Guthrie's production of *The First Gentleman* by Norman Ginsbury, New York, 1957.

Bunty writes cheerfully of her Dutch trip & visits in s. of England. I do think she's enjoyed it & doesn't find poor Wendy [Guthrie] too much of a trial. I guess there are occasions when the Nurse's training to look on all fellow creatures as Cases is a big assistance.

To Mrs Peggy Butler at Maidenhall

c/o Shakespeare Festival, Stratford, Ontario. 7 May 1957

Dearie, I hope you had a happy birthday. How the years fly! We are now quite elderly persons – at any moment I'll be sixty. I suppose inevitably as old age comes and one's seniors have already crept away and the contemporaries begin one by one to disappear, life becomes more lonely, but then, I guess, one has oneself become more detached so that the pain of loneliness is not so sharp; also that one realises that physical loneliness need not cut one off from spiritual & imaginative contact with all the people and places and things which are unchangingly dear.

It's nice to be back in Stratford again and to be made to feel *really* welcome by so many friends & acquaintances. The theatre in its half-finished state looks very impressive. Geo & Annette are with us, much enjoying, I think, the novelty and seeing many old friends. I think next week we'll go for a night or two with Brenda & Robertson Davies[32]. Brenda was for 2 years Asst. Stage Manager under George at the Vic. And they are great allies.

Oh! I very stupidly destroyed your letter about curtain material. Sorry. Please repeat. The choice is bewilderingly large.

To Mrs Peggy Butler at Maidenhall

The Park Plaza Hotel, Toronto. 18 May 1957

I've stayed here overnight en route from day's filming in Ottawa – half hour interview about *Twelfth Night* filmed for issue by Canadian Adult Ed. Board – to be on hand to "welcome" Siobhán McKenna this aft. & attend a press conference at 5. Then, I hope & believe, we shall all drive up to Stratford – "all" being Siobhán & (I think) her boy aged about 10, Michael Langham, Tom Brown, A. M. Bell (the President of Festival Board), Mary Joliffe, the Press Representative, & Yours Truly. Rehearsals start on Monday & will last six weeks. *Hamlet* opens July 1 with Christopher Plummer directed by Michael; *Twelfth N.* July 2 by me with Miss McKenna.

Toronto is incredible. Since last year this hotel has added another wing (14 storeys) of 500 rooms & a whole series of bars & restaurants; there are two other immense new hotels in the centre of the city and endless new vast glass boxes of apartment houses, offices & so on in extremely "modern" style – Swiss influence, I'm told – masses of glass

32   Distinguished Canadian author, influential in the establishment of the Shakespearian Festival.

Siobhán McKenna played Viola in Guthrie's production of *Twelfth Night* at the Festival Theater, Stratford, Ontario, 1957.

and balconies, very rectilinear. They look very new & daring right now, but I have a notion that in 10, if not 5, years they'll be frightfully "out". There's nothing so dated as yesterday's Dernier Cri. I think when today's infants reach university age they'll look at all these glazed boot-boxes and cast up their eyes and say "Well, for Dernier Crying out loud!"

But with all the expansion, Canada still has a simplicity, or so it feels to us, that the States has lost – there isn't the all-pervading feeling of disrespectability. Perhaps this is no more than that Ontario is still predominantly populated by people of Scots & Irish extraction and so the physical types and standards of behaviour and ways of thinking are more familiar. In an undercover way the Immigration Policy of Canada is grossly illiberal – ostensibly it's as nice as pie but in fact the door is open to respectable Scots and solid blond Dutch & Swedes but somehow convenient reasons why blackeyed Sicilians and greasy Armenians just don't get in, except in the very thinnest trickle.

To Mrs Peggy Butler at Maidenhall

c/o Shakefest, Stratters, Ont. 3 June 1957

XII Night coming on well, I think a very strong team and Miss Siobhán *much* better at acting and less the gifted "folk actress" than I feared. When she first came she briefly tried on the wee barefoot colleen act, but she very quickly and sensibly realised that it might work in New York but was totally unsuitable in Ontario.

The new [theatre] building comes on fast. "Everyone" says it will be ready in time. It doesn't look as though that will be possible but certainly every day now one sees obvious progress. A gifted lady sculptress has asked to "do" my head and sittings are to begin on Wed. right here in the garden. I think it'll be embarrassing at first because all the neighbouring children will swarm around and give advice and keep up the excitement. The lady is reputed to be very good and has the rather unglamorous name of Ursula Haines. If the bust is any good the Board of the theatre has an arrangement to buy it and put it in a niche; and Miss Ursula is then to be commissioned to do one of Tanya for another niche so that we shall scowl down upon the audiences like Zeus and Hera.

To Mrs Peggy Butler

c/o Shakespeare Festival, Stratford, Ontario. 6 June 1957

We are now in our last week before the Opening. Rehearsals now occur in The Building – but there still remains a great deal to do. In a project of this size it's amazing how one small omission can create widening rings of confusion and delay. For instance, no one remembered that if entrances were to be made by the actors from the periphery, down aisles, then when doors open light from the periphery would flood disconcertingly into the darkened auditorium. The outer wall of the periphery is almost entirely of glass so a major blackout problem has arisen just at the most inopportune time.

XII N. will, I think, be ready. Tanya's dresses are some of her very best – "Cavalier" period, with huge lace collars and cuffs and very sombre colouring. Orsino Dept. in deep Van Dyke brown and brown madder; Olivia Dept. in black mourning until the finale when the ladies all appear in azalea colours – canary, yellow, orange, flame-pink and (very successfully clashing) bluish rose-pink. It's a period which on the stage usually appears extra fussy and velvety and "picturesque" in the Fred Terry style. So it's nice to see it done with great elegance and authority – the "authority" emerges in eschewing all, but ALL, the more obviously flauntingly picturesque features of the period and concentrating on material & workmanship rather than trimming & feathers.

Send curtain measurements.

To Mrs Peggy Butler at Maidenhall

c/o Shakesfest, Stratters, Ont. 16 June 1957

Our plays are coming on ... am too close to *XII N.* to know if it's any good or no; but think the Team is a very strong evenly balanced one. Siobhán is being delightful as Viola – a very simple and charming "gracious" person.

Hear from Eddy & Bunty that Becky is decidedly more mobile; but hasn't yet attempted the stairs. Have you had your half of the valuation money?

To Mrs Peggy Butler at Maidenhall

c/o Shakespeare Festival, Stratford, Ontario. 4 July 1957

The plays have now opened – & successfully. *Hamlet* [Christopher Plummer], an interesting, but rather over-intense & overstrung first perf: will be really good in a fortnight. *Twelfth N,* which came second, scored heavily because the audience (75% the same people as the previous night) thought it such fun, which it was, to see the serious characters from *Hamlet* being funny. Notices and biz are v.g. so one and all are settling down (pretty exhausted I must confess) to ironing out creases in the performances and to planning the Next Moves.

The Dedication had a simply splendid feeling of Occasion. The new theatre seats 2,000; and I guess there were another 500 sitting in aisles and standing in doorways; at least another 1,000 in the corridor which runs round the auditorium, and another 1,000 standing outside in the park. The actual service was a weeny bit of a disappointment. We paid dearly for the Eminence of the Divines. The head Presbyterian was an aged Highlander called Ian McKinnion who looked as if he had a ripe damson in his poor old mouth since birth (80 years agone). He opened the proceedings by groaning out in a voice of ashes "O be joyful in the Loarrd all ye Lahnds!" The Romanist, in resplendent robes of puce watered silk was an overfed butcher in pince-nez. He read a little address commending the Festival for "the proper administration of culture" and saying all the dreariest most platitudinous things in the most objectionably authoritarian manner. A disgustingly lascivious-looking Père Poisson jumped about conducting six snot-nosed ill-conditioned and nervous "Lads" (in hired dance-band outfits too big for all of them, white blazers, made-up bow ties and black trousers with braid down the side) in a glee-club tradition in slow waltz-time & close harmony – of entirely unsuitable sectarian words on the lines of "Mary, mother of angels, queen of the skies, intercede for us in the name of the bleeding wounds".

The Anglican ARCHbish was far gone in Dotage and gave the impression that he was only held together by ill-knotted string and masses of Scotch tape. The Chief Rabbi spoke earnestly, audibly and dully. But thick muddy boots appeared beneath a creased and dusty gown and the good man exuded the odours of sanctity & halitosis. Then arose the Rt Hon Leslie Frost, Premier of Ontario, in a sharp, tight-fitting ensemble of ginger-coloured Dacron and a floral satin tie. He commended the business enterprise of the community, quoted (inaccurately) statistics on the dimensions & cost of the building and endeavoured (unsuccessfully) to magnify the degree of support accorded by himself and his cabinet. However, proceedings were immeasurably bucked up by the final and chief speaker, the head of the United Church of Canada (an uneasy but wealthy amalgam of Methodists, Baptists and renegade Presbyterians & in my opinion the only practicable solution to Protestant schism). He is a brisk, plummy, sixty-ish Ayrshire Scot who looked like a cattle-dealer who'd dressed up in Academic Robes to amuse grandchildren. He gave a thoughtful, forceful, witty & punching address on the relation between church and stage – it was absolutely and perfectly à propos – Christ's Church militant here in Earth but tolerant, wise and funny. When he said "The Bride of Christ too often appears as a minatory scold" the whole audience laughed, with the exception of the Presbyterian, who looked as if a scourge had been applied to his back; and the R.C. Prelate who looked like he'd taken a blood-fit that second.

Such a nice letter from Peter [Norah Kesteven] recalling this time last year. I miss our old darling [their mother] constantly and dream of her almost every night – but happily. Don't, and I'm sure you don't, wish her back with us. I realise that the inevitability of "bereavement" is not a cause of grief. One thing which I admire about R.C.ism is the constant insistence that Life is Preparation for Death; that, consequently, death is the fulfilment, not the destruction of life, its complement rather than its antithesis.

I'm going to New York (flying) next Sunday for 3 nights to see representatives of Theatre Trades Unions, appointments arranged by N.Y.Times who want an article on the Economics of Broadway Production. I'm supposed to combine some first hand knowledge with a reasonable degree of objectivity. I think it will be interesting to attempt.

The meeting with the Trades Unions was to have a direct influence on the establishment of the Guthrie Theater in Minneapolis six years later – far removed from the restrictive practices of Broadway.

To Mrs Peggy Butler

c/o Stratford Shakespearian Festival, Ont. 27 July 1957

Was down in Toronto for a TV thing last Monday & got your curtain stuff! Do hope you like it. It seemed to me suitably kitcheny but also gay & nice colour. *If there's duty to pay please let me know.* We've had quite a succession of guests – mostly friends from N.Y.C. to see the plays. Tues. I go to N.Y. and on to Boston to lecture at Harvard. Might hop over to M. Vineyard & stay night with Lilian Hellman who might return with me here. Lola Kipnis has been very ill; & Abe Polansky was taken ill on way up here & had to sink down on a bed of pain in Syracuse, New York State.

To Mrs Peggy Butler at Maidenhall

c/o Shakefest, Stratters, Ont. 16 August 1957

Very pleased & relieved to know you're out of Mrs Carver [knee surgery]. Thank goodness. It has been a *very* pleasant quiet leisurely summer, but where has it FLOWN? Peaches, nectarines, grapes & cantaloupe "abundon", hummingbirds hum and dart like the most exquisite flying jewellery and the violent brilliant florescence is wonderful. Our lawn is visited now daily by a neighbour's tame ROOK – repulsive at first, it has now greatly endeared itself with its chatty ways and insatiable demands for attention! I have been busy on a free adaptation of Capek's *Macropoulous Secret* – just finished. Plans quite confused. Plenty of offers from N.Y. – will probably do a play there in autumn but definitely returning to A'kerrig at end of year for a full year. Last few days have been sitting up to a Russian government-sponsored visit of two Artists – a Hamlet and the Director of the Maly Theatre in Moscow. Suspect their *very* highly publicised visit here is really a back-hander at the American theatre, but it's been quite interesting and the two gentlemen – one young & lissom & almond-eyed, one elderly & jolly & fatherly & cross-eyed – have been hugely cordial. A pallid spectacled interpreter, also laid on from Moscow, has done a good job.

To Mrs Peggy Butler at Maidenhall

c/o Stratford Shakespearian Festival, Ontario. 1 September 1957

All plans changed! Now all films are off. Invited to do two plays at the Phoenix in quick succession. The Phoenix is N.Y.'s sort of nearest equivalent to the Old Vic – "popular prices" and a programme that aims to be good rather than just commercial. Plays are new version of Schiller's *Mary Stuart* and an adaptation of Capek's *Macropoulous Secret* by Yours Truly. If either is a big success it would finance our year at A'kerrig. If neither is, the fees will still be a help and reduce the gap caused by films. I now leave here next Tues. (5 days earlier than anticipated) in rather a rush. Judy will follow a week later having handed over house, coped with inventory, etc etc

In addition to all this we've had Max Schaffner (our fellow-tenant at Brooklyn Heights last winter) & a friend of his staying for a week. They've been very pleasant, easy guests but Max, being Jewish, is wildly sociable and likes (like Hubert) to "klatsch" from 11 A.M. till 4 the next morning. So for a week the house has been like a busy Club and the washing up would stretch from here to Mars. Of course each and all "give a hand" but the mere noise has been tiring. So, though we liked them very much, their departure this morning had its elements of relief.

We've gone and invested quite a sum in new carpets for A'kerrig. They're made here by one of the Festival Directors and he's given us a very very "special" price. Seemed to be an opportunity not to be missed so have Gone to Town on plain sort of haircordy stuff backed with rubber; they're "moth-resistant" and practically impossible to wear out. Getting a sort of silver grey green for drawing room; brown for study; "a soft green" (at her own request) for Bunty's room; and can't decide between scarlet or a very nice sort of bluebell colour for the morning-room.

To Mrs Peggy Butler at Maidenhall

c/o Phoenix Theater, 2nd Ave at 12th Street. 26 September 1957

Was VERY delighted to get your letter in your own, rather shaky, hand o' write. It was v. gallant & made me feel very happy. This note really does no more than amplify telepathic sentiments. I do hope convalescence manages to be a pleasant & not just a frustrating & fretting period.[33]

Am very biz with Schiller's *Maria Stuart* & consequently have no News. The play is well advanced as regards everyone having the words and what they're trying to do. Have no idea if it'll be an acceptable offering to the public – it's very romantic and high flown & the translation inevitably is apt to reduce purple passages to mauve. I think the real issue will be whether the two ladies – Mary & Elizabeth – are sufficiently interesting.

You'll be glad to know that at long last Probate has been granted [Mrs Guthrie's will]. The forms arrived last night from B. Murphy [lawyer] for me to sign. I shall go to Notary Public today if I can get an appointment. So it shouldn't be too long until you get your share. I would also like to go halves in the expenses of your illness. Will you discuss this with Hubert and let me know? RSVP.

---

33   Mrs Butler had been suffering from temporal lobe epilepsy.

To Mrs Peggy Butler at Maidenhall

c/o Phoenix Theatre, 2nd Avenue at 12th Street, New York. 30 September 1957

Hope you are going on satisfactorily. When will you leave Porto[bello Nursing Home]? Will you then go to M.Hall? How long do you expect to be bedded? All information gratefully recd.

Great excitement, but real *excitement*, here because the Soviet "Moon" is believed to be passing over the U.S.A. every 96 mins. It's been an immense coup-de-prestige for the U.S.S.R. 'cos the American man in the street has been sold for years the idea that he, and he alone of mankind, possesses technological "know-how". I think this has been a real, & maybe salutary, shock to public complacency. I suppose it's unimaginative & intolerant to expect a more mature Public Opinion from a public so heterogeneous, so insulated by geographic & economic circumstance from the mainstream of human feeling, and where there is, by European standards, so little hereditary leadership by an old-established Upper Class, the all-but-fossilised "steadiness" of Colonel Blimp is, one learns, a colossal public asset!

To Mrs Peggy Butler at Maidenhall

c/o Phoenix Theater, 2nd Avenue at 12th Street, New York. 9 October 1957

First let me say how glad I was to hear and know you really feel stronger – it was "between the lines" of the letter.

Second – you know your love for me is entirely, fully from the depths, reciprocated.

Third – I too have held off the topic of this terrible quarrel because nothing seemed possible to say without the likelihood of creating further difficulty and misunderstanding.

I won't mention again a word about wishing to assist financially. That such an offer should be construed by Hubert as "patronising" seems to me very sad, but so long as *you* don't feel that too, it doesn't particularly hurt. Hubert wrote – about a year ago – two letters full of such hatred,& with such undisciplined accusations of lying & cheating over money, that I was utterly bewildered. I appreciate that in a situation like this the Right is never wholly on one side. But in that case neither is the Wrong. And there, I suppose, the matter must rest.

I realise that between the two of us you are placed in a hopelessly passive position, and will, wittingly, do nothing to make matters more uncomfortable, but it seems to me that my mere existence offends Hubert, that whatever I do, or omit to do, will be offensive. Therefore I shall keep out of the way. Necessary to rush ahead into next effort and I must meet on *your* initiative, therefore; and you must not feel that my affection is changed at all if I do not try to arrange joint plans or meetings.

To Mrs Peggy Butler at Maidenhall

c/o Phoenix Theater, 2nd Avenue at 12th Street, New York. 14 October 1957

VERY glad to hear of you back in your own bed & own surroundings. This can only be a brief note 'cos we also are in quite a poor way. As I, on Sat after a nasty little go of flu (temp 104), so Judy collapsed. Her temp. hasn't reached the high peak that mine did but has stuck obstinately at 103 for 2 days and she lies abed like a sullenly burning brand, not feeling terribly ill or even uncomf. but terribly feeble. Meanwhile I'm creeping about feeling not un-cheerful but hopelessly weak. Very fortunately the success of *M. Stuart* makes it unnecessary to rush ahead into next effort.

Expect you've been reading all about the goings-on at Little Rock High, and, even more disgraceful, Jimmy Hoffa & the Teamsters Union.

To Mrs Peggy Butler at Maidenhall

c/o Phoenix Theater, 2nd Avenue at 12th Street, New York. 27 October 1957

Splitting headache as regular as the clock from 11 A.M. to 5 P.M. quite incapacitating. Rehearsals of *The Macropoulos Secret* have been postponed a week & I'm UNDER the Dr (at fearful expense!) undergoing dreadful pokes & pushes with medicated needles, swallowing pills of every conceivable shape & size & colour – mile a minute. It's a fearful bore & I suspect is "Nerves", but that doesn't make it any easier to bear.

To Mrs Peggy Butler at Maidenhall

Standish Arms Hotel, Colombia Heights, Brooklyn. 1 and 9 November 1957

I've taken enough pills to sink the Q Mary & am heartily sick of the whole business. There is no question of surgery. Pills, pills, pills – &

very expensive. I'm told they're anti-biotic, but have no conception of what that means, and think it's really best to swallow in Faith (blind) rather than knowledge (useful). *Mary Stuart* playing to excellent houses. *Macro Secret* being interesting to rehearse, postponed 'cos of Yours Truly (which was fortunately easy because *M Stuart* is doing roaring trade). No more – it's getting time for me to leave for work. Five mins thro' tree-lines streets, rather like Paris – houses of 1840 – then 25 mins in subway – much grubbier and more ramshackle than London equivalent – then another brief walk thro' "poor quarters" to the Phoenix. We lunch (the company I mean) at an excellent Italian place just down the road. One of the nice things about N.Y. is that it is a dozen "foreign" cities all in one – far far more cosmopolitan than any place I've ever been, even Toronto where they pour in daily from *all over* and will do so for years, a sort of outpost of Glasgow & Belfast.

To Mrs Peggy Butler at Maidenhall

Annaghmakerrig. 11 January 1958

Just a line to say that they've rung from Edinboro' to say that Sandy [maternal uncle] died, very peacefully, at one this morning. The funeral, not that the information seems very relevant, is at 2.30 on Tuesday. I don't think I'm going over for the funeral – it's such an expense; and what can one do? I think it better to make an effort with Wendy [Sandy's daughter], when and if she wishes some attention.

To Mrs Peggy Butler at Maidenhall

Montague Arms Hotel, Portstewart, Co. Derry. 2 March 1958

I'm here at the expense of Ballymoney Drama Festival, they run 13 nights with a diff. play each night. Haven't been here since I visited Hubert who was staying I think in this very hotel with his mother when he first began as Carnegie Librarian for Antrim. The place has grown quite a bit; but basically it has the same very grey, very very Northern feel – to me v. charming. I've been a long walk this A.M. along a wonderful strand & out to end of mole where the Bann runs out to sea. I don't think I've ever before seen a river actually meet the sea. It's impressive – a sort of death and resurrection in one.

Our London Season (mine 3 days; Judy's 5 days) was very nice. Geo. & Annette Chamberlain, delightful hosts. I had to spend most of the time with Bank & Accountants trying to determine what financial position really is – NOT easy because during last 3 years I've earned from many different sources, in several countries, all at diff. tax rates and all involving oh so much paper work.

Saw Julia in London. She came to party given by Geo. & Annette looking very elegant and *very* much the Young Lady About Town, but in a nice way – not at all loud or "Café Society" but very poised and entirely able to mingle easily with a group who were rather older than she.

To Mrs Peggy Butler at Maidenhall
Annaghmakerrig. 17 April 1958

We're all a little concerned – to say 'worried' would be too much – about Bunty. She has considerably aged. With guests present she just disappears from the conversation or else talks (during other conversation) in Baby Talk to the dog. She talks to, at, and about, it incessantly. Also we notice that her power of concentration is greatly less. She can't stick at anything for more than a few minutes. Of course this is only for your own ear. She's not being "difficult" or cross. But she is older and you must be prepared to find her so.

Becky is wonderfully better, seeing better & more cheerful.

Had an offer today to direct a new opera at La Scala, Milano. Rather gratifying & a very suitable b'day compliment – but dates will clash with Habimah.

To Mrs Peggy Butler
Annaghmakerrig. 11 June 1958

Murphy does at last seem to be getting to the very last stages of the wind-up [of Mrs Guthrie's will]. Meanwhile, do you agree to pay £25.0.0 to May Watson? – Alec Watson [farm labourer] was left this amount "if still in my service". Well, as you know, he'd already been called to a Higher Service. But since he and his father before him had worked here and since May is in low water don't you think we should give her the £25?

A very stiff and rather flustered old lady got out of the train at
Dundalk. Bunty. We both think she looks pale and feeble; and Anna
remarked the same thing. I think the real trouble is that she hasn't a
darn thing to do from morning to night – too stiff to garden; can't
concentrate on a book; just sits about in a sort of camping-out way
looking cross & miserable, & pouting at the weather.

To Mrs Peggy Butler at Maidenhall

c/o Migsie Davis, 53 Malone Road, Belfast. Undated, probably June 1958

All going well with *Bonefire*. I don't think the play[34] quite does, but do
think it's well acted. We rehearse this morning and then at 10.45 P.M.
– a bore, but the Orange Band, which is co-operating, can't rehearse
by day & the actors can only rehearse after their performance at the
Group Theatre, so …

To Mrs Peggy Butler at Maidenhall

Annaghmakerrig. 26 June 1958

Loved Julia's letter from London. It's splendidly long & vivid &
spontaneous – really easy natural writing, a real gift. Bunty read it
to Beckie whose only comment was a disapproving snort at all the
parties & running around!

Bunty is better; not so stiff and not nearly so grumbly and cross.
And – praise be – she has taken up some of her occupations again.
She now sits on a stool in the study at a sewing-machine with the
door wide open. But *busy* – not just sitting in a dejected heap.

To Mrs Peggy Butler at Maidenhall

Annaghmakerrig. 17 July 1958

The final a/c is now in the hands of the Death Duty authorities in
Dublin being assessed for Legacy Duty on the Residual Estate. Estate
Duty has been paid & Legacy Duty has been paid on all the specific
legacies. Murphy expects to hear from Dublin "any day now". *Bonefire*
got much better treatment than I expected – notices v.g. for acting &
prod. & not too bad for play; business excellent.

---

34   *The Bonefire* by Gerald McLarnon, Grand Opera House, Belfast, and Lyric Theatre,
Edinburgh.

To Mrs Peggy Butler at Maidenhall

Annaghmakerrig. 10 December 1958

Thank you *very* much for the Betjeman poems which I have not read and am very delighted to possess. It might seem more gracious to wait till after the Feast to say thank you; but we shall be in a flurry of forgotten toothbrushes, neglected Israeli visas and last minute duties. Life here is not uneventful – streams of visitors and last night a sit-down dinner for 22 persons when the Choir came to practice its carol for a Do at Killevan next Lord's Day: interminable hymns expressing the musical, poetical and theological ideas of 1853! Becky is really in rather good form. Daleys too have been socially enlivened because Lily [Becky's teacher niece] has given a party for her scholars, plus one past pupil, several Mums and two Dads, at Kilmore School. Sech a bakin o' cakes, sech a dressin' up of Big Ethel as Santa … it's all made for great interest & pleasure in which Becky has shared.

We had an Auction the week before and realised just under £50.0.0. out of chipped Delph, broken chairs, foul moth-eaten mats and the fragments of the morning-room over-mantle.

To Mrs Peggy Butler at Maidenhall

c/o Habima Theater, Tel Aviv, Israel. Saturday (Sabbath), 9 January 1959

We had a very pleasant journey indeed. The Theodore Heyl is new and specklessly spotlessly clean & wasn't crowded. The weather was fine & we had 4 hours in Napoli & were taken on a motor coach trip around the city and on to a volcano (Solferati? or something similar) not Vesuvius, but you go right down into the crater. Last eruption was 700 years ago but there are places where smoke still comes weaving up & mud boils – suitably épatant. The city is dreadfully crowded & poor but of course it's easier to be poor in such a climate than it is in Glasgow or Belfast and I must say the Neapolitans were quite living up to expectation (it was New Year's Day and a general holiday) and there was lots of loud brilliant singing in the streets & Catholic Repository decorations with paper roses and gilt twine.

We were met at Haifa by Fanny Lubitsch, the Artistic Director, & two others of Habimah management – we docked about 9 a.m. but by the time we'd done customs & immigration it was 11. We did the 90 miles down to Tel Aviv very fast by taxi in brilliant sunshine & thro' orange groves & palms (banana & date) with glimpses of a very blue – well, butcher-blue – Mediterranean. We're all three [Judy Guthrie & designer Tanya Moiseiwitsch] in a really delightful loaned apartment, *really* nice, balconies on both sides, north & south, tiled floors, nice furniture, comfortable beds and a fearfully grand non-resident housekeeper who speaks very good English & cooks like a cordon-bleu and buys in all our stores. So in all material ways we're on the pig's back. Only drawback is noise – it's a very crowded noisy city & we're right opposite a big Secondary School whose pupils, boys & gels, simply roar & squeal like beasts in a zoo. There's a stone-paved playground right opp. one balcony which is fun to watch as all the time there are gym classes & training in Singlesticks and games of basket ball. It's amazing to watch the young ladies at their gym. They're unbelievably busty and bummy and sedentary and all look as if they were called Beulah, but they dash & leap about and do things on The Horse, The Bars, The Ladder, that even Roedean would think quite splendid.

Work goes on at the theatre. Most of the cast very good – but Bassanio & Portia not happily cast – *very* bourgeois, but it can't be helped. It's hard work concentrating on the unknown lingo. I'm afraid the translation is pretty bad and very literal but they all use the word "old-fashioned": the language is changing & developing very fast. I gather this will sound as though the *Merchant of V* had been written by Bulwer Lytton. Oh well.

Tyrone and Judith Guthrie had no children. He took a truly familial interest in his only niece, Julia Butler, of Maidenhall, Co. Kilkenny, now in her early twenties and working in London as an interior designer. There she met Richard Crampton, a doctor from New York City working at St Bartholomew's Hospital, London. They discovered that they were both godchildren of Pamela Travers, author of *Mary Poppins*.

To Mrs Peggy Butler at Maidenhall
c/o George Chamberlain, 26 Wharton Street, London WC1. 3 April 1959

I've been meaning to write for ages but when *All's Well That Ends Well* is rehearsing [Shakespeare Memorial Theatre, Stratford-upon-Avon] we do 3 sessions a day – nine hours – at the end of which

I'm too tired to do anything but fall asleep. Now we're having a week "out" while *Othello* enters the last lap. But my other chores have been so behindhand that I had to stick to them – the book, my monthly "letter" for Montreal Star and a commissioned article for N.Y.Times – and yesterday night I was lecturing in Billingham, the New Town just outside Stockton-on-Tees, rather interesting, a sort of Workers' Garden City, rather nicely designed, I thought, but the newness of *everything* from trees to neighbours, must be a bit hard to live in.

What I really wanted to write about is Julia. Do you like her Young Man? Is it "serious"? If it might help her make up her mind, or even if it might just be pleasant, I would be very proud and happy if she liked to come to NYC as my "Secretary". I have to go there about April 27 for 10 days. And she could come too, free of expense. If that's too soon, shall be going again for longer, about Sept 5. It would be a chance to see potential in-laws without the problems of going on an obvious visit of inspection, and it would be a chance to sample, if briefly, the atmosphere of New York. Anyway, use your discretion whether or no, to broach it to Julia. And *of course* I shall not feel in the least wounded if the offer is not taken up.

Tomorrow we return to Stratford-upon-A and I must write, write, write at book which is rather badly behind schedule but is very nearly finished. I can't think of a suitable title – all the "light" ones sound fearfully flippant and common, all the serious ones fearfully pompous – My Life In Art sort of thing, which is out of all question! Work and Play; and *A Life In The Theatre*[35], are hottest favourites just now, but I'm hoping someone will dream up sumpin' livelier.

To Mrs Peggy Butler at Maidenhall

Memorial Theater, Stratford-upon Avon. 11 April 1959

I had to go to London y'day so was able to dine with Julia. She is prettily delighted to go to New York, and we all – Dick included – agreed it was a sensible idea to get an impression – both geographic & human – before being committed. He is a nice young man, as you say, very good looking but not at all in a flashy way, and did not give me,

---

35   *A Life in the Theatre* by Tyrone Guthrie (London 1960).

as do many young Americans, the feeling of blowing with every wind, of having no depth, no point of view about anything. His absorbed interest in medicine is a very heartening & endearing trait. And he gave me the impression of being a gentleman without being weak.

I had to go up to an emergency Vic Governors' meeting; present Chairman, Lord Esher, going to resign and they've asked me to take it on. The office is honorary. I'm very worried to know what to do for the best. It's quite an honour to be asked, but now that I've had the satisfaction of *being* asked, that's enough. I don't want the duties & obligations – the main one, in the short term, is to find more money out of the public purse. And that is just what raises problems: (1) I would rather be doing more creative & "artistic" work; (2) Annaghmakerrig. My inclination is to decline the job. But I feel that is putting my own work before what is, perhaps, an important responsibility. Nothing has to be decided quite at once. But one can't shilly-shally for long.

To Mrs Peggy Butler at Maidenhall

North British Hotel, Glasgow. 6 May 1959, following visit with niece Julia Butler to New York

I think it has all passed off & I'm sure has been a v.g. idea for Julia just to get a look at future in-laws & future environment. Louise, the wife, [Richard's mother] is a pretty little woman with gentle, quiet, good manners – smallish, dark, nicely and quietly dressed. I arrived early for dinner the evening we arrived. Louise was *dreadfully* nervous of the meeting and rather nice about it – "Don't think it's because I'm not eager to welcome Julia & to love her. It's just that I'm so anxious that she shall like us!"

Julia, natch, was very nervous too, but carried it off with great warmth and bel air. I was very proud of her.

Julia Butler and Richard Crampton were married a month later in Kilkenny. In the meantime Guthrie turned down the chairmanship of the Old Vic Theatre. He made Annaghmakerrig his permanent working base, surrounded by the almost feudal band of hereditary retainers – Burnses, Daleys, McGoldricks, McGormans and Maguires. Thence came many theatrical notabilities for meetings; it was here that the future Guthrie Theater in Minneapolis was masterminded by Peter Zeisler and Oliver Rea.

To Mrs Peggy Butler at Annaghmakerrig

Annaghmagkerrig. 7 June 1959

Just a line to say thank you for the wedding, and to congratulate you and Hubert on an *excellently* managed party.

As you know, I think a "white" wedding and all its strange mixture of golden bough, Christian sacrament, bourgeois vulgarity and solid good feeling is an unwise and unnecessary complication of what is already quite hard! But, since it had to be, it was a very, *very* nice white wedding. I know how flat you must now be feeling. But that will pass and life will go on. I think that's one of the really important facts which, through its sheer obviousness, we're inclined to overlook: life goes on. We don't always go on in tune or in rhythm of it; and then it's we – not the times – which are out of joint.

I won't ramble on as have an immense amount to do. "My publisher" keeps making rather sensible suggestions for amendments, subtractions & additions, which, tho' all small, trifling really, will add up to improvements & do add up to a hell of a lot of work. Oh it's so WONDERFUL to be HOME! Journey [from Kilkenny] was easy, tho' costly, in a grand & very warm hired Limousine with a dear old chauffeur. All the ones – Eddy, Becky, Bob, Seamus, even dreary old Lily – have been so genuinely delighted & moved to have us back – it's been a little upsetting. But the peace, the space, the healing familiarity.

Bunty is in bed – fibrositis – think she looks better today but has been really very poorly. Her great resource is to listen to "My Transistor" and then report with relish – & plenty of additions – the dislocation caused by the weather. Last night she informed us that "150,000 miles of roads in England were impassable" – this, so far, has been the Ace of Trumps – oh, if we except the freezing to death in his boat (as he delivered letters on an island in Upper Lough Erne) of the Postman at Lisnaskea.

Forgot to say – what should have been written much earlier – thank you for the Christmas Present: *The Country Girls* [by Edna O'Brien]. So far, Bunty is the only one who has read it & she thought it *horrid* & wishes it had never been written. I shall read it on the journey – I go to London tomorrow to begin Gilbert & S. Judy comes in a day or two but can't leave Bunty prone. We rehearse 2 weeks in London, then open *P. of Penzance* (which is the one they've been touring in USA) in a week at Brighton, followed by a week of *Pinafore* then open in London at Her Majesty's very early in Feb. After that back here, but not for long, 'cos of Robert Crean play[36] which rehearses in March.

Seamus [McGorman] *is* coming back – D.G. – they're to be wed in London and the first banns (of three) has been "cried" in Tottenham. Maguire boys have done *very* well in garden but are too young to be left unsupervised.

The break-up of Camlagh [Lady Rossmore's home] is dreadfully sad. Just like *The Cherry Orchard*. And "everyone" believes that, like Lopahin, Bobby Patton will GET the place. I can't see that that matters, but to the likes of May Haire-Forster [relict of Ascendancy] that's the real salt in the wound. Meanwhile – it's an ill wind – we are reaping a tremendous harvest of plants. Dot Rossmore, reasonably enough, sees no point in leaving them to a possibly unresponsive new owner. So we've been given literally truckloads of stuff – azaleas 50 or 60, laburnum, lilac and a lot of the biggish flowers like iris, dahlia, & that – oh & I don't know how many cherries.

Tanya [Moiseiwitsch] was here, for 2 nights only, to discuss final plans for stage at Minn. I took her to Nutt's Corner [Belfast airport] & called on Migsie Davis who is getting pretty old. I tried to make her come back with me but she's afraid of the cold (though nothing cd. be more arctic than her flat). The truth is that she won't face this place without Mrs G, & though that's most understandable, it's a pity, because she has so few friends, so few places to go, so few bulwarks of any kind.

To Mrs Peggy Butler at Maidenhall

Annaghmakerrig. 2 March 1960

I took a very low-spirited lady [Bunty Worby] to Belfast yesterday to stay a few days with Migsie Davis. *Nothing* was right. The weather, which I thought very pleasant, was "steamy", her glasses (worn because of conjunctivitis) were "AWFUL", the car "squeaked" and "bumped", the roads were "disgraceful", and, if ever we passed men working on

---

36   *A Time to Laugh* by Robert Crean, for Theatre Royal, Brighton.

the road or in the fields, Madam would say "I should *hate* to have to do that. Ugh! Isn't it awful!" However, the change will I'm sure be beneficial & a great peace reigns here.

Eddy [Daley] is going to retire, but gradually; and Seamus [McGorman] will take over, but gradually. Bob [Burns] knows & is quite happy. We're looking for another man to work outside and will not have great diff., I trust, in being "suited".

To Mrs Peggy Butler at Maidenhall

Annaghmakerrig. 20 April 1960

We have had a very social time as Dot [Lady] Rossmore came to stay over Easter and on Monday Mrs Voysey & her step-daughter Ella, who used to be Robert Donat's wife, and Ella's husband Richard Hall (a musicologist) came. Dot is *splendid* about washing up, emptying po's, or weeding groundsel, but, poor thing, is in sad nervous disorder & goes on & On & ON about their financial situation – or else, which is far more tedious – about "*what* Ann Leitrim said to Edie Devonshire and how Poopsie Northumberland was *diddled*, my dear, DIDDLED, by Tubby Westmoreland – but then everyone knows that Tubby is simply a Bolshie!". Belfast Telly to lunch and a weekend party on Sat. Mervyn Jones, son of Ernest Jones, Freud's biographer, &, from Dublin, actors – Jimmy Neylin, Mrs Ronald Ibbs & her cousin Josie MacAvin.[37]

To Mrs Peggy Butler at Annaghmakerrig

Stratford Shakespearian Festival, Ontario. 12 July 1960

A letter of mine must have miscarried because I wrote quite fully about Julia & Dick. We thought them *very* happy but both looking rather pale & tired. I hope you won't think it "interfering" but I suggest strongly that when you go over you don't stay with them in the flat – or only for a quite limited period. Maybe Julia will be disappointed if you don't go there for a bit, but it's really too small exc. for a quite brief stay.

37 Guthrie had directed Ronald Ibbs in *Hamlet*; his wife, Maureen Halligan, had played Ophelia. Josie McAvin was an internationally acclaimed film set decorator. James Neylin had appeared in Guthrie productions in London and New York.

You ask about our plans: *Pinafore* opens next Friday. Immediately after that I'm concerned with a TV programme (Canadian) of which I am author, about the S[tratford] Festival. Then July 25 we go to Minneapolis for 3 days; thence to Eugene, Oregon, where I have ten days of lecturing. Then back here, when not yet definite but probable will make a tape recording of *Pin*. Then, Sept 5, *Pin* opens in NYC at the Phoenix after a week's rehearsal to make 10 chorus replacements. Very soon after that we hope to fly back to A'Kerrig for a brief stay; back to Toronto to start rehearsals for Rob Davies' play *Love and Libel* approx. Oct 2. This is more of a Bradshaw's Guide than a letter but you requested the information.

To Mrs Peggy Butler at Maidenhall
Stratford Shakespearian Festival, Ontario. 24 July 1960

Pinafore is a succès-fou – here; but I think easily could be in N.Y. as well. It's excellently sung & acted & very gay to look at. We have negotiations in progress for a Videotape which may be extremely profitable but are by no means yet "in the bag".

In view of Eddy's condition, & fact that Bunty too is rather shaky, we have thought it best to cancel all New York plans for next year so as to be at home. It's financially sensible to do so because of success of *A Life In The Theatre* which is doing well in G.B. & still selling somewhat over here.

To Mrs Peggy Butler at Maidenhall
No address, Toronto. 12 August 1960

V.biz. putting *Pinafore* onto Videotape – not artistically rewarding (tho' technically rather interesting) tho' reasonably so financially.

Please write your plans & dates in case we can coincide in New York. We shall stay at the Standish Arms, &, if you & Hubert want & think it a good idea, could bespeak you a room with Harbour View. It is 20 min on Subway from Mid-Manhattan, 30 min from Julia, & about the same, if not longer, by taxi. But it is a great deal cheaper & quieter than comparable, more central, accommodation; & the View is truly glorious and can hold one pleasantly and quietly occupied by

Scene from *Love and Libel* by Robertson Davies with Robert Christie and Corinne Conly, Royal Alexandra Theatre, Toronto, directed by Tyrone Guthrie, 1960.

the hour. Also, having cooking & refrigeration arrangements saves a heap of money & energy otherwise rather pointlessly squandered on restaurants. I wish I knew more about your "arrangements", don't even know if you're boating or flying.

This would be Hubert and Peggy Butler's first visit to the United States, primarily to see Julia and Dick and to be present for the arrival of their first grandchild, Cordelia Crampton.

To Mrs Peggy Butler at Maidenhall
Stratford, Ontario. 13 August 1960

Just back from Eugene, Oregon, in the farthest N.W. simply *divine* geographically – great mountains & enormous trees, mainly Douglas fir; rather tedious professionally – huge, yawny, peach-fed hogs of students, and "professors" little better – the more one sees of U.S.A. the more scaring it is to think we are all politically tied to their lazy, complacent and materialistic chariot-wheels.

Quite tired, since previous day had left Portland at 7 a.m. & arrived Toronto 11 p.m. (By train it would have been 4 days & 5 nights!). Have a million letters to answer.

Bunty's letters tell NOTHING, but are well intentioned. I'm sure we are doing the right thing to be at A'kerrig next year. It *is* rather a wrench abandoning all other plans; but it certainly isn't as tho' environment or occupations were going to be anything but enjoyable & maybe even (spiritually if not pennywise) profitable! It's a bit fussing for you that there seems no mad rush to rent Maiden Hall. But, as you say, it could easily come at the 11th hour. [It did.] I was all agog to mention it to screamingly rich Minneapolitans, but, oddly enough, they seemed to prefer Florence or Miami (pronounced: My-yammy!).

To Mrs Peggy Butler at Maidenhall
Stratford, Ontario. 23 September 1960

Guess this is the last letter you'll get from me before you start – exciting. Perhaps when you arrive in N.Y. you'll give me a ring – make it a Person to Person call in case out & you get "through" almost instantly. The efficiency of the trunk telephone system really is one of the great advantages this continent possesses. See you in NYC. RING UP!

To Mrs Peggy Butler visiting New York City
c/o Basil Coleman, 69A South Drive, Toronto. 11 October 1960

Be *sure* and do the Round-Manhattan boat trip before the season discontinues. Be *sure* and do the El Grecos in the Met Museum. I'm assuming that with the Welch/Crampton circle you've enough social life, but if in error please correct and I can set various ones onto you who might be congenial. My last remaining Ivory Castles are in – natch! – the last stages of decay. Every day an ivy-clad buttress collapses and the wind whines and screams through the crevices. I

Paddy Chayefsky's *The Tenth Man*, with Don Harron (*centre*) Lou Jacobi, Jacob Ben-Ami and Jack Gilford, directed by Guthrie, New York, 1959.

think the man I'm now "under" is rather good – a Dutchman, quite young . It's simply at the back of beyond – way out to the very end of the subway and then way out again by bus into the purlieus amid slaughterhouses, Delinquent Crippleages, crematoria and Fowl Batteries.

Our rehearsals [*Love and Libel*] have started and are being pleasant – many old friends – but I haven't he greatest faith in the play's box-office potentiality. Never mind: there are other values.

To Mrs Peggy Butler visiting New York City

No address. 10 November 1960

Gideon[38] went very well last night to a most intelligently appreciative house. The press is all good exc. Kerr in H-Tribune, and he, tho' critical & saying (truly enough) that it's repetitious writes in a way that would make *me* want to see it. There is good interest at the B-office – not the mad success of his *The Tenth Man* but enough to ensure a good run & money back (barring unforeseen disaster) for investors. I have to go to Denver on Thurs (lectures & classes at the university) & thence to Minn: for Turning the First Sod.

Had another very homesick letter from Seamus McGorman [in England] so we can't help feeling a bit hopeful about his return to A'kerrig. It would make a *huge* alleviation to all sorts of anxieties. Bunty is well, boiler is working again, Fitches have visited, Bob is still in Adelaide Hosp but x-ray treatment has at long last begun.

To Mrs Peggy Butler visiting New York City

Pick Fort Shelby Hotel, Detroit. 14 November 1960

Our play [*Love and Libel*] is received in a *deathly* silence with plump, plump German-Americans scowling thro' thick glasses and ghurking after jumbo pork fries. This is a deadly but enormously rich place and more provincial than I've ever experienced – Belfast is a petit-trianon of elegant sophistication besides.

To Mrs Peggy Butler visiting New York City

Statler Hilton Hotel, Boston. 22 November 1960

With any luck we should be around N.Y.C. just about the accouchement & I hope I may be available to take turns at holding the Anxious Grandma's hand! & to squirt "Cologne Water" on the AG's fevered brow!

Play [*Love and Libel*] opened rather well here last night with human beings out front, not deadly Detroit automatons with their tiny

---

38   *Gideon* by Paddy Chayefsky, Plymouth Theater, New York. Guthrie had previously directed his exceptionally successful *The Tenth Man*.

minds concentrated, not on the matter in hand, but on how to make their silly ugly large product (the motor car or horseless carriage) fall to pieces the day after the guarantee expires. *L* & *L* opens at Martin Beck Dec 7. Unless otherwise informed I shall assume that you & H can use 4 seats – thought you might like to take senior Welch's – if too near the birth you might prefer to go later.

To Mrs Peggy Butler visiting New York City
Statler Hilton Hotel, Boston. 30 November 1960

Six seats will be available for our Opening [D.V.] at the Martin Beck Theater, N.Y., Wed Dec 7. When shall we meet? What about you have us to lunch or evening meal on Friday 9th? R.S.V.P. We leave for Minn on the Sunday and arrive at HOTEL ALGONQUIN N.Y. the previous (i.e. next) Sunday afternoon. I'll ring up.

Guthrie in the signal box of the abandoned railway station in Newbliss, Co. Monaghan, 1960 – later the office of Irish Farmhouse Preserves.

Tyrone Guthrie was offered a knighthood by Queen Elizabeth II in the 1961 New Year Honours 'for services to the theatre'. At Annaghmakerrig the departure of Colonel 'Simon' Fitz-Simon for his ancestral home at Glencullen and the death of the former farm steward Eddy Daley made it all the more urgent to persuade an apparently dubious former farmhand Seamus McGorman to return from England to take up the position of steward. The health of the elderly Bunty Worby and Becky Daley continued to decline. Hubert and Peggy Butler let their house, Maidenhall, and spent most of the year in the US with their daughter Julia, son-in-law Dick Crampton and new granddaughter Cordelia (the Mrs Welch referred to in New York is Dick's mother). Hubert Butler undertook a considerable amount of travelling in the US, which resulted in several published essays.

To Mrs Peggy Butler visiting New York
Annaghmakerrig. Christmas Day, 1960

Season's Greetings!

We got here last Thurs about midday. I went right round to Daley's. Found Becky & Ethel who were inclined to blubber when they saw me and then pulled themselves together. We were told the rosary of the past moves which were "peaceful" and considerably assisted by the presence of Lora (Daley, nurse), who, with Bunty splendidly in attendance, took charge & was able to confront the reality of Death [of Eddy Daley] with concentration on the pillow-thwacking, the sips of water & so on, which I guess elude the attention of the Voyager sinking downward, downward, to the Styx, but which mean so *much* to The Watchers, who want so dreadfully to feel that all that can be done *is* being done.

Shamus [McGorman] seems to be taking charge in the biggest way, the garden makes Kew look like an untidy, infertile mess, the boat-house has been trimly resurrected, a circular saw has been borrowed and we have more neatly piled logs than for at least 60 years – and he looks happy. So does Bob. So does John Maguire – this moment visiting chilly Burns' which we regard as a good indicator that he and Bob are working happily together.

I guess you are driving Julia up the walls with grandmaternal injunctions to do this, not do that … WARM it first … but that it's great fun for you both to be able to play at dolls together and really nice for Julia to have An Elder Woman to support the alarming transitions from the ordered white efficiency of the Hospital to the cosy squalor of the Native Hut, when suddenly she is alone with the responsibility … a great help, of course, to have a resident Dr – albeit young. ANN CORDELIA. Well. Of course Ann will do – BVM's mum and all that – but Cordelia. Well. Bunty and I can't understand why the poor child couldn't have been called something *nice*! – Marilynn, or Darlene.

To Mrs Peggy Butler visiting New York
Annaghmakerrig. 4 January 1961

Happy New Year! Hope Cordelia and her Ma are doing well. You know all news will be eagerly gobbled up.

Bunty, who has been roped in as a willing but monumentally inept private sec, and I, have been over our ears in "Knight-letters". We try to do thirty per day, but even at that rate, which takes more doing than you might imagine, we shall be at them for *weeks*. Judy and I have been quite poorly since getting back, we were both coughing and hawking like nobody's business.

Becky is very sorry for herself – it's understandable and pitiful; but really you'd think she was the only person in the world who had ever been the victim of a stroke, or ever been bereaved. Her appetite for sympathy, and for a new audience, are absolutely boundless and one tries to supply a bit of both. It simply doesn't occur to her that her failure to "get on" with the Daley girls is in the tiniest bit her fault. They are awful drearies – at least Lily and Ethel are, but I don't think they are the monsters of callous brutality that B. really believes. I think it's principally because she's bored – and they sure are bores – that she has to amuse herself with believing that they treat her so badly.

To Mrs Peggy Butler visiting New York

Annaghmakerrig. 9 January 1961

The knight business: would fain have declined the honour but everyone said it would be very ungracious and very 'enfant terrible' and that I must Be My Age; and certainly I can't see that it does anyone the least bit of harm – just one doesn't greatly "believe in" it. The nice thing has been the torrent of letters and telegrams – Mrs McCabe [Newbliss postmistress] can never have known the like. One day sixty letters came – largely from overseas – I think she has rather enjoyed it. Very nice letters from, among others, Kenneth Sandberg who last taught me when I was eleven. I had thought he had long been a denizen of Heavenly Mansions; but no; a clergyman at Wisbech!

Joe Hone was here for Friday and Sat nights. Had to go back Sunday aft in order to be present at first rehearsal Monday A.M. of new musical piece with the presentation of which he is connected. As far as I dared ask – just couldn't seem to be TOO spearing – it's not his own money; and he gets paid a weekly wage. To me it didn't sound a very interesting or ambitious project; but I guess it might easily make some dough and anyway it's all experience for Joe, of the kind which he evidently wants. He read to me and discussed at considerable length a synopsis for a film about Joseph and his Brethren which we had discussed before. I thought what he had done extremely impractical and pretty juvenile, but not *by any means* dull or untalented. He rather badly lacks "education" – is forever landing out with rather pretentious malapropisms, and French words which don't always quite mean what he means them to mean. I think – indeed I'm sure – in a year or two he will have the sophistication not to reveal so artlessly the chinks in his own armour; and also will, by dint of native wit, repair many of the chinks let by so scrappy an education. His clothes were sadly poor and in poor repair; but he had a good warm overcoat and I rather think the appearance was quite a carefully studied version of the Beatnik.[39]

---

39   Joe Hone (1939–2016) went on to publish several novels and travel books as well as the memoir *Wicked Little Joe* (Dublin 2009), which is mainly about his upbringing with the Butlers at Maidenhall.

Becky is fairly well. Naturally Eddy's departure leaves a very aching gap; and she and Ethel are far too à deux and mutually uncongenial. Bunty is nearly seventy six and begins to show it. She mostly sits with her feet in the study grate and listens to Lancashire comedians on her new radio. She was *very* good over Eddy's illness – a real tower of strength; but is, I think, now rather "feeling" the effort.

To Mrs Peggy Butler visiting New York
Annaghmakerrig. 29 January 1961

I've been helping Becky over her money, which causes her great – but not I think entirely unpleasurable – anxiety. With Hubert's aid she invested a portion of her fortune, which is not inconsiderable, but the rest, and indeed the greater part, has been sitting idle in the bank for twenty years. And the sole reason is that she thought it would be more accessible there in case of emergency. It is now going into the Leeds Building Society. It doesn't pay a v.g. rate of interest but the, to her, great advantage that they will cough up any or all of the investment by return of post.

She is naturally rather disturbed and agitated by not knowing what the plans of the Daley girls are. Joan is contemplating matrimony, though not I think immediately, and no one knows what the hell poor Ethel will want to do. I have, of course, said that they can stay on in the [farm steward's] house as long as they wish; and I expect Ethel will attend on Beckie till the last but it's not a congenial alliance between the pair of them. Becky intends, fairly enough, that Ethel shall have the residue of her property; but she doesn't know whether Ethel really has other plans in the back of her mind or no. There is a great deal of secrecy about little. It's all sad; and not easy for B.

I don't know if you remember – I guess not – but the cathedral in *Love and Libel* was represented by a very large, handsome brass chandelier. At the end I bought it in secondhand at a knockdown price; and it's just arrived. I haven't seen the packing-case, but they say it's as big as a cottage; and indeed the chandelier may be too big even for the dining room, for which it is intended. In that case I shall have to present it to Aghabog church.

Madame de Staël has been in the news for some reason, a new biog I guess. Anyway I was inspired to write these lines:

The trouble with Madame de Staël
Was a horrible pain in the baël
The upshot of this
Was Dieresis
Over which we must now draw a vaël.

To Mrs Peggy Butler visiting New York
Annaghmakerrig. 29 January 1961

On Saturday we leave for London for the Dubbing. I'll tell you *all* about it, if spared. Alec Guinness says it would make splendid fieldwork for an anthropologist. Two guests are allowed to witness the ongoings; so we've asked Peter Kesteven [cousin Norah] who has accepted with pleas. So we shall meet in our worn, mended, Best Clothes, looking as though we'd just WALKED all the way from a Manse in the Highlands.

Oh – I knew there was something I had to tell – not a nice piece of news: Chrissie [former parlour-maid]'s husband, Jack Howe, took his own life last Friday – all MOST shocking and unexpected and accountable. It is felt the only explanation that holds any water is that the long, long strain of her illness at last wore him into a nervous storm. He got up very early in the morning, took a carving knife out of the drawer, went out and cut his throat in the field.

Miss Christine Burns weds her rather nice, not very thrilling, Willie on April 12. A three tier cake is taking formidable shape upstairs and a Breakfast for forty is bespoke at the Lennard Arms, Clones. I think the young people would prefer something quieter, but, as always, the Bride's Mum can't bear not to make it An Occasion. I guess really that Nuptials are as good a reason as any for a party and it's very understandable for hostesses to want to break out and express themselves just once or twice in a lifetime. Pity it's *such* a tease for the b and b'groom and all the guests!

I was summoned to Radio Eireann a couple of weeks ago to have lunch with the new (American) Director of Irish T.V. He seemed to me to be the complete babe-in-the-wood as regards Ireland, and indeed most other things, including T.V. A very nice fellow – big and gentle and oh so idealistic. He's been in S. America for some years setting up radio and T.V. stations financed by C.B.S. I don't think he has even *thought* that there may be other ways of life – be they better or worse – than the Big Business pattern of U.S.A. I think, poor lamb, he's going to have a series of very disillusioning shocks when he tumbles to the fact that there very definitely is a Dublin Way of Life which bears only the dimmest resemblance as C.B.S. defines it. Maybe he's not by any means as simple a Simon as I supposed; but I think he is; and I think he got the job, which he is naively *delighted* about, because there was not a very strong field; and because he is a good Boston Catholic who only happens by the merest accident to be called Roth and not O'Brien or Curley.

To Mrs Peggy Butler visiting New York
Annaghmakerrig. Undated, post-10 April 1961

Burns nuptials evidently a smashing succès – sorry to have missed it/them. Bride & groom came back last Sunday very pink & self-conscious, having spent the honeymoon motoring – Killarney of cahss. The Present Display was impressive and a source of immense satisfaction to the Bride's Mum. Bob, I think, had truly enjoyed the romance, the poetry of it all, and blubs a little as he tells Mary has estimated the cash value of the presents and knows what she thinks, down to the last decimal, each Auntie and Cousin *ought* to have given, compared to their income. It's only fair to say that most vastly exceeded all reasonable expectations.

   Yesterday we fetched Rob Crean from Collinstown airport. He is a young American with a bun face & pop eyes & seven children who has written what I think a wonderfully interesting & funny play – far from ready – I think it's about the impact of the RC church on materialistic U.S.A. – not sure, nor, I suspect, is he. But it has *wonderful* characters & lines. He's here to try to finish it in a quiet "relaxed" atmosphere away from the hectic pressure of writing TV scripts to fill the mouths of the seven fledglings.[40]

40   Guthrie subsequently directed Robert Crean's *A Time to Laugh* at the Theatre Royal, Brighton.

To Mrs Peggy Butler visiting New York

Annaghmakerrig. 12 May 1961

We have the boat in action on the lake & Jack Merigold (Stage Manager, Stratford, Ont.) is a keen angler & I have been rowing for him quite a bit. Bunface is still writing away and one way & another we've been quite sociable.

I am CONDUCTING (!) at the request of that goat Chancellor Williamson a Hymn Festival in Clones Church. A choir of about 30 or 40 – sweetly eager but totally inexperienced chanteurs. We've had 3 *long* practices – 'pract-eyes-ez' - & a Sunday yowl-out of hymns & a unison spoken Magnificat. Maureen Burns & I sole representatives of Aghabog; but 3 from Newbliss; a whole raft from Clones & Newtownbutler & odds & sods from elsewhere – oh & a bevy of tiny, youngish, infinitely mild clergy.

Christopher Fitch [Fitz-Simon] brought Migsie Davis down from Belfast the other day for lunch & the afternoon quite a successful occasion.

To Mrs Peggy Butler visiting New York

c/o Festival Theatre, Stratford, Ontario. 21 June 1961

We've started *Pirates of Penzance* – a v.g. group. Last night the theatre opened with a really splendid perf of *Coriolanus*. We've cancelled our tickets for *Henry VIII* tonight & *Love's Labours Lost* tomorrow because I'm really not well enough for the effort after a day's rehearsal of *Pirates*. Silly & a bore but just has to be faced. I get very breathless & exhausted rather too easily. I'm under a quite nice ear, nose & throat specialist – all Drs seem agreed the trouble is not heart but bronchial due to swallowing mucus produced by inflamed sinus. I do resent not being able to get going properly till midday – in the morning I'm just choked & can do nothing but gasp & feel feeble. *Don't allude to this*.

I was a week in New York absolutely buzzing like a bluebottle. Didn't even ring Julia. There was no hope of meeting & jolly screams on the telephone are such a tease. It was very trying, hot, damp weather – one evening the entire electric system conked out in central Manhattan. It was quite weird – no light, no heat, no air-conditioning, no elevators, no subway, no traffic-lights, even no T.V.! It was rather reassuring to see how *nicely* the public took it all. Suddenly, instead of the screaming, pushing, spoilt New Yorkers, people were calm & steady & kind to one another – & *even* considerate of the infirm.

To Mrs Peggy Butler visiting New York

Standish Arms Hotel, New York. 19 September 1961

Well, here we are in our old abode. The view is *wonderful*; &, oddly, I thoroughly enjoy commuting by subway; & Judy enjoys the cooking.

Our departure from A'kerrig was distinctly fraught. Seamus McGorman skipping off is a fearful blow. He may come back. We shall see. [He did.] The two Maguire boys are young enough not to be quite on their own & neither is old enough for a car licence; so, with Bob Burns away in hospital it really is rather isolated for poor Bunty and when things aren't *just* as she's accustomed to have them – well, she's about as flexible as a biscuit! And is now very easily rattled & distressed. Judy has been quite seedy since we got here. We thought it was just the fatigue of the flight plus the fuss of departure but it's obviously been more than that – probably one of these "li'l virus infections' they're always gabbing about here. The temp. when we arrived & for 2 days after was high in the 90s, with oh such "humidity", the air was wetter far than water. It was like living inside a very hot lemon-sponge.

I rehearsed *Tenth Man* road company for 3 days – well, sort of supervised the very nice young Israeli man who's really doing it. It's going off on a long, long tour and is supposed to make all our fortunes. The Co. is excellent. Now we've started Gideon. Frederic March (Angel) & Douglas Campbell (Gideon) – a lot of the play is just between the two of them so they'll rehearse alone for a week. If *Gideon* goes well we shall have quite a lot of free time in Philadelphia. We might do some sightseeing. Of course if the play's in trouble I shall have no time at all.

Pirates is on at Phoenix – v.v. good press. It too goes on the road later, for 8 weeks, then, plus Pinafore, to London, England, in the new year.

To Mrs Peggy Butler visiting New York

Standish Arms Hotel, New York. 29 September 1961.

I've written (congratulating) Joe [Hone] – no, you hadn't written engagement before – in the most cordial terms. Very glad to hear that you & Hubert approve of Miss if she is a wise and steady person that will do him all the good in the world. His trouble, I'm sure, is that he has known that he has never been a really essential part of anyone else's life; and that makes it difficult to hitch onto life in general.

Meanwhile, *Gideon*,[41] which should be a thrilling & interesting piece of work, is just a wee bit more than I feel able for, so it's all rather a struggle. Judy spends part of every day at the beach – normally Brighton Beach, wh. is near Coney Island – wild in summer but v. quiet already with most of the summer flies in hibernation. *Tenth Man* tour opened in Washington y'day with acclaim. Booking is huge & far in advance and Arthur Cantor [impresario] says we shall all make our fortunes & that I can "endow Cootehill" – an ambition which I especially cherish!

To Mrs Peggy Butler at 239 Kenyon Avenue, Swarthmore, PA
Standish Arms Hotel, New York. 15 November 1961

Back here after very nice restful 2 days with Lola Kipnis [playwright] in Westport. Having a hectic 2 days & leaving for Denver at 9 tomorrow morning. Judy, Tanya, Douglas Campbell & Oliver Rea proceed to Minn on Sunday where we all partake in the Ceremonies of Cutting the first sod!

To Hubert Butler visiting New York
Annaghmakerrig. 28 December 1961

I hope your NY/Welch/Hotel Xmas panned off well. I am sure the Welch's will have done all poss. to make it so. We had a nice time... actual Xmas Day a little marred by the infirmities of eld. Miss Worby *crippled* by fibrositis & alternating very low & very snappy & rude! Geo Chamberlain (now over 70) very feeble & low with a cold; Annette (at a Difficult Time of Life) very jumpy & "odd"; Freddy Crooke low with a cold; Judy ditto; Yours Truly inclined to have diarrhoea (it can't be spelt quite like that!) owing to intensive & continuous cold. Then Paddy & Dot (Lady) Rossmore came to lunch & were both dreadfully – but DREADFULLY – low over impending demolition of Camlagh

---

41   Guthrie's production of *The Tenth Man* by Paddy Chayefsky had run for over a year
      in New York. *Gideon* was Chayefski's new play.

House. So the gaiety was a wee bit false. Now Chamberlain et Cie have gone & Tanya is here very briefly and mainly on biz.

You certainly seem to be flying around. I think you'll like Chicago – it's so lively and vigorous. Delighted you think P so much better – long may the improvement continue.

Over the previous five years Guthrie, with the New York stage-director Peter Zeisler and impresario Oliver Rea, had been making plans to establish a permanent repertory theatre removed from the commercial procedures, trades-union regulations and general mindset of Broadway. They sought submissions from cities with a strong existing artistic infrastructure plus the money and the will to create and maintain such a company. Minneapolis was selected as having the necessary qualifications in abundance. In Ireland, plans were under way to renovate a vacant estate cottage for Seamus McGorman, returning from England with his family to take up the post of farm steward, while Becky Miles and her niece Ethel Daley remained in the adjacent cottage.

To Mrs Peggy Butler at 239 Kenyon Avenue, Swarthmore, PA
Annaghmakerrig. 1 January 1962

Happy new year! You asked about the sod-turning in Minneapolis. I arrived at Minn of a Sunday evening in November from Denver (having spent the morning motoring in the Rocky Mountains) & was met by Oliver Rea, Judy & Douglas Campbell, oh, and Tanya [Moiseiwitsch], who'd arrived half an hour earlier from N.Y.C. Oliver spends half his time now in Minn & has a hired car so he drove us to motel where we were all putting up. Then we went to dinner with the local man in charge of the office & the promotion. That was alright exc. that when discussing the procedure for next morning he announced that he was arranging for Yours Truly to be photographed "driving a bulldozer on the site". This lead to a near row between him & Douglas. Douglas started giving him all sorts about the silliness & vulgarity of the idea. Luckily he is rather a gentle, mild little party, otherwise.

The ceremony was at 8.30 a.m. on a day of bitter, bitter black Prairie cold with a screaming wind & a sky the colour of pewter. Hot coffee & doughnuts were served in the kitchen of Walker Art

Gallery (adjoining the site) then we adjourned with chittering teeth & stood under a pretty elm tree which was about to be uprooted as the first step in preparing the site. John Cowles (Chairman of the Committee) made a very brief, sensible, to the point little speech & handed me a – Snow Shovel! with which I was to cut a stiffly frozen Sod. I attacked it with utter determination really to scoop up an adequate, if token, amount of earth – & panting heavily, & near black in the face, did succeed in hoking up enough soil to plant two hyacinths. Then, still panting, made a v. brief (but *serious*) speechette. Then a vast Behemoth rushed at the poor tree & literally pushed it out of the ground.

Then there was a press conference and a lot of terribly boring but I suppose necessary "speaking" for the telly, & photographs. Then there was a celebratory Luncheon with the committee – at the Minneapolis Club, very grand, and fabulously fabulously OLD – way back to 1897. Rather pleasant occasion - & hardly was that over before it was time to attend the Tea Party given by the very nice & supremely capable wife of the Chancellor of the University – for us to meet the "McKnight Fellows", graduates of the Univ. Drama Dept. who have been awarded scholarships to join the theatre – one actor, one on the business side, one in design and one to study production – as sort of apprentices. They seem to be 4 very nice, eager, high-souled splendid young things – all except the Business One who has a very long thin nose & thick glasses & uses words like Usage=use, Commence=begin & Weather Conditions = weather; & who will almost for certain turn out to be the Pick of the Basket, far, far outstripping the splendid young gods & goddesses with white regular teeth & fine co-ordination.

The Chancellor's residence – high on a bluff over the Mississippi – is quite something. It's white, sort of Colonial-Queen Anne style, with a portico & big rectangular painted windows. In comparison, Buck Pal is a HUT with clay and wattles made. The Chancellor-ess, a very handsome, merry, really charming lady runs it with the aid of two non-resident, part-time cleaners. She has three delightful children of school age, is "on" I don't know how many committees; she obviously thought nothing of giving a tea party for about 60 guests, having been at the sod-turning at 8.30, the Luncheon at 12.30, & no doubt going on to several other events in the later course of the day. Extraordinary.

To Mrs Peggy Butler at 239 Kenyon Avenue, Swarthmore, PA
c/o Geo & Annette Chamberlain, 26 Wharton Street, London WC1. Undated, early 1962

"The Accolade". P.K. [cousin Norah Kesteven] came up and "did" it with us. We met at 9.45 in the lobby of the Hotel Rubens which was full of old ladies in grey BAWLING into one another's hearing aids. Annette [Prévost] drove us down in state in their Consul and had ordered Flowers – a hyacinthine spray for Judy & a red carnation for me. She had also lent Judy her best (black suede) gloves & best handbag (black "leather" but very quietly good) and J. had a quite grand black *sort of* hat bought in N.Y. – a piece of gauze with black appliqué "petals". Peter [cousin Norah] was in a dark tweed coat with a fur collar and a modern but simply frightful feather hat of elaborate simplicity – not feathers at all I think but very convincingly wrought plastic. We walked round to the Palace by coming thro' a side gate, found ourselves ahead of several hundred others who had known no better than to Queue at the main gate.

It was rather fun seeing the inside of B. Pal. You go through the Façade into a courtyard with a big Porte-Cochère over main door which leads into a v. grand hall *full* of footmen in scarlet tailcoats. Then "Recipients" were marshalled up one stairs & "Spectators" up another. This meant that P & J were conducted straight to the scene of operations & got v.g. seats as near as anything to where Q. Mum was going to stand. I was marshalled into a very handsome sort of "Gallery" lined with portraits, mostly of obscure Hanoverian princesses but one splendid Van Dyke and the Winterhalter group of Q Vic & P Albert surrounded by very pink Royal Kiddies – much seen in Repro in old-fashioned boarding-houses.

After rather too long a very tall, very grand, elderly Life Guard's officer, in what Ouida would call Full Regimentals, came and told us what we were to do – when to step forward, when to bow, when and where to kneel, when to bow again after the Royal shake-hands, when to step back, where to go then. All seriously & sensibly & in very upper class choice of monosyllabic Saxon words. Then we were formed into lines like a very elderly dancing-class & waited to Move Off.

Then we moved off – down another long gallery with more Regency sofas, more Early Victorian crimson Denmark pelmets, until we came to a halt before *the* most enormous Rubens with big rose-pink bare ladies carrying-on with burnt-Siena satyrs amid piles of fruit, dead birds and raw carcases – *wonderfully* painted but not at all the thing if one were feeling even the weeniest bit bilious. Well then from another part of the forest were heard the strains of God Save played with less rhythm than you could believe possible; and there was a frou-frou from ladies & gents rising to their feet and pushing back their chairs as one knew that Q Mum had made her entrance & the Ceremony had begun.

By degrees the Queue moved forward and now, under Haydon's Christening of the Infant Prince of Wales, I could see into the big room where it was all going on. It's a hideous great room with a tunnel shaped roof; at one end in a gallery, against gold organ pipes, the Band of the Life Guards resplendent in scarlet & gold playing endlessly and very very poorly. They have to play soft enough not to be rowdy & interruptious, but not loud enough to drown the creaking of royal stays, the snapping of elderly tendons as Recipients fall to their knees, the Vapidity of Sweet Nothings which Royalty has to utter to each flustered Recipient. The Bandmaster was oh so plump and pink & white, and conducted in a dainty, wand-waving rumpetty-tumpetty style. One expected the Overture to Iolanthe, the Merrie England selection & a pot-pourri of Schubert. But no: it was Haydn, Mozart, then, rather abruptly, Oklahoma!

Down each side of the room were tiers of seats, sideways on to the spectacle & in the middle, rows of chairs as in a church only the chairs were gilt Ballroom type. I should think there were 750 to 1000 people there. At the apse end, so to say, a sort of Howdah of extreme ugliness – vaguely Indian, I think, in "inspiration", which made a sort of baldachino over two simply frightful great clumsy thrones with red velvet lodging-house curtains & a huge lion & unicorn in repoussée embroidery on a shield above and behind the thrones. There was Axminster on a Daïs, & beefeaters, most of whom were in pince-nez that didn't accord too well with their ruffs & halberds & gave an air of Amateur Gibert & Sullivan. Oh, & there were great clumping candelabra – everything you can think of that made it look like a throne-room in a Cricklewood film set in 1926.

Queen Mum – dumpy but most charming – stood on the daïs, and bevies of grand officers (the very lowliest of whom was a Duke and the very youngest 77 years of age) titter-tottered and didder-doddered about with trays of medals & ribbons and an altogether too realistic sword with which she clapped Knights on the shoulder – right, then left. The Lord Mayor of Bolton – or was it Barrow-in-Furness? – made to rise after one blow and very nearly had his ear cut off. Recipients had to approach from the Q's rt. side; wait behind an aged Marshall until one's name was called by another aged Marshall, then advance, bow, kneel – upon a sort of velvet commode with a handle which made the operation sensible for even the goutiest dotard, get your two whacks with the sword, shake hands with Her Majesty, exchange a few very conversational nothings, shake hands, step back 3 paces, bow, push off. Simple enough, but you'd hardly credit how many forgot to bow or refused to "back", like excited cart-horses. I did my routine correctly but when asked "What are you going to do next?" I couldn't remember. My mind, as they say, was a blank. But then I blurted out (untruly) "Going to America" and started to burble about Minneapolis.

We got a cab & went to Brown's Hotel where Geo, Annette, Kenneth & Gwyneth Rae joined us for lunch. It was very cosy & jolly.

To Mrs Peggy Butler at 239 Kenyon Avenue, Swarthmore, PA
Theatre Royal, Brighton, England. 25 January 1962

We're ensconced in a delightful flat overlooking the sea lent by Murray MacDonald [impresario] who is in U.S.A. Judy has had 'flu, short but sharp, & is somewhat "pulled down". *Pirates of Penzance* opened with the greatest of éclat on Monday – most satisfactory raws o' lawter & cheers at the end. *Pinafore* opened last Thurs. All press v. good exc Tynan in Observer who hated the Opus, but thought it well done, & Financial Times which hated everything about the evening; rest were all favourable.

We go home on Friday. Joe [Hone] is there right now, I hope; is to be installed in the Blue Room to WRITE – what the Writing is, I don't know, but doubtless all in in due course be revealed. Seamus is back; & we must set work in hands as soon as possible to turn Laundry, Coal House, & Eddy's Bedroom into a "Duplex" – think with

Farm cottages at Annaghmakerrig. The McGorman family was installed in the nearer in 1962 while Aunt Becky and Ethel Daley remained in the other.

a little titivating it can be v. nice as all faces south. We'll probably move laundry sinks into Breakfast Room which has already sunk into a rather slummy "Airing Room"-cum-store for cardboard boxes & ten thousand other articles which are just too good to throw away but never seem to "come in". One couldn't obviously push Becky & Ethel out into the snow. And, looking ahead, the property is surely more "possible" as a series of moderately detached residences than as a single, rambling, shambling Palazzo.

I wonder when Hubert gets back from the Far West. How very interesting to meet Eudora Welty [Pulitzer-prize novelist]. All his tales will be of great interest and I hope there'll be plenty of filth about weird rites in Californian garden suburbs. If you want an interesting novel (don't be put off by the title which is an obvious aberration) read *The Heart is a Lonely Hunter* by Carson McCullers – about a group of interesting mixed characters in a town in the Southern States of U.

To Mrs Peggy Butler at 239 Kenyon Avenue, Swarthmore, PA
Annaghmakerrig. Undated, February 1962

We have had an agitating night. Bunty took a heart attack. She went to bed in quite good form between 10.30 & 11.00. At 1 (approx.) she came to our room & asked Judy to come to her. J. found her very breathless & frightened & inclined to be sick. I rang Dr Gunn – OUT; so rang Dr Maguire – also OUT. Very fortunately we have Isabel Lencke, née Scaife, Christopher & Gillian's niece & her daughter Stephanie staying. Walter Lencke (Isabel's husband) died last summer & they are feeling very bereaved & Stephanie's had flu, so they're by way of recuperating. All this is preamble to fact that Stephanie's a Nurse, nearing the end of her training at St Thomas'. So she was VERY helpful. Maguire came about 2.30 (A.M.) with his wife – also a nurse. Bunty was by now extremely collapsed & we none of us thought she'd pull through. I don't think she was in great pain any of the time but great discomfort & frightened & *very* low, also VERY cross! Maguire gave her I don't know how many injections of this, that & the other, incl. heart stimulant, heart sedative, pethadine & morphine – I think honestly he just pumped into her anything he could think of in the order they occurred to his kind but sadly un-reassuring mind. However, all credit to him, she rallied and is still alive (11.30 A.M.) & comfortable & declares she is MUCH better. Stephanie says her pulse is anything but reassuring & clearly doesn't take a rosy view.

To Mrs Peggy Butler at 239 Kenyon Avenue, Swarthmore, PA
Annaghmakerrig. 23 February 1962

I know you'll be anxious to hear Bunty is a little better but still in a v. grave condition – I don't know well enough what it's all about to embark upon explanation … something about CLOTS, which may move &, I think, other clots might join. She ought to be where tests of her blood can be taken & electrocardiogram used to test heart – but it's out of the question to move her – yet. She is comfortable, even cheerful; & is being kept ABSOLUTELY quiet. Stephanie Lencke is being splendidly responsible, but it's not exactly a holiday for her, poor girl. All are rallying round very well, incl Joe [Hone] who sat up with the patient from 1 A.M. to this morning. We take this duty in turns. I fancy when/if she's well enough to move, the Dr (Maguire, who's done well) will send her to Hospital, but whether Monaghan or Dublin we don't know.

To Mrs Peggy Butler at 239 Kenyon Avenue, Swarthmore, PA

Annaghmakerrig, 25 February 1962

Bunty was removed to hospital last night. The fact that she was fit to move indicates a considerable improvement. She's in a private room in Monaghan Hosp. Stephanie, who's inclined to take the gloomy rather than the roseate view, says she'll be in hosp. from 4 to 6 months. I just don't know. And of course there is considerable likelihood of further attacks. Ambulance came about 7.15 + stretcher, hot bottles, blankets & a very nice competent nurse as well as the driver. Bunty was fully conscious but heavily under the influence of sedatives so didn't fuss at all. Stephanie went with her & Joe took own car for shopping in Monaghan & to fetch Stephanie home. He has been most co-operative & helpful, & room NOT a slum; but he is – rather tragically – essentially a soloist. A helpful marriage might do wonders. But I question whether, with his background, he has it in him to be a real *partner*.

To Mrs Peggy Butler at 239 Kenyon Avenue, Swarthmore, PA

Annaghmakerrig. 2 March 1962

Bunty is, if anything, better. No one can predict the immediate outcome and, if there is to be a long term view, it isn't rosy. No use thinking far ahead.

Joe & Lenckes still here. Robert Crean, author of the play I'm about to do [*A Time to Laugh*] has now joined the party; & Lewis Allen, the American end of the management for Crean play, probably comes tonight. So we are very much House Full, & in addition have Eddie McPhillips (electrician from Drum) & Asst. Electrician every day for midday meal. Mercifully Anna [Kelly, cook] really enjoys the bustle. Crean, Allen & I have to leave next Thurs. Judy, I think, will stay anyway for a while so as not to leave Bunty; & I think Isabel & Stephanie may stay a bit too.

Simon & Ailish [Fitz-Simon] came to supper last night. They have let Glencullen for 8 weeks & are paying A Round of Visits, beginning with Mattie & Marc [Killen, in Monaghan]. Simon was delightful; A at her very very worst. She gave a display of what one can only suppose was meant to be Fascinating Woman of a Certain Age ENCHANTING an intellectual circle – which meant that she talks non-stop pretentious rot &, literally, shouted down all competitors. Two gins & a captive audience are too much for her equilibrium.

To Mrs Peggy Butler at 239 Kenyon Avenue, Swarthmore, PA
Annaghmakerrig. 6 March 1962

We've been to Monaghan hospital today & the news is not good. Friends are rallying with fest. cards & notes. I've telephoned to Geoffrey Steele [Bunty Worby's cousin] & said we think he ought to come over; & I've written to her brother-in-law Stanley Maynard, at Morcambe, saying if he wants to come that Judy will meet him in Belfast. I have to go to London tomorrow to start of Ron Crean play. It's all rather dreary & unsatisfactory & *quite* inevitable.

Bunty Worby died in Monaghan Hospital while Guthrie was away. After his return he arranged a scattering of her ashes at her Annaghmakerrig rock garden. She had been housekeeper and companion to Mrs Norah Guthrie since 1931 and had become a member of the essential household, amounting to family.

To Mrs Peggy Butler at Maidenhall
Annaghmakerrig. 5 May 1962

Stephanie [Lencke] is still here & I think very happy & distinctly less crushed & nervy. I think she'll go back to St Thomas' next week. Dot Rossmore left y'day in last stages of nervous agitation. It has all been truly hateful for them – much worse than the *Cherry Orchard* – and matters are made so much worse because of the case-book love/hate tension between Dot & Paddy. One could fill a book.

Talking of tensions, I'm having a Regrettable tension with Migsie [Davis]. Each of us thinks the other is being completely self-centred & unreasonable. No doubt the truth is somewhere in between. So far no High Words have either been written or spoken – so maybe, if we can keep our foolish old heads, it will eventually blow over. Sad.

We [Guthries & Stephanie Lencke] had a nice evening with the David Grenes.[42] The humble cot is very unattractive indeed. Pointless

42   Professor David Grene of the University of Chicago had a farm in Co. Cavan about thirty miles from Annaghmakerrig.

situation, sitting as it does plumb on a dirty road facing a large cow-byre in a dank, rushy hollow. We arrived a few moments after the w.c. had catastrophically overflowed. So the house resounded to whacks & bangs & wheezes & gushes and the cries of the Plumber to his Mate. Ethel (Stephanie says she's Spanish, Judy says she's a negress – &, of course, Ethel is a thoroughly Spanish name!) was in 5th Position on the doorstep in an elegant grey one-piece; David was in the byre, in dung from head to heels. After a very cordial greeting he finished milking, she dealt with the plumber, and we sat at a dirty kitchen table on three rickety kitchen chairs. Very soon, however, they joined us & were most interesting & pleasant; tho' the meal – monster gobbetts of ¾ raw cow – was The End, the conversation maintained itself on a high level in the Sophocles Dept.

Evening really far more congenial than the subsequent one at Glaslough [Castle] where the surroundings were certainly ancestral in a big way, but one yawned at endless anecdotes in Etonian drawls about what King Alfonso said at Crockfords in '23 and how poor Poopy Pembroke "blotted his copybook with Q Mary so of course, poor fella, he never got the Garter".

To Mrs Peggy Butler at Maidenhall

Annaghmakerrig. 6 June 1962

There are great parochial doings. We are undergoing a MISSION in Cootehill, which means that every night of the week we leave at 8.00 for a service in Cootehill church (rather charming), which isn't as excitingly different from ordinary Evensong as one had hoped. We plough our way thro' Magnificat, Nunc Dimittis and *several* hymns and are eventually rewarded by a preachment from My Lord Bish of Clogher. He is rather a splendid man of compelling personality; and gives forth his sermon with masterly bel-aire and noble simplicity (he's an ex-farm-boy from Fintona, Co Tyrone) which leave one with the impression that something deeply felt has been said, but which afterwards leaves no coherent impression whatsoever. However it is rather stimulating & pleasant to be part of a *packed* congregation of OH such rugged, solid, splendid great types – and when we all pour out at the end into Church St, Cootehill, looking like A Promised Land in the golden dusty twilight it is truly & movingly "beautiful" & just what I would like to paint, if I could paint.

Tomorrow we have invited every man, woman and child in the parishes of Killevan-Newbliss-Aghabog to tea at 6.30 "to meet the Bishop of Clogher". Eighty-six households have had invitations (at a cost of 29/- postage) but many are too old and many will have milking and other chores. We think somewhere between 30-50 will turn up, but food, cups, plates etc are ready in the background for more, if need be. PRAY for fine weather! The staff (minus Bob, who, alas, is back in the Adelaide Hosp with a recurrence of dermatitis) is adoring the stirabout – paths have been scraped, edges of grass clipped, carpets brushed, furniture polished and Anna is in a seventh heaven of Artistic Creation surrounded by featherlight "sponges", bronze-gold "egg-cakes" and other delights.

Lizzie Black (ex-Sextoness) died last night. No details yet, but we suspect cancer for which she had an operation something over a year ago. She's been feeble for some weeks & much trouble by blisters, but the end was sudden. Burial tomorrow. A prelude, as 'twere, to our Garden Party, to which she was a bidden guest. So there we are – 'twixt grave & gay; flutes & garlands at the sepulchre, black weeds at the feast.

Conor Farrington [playwright & actor] and his able tartar of a bride [Meryl Gourley, actor] came up for Sunday night and were very pleasant. I think he would quite like to use me as a professional god-parent – a rôle I am entirely willing to play. It's rather interesting how the females in that family are so, so much stronger than the males: little Mrs F just spins plump Tony like a top; and I make no doubt that Oonagh is whipping her Mexican husband like a refractory mule. And here's Conor hitched to what seemed to us a nice, and highly intelligent, but formidably determined young person.

Have you a boy kitten, about 6 months old, who would make a suitable mate for White Currants, who turns out to be a female?

To Mrs Peggy Butler at Maidenhall

c/o Benn Hospital, Belfast. 16 July 1962

My week has been of a sacred calm, a pale dove-grey monotony. I think the streptococci are at last, after a desperate rearguard action, in retreat. My nose still runs rheumatically, but the tendency now is for streams of living water, not thick egg custard, and I feel much livelier.

Migsie Davis has been *very* good & faithful but I'm sorry to say she's greatly failed and is, I fear, finding her daily routine to be too much. Don't know *what* one can do to help. Matron & Sister are old & tried friends which is a huge help. Right now a dignified coloured girl of about 20 is Doing the room – she's tall & slim & makes the little nurses seem very plebeian – it's odd to hear a strong Shankill Rd accent come out of her coal-black face!

To Mrs Peggy Butler at Maidenhall

Annaghmakerrig. 24 July 1962

Much enjoying being at liberty; but don't feel equal to much exertion. Think I am getting gradually right. Can't come down to you yet 'cos of fruit picking – *nothing* like on your scale but enough to make it imposs. to leave.

Alex & Merula Guinness came unexpectedly for weekend which was nice. Dot Rossmore in thoroughly over-wrought stage is leaning rather too heavily on our support; all very sad and interesting; but none of it the sort of spiritual responsibility that one wants or really feels called upon to support.

Gilbert & Sullivan [*Pirates of Penzance* and *HMS Pinafore*] doing v. well in Los Angeles.

It is likely that an example of local enterprise manifest in a new textile factory in Clones, seven miles from Annaghmakerrig, gave impetus to Guthrie's long-standing idea for a fruit-preserving industry that would make use of natural resources and help combat a dire lack of rural employment. The plans, their fulfilment and the ultimate collapse of 'the jam factory' occupied much of his energy over the coming years.

To Mrs Peggy Butler at Maidenhall

Annaghmakerrig. 1 August 1962

We've had such an interesting afternoon going over the Ernetex factory in Clones. It's a most fascinating & impressive victory of humble persistent common-sense over inertia. No doubt there are large and sinister flies crawling about in the ointment but one hasn't seen them – yet; & they haven't been able – yet – to check the impetus.

Go to London tomorrow for 5 nights & Steeles arrive. Geoffrey S. is Bunty's executor; so, while here, they must finish the disposal of her (not extensive) belongings. The clothes are already dealt with (by Judy at Geoffrey's request); all that remains are books; & a few little trinkets & pieces of china.

To Mrs Peggy Butler at Maidenhall

Annaghmakerrig. 11 August 1962

Got back from London last night. Steeles are here – OH so decent and kind. Meriel is not very well – horrid rash as a result of some kind of sedative pills – she is much more intelligent than good, gentle Geoffrey whose eager English manner and high-pitched Haw-Haws of mirth at remarks or events which aren't even faintly funny *might* eventually "get on one's nerves". But they are happy, totally easy to amuse, do a lot of useful work. It's not an imposition of the kind which the Dewhursts inflict.

I feel better. Nose not so runny and have more energy & interest & don't get so immediately breathless.

To Mrs Peggy Butler at Maidenhall

Annaghmakerrig. 1 September 1962

Thank you for kind, prompt & early enquiry about FIRE. Might have been *much* worse. Some damage to chimney of Burns apt. [in Annaghmakerrig house]. We hope it will be covered by insurance. No one was hurt; no carpets, pictures, rugs, furniture, even singed. The Clones Fire Brigade with pealing bell dashed out in really splendid style but the conflagration had been initially subdued by Seamus, Maguire boys, Nicholas & Christine Fenke [house guests], Judy, Isobel, Mary Burns doing a chain of buckets from bathroom & lily pond. Several barrow-loads of burning soot were removed; & the slates were so hot that they hissed & steamed when water was poured upon them. Wasn't it a mercy it didn't happen in the middle of the night, nor in a high wind.

Jam Biz: oh such a lot of to-ing & fro-ing but not without results. We are now going to start BOILING on Mon or Tues week – in

Mullena Creamery, a disused member of the Lough Egish Group – about 4 miles out of Castleblayney on the way to Carrickmacross. We have a huge steam pan and can hire the boiler at Mullinea. A splendid Presbyterian Mrs Gilmore of Monaghan, who has been a jam-cook, will do the boiling (unpaid; in the embossed, engraved, silver tea-tray Dept.) and Volunteers (we hope) will put into pots & convey back to store in Newbliss. There is to be a Public Meeting in our store on Monday night, when an expectant public (consisting I fear of the c'ttee and a handful of their/its buddies) will be told what's in the wind and asked to offer goodwill & assistance, but *not* – at present – to open their purses. Dr Craig was v. pleased with my condition. Tanya [Moiseiwitsch] went up with me to Belfast as we had a lot of biz to talk as we went. After the Dr we went to tea with Migsie Davis who was v. pleased to see T.M. whom she partic. likes. She begins (Migsie I mean) to be a really old lady – sad; & getting very cranky & "odd", inevitably. The routine is unbelievably restricted, not by poverty, tho' she is very poor, but wilfully, by conservatism. Fortunately she is under the impression that she is MADLY busy. In fact she hasn't one thing to do; & makes occupation by tramping out twice a day for meals. But when I upbraided her for not writing to Becky, who is inclined to be pouty 'cos of M's neglect, she said, "Child, dear, how can I? I haven't a single minute to myself!"

To Lady Guthrie at Annaghmakerrig

c/o Mr & Mrs A.M. Bell, 23 James Street, Stratford, Ontario. Undated, September 1962

Saw *Macbeth* last night, not good. See *Cyrano* tonight & on to supper with Plummers. Lunched y'day with Doug Campbell to see Ann & the children. Dick is a very nice boy, responsible, sensible; Tessa, very, very pretty is a Madam of the first water. Before the theatre Dama (Mrs Bell) gave one of her dinners – Jarrotts, Andersons, Helen & M. Langham & T. Moiseiwitsch.

Plump executives wave from their cars & cry "Hi, Doc!" and ladies, more dessicated than cornflakes & rouged like oriental sunsets wave from rockers on doorsteps & cry "Hi, Doc!" It's rather ingratiating. Langham is well & now that the decision has been taken [to renew his contract] is rather looking forward to starting a new phase here. Now

I'm going out into the Bell "yard" to finish a chart of who-appears-in-which-scene of *Hamlet*, begun way back & never completed. Leave here at 10.30 on Sunday A.M. due Minneapolis about five something. Write to Vineland Place.

To Lady Guthrie at Annaghmakerrig

c/o Mr & Mrs A.M. Bell, 23 James Street, Stratford, Ontario. Undated, September 1962

Saw *Cyrano* last night – hateful play but [Christopher] Plummer is simply splendid; so is the prod; so are the designs. The Co. rather uneven with Douglas [Rain] wonderful as the pastry-cook & Toby Robins nice but OH so common-place & lower middle class as Roxane.

To Lady Guthrie at Annaghmakerrig

Concord Hotel, 65 South 11ᵗʰ Street, Minneapolis. 9 September 1962

Hard at it, & now in a minute we [Tanya Moiseiwitsch] are off to dinner & a meeting with newly created Large Committee – bank presidents from Bismark, N. Dakota, & stuff like that who are to be the NUCLEI in many & far-flung bivouac & arrange for busloads of citizens to bump & grind over dusty miles. The building begins to look exciting – very: one can't work up the same head of steam as over Stratters, mainly because it's the second time & partly because it's not such a big frog in a small puddle. Nevertheless it looks quite thrilling. How good that Maureen [Burns] wants to take over from Margaret [Maguire, on domestic staff]. It won't last but will "tide over". How can we get out of going to Joan [Daley's wedding] reception? You must think up a previous engagement which permits attendance at the edifice [church] but utterly prevents a four hour séance in the Westenra Arms.

To Lady Guthrie at Annaghmakerrig

c/o Kipnis, Apt 5D, 8 East 48 Street, New York City. 20 September 1962

Thrilled to hear of Jam progress. Tell Joe [Martin, Manager, Irish Farmhouse Preserves] I have followed up letter from Mr Patrick Sullivan who turns out to be the Vice President of General Dynamics. And G.D. is a tiny concern about the size of I.C.I. & Austen Motors put together with a 20 storey building on R'feller Plaza. Mr P.S. is a James Cagney type who took me to a drink at the Athletics Club & will I hope be helpful with grand introductions. His advice is not to try and achieve large promotion (which we couldn't afford anyway) but to *infiltrate* thro' snob appeal. He thinks it a serious error that we haven't fancy jars. There was talk about introductions to Mr Boland [Irish ambassador to the U.N.] & the President of Aer Lingus who would use our jam on their planes. Agents are appointed in Stratford [Dama Bell] & Monterey who will do or die. Also endless people make vague promises to buy. Report this to Joe, please: I wouldn't want to be thought idle while others toil at Mullinea!

I think we have a Co. [for Minneapolis]. Cronyns [Hume Cronin & Jessica Tandy] are definite; also a John Cromwell – a splendid 70-year-old of high repute (Player King in *Hamlet* & Seigneur Anselm in *Miser*); Voskovec is highly likely (Polonius et al) & an interesting younger group. The outstanding gap is in the Young Gel Dept – nothing turns up but loud painted hussies & neurotic jumpsies with dirty hair & black stockings.

To Mrs Peggy Butler at Maidenhall

Annaghmakerrig. 2 October 1962

Hope Paris is going to be nice. Looking forward to hearing; but you needn't make writing an effort. I got back here to find JAM JAM JAM. 1,000 pounds of rhubarb & ginger had been achieved; & 1,000 pounds of plum was achieved (in one tremendous day) last Sat. I really admire Joe Martin]. Now we're at the b'berry jelly. Yesterday we picked all day – luckily in divine weather. Judy, Seamus, Bob, the 2 Maguire boys, Anna, Maureen & the three Maries (M. Burns, M. McGoldrick & M. McGorman) oh & Yours Truly picked amongst them 10½ stone. It was very gay. Today they are "dripping" at the Creamery; tomorrow we hope to boil.

Ann Maguire's wedding tomorrow – Judy is even now binding the bouquet – & Joan Daley's nuptials, which I missed, were a tremendous event – 45 persons (incl. Lady G) sat down to a champagne lunch in the Westenra Arms, Monaghan. We're going to a grand Dinner Party chez Peter Montgomery and spending night with Gloria Belmore at

Castle Coote. She is quite a decent spud – sadly & recently widowed – with a crashing 'Strylian accent. I could quack on like this for hours. Have a heap of necessary letters of the dullest kind – forms to fill re Fire Insurance, forms to fill re grant on new pump, forms to fill re grant on Seamus' Bijou Residence & so on & so on.

To Mrs Peggy Butler in Paris

Annaghmakerrig. 10 October 1962

Tomorrow I go to Dublin with Joe Martin to see Childers [local Dáil Deputy; later President of Ireland] & try to find solutions to various jam problems like printing, packaging & shipping; and I go to the Abbey Theatre at night. Did I tell you I'm being employed by Mr Mervyn Wall & the Irish Arts Council as a sort of Spy or Sneak & have to Report on the Abbey. Alas I missed Miss Mooney & *Long Day's Journey*. I saw it in New York where it was spoilt by inadequacy of Mrs March, though he (Frederic March) was splendid & so were the sons. In London it was far better with Gwen Ffrangcon Davies in that very fine part.

Next to Joe Hone's piece [*Fursey*, musical by Fergus Linehan from book by Mervyn Wall] to show respect. It seemed to me signally to lack direction. The script was much better than the perf. which was the epitome of Dublin middle-class would-be elegance. Only fair to say the house was packed & enjoyed it all thoroughly. Was rather interested to meet Joe's "patron" John Ryan & to find him a good deal more *respectable* than I had uncharitably supposed.

Afterwards Joe, I, & a rather intense, not quite young, American lady went to a late-night one-man perf. from works of S. Beckett by Jackie McGowran. It was a brilliant perf. – in the Coterie Dept. – but wonderfully done. I don't know what to think about Beckett. I can't read him. But 'interpreted' like it was there, he certainly seemed to have a good deal of meaning.

Amused to hear about Leixlip Castle & fitted carpets. Have met Desmond & Mariga [Guinness] at Rossmore & did not care for them *at all*!

Love to Hubert. I hope that he too is finding Paree gai. Very nice to think of you in such charming & elegant surroundings.

To Mrs Peggy Butler in Paris

Annaghmakerrig. 17 October 1962

This will be my last letter before beginning *The Alchemist* at Old Vic. Lovely weather & enormous poundage of b'berries has been picked – nearly 40 stone for jam alone, besides endless small collections for our own private jam, bottling, puddings, etc.

I saw *And Him Stretched* [play by Patrick Galvin] as part of my spying for Arts Council. Thought the whole thing far the best & liveliest offering yet seen. I guess the author will probably feel gradually less & less need to shock the pants off his uncles & aunts, but he has real talent. The weakness, I thought, was the complete lack of any positive philosophy. The young man who leaves for England will be just as dissatisfied there, because he carries a built-in grievance. Screams of anger & shafts of satire unmixed with aspiration of hope of any kind (even in a hereafter) make a rather unfilling banquet. I suppose the dying, or the dead, man was meant to be an Allegory of The Revolution or Patriotism or sumpin'. I don't mind that not being clear – after all, if you're to dot every eye there's no point in allegory or symbolism. But there seemed no symbol of the future; & I reckon if there's a past & a present it's reasonable to presume a future.

Thinking Joe's piece over I rather wish he wasn't in that milieu, but don't know what one can do. I can't find him a job at M'polis; and I think it wrong to "interfere" unless one has a very positive plan to propose. He has obviously scurried around most industriously publicising the rotten thing – in a rather vulgar way, but that's not quite the point; he *had tried* – real hard. Christopher Fitz-Simon, who hasn't, I think, Joe's potentiality, has played his cards much better – so far; and in the face of mighty little parental encouragement. Joe – I guess this is hereditary – is bedevilled by Grand Ideas. Christopher just works away with rather poor cards and quietly takes tricks with the three of clubs.

We've asked Wendy [Guthrie cousin] for a week before Christmas and are dreading it but feeling very righteous. There's nothing here to occupy her and she'll feel the cold; persons of low birth always do. She must just whack the be-Jesus out of the piano; and I have to go to Dublin (Arts Council) & will take her for the jaunt.

To Mrs Peggy Butler at Maidenhall

Annaghmakerrig. 14 December 1962

> Wendy … wait for it! … rang the night we arrived back to say that
> the weather was really so terrible that she'd rather wait & come later.
> For one terrible moment I thought it was you doing it in a bittersweet
> jest. Then relief came flooding in "like the close of an Angel's Psalm"
> (Adelaide A. Proctor) and we've been swimming ever since in a kind
> of pink aura.

To Mrs Peggy Butler at Maidenhall

Annaghmakerrig. 29 December 1962

> We had a nice Xmas Day – Tanya & her delightful 71-year-old-
> Austrylian-mamma staying, & Paddy & Dot [Lady] Rossmore for
> lunch. The main festive event, however, was the Party for those who
> helped to make the jam. Over 40 guests of the most diverse ages,
> types & backgrounds. It was a wee thing sticky at first when all sat
> round, mute as toads, looking some panicky, some near tears. But it
> very soon got going. We had a radiogram (loaned & presided over
> by Phil McCabe, a 17 year old son of the Post Office) & dancing –
> the TWIST – in the hall; a huge fire; and an electric stove and the
> new chandelier ablaze in the dining-room where hugely grand
> Refreshments, all done by Judy & Anna, were ranged: sandwiches
> of many, varied & luscious ingredients; elegant tiny sausage rolls;
> jam tartlets of many hues; Xmas cake lousy with marchpane; &
> champagne glasses with ruby, emerald & amber jellies. There was Pop,
> lemon & orange, for Pioneers; & chalices of hot crimson claret-punch
> for non-Pioneers. The drawing-room, candle-lit, for non-dancers,
> looked very pretty & Daisy Kennedy (Tanya's mum) Held Forth with
> Strylian Anecdotes (when excited, her grand English accent slips way
> back into the outback behind Ad'lyde in the most endearing way) &
> glamorous reminiscences of Caruso, Melba, Ramsay MacDonald, et
> al, which were meat & drink to Guard Horan & little Miss Finnegan.
> The Protestant Lion (tiny Rev Lumley) lay down with the Catholic
> Lamb (tiny Father McCluskey who looks about 12 years old & is
> rather forthcoming). Joe Martin made a splendid speech thanking Mr

& Mrs Gilmore of Monaghan who were the guests of honour 'cos, tho' "professionals", they had graciously come & cooked the jam for us free of charge. Judy presented Mrs Gilmore with a pot of Scilly Whites [daffodils] in glamorously full bloom. Mrs Gilmore made a speech of thanks "from the full heart" and amid cheers & spontaneous musical outbreaks they were waved away into the starry magic of a frosty night.

12

**GUTHRIE THEATER,
QUEEN'S UNIVERSITY
AND THE JAM FACTORY**

Guthrie's first season with the Minnesota Theater Company in its new theatre took place in 1963 to widespread acclaim. Guthrie was Artistic Director, Peter Zeisler Production Director and Oliver Rea Administrative Director. In the same year Guthrie was installed as Chancellor of Queen's University, Belfast. The plans for the rural jam factory in Newbliss, Co. Monaghan, came to fruition with local entrepreneur Joe Martin appointed as manager. Guthrie's brother-in-law, Hubert Butler, an experienced market-gardener, strongly advised against the project for reasons of climate and soil but more significantly because he believed the commercial producers would not allow even a small rival to succeed. Tensions between Guthrie and his sister Peggy Butler surfaced from this issue. Guthrie wrote his will, but did not notify his immediate relatives of radical property disposal. It is remarkable how Guthrie, while addressing rising family disagreements, continued to report blandly in his letters on his theatrical enterprises.

To Mrs Peggy Butler at Maidenhall

Annaghmakerrig. 23 January 1963

I went today to Dublin with Joe Martin to see lawyer about flotation of Jam Co, & the roads were alarming – it was more like sledging than motoring. I'm glad you're going to Spain. Have a lovely time – the change can't fail to do good. I've had a delightful, long, merry letter from Julia, thanking for my Xmas one. I won't send it on as there's no "news" you won't already know & I think that the feeling that one's letters are being "bandied about" – even among loving intimates – is rather daunting to the correspondent. Indeed I wonder if a public reading at the Market Cross would be easier to take than the scrutiny of the loving intimates.

Will you consider taking shares in the Jam Co? entitled Irish Farmhouse Preserves Ltd. Shares at £1.00 each. *Let me know if you're interested.* I don't think you'll get any interest for first five years or so; but eventually I can't see why the enterprise shouldn't prosper. Our first tangible impact is that nearly 30 neighbouring farmers have bought blackcurrants to grow for sale to us in due course. We take 30 lbs of sample jam to N.Y.C. next Monday and shall see what we shall see.

To Mrs Peggy Butler at Blanes, Spain

Minnesota Theater Company, Minneapolis. 23 February 1963

Sorry you feel unable to take shares in Jam Co. and far sorrier you feel "excluded". Do not intend to answer that part of your letter. On paper we are both too fluent, too apt to try some debating points, too eager to justify our own points of view & conduct. Our love for each other is intense, profound & unchangeable. Don't keep prodding me with my ingratitude to underappreciation of & frequent insults to Hubert. It doesn't help any of us. You can easily ring from me an admission that I am jealous, unjust, etc etc. What good does that do for any of us? If H & I were cast together on a desert island we should manage a perfectly adequate & co-operative relationship & live & die in a brotherly amity which we cannot, *at present*, achieve in more complex & sophisticated environment. For just now, & without malice or over-anxiety, let's leave ourselves be – hatchets unburied, nettles ungrasped, red herrings unpursued. Share this with H. I think he will "understand" & agree.

We are comfortably established here in the attic flat of "the Oliver Rea [co-founder of the Guthrie Theater] residence". Our suite has been charmingly done up with white paint, has lovely polished floors & consists of bedroom, sitting room, bathroom-cum-aunt & very small but highly adequate kitchen. It is sunny, and a flat roof over Rea's kitchen will come in handy come summer. At present it's apt to be "twenty below" in the shade or when in teeth of wind is like being MINCED with a steel sword. Theatre building coming on; & demand for season tickets very encouraging. There are being, and will be, crises, so far not insurmountable but, coming one after another, a little wearing. But of such is a new enterprise created.

Guthrie helps to
stir the pot in
the Newbliss jam
factory, 1963.

To Hubert Butler at Blanes, Spain

Minnesota Theater Company. 25 February 1963

> Your very nice jam letter reached me today. I appreciate *very* much your troubling to write & to giving the matter such thought.
>
> In fact, I am perhaps less involved in the project than you suppose. Joe Martin will have the chief responsibility, not I. I've only helped to set the ball rolling; but cannot – & do not want to – contend with the management. I think I can be useful as a sort of substitute Daddy to Joe (in the Advice & Steady-on Departments); & can also be useful with contacts & publicity on this side of the water. But I have no intention, and have made this quite clear to Joe & the rest, of being involved to the exclusion of other activities which are no less important, being what one knows a bit more about. In the long term I think it highly likely that we will seek to be absorbed in Lamb's or William's & Wood's or one of the larger concerns. But in short term we must start something ourselves or no one else will.

None of us, however ("us" meaning the Newbliss group) are under the delusion that we are anything but Babes in the Wood, nor that, in the process of learning, we shall not suffer setbacks, rebuffs & disappointments & make terrible mistakes. We are not, however, proceeding in a reckless way. The samples met with a good reception in N.Y. but we are not under the impression that we have therefore collared the coast to coast market!

PLEASE don't think that any of above implies very smallest resentment of your wise & cautious letter. Quite the contrary. I am very happy that you are interested; & anxious that you continue to be so.

To Mrs Peggy Butler at Blanes, Spain

Minnesota Theater Company. 12 March 1963

The Co. is all assembled & rehearsal in full swing. We are endeavouring to *practice* Integration so have a black Horatio and a perfectly lovely young black (called Janet MacCachlan) among the young gels. We shall make absolutely no point of their colour and indeed I think in artificial light no one will especially notice. Neither is the thick-lipped type and both have great "air" & speak better than most of their white confrères.

The theatre is quite disappointing outside – a glass box with iron bars and sort of cement buttresses which aren't functional at all, supposed to supply "design". The result looks like any and every minor airport. The interior is distinctly interesting & will, I think, work well. The seats are comfortable, but not too much so, just right; but a little spoilt by being upholstered in a multiplicity of bright "shades". The material is nice – sort of thick wool tapestry – & the more subdued colours – olive, grey, buff, etc – are delightful; but against Tanyas's wish (who is officially consultant) the architect has included seats in cherry-red, peacock, à la Grace Sheppard – which makes a quite garish & common effect. However, as they'll only be visible when the house is empty it doesn't terribly matter. But it does matter that one has small confidence in either the architect's taste or his integrity.

We open May 7 *Hamlet* – May 8 *Miser* – then 5 weeks later *Three Sisters* and 4 weeks after that *Death of a Salesman*. I hope to return home a few weeks after *3 Sisters* (Douglas Campbell directs *Salesman*).

To Mrs Peggy Butler at Blanes, Spain

Minnesota Theater Company. 29 March 1963

> We had another blizzard two nights ago. Walking to the theatre
> yesterday I fell down 6 times in about a minute & a half. It was on
> a very steep downward hill & I sat with a fearful bump, rose and
> promptly sat again – SIX times! It's at these times one realises the
> onset of old age. I was quite "shaken" and felt tired and done for, for
> the rest of the day.
>
> Poor Tanya had to fly back to London on Sunday. Her sister,
> Sandra, rang me early that morning to say that Benno [Moiseiwitsch,
> distinguished pianist] had suffered a bad stroke and would I "break the
> news" to T. It was not entirely unexpected. He is in the mid seventies
> and had been "not very well" for some time – though still banging away
> a mile a minute on the instrument. Sandra said he was just conscious
> but quite unable to communicate intelligibly – just kept muttering
> away in Russian, which they none of them understand. Poor Tanya left
> in great sadness but very sensible and collected. She's due back this aft.
>
> *Hamlet* gets on. The theatre is getting ready & we're already working
> in the rehearsal room. There are the inevitable 1001 problems of a new
> building, e.g. the air conditioning makes a noise like a mighty rushing
> wind so that we can't hear the actors speak. If turned off, blessed peace
> reigns but everyone shortly but surely STIFLES. I'm reading Kafka
> for the first time. It's fun to be in be-ruffed, stove-heated, gemütlich
> Jewish homes in Prague 1910 – & eerie to think it's all utterly, utterly
> *gone*, but I don't know yet what to think of the Œuvre.

To Mrs Peggy Butler c/o Christopher Fitz-Simon at Teilifís Eireann, Dublin

Minnesota Theater Company. 1 April 1963

> Midsummer weather in naughty, flighty Minneapolis, and we're back
> from Palm Sunday service at the Episcopalian Cathedral of St Mark
> – just 12 minutes walk – and such a good sermon from the dear Dean;
> and such a full house with masses of the nicest people in new hats.
> And then, after church, if we didn't bump into the dear Ropers (British
> consul and nice but rather t-psy wife – a lady at a v.v. diff time) who
> asked us back for a marie biscuit & a glass of sherry. It was almost –
> but Ah not quite, not even quite – like being back in dear old T. Wells.

Give love to Christopher. Hope he's well and reasonably content with Teilefís Eireann. Hilton [Edwards, Head of Drama] I hear has left the sweet, safe containment of TE and returned to the open market. Does that perhaps move C up a notch on the promotional ladder?

To Mrs Peggy Butler at Maidenhall
Minnesota Theater Company. 13 April 1963

V. interested & pleased to hear Julia is expecting again; & will, of course, be "discreet" tho' just who is going to get into a stew about it in the Upper Mid West isn't quite clear!

To Mrs Peggy Butler at Maidenhall
Minnesota Theater Company. 19 April 1963

End of a long, exhausting day of fittings – 20 uniforms made by Western Costume Co of Hollywood who have done a superb job & sent a v.v.g. Hungarian tailor "over" (by air) to supervise the try on. There are many alterations but all minor & Tanya & I are hugely relieved as we were inclined to believe that the job couldn't be done adequately thus, at long distance. We're getting now to a rather strenuous stage & I dare say I shan't write much more till after our "Openings". It's 8.0 p.m. & I've to go out & rehearse – we have a tiring final session each day 8.30-12.00 so as to work on the stage when it's quiet & no workmen about.

To Mrs Peggy Butler at Maidenhall
Minnesota Theater Company. 23 April 1963, Shakespeare's b'day

Do hope that H is on his feet again & able to take pleasure in the Debate [Kilkenny Annual Debate organised by Hubert Butler] & surrounding goings-on. I am sending (by surface mail) the Picture Supplement of local (& very feeble) Sunday paper. It has a rather alarming colour portrait of Yours Truly "relaxing" but looking old, feeble and panicky among the desperately bright upholstery which the architect has seen fit to provide. We *are* inclined to panic about the acoustics which are cathedral-like and make rapid speech a ringing blur. I dare say when carpets (delayed) are down and various mysterious "baffles" in place, that all may be well. But the trouble is that the soi-disant acoustic Expert, who talks extremely big, is just a polysyllabic dullard. He makes hit-or-miss experiments to the accompaniment of mumbo-jumbo that wouldn't take in a child of nine (but does take in the Vice Presidents of multi-billion dollar Corporations) striking on wee gongs and then LISTENING with an air of important abstraction and then making pronouncements full of words like Decibel & Reflective Surfaces which merely reiterate what everyone already knows – that the place is sort of echoey.

To Mrs Peggy Butler at Maidenhall
Minnesota Theater Company. 6 May 1963

Here we're trembling on the very brink of very brink. *Miser* had a "preview" last night – a packed house of invited guests, the construction workers who put up the building, with their ladies, & groups of policemen, firemen & other employees of the city. It went – thank goodness – to volleys of delighted laughter and was clearly enjoyed enormously. Tonight a similar audience sees *Hamlet* & tomorrow is the Opening. There is a feeling of rather anxious Optimism. We can but wait. Silly as it is, it's impossible not to be anxious.

Yesterday afternoon we had the Dedication. A Lutheran, a Rabbi, a Monsignor. The Lutheran (numerically easily the dominant sect) spoke the dedication, a very short, very simple, very moving little prayer written by himself, a lumpy little figure in too short trousers with huge dirty brown shoes. The Rabbi did a Litany composed for the occasion. Monsignor Shannon (Irish-American, clever as paint and less worldly than many) spoke the Address – hugely able and not unsympathetic – why is it so much easier for duffers to be "sympathetic"? There were 2 popular hymns, roared with splendid élan by Distinguished Congregation; the actors spoke Psalm 118, rehearsed to the last hair by Yours Truly and run off with huge aplomb & zeal; and a Lutheran choir, the best in the Region, sang a Schubert piece (loud but not loud enough, it needed 1,000 voices rather than 500), & a Nunc Dimittis by Gretchaninoff, which I'd never heard before; it was simply splendid & perfectly "rendered". The whole occasion was simple & moving & a highly suitable beginning.

To Mrs Peggy Butler at Maidenhall

Minneapolis Theater Company. 14 May 1963

The Openings [*The Miser* and *Hamlet*] passed off all right but were fearfully exhausting – what with anxiety, what with never being off one's feet & I've pulled ligaments in R ankle – nothing alarming but v. painful and draggy by end of day.

Neither performance was quite as good as the Coy. could achieve, partly nerves, mostly fact that First Night audiences (mostly v.v. rich & elderly) had come far more for the Occasion than for either play. They sat in dresses, ordered specially from Paris months before, wondering why the McNutts & the Schoefflers weren't present and counting one another's pearls. However it never came anywhere within hailing distance of catastrophe. It was all mechanically smooth as silk, just rather piano and dull. Since the openings Lola [Kipnis, translator], Tanya & I have been absorbed in final prep. for *3 Sisters*.

To Mrs Peggy Butler at Maidenhall

Minneapolis Theater Company. 4 June 1963 – what was the Glorious 4th of June?

3 Sisters coming along well, I think. It opens in 2 weeks time and very soon after that we head for home. Have to be in Winnipeg (if you'll excuse the familiarity – it should be Winifred Margaret) for a night & N.Y.C. for a day and a night, but hope to board a plane on night of June 24 for Shannon.

To Mrs Peggy Butler at Maidenhall

Minneapolis. 8 June 1963

We've had a mild haroosh again over my health. However, cardiograph & x-ray gave rather reassuring messages; so after 2 days of VERY thorough & conscientious "tests" I was out on condition that I "keep very quiet" till Tues, when I may go back to work.

As it happened, *3 Sisters* was very well along, & my absence really won't have mattered. Good old Douglas [Campbell, director for *Death of a Salesman*] flew back from Stratford and is taking charge so all's well that ends well. I don't feel too bad about Duggie because the family are all joining him here any time now. They're all coming +

household gods, Teresa's cat, Dirk's tropical fish & goodness knows what beside, travelling by Great Lakes steamer thro' Huron, across Superior, to Duluth. Doesn't it sound fun? And Douglas will meet them at Duluth which isn't much above 100 miles from here.

I have read a Life of Lady Gregory championing her passionately in the face of those whom the authoress suspects to have deliberately pushed her into the background to the greater glory of Yeats. But all those early Abbey triumphs have been rather over-documented. Neither Synge nor O'Casey wears well. And Yeats, tho' a great poet, was nowhere near a great playwright. I'm inclined to agree with the lady that Lady G is rather due a come-back.

To Mrs Peggy Butler at Maidenhall

Minneapolis Theater Company. 18 June 1963

3 Sisters opens tonight. I think it is well done; remains to be seen if M'polis will care for it. We're in quite a whirl of last arrangements here – a great deal to settle both for Judy in the domestic sphere & for me in the professional. Went to Dr yesterday; & showed marked improvement in various "tests"; but am told still to continue on reduced dosage of some cortisone compound which (so the rather nice Dr says) is helping to "keep me up" during efforts of *3 Sisters*. Judy, who also was "seen", is suffering from long-standing lung & chest weakness, has been given the inevitable antibiotic medicine & charged to cut down & eventually abandon smoking. Truth is we're all getting old & starting to break up. And the further truth is that, if one concentrates enough on Spiritual Values, it couldn't matter less. But it's easier said than done.

Becky will have much enjoyed your company [at Annaghmakerrig] and the wee outings; & was certainly due a bit of divarshion. The time spent just sitting in that kitchen with poor decent deadly Ethel must often hang intolerably heavy.

To Mrs Peggy Butler at Maidenhall

Annaghmakerrig. Undated, June 1963

Lovely weather. We're cutting hay. Seamus [McGorman] has a new baby girl. Jam getting hectic – this day week is D-day for strawberries

– 2 tons of. The price of sugar has risen catastrophically (for reasons which a nice man at the Sugar Board explained very clearly & which I thought I understood at the time, but now find I don't at all!) & instead of getting a rebate for export we pay MORE. However, I think, tho' our profit per pound will be woefully reduced, we shall still make a profit but only just.

I'm v. busy journalising. The fact that next year will be the 4th centenary of Shakespeare's birth is turning out to be worth hundreds of pounds to me. Opens our eyes to the commercial desirability of Mother's Day, the Assumption of the B.V.M., and so on ... quite apart, of course, from that Grand Jamboree of Retail Trade which we have made out of the birth in the manger.

To Mrs Peggy Butler at Maidenhall

Annaghmakerrig. 2 July 1963

Feeling very OLD! [and] distinctly tired 'cos Joe [Martin] and I left y'day for Dublin where we flew about shopping for the jam factory – a pump, a wash-hand basin, 3 sort-of bidets for washing fruit & jampots... oh endless hardware. The goods shed [former Newbliss Railway Station] is transformed into a snowy dream of functional elegance with, attached, a Refrigeration Chamber. We got back just a leedle late for the Grand Reception, given by the Newbliss Development Assn. to welcome home Sir T. & Lady Guthrie, in the ballroom (crystal chandeliers, spanking parquet floor & rosebud wallpaper) of the Creighton Arms, Clones. A buffy supper (excellent), tea, orange pop for Pioneers, whiskey for others, a gracious speech from Father McCluskey followed by dancing by the younger people while the serious lined the wall & chatted rather congenially till nearly one o'clock. It was all amazingly & amusingly different from U.S.A.

To Mrs Peggy Butler at Maidenhall

Annaghmakerrig. 11 July 1963

Jam. Jam. Jam. Spent almost the whole of y'day screaming into the tel: & repeatedly getting cut off in the middle of cross-channel calls to manufacturers. A firm in Yorkshire is supplying us with 20,000 glass jars of special design, which hadn't turned up; another firm in Dorset supplies 20,000 screw caps, which hadn't turned up. Yorkshire was brisk & businesslike & was able to explain everything satisfactorily & the jars will, I think, be delivered today. Dorset couldn't have been dimmer. "Well actually we would have written you actually but we'd lost your address actually. The caps will reach you next week." After screams & thrashings from me it was agreed that ½ the quantity would be put on a plane at their expense. But the general air of couldn't-care-less fully explains any lag in British exports.

The strawberries are a problem. Many growers have lost a great deal of their crop 'cos of the damp, sunless weather. Out of a consignment of two tons delivered to us y'day I should think ½ a cwt. were already mouldy. And I don't think it's anyone's fault. We shan't get our quota for this year. The big growers mostly work under cross-channel contract; the wee growers are really too much trouble. You struggle out to Emyvale to lift 25 pounds to be told that they're awfully sorry but, owing to Cousin Florrie's death, they forgot to pull.

Going to Belfast tomorrow, primarily to see Jack Smyth (Dr) as we're still rather unsuitably wheezy.

To Mrs Peggy Butler at Maidenhall
Annaghmakerrig. Undated, August 1963

We were in England for three nights last week mainly for Judy to be present at casting conferences for [new production of] *Queen Bee* which now goes forward full steam ahead. They rehearse in about a fortnight and open in Windsor September 15. Dame Sybil [Thorndike] and Lew [Casson], latter much nearer ninety than eighty, are in great form and fly by helicopter, which they LOVE!, to and from Chichester where they are appearing in *Uncle Vanya*!

Had hoped to suggest coming to you next week but really the demands of the jam are endless. We reel and lurch from one crisis to another – so far the boat, though rocking alarmingly, has not foundered. Production is going at well over two thousand pounds a day; and great towers of newly filled jam-pots rise like miniature ziggurats all over the shed. Thirty persons are in daily employment, ten or twelve grown-ups and the rest youngsters at a slave wage under the supervision of ex-Sergeant Horan who marches up and down the long table whip in hand.

Religious faction has already raised its ugly head. The Protestants look on it all with disfavour; I think for no better reason than it got started by predominantly Catholic help. Rev. Lumley has left and his successor [Rev Styles] is getting a backwash of parochial disapprobation of Lumley's rather too wholehearted support for the scheme. He (Lumley) rather unwisely last year gave the Orange Brethren a bellyful of jam and the need to co-operate with Catholic neighbours rather than play at soldiers in orange sashes. It was brave and RIGHT and I honour him for it but it wasn't very wise and has sown dragons' teeth. Never mind. When/if we start making money and buying local fruit at a good price the tune will change.

Christopher Fitz-Simon was up this week for the day with a young lady poet from Grand Rapids, Mich., now resident in Dublin. They attended a Meeting re. jam in Newbliss and both took modest shares in the enterprise, which was good of them. In view of my impending dep. for Minneapolis and Joe [Martin]'s intense preoccupation with the cooking-pot (he and young Larmor and Phil McCabe stand in white aprons with sort of paddles in their hands looking like three Witches in clouds of hissing steam) it's moderately unlikely that I can get away.

Becky is fairly well but is, I fear, gradually feebler. Did I tell you that she and I conducted correspondence with her Bank Manager and she is QUITE a well-off woman. This was, I think, a great pleasure and relief to her. She feels now that if she wants to have a little burst of extravagance (of course she never will) it would be possible, without robbing Ethel of her deserved legacy.

To Mrs Peggy Butler at Maidenhall

Annaghmakerrig. 8 August 1963

Please thank Hubert for v.nice letter & helpful advice re. jam. I should like to bring Joe Martin down to see your local affairs – canning of veg. etc, either just before or just after Raspberry season. We have a lull pending in about a fortnight (end of soft fruit) and hope, between that and the b'berries, to do the labelling, packing & dispatch of the near 100,000 pounds which by then will have been made.

We have James Devlin – little *very* gifted hunchbacked actor from Belfast – staying for a few days: he's recuperating from a (not very bad) heart attack, returns tomorrow. I don't expect to be long

Summer workers at Irish Farmhouse Preserves in Newbliss Railway Station supervised by Sergeant Horan.

away & I hope if humanly possible to attend *Queen Bee* opening at Windsor, Sept 15.

To Mrs Judith Guthrie in London

Minnesota Theater Company. 20 August 1963

> Biz at the theatre is booming – hardly a seat for the rest of the season. Morale of the Co. v.g.
>
> Saw *Hamlet* last night – greatly pulled together & Geo [Grizzard] much more confident & various.

To Mrs Judith Guthrie in London

Tyrone Guthrie Theater, Minneapolis. 25 August 1963

> We have now decided our next Season's programme (strictly confidential): open with *Henry V* & *Saint Joan* which seems to me rather elegant since they view almost the same period & the same war but with the sympathy first on the Red side, then the Blue. Grizzard will play Henry; Ellen [Geer] St Joan. Next, *Skin of our Teeth*,[43]

---

43   *The Skin of our Teeth* was not produced; it was replaced by *The Glass Menagerie*.

probably with Hal Holbrook; last, *Volpone* with Douglas [Campbell] as V and Grizzard as Mosca. Then – this is the most interesting part – we plan to do the *Oresteia* (*Agamemnon, Choephoroe, Eumenides)* for a limited off-season period in the T.G., then for a tour of universities under rather grand auspices. This I like very much. The only actors approached so far are Grizzard and Pasteur who profess themselves thrilled with their parts! Tomorrow we see Ken Ruta, Lee Richardson, Paul Ballantyne, Clayton Corzatte and the Campbells. I think most of them will want back. So next year's Co. will be v. like this year's, minus Zoe [Caldwell] (who doesn't want to return alas), Cronyns (who'd like back in '65) and Dick Coates (for whom we have no suitable parts). New will be Douglas Campbell, Hal Holbrook (much interested but not yet "in the bag") and a Comedienne for Sabina & Lady Politick. Peter [Zeisler] & I fly to San Diego next Sat to see Ellen Geer and her husband for whom, if he is O.K., there are parts.

Receipts in the middle of last week passed $600,000 & total expenditure is not expected to be more than 650 or 600,000 which we should achieve the week after next. So there should be a surplus at the Season's end of at least 50,000 with the Ford Foundation guarantee untouched.

D/Salesman: I think Duggie's done a good job [Director], Jessie [Jessica Tandy] is quite miscast – far too Anglo & ladylike, Hume [Cronyn] is immensely capable, Lee Richardson & Paul Ballantyne & Ken Ruta are first class. Coates passes.

American Educational Theater Conference (1000 delegates from all over): am to be the recipient of An Award. Oh these awards & Prizes & Citations: you'd think we were all in our early early teens!

A Life in the Theatre has been brought out "in paperback" – the cover is in pink & nile with an abstract design of amazing triviality. Still, it's nice that they evidently think it still has a market.

To Mrs Judith Guthrie in London

Tyrone Guthrie Theater, Minneapolis. 29 August 1963

A Blow: I don't think I can possibly achieve the Opening Night [of *Queen Bee*] at Windsor. The new McKnight Fellows have been scheduled to come here for a Reception – Sept 17, 18. I *must* be there;

The Guthrie Theater,
Minneapolis, 1963.

& the date can't be changed. It's most disappointing. No one to blame. Ann & Douglas [Campbell] will be there. Oh dear, I wish I could be there too.

Had a very wearisome 3 days with the American Educational Theater Ass. Convention. Most of them crashing bores – some very "nice". Plenty of lip-service was paid [to the Minnesota Theatre Company] but they really were a drunken audience who whooped like hyenas at the more obvious jokes & dozed thro' the dry bits! We all never stopped sitting on panels, attending lunches, giving lectures.

Tanya is very well & full of grand offers which she's refusing. It's rather interesting how suddenly she has turned into a grande dame of design and how enormously she has gained in confidence & authority without losing her genuineness and humility. Nice.

Must go now to rehearse *3 Sisters*. Jessie [Tandy] is back and walking without a stick.

To Mrs Peggy Butler at Annaghmakerrig

Minnesota Theater Company. 3 September 1963

Very busy here – plans for next Season; which involves endless juggling upon which depends the livelihood & contentment (or discontentment) of 30 or 40 people so it's all rather a worry. The Season is ending in spanking style – 100% full last week and hardly a seat available for rest of Season, 3 weeks. We should show quite a nice profit which is good for the first year.

Just back from San Diego (Calif.) Such a lovely flight over the Rocky Mts. How I wish there'd been time to do it by train. San D itself is FRIGHTFUL. It's a sort of Bournemouth except palms instead of pines, & senile & silver motels instead of Boarding Houses, but similar hordes of retired tradespersons creeping about & sitting on seats looking at the sun sinking into the sea. The Pacific Ocean, tho', is even drearier than the English Channel – grey sand like a wet shroud. The tradespersons sit and look at it chew bubble-gum while they plan their embalment and interment at Forest Lawn.

To Mrs Judith Guthrie in London

1908 Grand Avenue, Minneapolis, Minnesota. 19 September 1963

Hope Joe's [Martin] pleurisy is better. I am eating a bottle of our raspberry which doesn't seem quite full enough & therefore made a poor impression as a sample. It's excellent: good consistency & not too sweet.

To Mrs Peggy Butler at Maidenhall

Annaghmakerrig. 15 October 1963

Last night we went – wait for it – to *Blossom Time* at the Saint Louis Convent in Monaghan as guests of Mother General who is celebrating her Jubilee – well, 50th Anniversary! – as a Nun. All most interesting – but a tiny bit long for now. A girl Schubert, girl officers of the Imperial Guard & splendid Sister-Claire-of-the-Wounds beating the be-Jesus out of the tymps.

Now to Clones, where I'm going to make my Will (!)

To Mrs Peggy Butler at Maidenhall

c/o Geo Chamberlain, 26 Wharton Street, London WC1. Undated, November 1953

> *Queen B* [by Judith Guthrie] is not coming to London but ends
> in B'ham tonight. Quite a thunderclap to one and all because the
> receptions have been good everywhere. "The management" has
> been rather secretive & un-candid which is odd because Murray
> (MacDonald) is an old friend. No doubt reasons will eventually be
> revealed. The authoress visited them all at B'ham on Thurs. night &
> found it going excellently to a v.g. house; & the Coy. rather inflamed
> by the discontinuation. However, Murray is completely within his
> legal rights, it's just that it wasn't "handled" frankly or nicely. But
> there's bound to be A Reason.
>
> Thirty thousand pots of jam left Newbliss last Monday and are
> now, I trust, AT SEA, in the hold of the American Importer (name
> of ship). The labels only reached us a week before the cargo was due
> on board. So, as you can imagine, it was all hands to the paste in the
> hugest way. Everyone rose splendidly to the Emergency; indeed I
> think it was enjoyed in spite of fearfully long hours.
>
> *Coriolanus* [for Playhouse, Nottingham] beginning to shape quite
> well; it's a v. interesting piece, which I've never done and have seen
> seldom.

Guthrie's sister Peggy Butler had evidently enquired about producing a play by
William Congreve at the Kilkenny Beer Festival because Congreve had been
educated at Kilkenny College, late seventeenth century.

To Mrs Peggy Butler at Maidenhall

County Hotel, Theatre Square, Nottingham. 12 December 1963

> I think Congreve totally daft, for the occasion – is it really to be called
> Kilkenny BEER festival? it sounds so galumphing and German and
> will alienate many people who disapprove of drinking. [Congreve]
> far too sophisticated; also death unless done with batteries of
> professional skill and weight, absolutely not for a gifted young "group"
> from Dublin having glorious fun. The best contact there would be
> Christopher O'C Fitz F. He's very shrewd & sensible. I think Son-et-

Lumière is an anaemic bore but many think otherwise. The Procession could be delightful but would be very apt to be just commercialised & awful – "Floats", motor-propelled, with Pooty Gels shivering in butter-muslin (mauve, pink, yellow & Cambridge blue) on a damp, grey night. If the whole thing is being got up, as you say, under aegis of Smithwick's [Brewery], you simply couldn't make the "cultural", or even "jollification", aspect outweigh the commercial. And if Tourism raises its ugly head & Ireland of the Welcomes gets cracking, then there'll be a welter of scarlet & emerald colleens with harps & spinning-wheels and cardboard Round Towers. I think if you try to be ambitious there'll be trouble.

To Mrs Peggy Butler at Maidenhall

Playhouse, Nottingham. 14 December 1963

Very sorry you've been abed. I'm rather feeble too. Rehearsals are rather a tonic. If you have to think of other things & get interested & diverted, the ailments diminish. Truth is we're all starting the BREAK-UP. Rehearsals have been in London in a warehouse back of St Bart's at the top of 84 stone steps which I have found quite a struggle. Weekends have to be devoted daffedly answering the 20 or 30 boring accumulations – "Will you lecture at Oxford College, Mississippi?" – "I am a girl of 17 with two heads & no brain, how do I become a STAR?" – "I have a very old and very beautiful and very valuable edition of Shakespeare published by Collins in 1910, should I send it to Sotheby's or would you care to purchase it for 20 Guineas?"

To Mrs Peggy Butler at Maidenhall

Annaghmakerrig. 20 December 1963

The installation [as Chancellor of Queen's University] was really rather fun – helped by radiant weather. The Procession was quite impressive, with the L. Mayor in v. grand robes, preceded by his mace-bearer, leading a bevy of scarlet Aldermen, followed by at least 150 Academics in bright hoods & flowing gowns including 6 or 7 splendid iron grey Lady Dons (Mrs Pankhurst's influence takes a while to spread) followed by the Chancellor, a very tall upper-class gentleman called Michael Grant, in black watered silk with Cambridge blue

Sir Tyrone and Lady Guthrie welcome Queen Elizabeth II to the Queen's University of Belfast where he was chancellor, 1966.

facings, followed by *my* mace-bearer (a tiny physicist in a rose pink hood staggering under a great knobkerrie of solid silver), followed by me in black damask loaded with gold embroidery, followed by my Page – a twelve-year-old in absurd black velvet Lord Fauntleroy get-up with buckled shoes & cocked hat.

We waddled the length of Whitla Hall while the university organist (Professor Philip Cranmer, a *dear* boy whose father sang the bass part in *The Immortal Hour* in a Birmingham accent and a voice like a charcoal biscuit) ... while dear Philip at the organ belted out a "specially composed" march of unmatched discordancy – it sounded like Saint Bernard dogs romping on the keyboard. After that there was sherry sherry all the way with greybeards bending over one's hand and saying "Chencellurr!" Then a Reception in the Great Hall for Convocation – theoretically all graduates, in fact a collection of about 250 SPOOKS which no city but good splendid old Belfast could muster –bustling with Righteousness & Consciousness that the Lord was on their side.

There's a lot of prep to be done – it's a life-appointment so I hope I needn't feel too pressed for time – I think perhaps I can be a little helpful in steering Queen's towards being a thoroughly liberal influence in the North. It is now a much larger, more rich & influential an institution than 30 years ago. An immense building programme is afoot.

Becky is rather well. She, the McGormans, Burns', Ethel & Anna gave us a Party in the kitchen last week. Sherry & whiskey (at their expense) were broached, one of those terrible little Ladies' Fireside Companions (hearth-brush, tiny shovel, tinier poker and tiniest tongs on fancy stand) was presented and Becky Made a Speech – very well. All in aid of the Chancellorship which has given more pleasure locally than a Beatification.

The second season at the Guthrie Theater in Minneapolis proceeded successfully with Guthrie's productions of *Henry V* and *Volpone*. He also directed *Six Characters in Search of an Author* at the University of Minnesota. His book *A New Theatre* was published. At home, the jam factory hovered between triumph and disaster. The disclosure that he had willed the mansion and agricultural estate of Annaghmakerrig to his farm-steward Seamus McGorman created intense family feelings of betrayal, his sister Peggy Butler having understood that she was co-inheritor, objecting primarily to the absence of consultation. She felt that in the event of her family not wishing to retain the property he should have considered 'some useful scheme' such as a youth hostel. A meeting at Maidenhall ended in Guthrie fleeing from the house.

To Mrs Peggy Butler at Maidenhall

Annaghmakerrig. 3 January 1964

Was in Dublin y'day with Joe Martin on jam biz & ran into Joe Hone with Miss Jacky. They pressed me cordially to join them for a drink but we had other fish to fry & couldn't accept. I thought Jacky looked wholly respectable & not a bit Beatnik which we had secretly feared! She struck me as a bit older than Joe. But maybe that's quite a good thing. What nationality? and what's her occupation? Christopher Scaife [Guthrie's oldest college friend] is being a delightful guest – wholly self-sufficient but very joining-in when wished. He has a fire in the Blue Room & writes there most of the day and we meet at meals in the evening. I have now finished my book, barring the copying & revision, and the revising is rather a pleasure & chiefly consists in keeping down adjectives and striking out SIX in front of every noun.

To Mrs Peggy Butler at Maidenhall

c/o Oliver Rea, 1098 Guard Ave S, Minneapolis. Undated, 1964

Just back from 10-day lecture tour. I'm not going to embark on theme of *will* "(Uncle's Will" is the oldest dramatic theme in the world after "Boy meets Gel") until I get home & can consult Baldwin Murphy [Solicitor]. I was under the impression that Annaghmakerrig was mine; but I may be wrong & don't, anyway, want to be unduly possessive. I thought, and think, that it's a wise & more equitable plan to leave Julia money, rather than the Place. But natch I want to leave things in the most acceptable way to all parties concerned.

It was rather nice getting a blick of Charleston, Carolina – my first time in The South. A nice Lady (with a capital L for Upper Class) took me on a brief architectural tour and ran off EVERY cliché of White Ladies talking about Negroes, incl.: "I love them. I was brought up by a nanny whom I just adored. She was my second mother" till finally, as we passed a new housing estate, she announced that "Of course, any place *they* go gets run down and dirty. They keep coals, my dear, in the bath!" (As the houses are all heated, *they* must import their bath coal at great expense & solely for ornament.)

In Calif. there were roses & arum lilies & acacia trees (wattle to you) all in full bloom and it was warm enough to eat on the paddy-oh. But, even so, I LOATHE it! [Hollywood] city is repellent, the more so because natural surroundings are spectacularly lovely and climate simply dreamy.

To Mrs Peggy Butler at Maidenhall

Minnesota Theater Company. 5 March 1964

Just a line to say that all is going reasonably well here. Apart from starting rehearsals in the theatre I have been writing mile-a-minute for the N.Y. Times (very remunerative) and "putting finishing touches" to my book – and oddly long business – checking statistics, quotations

& so on – fiddly, but rather pleasurable IF there were long firelit hours in a book-lined study; but just a bore when it has to be done at the end of rather too long a day.

Joe Martin has been ill in N.Y., a heart condition brought on I fear by the ceaseless hard work and anxiety about the jam. I'm going to ring him now and, if he's still in N.Y.C., am going to ask Dick Crampton to call & give him the once over.

To Mrs Peggy Butler at Maidenhall

Minnesota Theater Company. 21 March 1964

Joe Martin is back at work, has started on expansion & improvement of factory. We had 6" of snow last week. I was supposed to lecture in Oxford, Ohio, & had started thither by plane. After 30 or 40 mins. We turned around because neither Chicago, Milwaukee, Cleveland or Detroit were fit to land in so we were back in Minn. after an hour or so.

To Mrs Peggy Butler at Maidenhall

Minnesota Theater Company. 24 March 1964

I think it wiser not to keep up a correspondence in which your letters seem to me acrimonious and selfish, as mine evidently do to you. So do let's wait to discuss it fully and without acrimony when we can *talk*. If you want Julia to discuss the matter with us, in your place, we shall be very happy. *Of course* I do not intend to treat her unfairly, unkindly or even ungenerously. If she, or you, have a legal claim on the place, if Judy predeceases you, then that settles the matter. You have made it fully clear that you are hurt and angry at what you consider my "selfishness", "unreasonableness" and "irresponsibility". Repeating these charges in letter after letter does not help to clear up a situation which you seem to think I don't take seriously. I do take it very seriously; but I know that angry, or worse, "grieved", letters are only inflammatory.

The weather continues charming.

To Mrs Peggy Butler at Maidenhall

T.G. Theater, Vineland Place, Minneapolis. 12 April 1964

Just back From Chicago where I was "Speaking". Such restful and delightful train journeys – 7 hours each way, 4 of them winding along banks of Mississippi River.

Hubert's letter much appreciated. It was courageous to embark on such a turbulent sea and the reasonable, friendly tone deeply acceptable. It even makes me wonder whether out of this sickening Hurluburlu a better mutual understanding between the four of us may emerge. But, though tempted to start explaining reasons for leaving A'Kerig to Seamus ... I know that you think the matter was not reasoned at all but was one solely of impulse ... I am not going to do so.

The serious issues involved seem to me quite impersonal. They are – as I see it but I'm fully prepared to see them otherwise – 1/ A matter of general family policy in respect of property; 2/ A matter of how this particular property should be bequeathed to the general advantage. And I think you were wrong to go in for emotional and highly provocative WILL-BRANDISHING. I was wrong to be provoked. And I do apologise for that.

Naturally, if your legal claims can be entertained, then I have to give way and make what compensation I can to Seamus for having raised his "expectations".

In all this controversy, you and, apparently, Julia and, for all the kind and reasonable tone of his letter, Hubert, assume that you are the wronged parties. You have placed me in the position of Defendant and are grieved that I do not accept this position & offer apologies for heartless, thoughtless & irresponsible behaviour. I don't see it that way at all. I thought (and think) that I was making thoughtful and careful provision for my decease. It is true that I didn't consult you. But this, though maybe mistaken, was not unpremeditated.

I'm not saying that my present Will is necessarily the wisest way of arranging things. But it has been the product of some thought and feeling. There. Enough. I absolutely refuse to stand in the pillory as a totally thoughtless, unfeeling, silly, "theatrical" star.

I'd like Julia to see this letter – & of course, Dick too. Does no harm for young people to have the written evidence that old people are still excitable, quarrelsome children. And, if they have half the sense I credit them with, it will in no way diminish the Respect with which young people should regard those who have preceded them on the journey.

To Mrs Peggy Butler at Maidenhall

Minnesota Theater Company. 19 April 1964

> We've had five dress rehearsals in a row of *Henry V*, if not good at least ready. A public dress rehearsal tonight – invited friends & well-wishers – then 3 weeks of matinées sold out to Mpls. & St. P. Education Authorities who send, literally, tens of thousands of teenagers in busses. A v.g. lively, alert audience last year; & I don't see why not again.

To Mrs Peggy Butler at Maidenhall

Minnesota Theater Company. 7 May 1964

> The [Kilkenny] Beer Festival – *such* a glamorous name! – is, I can see, a help as a focal point for various "cultural" & semi-cultural events. I couldn't be less surprised that Congreve is OFF. Have you met C. Fitz-Simon's intended? The nuptials, I hear, are at Hammersmith at 10.30 so I assume she's a Romanist. What of Joe [Hone]'s engagement? I heard from him a day or two ago but there was no word of the wedding or of Miss, so I though it better not to allude when writing back.

To Mrs Peggy Butler at Maidenhall

Minnesota Theater Company. 20 May 1964

> Peter (Kesteven) wrote that she had been at C.Fitz-Simon's Nuptials but, characteristically, left it at the bare fact – no, she said "Ailish looked gaunt in black lace"; but it's really the bride's appearance, parents & background that one's curious about.

To Mrs Peggy Butler at Maidenhall

Minnesota Theater Company. 10 June 1964

> Please write to anyone you know who might be helpful, to go to Harrod's, London, and ask for Irish Farmhouse Jam.

To Mrs Peggy Butler at Maidenhall

Annaghmakerrig. 17 July 1964

> Off to factory, where All Hands to the hulling of strawberries – they, raspberries & b'currants are all ripe at once & arriving in vaster

quantity than we can manage. To make matters worse our boiler went wrong at the height of the crisis & was out of commission for 36 precious hours. Now we are working day & night shifts round the 24 hours. Yesterday over 80 boils were achieved – that's about 10,000 pounds of jam.

Migsie [Davis] is here – enfeebled but splendidly alert. Also James Cromwell, son of one of the actors at M'polis [John Cromwell], a very nice lad. He's six foot six and a half inches and EATS more than anyone I've ever known. Freddie Bennett – once an actor at the Old Vic – arrives tomorrow. He's recently been sadly bereaved. He's very stalwart & will be a help with the fruit – one hopes the picking & fresh air & so on will be restorative.

To Mrs Peggy Butler at Maidenhall

Annaghmakerrig. 14 August 1964

It seems we are both – and I guess Hubert and Judy too – in the grip of passions which we do not understand and cannot control. I *can* understand that you should be wounded at not being consulted, but not to the extent of bitterness and fury, which you evidently feel. It never crossed my mind that you should feel that Annaghmakerrig was partly yours. In my opinion the will makes it perfectly clear that this is not so; and Mrs G on various occasions explained to me (and I thought to you) that she was not leaving it to us jointly because she considered that might be a cause of friction. If you think I am wrong about this, do let us agree about a solicitor and get his opinion. I have already consulted Baldwin Murphy, who may not be Socrates but is a very experienced drafter and executor of wills. In his opinion Annaghmakerrig is, without the slightest doubt, mine not merely during my lifetime but to bequeath it as I think right.

I did not think it right to leave the house and land to you because you have Maiden Hall; nor to Julia because I presumed that should she ever want to live in Ireland, Maiden Hall would be hers. [Judy and I] both felt that we should do what we could to keep the place used and occupied, if possible by someone whose roots and interests are in this locality.

I have – and I admitted this the other night and do so again – been inconsistent in that I did not discuss it with you beforehand.

This was very silly and I regret it infinitely. I didn't discuss it with you beforehand because I didn't want to risk another disagreement with Hubert. I thought, and think, that whatever disposal I make of my property he will feel as he felt over your marriage settlement, then over Aunt Sue's will and then over the execution of Mrs G's will, that I have insufficient consideration of your interests. Finally, there is the question of my continually trying to "domineer" over you. I may have domineered a bit when we were children, because I was nearly five years older, but I cannot accept that I either have done so, or have attempted to do so, in any single way, for the last forty years.

Love, not quite as ever; but I try to hope that out of mis-understanding and mutual unkindness, an even deeper love may grow.

To Mrs Peggy Butler at Maidenhall

AK. 17 October 1964

I'm off to Minneapolis on Tues. Not eager to go but can't be avoided. We shall have to have another attempt to settle our disagreement. But I simply can't face the boiling passions – yet. Nor, I'm sure, can you. Dewhursts [English cousins] arrived today with formidable amount of luggage. Michael is walking not too badly. If only he wouldn't talk in this loud boisterously encouraging way about nothing! Molly seems a bit better, I think, less twitchy & eerie.

To Lady Guthrie at Annaghmakerrig

University of Minnesota. 22 October 1964

I've had lunch with the Drama Dept. (teachers only) followed by rather too long with Dr Maxine Klein who's a tall Hilde Wangel with black hair and a nervous over-emphatic manner while she told me of her rehearsals of *Dame aux Camélias* in which Murgreet had to show the characteristics of a Swan while Almond did ditto ditto as a Greyhound. Such blathers.

6 Characters made quite a good start last night. All principal parts quite well cast if, inevitably, too young. But the talent is v.g. & enthusiasm (as yet) v. high.

In October, addressing students from Dublin and Belfast in his capacity as Chancellor of Queen's University, in Belfast City Hall, Guthrie gave grave offense to the Unionist establishment by describing the Irish border as "senseless". There were loud calls for his resignation.

To Mrs Peggy Butler at Maidenhall

University of Minnesota. 27 October 1964

Thank you for nice warm back-up letter over the Chancellor crise! My speech *was* indiscreet and it *was* naïve to suppose that coming right on the morrow of the Divis St riots and the eve of gen. election it wouldn't be taken as a piece of political partizanship. I shall have to face a desperately uncomfortable show-down with the Vice-Chancellor & Pro-Chancellors, who have behaved (I think) in a silly & disloyal way – but in a horrid & depressing way is *very* interesting. I can't decide whether, or no, they intend to manoeuvre me into resigning. I have no intention of doing so; it would precipitate a worse crisis because all the non-Unionists would say that "the establishment" was pushing out the too-liberal Chancellor. It's a storm in a kettle I truly believe and best course is to do – and say – as little as possible.

I'm writing this in a lovely sunny upper chamber of the Faculty Club at the top of a vast building perched on a bluff on the mighty Mississippi. My duties are light – rehearsals 7-10 p.m. and by day I visit various of the myriad classes of the Drama Dept. Did you see Brian Friel's play in Dublin? *Off to Philadelphia.*[44] He wrote a lot of it here. He was "attached" to us for about 3 months last year.

Thanks again for yours. It's very comforting to feel that you and Hubert would be behind one in a crisis of the kind.

To Mrs Peggy Butler at Maidenhall

Guthrie Theater, Minneapolis. 10 November 1964

Here till the end of Nov getting up *6 Characters* at the University and trying hard to help the Drama Dept at the U decide what it's really trying to do. At present it's a darling little Silly that doesn't know what

---

44   The correct title is *Philadelphia, Here I Come!*.

it is, like the blue fairy lights at the end of *Peter Pan*. As there is a staff of about 15, mostly learned doctors; graduate-students to the number of 80; and literally hundreds of undergraduate "Drama Majors" (not to be confused with Drum Majorettes) it's time they all made up their minds. We return (via Canada) at the beginning of Dec.; & I'm getting an Hon. Degree from T.C.D. on Dec. 3.

To Mrs Peggy Butler at Maidenhall

Minnesota Theatre Company. 26 November, Thanksgiving Day, 1964

Six Characters opened last night at the University. We're going in an hour or so to Thanksgiving Dinner with Tanya to the Barton Emmets. He's a great nephew of Posy Emmet who was a daughter of Judge Emmett who befriended our grandfather in New York and was himself a nephew of the Patriot. Our grandmother presented Posy in ostrich feathers to Victoria the Good! Small, small world.

P.S. Didn't explain that Bart Emmet is manager of the theatre – the brain of a pea-hen but "OH so kind and TRULY good".

To Mrs Peggy Butler at Maidenhall.

Annaghmakerrig. 11 December 1964

I cannot bear the shadow that hangs between us over the future of A'kerrig. I think, I *know*, that I was wrong not to consult you about the disposal of this place. And it's still not too late to do so.

I think, if you agree, that Judge Peter Smithwick [Kilkenny lawyer] should be present. I have to be away the whole of next week but have to be in Dublin either 21, 22 or 23. I want to say that I can't, and don't, promise to meet all your wishes but I will do my best to do so & to see, & respect, your point of view. But if the meeting is not just to be another calamity we must *both* be determined to avoid emotional outbursts and recriminations.

13

WHAT BECOMES OF ANNAGHMAKERRIG?

The discord between Tyrone Guthrie and his sister Peggy Butler about the disposal of Annaghmakerrig persisted. It is not difficult to detect an element of needling in his letters, particularly where he lists his theatrical distinctions and academic honours as if demonstrating in a veiled way that his achievements – and his circle of acquaintance – were more lustrous than those of the Butlers. (He would have been distinctly aware of Hubert Butler's superior intellect.) He was keeping in touch with his niece, Julia Crampton, in New York, in a less sardonic manner concerning the terms of his impulsive will. In the 1965 season at the Guthrie Theater, Minneapolis, he directed *Richard III* and *The Cherry Orchard.*

To Mrs Peggy Butler, staying in Paris
Minnesota Theater Company. 17 February 1965

> We arrived here last night & your p.c. from Paris was here. Very glad you are enjoying it. Saw Dick & Julia in N.Y.C. – not the easiest visit since that charming evening at Maiden Hall.[45] I said I was sorry that precipitate will [bequeathing property to Seamus McGorman] had been made, and was fully willing to reconsider & would welcome their suggestions for better/wiser use of A.kerrig. They said they would try to think. Dick was very tactful throughout. I think – but only think – we parted friends. I shall write in a while and discuss what seem to me various (not very sensible) possibilities, not because I think they are even possibilities, but to try to show that their suggestions and advice really *are* wanted.

45   A reference to his visit to the Butlers' home when he had been asked to leave the house.

I've had two wounded little notes from Hubert, because I deputised for him at a meeting in C'blayney a few weeks ago. The Secy. asked me to do so and I assumed (apparently wrongly) that Hubert had asked to be released and that by taking his place I was being helpful. As it turns out, he wanted to come, & feels that I deliberately usurped his position. Seems we've got onto conflicting wavelengths and that every word and deed is liable to (mutual) misinterpretation.

My memories of Paris are principally of one very pleasant brief autumn trip as guests of Garson Kanin and Ruth Gordon[46] with a splendid luncheon to meet Thornton [Wilder] & Alice B. Toklas, topped off with AMAZING visit to Alice B's apartment, which had something to do with Kristina of Sweden and was stuffed, but STUFFED, with Picassos – wall to ceiling.

To Mrs Julia Crampton in New York

Minnesota Theater Company. 2 April 1965

I have had a very long letter from your father, a very nice letter, trying to be fair; but full of what *I* think to be misconstructions of my motives, and more particular Judy's, in the matter of the disposal of my property. I therefore want to tell you quietly what my conscious thoughts have been. I am aware that these may be, as your father implies, no more than rationalisations of sub-conscious urges. That being so, I don't think it a bad idea that you should know at least what the conscious thoughts have been.

1. Before making a will I *should* have discussed the disposal of Annaghmakerrig with your mother. I have admitted this; and asked her forgiveness – more than once. Your father and I have very different views about the disposal of property and had already disagreed (years ago, just after the war, I think) about how Aunt Sue had disposed of hers. I didn't think he would agree with what I planned to do and didn't want a quarrel. Your parents also suppose that the plans for A'kerrig were inspired out of jealous malevolence by Judy. This simply is not so. It was my idea to leave the place to Seamus [McGorman]. She neither thought of the plan nor ever urged it. If blame there is, it must *be laid entirely* at my door.

---

46   Garson Kanin was a distinguished US writer and director; his wife Ruth Gordon was one of Guthrie's favourite actors.

2. I did not leave A.Kerrig to you for the following reasons. (A) You will be the heir of Maiden Hall. If you want, as may well be in the future, to spend time in Ireland, you will have a home there. (B) You have married an American who is busily and usefully employed in America. Therefore it is reasonable to suppose that your children will be brought up as Americans. (C) The maintenance of Annaghmakerrig costs money. For some years before Mrs G died I had been helping her financially, a fact of which, I believe, your parents are aware and of which there is no need to remind them. When Mrs G died and I inherited, the expenses were such that we could only afford with difficulty and by giving up our place in Lincoln's Inn. Since then both my income and my capital have very substantially increased so that is no longer a problem. (D) Your parents, apparently, find it very hurtful that I should consider Seamus a suitable person to have the place. I do not see why it should be so hard to understand: he is working very hard to maintain and improve it. It seems to me only suitable that I should wish to reward him. I know that he feels, as I do, a great desire to see the neighbourhood more prosperous. I want to enable him to make the best contribution to that end.

I appreciate that, if he owned it, he would neither wish, nor be able to afford, to live in the genteel style which we have inherited (only since the 18c). I should be sad to think of harness and hay in the drawing-room; but I'm not convinced that this is sadder than seeing it maintained at considerable expense for the Family to enjoy for maybe two or three weeks in the year. There may be other alternatives.

3. Now for the future. The last thing that I want, or that Judy wants, is that our property should be a cause of hurt feelings to anyone. There is no legal reason, and no moral reason that I can see, why I shouldn't make another will. I can leave Annaghmakerrig to you, and, to compensate Seamus, leave him money. But I shall only feel that this is a responsible step if you and Dick help me to search for a sensible and public-spirited use for the place, i.e. not just a second holiday retreat (believe me, this is NOT intended as a jibe) for comfortably-off Americans. And we shall be grateful when, and if, you help us to make what we all agree to be wise plans.

I know that all this doesn't arise from greed for the property which is, as we all know, a financial liability, not an asset, and is likely to remain so during the lifetime of us all. It is a symbol of emotional stresses amongst the four of us of the older generation. This long letter is written in the hope that such stress may not involve you, the hope that the air may be a little cleared between you and me.

To Mrs Peggy Butler at Maidenhall
Minnesota Theater Company. 1 May 1965

This is to wish you many happy returns of your birthday. I think of you *constantly* and wonder how to heal the chasm that seems to have opened between us. I wrote to Julia about 6 weeks ago – the Sunday before Palm Sunday to be precise. My letter crossed a nice one from her. But I am disappointed & surprised to have had no further word. No doubt she is preoccupied; and I simply cannot believe that my letter, which was intended to be pacific, affectionate & co-operative, has been taken 'amiss'.

Richard III & Congreve's *Way of the World* (directed by Duggie Campbell) are playing to schools right now & open to the public next Mon & Tues. Spring has arrived. It's beautifully warm, snow gone, trees beginning to bud. I was in Kansas City a day or two ago. It's 600 miles south of here & the trees were out, also lilac, viola, dogwood et al. No more. I just wanted you to know that your birthday was remembered & with unchanged, though grieved & puzzled, affection.

To Mrs Peggy Butler at Maidenhall
Minnesota Theater Company. May 1, 1965

I had a very brief but nice note from Julia two days ago. Sorry to hear Cordelia had had scarlet fever. We've had floods & a tornado, latter very sensational. One or two outlying suburbs look like Ypres 1916 but central Minneapolis was only frightened, not hurt.

To Mrs Peggy Butler at Maidenhall
Minneapolis. 29 May 1965

I shall be 65 in a week or two; and begin to be quite conscious of waning energies. But if we die tomorrow it makes absolutely no difference to the love I feel for what you mean to me. I won't pretend that I have not been devastated by the recent manifestations – notably what I consider quite unmerited hostility to Judy – there's no use pretending that after all this our relations can ever be quite as serene and as mutually trusting as I know we both hoped & believed they would always be. I don't think we can struggle out of the impasse so long as you continue to believe that you are the injured party. Believe me, you've given as good as you've got.

I simply hate this estrangement – it's a nightmare which haunts me night and day. I KNOW that the property is not the cause of the wounds. I know very well that you are not greedy for property. On rational grounds I am still quite honestly totally unable to see why it has all made such a mutually wounding situation. I do realise that the importance of the whole business is symbolic and is connected with jealousy; and is way out of our conscious control. I shall try hard to discuss it all affectionately but realistically *with Julia*.

Do try & see Beckie. Accounts of her are not good. If you don't want to stay at A'kerrig that's alright. But if you do, just call Anna, who'd like to make things ready.

To Mrs Peggy Butler at Annaghmakerrig
Minnesota Theatre Company. 16 June 1965

We opened our third production – *Cherry O* – last night. V.v.g. recep & press today, all that heart could desire.

On Sunday we fly to Chicago; thence by train – two days & two nights – to San Francisco; thence fly to Sydney, breaking the enormous journey at Fiji. Then from Sydney right across Strylia to Perth where I'm asked to give advice about some Shakespeare Festival project. Then back here where I do a few things in the University. We hope to leave for home about mid-August.

Good news of the jam. You know we got our Govt grant & have built a large annexe onto the Rly Station. Now we're installing deep freezers which one HOPES will greatly ease the frantic pressure during the fruit season; and should enable us to more than double production … that's a split infinitive & instances the terrible corruption on the language of living in the U.S.A.

To Mrs Peggy Butler at Maidenhall

Annaghmakerrig. 12 August 1965

I had meant to ring last night, but Steeles are here and seem to telephone continuously to all parts of the British Isles. As you know, Geoffrey is Bunty's godson; and having them is partly an act of piety to her memory. They are oh so decent, but terribly "English" – giggly wee jokes about little, with no real humour or even meaning to them – the boys (much enjoying water-ski-ing and make quite a good dash at it) are nice enough creatures but their accents grate and there is a formidable lack of even the smallest symptom of "culture" … "pictures" mean the coloured ads in the glossy mags; "music" is strictly pop; Geoffrey is a quiet, mild, spectacled lower-middle-class anaesthetist – OH so right-minded in a right-wing style; and ever so decent and kind and good but D E A D L Y. Meriel hasn't come – the reason is slightly wrapped in mystery because she's the one who really finds things the most congenial here and is a good deal more intelligent than the gentleman-part. But they ARE decent; and do seem to want to come which I suppose is rather flattering.

My TV business went off alright, I think. If interested, it's to be on Oct 4 on B.B.C.2 which not every set can "get". Apparently "they" were quite pleased with it and are making it the "Pilot" of the series [*One Pair of Eyes*] which include quite grand people like David Cecil. Being the pilot is a mark of honour like being asked to lead the party which storms the Heights of Abraham or to lead the Quadrille with Milady.

To Mrs Peggy Butler at Maidenhall

Annaghmakerrig. 27 August 1965

So very glad Julia & Dick are planning to come here. We can then, I trust, discuss possible "arrangements" for the future of this house; and will, I know, all endeavour to do so with calm & good humour. Hope to see you soon and, let's hope, with some clearance of the atmosphere which I find at present – & I'm sure you do too – an almost ever-present depressant … that is not a euphonious sentence but is the truth.

To Mrs Peggy Butler at Maidenhall

Annaghmakerrig. 1 October 1965

We've induced Becky to venture downstairs. Mrs Killen's litter (wicker chair on 2 rattan poles) has been dug out of Big End Room & she ascends & descends the stairs in it. She's been a number of small expeditions in the car and it all bumps her back a little more into circulation with evident advantage to spiritual health. The relation with Ethel is a real problem to which I see NO solution.

We have bought a gramophone – beg pardon, Record Player! So far we have only one record – Verdi's Requiem – but it's ve'y ve'y splendid and bears repetition; but by degrees we hope to expend the rep. Such lovely weather. Only jam crop is blackberries but we despatch 7 ½ stone to factory today & hope for at least as much again.

Tanya is here for a week then she & I cross to England & go to see Ben Britten in Aldeburgh. We're doing *Peter Grimes* at the Met in Jan 1967 but the designs have to be ready a *year* ahead.

To Mrs Peggy Butler at Maidenhall

Annaghmakerrig. 6 November 1965

Just a belated line to say thanks for B & B & *much* enjoyed trip to Wexford [Opera: *Don Quichotte*]. I've been considerably "on the go" ever since & only got back from Belfast late last night. It was nice seeing Hubert looking so well; better, I thought, than for some time.

I saw you, almost touched you, on Kildare St on Wed aft. – or was it morning? But was too occupied steering thro' the maze of cycles, busses & pedestrians to do more than utter a scream, which you didn't hear. Was en route with Joe Martin to meet our third jam director, Pat Lynch, who is Prof of Economics at the National University & also (somehow) Chairman of Aer Lingus. Off to Canada tomorrow. Judy comes with me to London & returns on Friday.

I shall try to see Julia while I'm on that side; & we thought we might jointly go to see P.L. Travers who's at a ladies' college (forget name – think it's somewhere up the Hudson).

Pamela Travers, author of *Mary Poppins*, a family friend of the Butlers and godmother to both Julia and Dick, was Writer in Residence at Radcliffe College, Cambridge, Massachusetts. She had suggested that Annaghmakerrig should become a workplace for writers and artists on the lines of Yaddo or the MacDowell Colony in the US. The meeting was not immediately productive but paved the way for later plans that resulted in the foundation of the Tyrone Guthrie Centre at Annaghmakerrig.

To Mrs Julia Crampton in New York
Annaghmakerrig. 4 December 1965

Hope you got back alright after we had parted. I think it must have been "our" shuttle that crashed the very next day. I got to Westport in good order, had a great Sunday, then had to fly to the coast for two nights & two days of fearfully tedious business meetings. Then to Ottawa for more, but much more interesting meetings, then home where I had to turn right around and attend more meetings – University [Belfast] this time. So this is the first moment of leisure to write.

I shall explore possibilities either of some collaboration between Queen's U. Belfast & Trinity [College, Dublin] to consider eventual use of this house for whatever purpose they might jointly suggest – probably for free holidays for lowly-paid "intellectuals" or people working on special projects; OR collab. between Arts Councils of North & South. The latter seems to me a little more appealing because it *would* be a very suitably peaceful haven for writers, painters, etc, who *need* a bit of quiet & a bit of space (both very hard to obtain on limited means) and for whom far less is provided than for university people. The trouble in either case is lack of funds. I can leave something but not nearly enough. And all these bodies will be (rightly) reluctant to take on something which involves expenditure since they are all hard pressed.

I think and hope you'll agree that if we could try to make the whole scheme involve North/South collaboration it would be valuable. I don't want to make moves without your full agreement.

Eventually we shall have to discuss plans about furniture. At present, my arrangements for Judy, if she survives me, are to have use of all during her lifetime or for as long as she wishes. My feeling is that, if some such scheme as we hope goes through for the house, most of the contents should remain, rather than whatever body takes over should decide to furnish it in the very cheapest, most "institutional" style! I'm sure you agree. What Judy & I feel is that, after we go, we should like Peggy or you to take whatever you feel has particular sentimental or family value, but leave the house pleasantly and comfortably usable by whatever Inmates eventually come. Don't you think this is right?

I have left instructions that eight or nine people are to be given "mementoes" when I die. The choice is left to my executors & the idea is not that they be objects of partic. material value.

To Mrs Peggy Butler, c/o Dr Geo. Clarke, Presteigne, Radnorshire, Wales
Annaghmakerrig. 15 December 1965

This brings loving Christmas/New Year wishes. I got your whereabouts from Beckie who was very pleased with your card. I don't think Ethel is equal to taking a letter from Becky's dictation, even if the technical problems of the dictation were soluble the temperamental ones of the two ladies are insoluble. The faults aren't by any means on Ethel's side, tho' she is utterly maddening.

Julia & I flew to Boston to see Pamela Travers. She gave us an egg to our tea & encouragement (firm) to make a co-operative plan about this place; but she is not able to be personally a bit helpful and does not think (with which I agree) that American trusts will want to endow an Irish trust except for American purposes. I have written to Julia with alternative possibilities but will take no steps till I have her reaction. I think and HOPE that I have convinced her that there was never any intention to ignore her interest or cut her out of a substantial share of such worldly goods as I may leave.

I don't propose to discuss the plans with you or Hubert. If Julia cares to do so she is, naturally, entitled to do so. But between *us* it has all become so hopelessly emotional & unbearable that I think it can only be a source of even more unhappiness. I only ask you to believe that 1. Julia's feelings & interest and 2. The useful &, if possible, fruitful use of A'kerrig in future, are all Judy & I want to try to achieve in the disposal of the property. Let's try and forgive the whole affair. It can't, & won't, ever be possible to forget it. But we can agree, can't we, that all have been jealous and unreasonable and consequently unkind. Let's therefore assume that's what's past is past; and that we'll do better hereafter.

Guthrie's correspondence with his sister Peggy continues mainly from Annaghmakerrig where Becky Miles' final illness is the main topic. In 1966 Guthrie directed only one production each in the United States and Britain – George S. Kaufmann & Edna Ferber's *Dinner at Eight* at the Alvin Theater, New York, and Shakespeare's *Measure for Measure* at the Bristol Old Vic. The vexatious *leitmotif* of the disposal of the Annaghmakerrig property permeates all other topics. Guthrie reluctantly accepted Pamela Travers' suggestion that the house become a workplace for writers and artists. He had difficulty in envisaging the practicalities. He was also in consultation with An Oige (the Youth Hostel Association) with the possibility of a hostel in view. His health continued to be precarious, not helped by increasing anxiety about the financial affairs of the jam factory. His old friend Migsie Davis died in Belfast.

To Lady Guthrie at Annaghmakerrig
New York. No address or date, 1966

To reply to your thoughts about Ethel [Daley's] future, I think probably when Becky goes one of the girls (Joan or Lily) will have her to visit for a while. I think we must encourage in every possible way that she doesn't drift from Regan to Goneril as (moderately) useful servant. I think, if asked to help, Migsie could find her a job [in Belfast] in six minutes flat. And we can, I feel, recommend her as totally shiningly, HONEST, if not either very energetic, intelligent or methodical. If, after the demise, the girls don't come through & take her back to their houses, she must come to us for a while; but absolutely not as anything but a guest; it can be called "till you get sorted out & get over the shock".

To Mrs Peggy Butler at Maidenhall
Annaghmakerrig. 19 January 1966

We are going to spend 10 days with Chris Scaife near Beirut. It's his last year there before retirement (to small farmhouse near Florence) as he wants us to see it all with him before he goes. Did I tell you that he has totally lost the sight of one eye? Detached retina – I fear they made a hash of him in Bart's Hosp where he underwent five horrid operations last year. Needless to say he is amazingly philosophical &

courageous and makes as light of it as his war-crippled arm. He can read "a bit" & drive his car "slowly" & only has headaches "sometimes". After that I shall be 3 weeks in Bristol, getting up *Measure for Measure* for Bristol Old Vic. I've had a very nice letter from Mrs Crampton [Peggy's daughter Julia] approving my suggested (but far from realised) plans for A'kerrig. We have enough money for our lifetime but NOT enough to make anywhere near an adequate endowment; and no Good Cause will be able even to consider using the place if it costs money. I don't think Julia has fully grasped this; and I don't think you have grasped it at all. Rates, right away, are £150 p. a. and if the house isn't heated, which, while all the wood is about is a matter of labour rather than fuel, there has to be at least a caretaker. And that's before one even starts to think of the needs of whoever might be the incomers.

When I lie awake, as I do rather a lot when sinus is kicking up, I think how ironic it is that you and I should have so fallen out over the disposal of property. Of course I know that was only the apparent cause, the root cause is far less conscious & more complex. Perhaps it will leave us wiser, though scarred. It will be wisdom dearly bought. I had meant this to be a cheerful, newsy, chatty effusion & it seems to have got into a minor key. Don't think that I'm "depressed". It's not the case. I hasten towards the sepulchre with a great deal of cheerfulness, even contentment. Autumn was ever my favourite season.

To Ms Peggy Butler at Maidenhall
Annaghmakerrig. 14 April 1966

Becky is much the same. It's hard to see much change from day to day but I think she is quite a bit feebler and the effort to achieve "the chair" becomes more pitifully exhausting.

It makes a strange obsessing, but not by any means entirely sad, atmosphere. In a way it's rather thrilling & ennobling to see the spirit being *gradually* released from the trammels of mortality. She grumbles incessantly & the relation between herself and Ethel is utterly weird. But I think poor Ethel has become the symbol of all her misfortunes & frustrations – not exactly the symbol but the embodiment – & being bad to (and about) Ethel is the equivalent of taking revenge upon, being quits with, misfortune.

To Peggy Butler at Maidenhall

Annaghmakerrig. 27 April 1966

We can't immediately rise out of what you call this slough of disagreement. Later, perhaps; and I think our great mutual affection will be strong enough to stand the strain. But the disagreement is deeper than just about the disposal of a property. We will co-operate with Julia and Dick over the future of A'kerrig and I think we can reach mutually acceptable decisions IF you and Hubert will keep out of it. Your jealous resentment towards Judy and my ditto ditto towards Hubert is, I believe, the sub-conscious background of the whole trouble. Because of this he and you ought, in my opinion, to leave us to settle the future of our home with the younger generation.

Rumour hath it that y'day Becky caught Ethel a thwack on the back of the head with her stick. I'll investigate and add a stop press report.

No, she just threw a mug at her. Ethel is being nice and "understanding" but oh dear she's having a hard vigil. I wish it could end.

To Hubert Butler at Maidenhall

Annagh-ma-Kerrig. 9 May 1966

Of course we shall be only delighted if Julia can follow up Pamela Travers' suggestions [for Annaghmakerrig]. And we shall also be happy if my impression of our meeting with Pamela was wrong. But I thought that she was much preoccupied, and fully committed financially, with her own plans, which were concerned with her own house in London. But, if Julia is willing to follow any American leads which Pamela can supply, or any of her own, with a view to financing A'Kerrig as a home for artists & writers, naturally we shall be delighted.

It *is* our house; and, while Peggy will of course get any financial advantage to which she may become entitled under the terms of Mrs G's will, your implied right to decisions about the future of the place are hard not to resent. I am attached to Julia, and even were there no blood-tie, I couldn't but like and respect both herself and Dick. I cannot, however, see that they have the slightest claim, legal or moral, to possess A'kerrig. Julia has a sentimental right to be interested in its future; and I have a duty to respect that interest; a duty which I had neglected, but which I am now trying to fulfil. I am wholeheartedly delighted that they are interested and will help to make a mutually acceptable plan. Julia, Dick and I agreed that to be a part-time holiday-home for the Cramptons was not a suitable future for the place.

Incidentally, and I have never before asked the question, what do you envisage for the future of Maidenhall? Surely it is the more logical holiday, and perhaps eventually year-round, home for the Cramptons. We had, perhaps wrongly, taken it for granted that Maidenhall would eventually be Julia's.

To Mrs Peggy Butler at Maidenhall

Annaghmakerrig. 7 June 1966

I've been in hospital – had to have polyps removed, very far up & back necessitating general anaesthetic. It all meant cancelling the first part of [a] Canadian trip, natch the more interesting western half. But can't be helped, and, in a way, it's better because of being available for Becky who depends on us more than somewhat. She's quite able to "take things in" but no longer feels very much other than what touches herself. Thought it better she should know about Migsie [Davis]'s death, otherwise one gets caught up in a perfect web of prevarication & concealment.

To Mrs Julia Crampton in New York

Annaghmakerrig. 30 July 1966

This is a brief progress report on relations with the Arts Council[s]. And I'm sorry to say that there is very little progress. Members of both Councils are mostly on their hols. but in both cases the attitude is distinctly favourable. Three members of the Eire Council came to lunch this week to look us over & discuss the project – Terry White & Bobs Figgis, both of whom I think you know, and Dr Conor Maguire, retired Lord Chief Justice, very distinguished but *very* old. I think a similar group from the North plan to come soon. They none of them think we can move *fast* – & I suppose one can't expect it of public bodies.

I was distressed in a passage in a letter from your mother (an otherwise friendly letter) in which she says "Julia says you've sent a codicil in which she has to agree to most of the furniture remaining in situ, and, if the Arts Council plan goes through, no word of a pied-à-terre for her when she needed it". I trust she has, as they say, taken you up wrong; because I thought my covering letter had made it entirely clear that you didn't have to agree to anything. The codicil was sent for your comments. About the pied-à terre, I hope you agree that in the whole scheme this is a detail, not a principal item, and the time to discuss it is when/if we get down to details with the architect. The whole situation is so touchy and emotion-fraught that the most harmless sentences and remarks seem to give mortal offence. So please be frank in your dealings with me and don't, if you disagree with any proposal, keep silent with me. If you don't like the codicil, say so; and say why; and propose an amended version. But please bear in mind that it's only to tide over the period of negotiation with the Arts Councils, in case I die suddenly before all is agreed.

I am most anxious that you should feel that we are jointly taking responsible, sensible decisions.

To Lady Guthrie at Annaghmakerrig
Gorham Hotel, 136 West 55th Street, New York City. 22 August 1966

I think Seamus [McGorman] would really be considerably relieved if Bob [Burns] works mostly (not entirely) indoors. And I believe Bob will accept this happily if (1) he's not totally changed from one job to another, & (2) it's put to him that doing so is helpful to all of us.

Ever so nice letter from [Michael] Langham regretting my inability to go there [Stratford, Ontario] next year. Rehearsals plod on quite well here. Blanche Turlea & Walter Pigeon [in *Dinner at Eight*] *will* know their words – very nearly so already. Ms Arlene Francis is a great, big, quite handsome, head on two feet – *highly* capable.

I have seen Charlie Baker, he thinks he can get money from Glenville who is now the richest person in the United States; failing him, Arthur Turchell. Please tell Joe [Martin] I am hopeful of getting new investors.

The financial problems of Irish Farmhouse Preserves were becoming acute; Guthrie felt bound to seek funds in the US. The long-time cook-general at Annaghmakerrig, Anna Kelly, announced her departure to get married.

To Lady Guthrie at Annaghmakerrig

Gorham Hotel, 136 West 55ᵗʰ Street, New York City. 1 September 1966

Well, Anna! Naturally the time had to come! Give her my love & gratitude for the kindness and thought as well as energy, nice and endearingly eager to show friendship to us as her friends.

Had a v. good day today at *Dinner at Eight*. They're all beginning to get on top of the words & to Act. According to Lola[47] there is now advance booking of $400,000 & it simply can't NOT be "a success".

To Lady Guthrie at Annaghmakerrig

c/o Lola & Sonia Kipnis, Westport, Conn. 3 September 1966

Dept. of Absolute Candour: I have been having some breathless attacks, not nearly bad enough to stop me working but bad enough to be a nuisance. I had a cardiograph & a complete going-over. The cardiograph shows some degeneration compared with 6 years ago, but not alarming. This very hot, muggy weather is not helpful. My spirits are excellent, I'm enjoying the work & am not finding it "too much".

You might ring Joe & tell him that I am exploring several possibilities to get investors and am quite hopeful but have no one yet "in the bag". Tell him I know the urgency BUT I can't press people to move at any but their pace. Lester Osterman has promised to invest. Franklin & Sam Friedman have both said "Yes" but I don't feel, nor does Lola, that we can count on them for more than $1000 each, & we need $75,000! Lola is v. sceptical. Did you give the cheque for $3000 to Joe?

To Lady Guthrie at Annaghmakerrig

Gorham Hotel, 136 West 55ᵗʰ Street, New York City. 3 September 1966

I've got to cough up 1,500 words about *D at 8* in place of Miss Ferber who said, reasonably enough, that she felt too old. She is well over 80. She came to a rehearsal on Thurs & was extremely affable, gave terse (mostly) sensible, shrewd notes & professed herself graciously pleased.

---

47 'Lola' – Guthrie's friend the Russian writer Leonid Kipnis – was associate producer of *Dinner at Eight*.

To Lady Guthrie at Annaghmakerrig

Gorham Hotel, 136 West 55th Street, New York City. 14 September 1966

> The play is pretty ready. With intervals, it looks as if it would play very little under three hours which is too long for this kind of evening. So yesterday Miss Edna & I spent 2 hours cutting. She is being extremely pleasant and sensible and co-operative but owing to age is very slow.

To Lady Guthrie at Annaghmakerrig

Gorham Hotel, 136 West 55th Street, New York City. 16 September 1966

> Will you please write a cheque for £3,000 to Irish Farmhouse & find out what Joe wants done with it. I think he wants to open an account with a bank other than the Bank of Ireland, Clones. Find out. A substantial cheque should now have come from Canada and Jim [Barr, stockbroker] will be sending another large cheque on Sept 27 so our account should be O.K.

To Lady Guthrie at Annaghmakerrig

Gorham Hotel, 136 West 55th Street, New York City. 17 September 1966

> Last night's dress rehearsal [*Dinner at Eight*] was pretty dreary; interminable waits between scenes; ½ hour intermission fraught with bangs, crashes & curses. Miss Ferber "kicking up" about last set which she doesn't like. She was "handled" by Lola – very firmly. "You may not like eet, Mees Fairbair, but yore taste ees not everyone's taste!" Total TOTAL collapse of small angry party.

To Lady Guthrie at Annaghmakerrig

c/o Lola & Sonia Kipnis, Westport, Conn. 18 September 1966

> Our first preview (packed) passed off reasonably. Curtain didn't rise till 8.50 and didn't come down till 12.00 midnight with an *interminable* intermission (scenery diffs) but the audience stayed & in a dull way enjoyed itself. They seemed entirely to miss the "high" comedy, comedy of manners sort of thing, but loved the melodrama – e.g. suicide of film star, fight between butler & chauffeur. Only the most obvious "jokes" got laugh; & only very broad noisy acting was accepted as Acting. However, I'm nearly sure that when, as we will, get the

changes working really fast, that it will be a "success". Remembering *Matchmaker* previews, last night's was an audience of Ciceros, Socrates, Jane Austens and Virginia Wolves.

To Lady Guthrie at Annaghmakerrig
c/o Lola & Sonia Kipnis, Westport, Conn. 22 September 1966

We have now got the playing time down to 2½ hours.

I'm not going to be able to finish up the Jam biz as soon as I'd hoped. Arthur Cantor, who is being genuinely helpful, is taking me to a lawyer on Wed, & as I leave for Toronto Thurs we won't be able to put the lawyer's advice into practice till I come back. As you can probably sense, I feel a bit more "flustered" and "under pressure". One feels such a goat to allow it to "matter".

To Lady Guthrie at Annaghmakerrig
c/o Master's Lodging, Massey College, Toronto. 30 September 1966

The [New York] opening was rather troublesome. The first act was v. sticky but the Co. kept its collective head very well & conquered in Act 2 which plays to a v.g. climax. The notices were 3-1 in favour but the bad one, alas, was the N.Y.Times (Walter Kerr now) which is the only one with any weight. However, the "advance" will ensure solid good biz for some weeks.

Arthur Cantor is being v. helpful over [jam] shares & I have two or three "prospects" as well as those who he is approaching.

Dinner at Eight ran for four months at the Alvin Theater. Helpful advice and contacts in the US failed to realize substantial funds for the Newbliss jam factory.

To Mrs Peggy Butler at Maidenhall
Annaghmakerrig. 22 October 1966

I do think you should write to Becky. She may hang on for ages longer or she may not. I notice hardly any change since I went away. Sometimes she is too weak (or disinclined) for conversation but in general she is completely lucid, and fully able to take in not only what you write, but the fact that you've written.

Guthrie (*right*) and Judith (*centre*) with the playwright Brian Friel (*left*), his daughter Judith and other guests at Annaghmakerrig, 1966.

Ethel is a problem. Becky *never stops* complaining about her (we're convinced the complaints of mistreatment – beatings, curses, neglect – are unfounded) but the place is dirty; and Ethel's stupidity must, when she is daily and nightly companion, be abrasive. The Daley sisters are utterly useless; when I got Mrs McGoldrick to go in for a night, it was Becky who put her out, with queenly but rather hurtful dignity: "Thank you, I think I prefer my niece to attend me"!

To Peggy Butler at Annaghmakerrig

Annaghmakerrig. 10 & 12 November 1966

We go to Belfast for opening of Arts Festival at Q.U.B. and back next week for Reading Aloud [Eugene McCabe's play *Swift*] which I'm arranging and then the Queen's senate and after the reading Brian Friel (accomp. by delightful wife & 3 children) Dame Flora [Robson] and two nice American stoodents return here for weekend.

At the Festival Club (a Nissen Hut with adjacent elsans![48]) had glasses of beer with Eugene & Margo McCabe who had "come up"

---

48   Portable lavatories.

from Clones. Then we all went for about 10 mins of a choral recital by the McCready Singers, a group of Romanists in hired tuxes and home-made peacock sateen gowns who stood in a row and sang exceedingly highbrow & complicated modern church music simply beautifully. They follow the plough and swing the churn and tend looms in or near Lisburn & Mrs McCready 4'1" in high heels must be a Genius! Next morning I conducted a Seminar on The American Theatre with a perfectly weird mixture of very Northern Irish students; itinerant USA beatniks; Malone Road Laydies; Rotarians; and a small group of Psycho-Analysts led by two (need I say?) Austrian refugees, passionate disciples of Vienna's Own Sigmund Freud. Then we had a wine-luncheon with old Mrs Mihail McLiammoir[49] who gave a DISPLAY of stupendous accomplishment and charm. Then a brief call on Mrs Mayo Davis (Migsie's brother Fred's widow) then home through a twilight of damp gray wool.

---

49   Micheál MacLíammóir, in Belfast to perform *The Importance of Being Oscar*. Guthrie cast him as Jonathan Swift in Eugene McCabe's play at the Abbey Theatre in 1969.

Len Cariou as Orestes in John Lewin's version of Aeschylus' *The House of Atreus*, directed by Tyrone Guthrie and designed by Tanya Moiseiwitsch, at the Guthrie Theater, Minneapolis, 1967.

14

THE HOUSE OF ATREUS AND THE HOUSE OF GUTHRIE

The Irish Farmhouse Preserves project did not prosper. Guthrie undertook US lecture tours in the spring of 1967 and the autumn of 1968, the proceeds of which went to bolster the jam factory's flagging finances. He directed two productions at the Old Vic – *Tartuffe* and *Volpone* – and two in Minneapolis, *Harper's Ferry*, a new play by Barrie Stavis, and *The House of Atreus*, adapted from Aeschylus by John Lewin, generally considered to be his greatest stage achievement ever.

To Lady Guthrie at Annaghmakerrig
No address, USA. February 1967

> Ask Joe [Martin] to make a note of each cheque that he gets so that we can check with lecture list eventually. Well, I've now been on the road for a week and am holding together very well & beginning to give the lectures with less nervous effort. On the whole the people I deal with are very nice, serious "good" people sincerely trying to make themselves useful to their students. One does get rather a lot of American hot air on the lines of: Utilization of cross-fertilization patterns of technique.

Postcard to Lady Guthrie at Annaghmakerrig
Emporia, Kansas. 7 February 1967

> Flat, flat country with rather marvellous wide horizon. Wealth gushes out of oil wells & the grazing is some of the richest in the world.

But – so far – the wealth hasn't done much for the drabness & total provinciality of the hideous little towns.

To Hubert Butler at Maidenhall

Hotel Sawnee, Brookings, South Dakota. 8 February 1967

Your letter (undated, but written, I guess, just before Xmas) caught up with me at Boulder, Colorado. The fact that you wrote – & with concern – makes me very happy. I simply hate the feeling of estrangement & "difficulty" between us.

What you say about the Jam Factory may all be perfectly right. I am under no illusions that we shall establish a great industrial empire in the ex-Great Northern Railway premises at Newbliss. But I think that the attempt to provide some activity and hope there is worth making and worth sticking to. Better, to my way of thinking, than just drifting along under the laissez-faire incompetent leadership of unconcerned Upper Classes and nest-feathering rogues.

Meantime we aren't doing badly. Before next season's fruit is ripe we shall fulfil a £30,000 order from San Francisco that will more than finance the purchase of the next fruit crop; and what I make on this tour will more than pay for the extension to the plant and various bits & pieces (e.g. a labelling machine) which we need to increase production. Joe Martin is NOT perfect. But he has courage, intelligence and the practical know-how which I so signally lack. BUT, so that you may know that your letter has not just produced a "contrairy" reaction, I have told Joe that I am quitting at the end of this summer.

I'm standing up well to the (very moderate) strain of this tour. My heart is NOT in the very best condition; but at 67 you and I can't expect to do quite all that we used to. I let Younger People carry my luggage and make my arrangements, and, in general, carry on like a helpless elderly parcel. So far this is the most primitive place I've been to. A tiny town at the back of beyond with an ENORMOUS State College where fat spectacled boys and pale spectacled gels (off the vast rolling cornlands) are being turned out as morticians, beauticians and Lutheran Pastors (Jesusicians). One is getting a weird blick at the enormous number and variety of American Cahliges. And it's impossible not to be touched and impressed by the *vast* expenditure of money & effort to achieve in 200 years what Europe has taken 2,000 to achieve.

To Mrs Peggy Butler at Maidenhall

Annaghmakerrig. 22 March 1967

I'm home. Quite exhausted but nothing that a little rest won't put to rights. Becky is still here but only just. She now dozes a great deal and is, we think and hope, rather happier than a while ago. There is less vilifying of Ethel.

My tour was really most interesting – such a diversity of colleges. Of course the shine is taken out of travel by the monotonous standardisation of planes & airports. But it was rather interesting to leave Fargo, N.Dakota, with the thermometer at 32 below freezing point and arrive in mid afternoon at Noo Orleans with the temp: 89 – azaleas everywhere in that rather unattractive "cerise" shade, and a huge vase of sweet peas on the Hertz Desk at the airport. I hope it won't be necessary to go away until we leave for M'polis April 10.

To Mrs Peggy Butler at Maidenhall

Guthrie Theater, Minneapolis. 22 April 1967

Well, we are ensconced in 2 rooms + aunt & tiny but nicely "appointed" kitchen in HUGE palazzo handy for the theatre. The chatelaine is called Mrs Mildred Van Horne. The furniture is a mixy-maxy jumble of faded Van Horne grandeurs of 1905 supplemented by Salvation Army jumble but all quite supportable for a limited time.

Tanya arrived last night from Stratters (Ont.) – she is commuting between us this year. A real pleasure to witness the pleasure her arrival has given to one and all; & a pleasure to have seen her develop over the years from the talented but dreadfully self-doubting daughter of two large and overwhelming Personalities into the modest, lion-grey, but totally authoritative lady whom younger designers regard with the most winning mixture of reverence and affection. I think her *Oresteia/ House of Atreus* designs are really masterly; however it turns out it will be a staggering and hugely interesting eyeful.

To Mrs Peggy Butler at Maidenhall

Guthrie Theater, Minneapolis. 9 May 1967

Judy hasn't been a bit well. She gets an "allergy" from the elm pollen; & as all streets around here are lined with rather lovely elms there's no escaping it, & runny gummy very sore eyes result.

House of Atreus rehearsals are being very exciting – so far only chorus at work (as main concentration is on Barrie Stavis's *Harper's Ferry* which opens first) but 16 splendid persons of both sexes (men appear as women; & later women as men) yowl and scream with glorious abandon. I think you would be very interested in Tanya's work; the false faces are really something – very primitive and strong – not quite Dear Sir Frederick Leighton's notion of the Mediterranean, tho' of course we shall return to that: prettiness and pale mauve chiffon are never "out" for long.

To Mrs Peggy Butler at Maidenhall

Guthrie Theater, Minneapolis. 17 May 1967

I cut my shin rather badly way back at *Dinner At Eight* [New York, 1966], walked into an open cupboard door in a barber's shop. "They" say there is some vascular stasis (which being interpreted means that the blood ain't flowing quite right) which could lead to phlebitis & thence to – oh horrors! – a CLOT. So I have to keep the leg UP; at rehearsal I lie on a *stretcher* feeling more than a bit of a fool. *House of Atreus* being a great interest & pleasure.

To Mrs Peggy Butler at Maidenhall

Guthrie Theater, Minneapolis. 26 May 1967

The leg was swelling up rather alarmingly at the end of each day & looking very purple & inflamed. I have been provided (at great cost) with a SURGICAL STOCKING – one of those pinky beige affairs which one sees on fat ladies who have had nine children in eight years. Truth is we are all Breaking Up. And, as in my case, the allotted three score years and ten are nearly up it's hardly to be wondered at. Mentally I think I'm still quite brisk – knowing nearly all the time WHO I am, & quite often WHERE; tho' really very, & increasingly, uncertain as to WHY.

Douglas Campbell as Clytemnestra and Robin Gammell as Cassandra in *The House of Atreus* at the Guthrie Theater, Minneapolis, 1967.

To Mrs Peggy Butler at Maidenhall

Guthrie Theater, Minneapolis. 9 June 1967

Just a wee line to cover the Wartburg, Iowa, programme [Conferring of honorary degree]. Iowa is glorious country – some of the best farming country in the world – rolling wide lands with lovely great calm rivers (all polluted as sewers) and great elms & oaks. It is populous – big, prosperous, solid-looking farms but no large towns, lots of little places about the size of Monaghan, as is Waverley, where Wartburg Coll is the principal industry & source of income.

It is all incredibly *provincial*. The local papers report local Pretty Weddings and Impressive Obsequies, local crime, local trading, local church matters. Foreign news is scarcely covered at all, & "foreign" doesn't mean news from Turkey or Terra del Fuego it means news from outside Neshawa County, Iowa. And this attitude seems perfectly compatible with air-conditioned cow-byres, HUGE Cadillacs, European holidays. One "does" Europe in 2 weeks during which one visits 11 countries, 47 cities, 41 cathedrals, 2 art museums and 19 factories, but one does not make the least attempt to speak any language other than one's own, nor to stay anywhere except in Hilton Hotels nor to eat the food with which foreigners stuff themselves

– one eats Hamburgers, Cole Slaw & Ice Cream thrice daily washed with good old American Cawfee. At the end of 2 weeks one returns to Waverley utterly dead-beat but with a sense of triumph – one has SURVIVED, one has not been "diddled" more than 2ce by those artful Europeans, one's convictions are redoubled that, in all of His wide universe there is nowhere to compare in beauty, prosperity, intellectual (and especially moral) achievements with dear, good, old Waverley, Iowa. And, to be fair, they will work like beavers to keep Waverley "at the top of the heap" – unselfishly, nobly. But that's why they resent having to abandon their serious, sensible endeavours at self-help, self-improvement, to go and pull Foreigners out of the mess which, owing to incompetence & especially wickedness, they get into every 20 years.

You probably imagine that when the ceremonies were over we sat down to strawberries & cream (it's the foremost strawberry-growing region in the world) & cold salmon & a glass of champagne. You would be wrong. After the longest prosiest Grace we sat down to Hamburgers, Cole Slaw, & Ice Cream, washed down by jorums of Cawfee.

To Mrs Peggy Butler at Maidenhall

Guthrie Theater, Minneapolis. 18 June 1967

Harper's Ferry has opened & had rather bad reviews but the audiences are quite large & very attentive. *House of Atreus* is being intensely interesting to prepare. But I just hope the public understands some of the things we endeavour to convey. It will be wildly pretentious; but it's rather pretentious even to attempt to stage a work conceived on so august a scale.

We shall be here till about Aug. 1; then to Stratford, Ont., for 2 weeks to see the ongoings & for Tanya & me to prepare designs for *Volpone* at the National Theatre (British) in Jan. I'm going to do *Carmen* in Düsseldorf next year with a contralto from Dublin called – wait for it: Mignon Dunn. The text will be sung in Deutsch with an enormous chorus & no expense spared – Sevilia am Rhein.

To Mrs Peggy Butler at Maidenhall

Guthrie Theater, Minneapolis. 29 June 1967

Have to go tonight to see perf. of *Harper's Ferry* which I haven't looked at for a week or two. It has not been a success; practically all reviewers found it heavy & dull. But it "goes" well; and the business keeps up quite reasonably. It is a bit stodgy; but rather noble and moving, I believe. *House of Atreus* is getting ready. It's very, very extreme & will either be rather splendid or pretty ridiculous. There is always that risk if you try to be "primitive". I think it will depend more than anything whether Tanya's stuff comes off. It's very daring. Athena (Douglas Campbell) is an enormous (10 foot high) seated figure which is pushed on in a sort of bath chair. He sits (or rather leans) inside a huge encasement of plaster – only the head and arms (with enormously magnified hands) can move. It is intended to look (& I really think will) like a colossus in pink Parian marble – with a huge cloak of canvas stiffened in plaster of Paris floating out like the winged Victory of Samothrace.

The Furies have been rather an anxiety too. They wear shapeless baggy garments stuck over with strips of black & grey polythene, & masks which look like petrified sponges or toy snouts made in lava. They don't have to speak much – just lie about in a heap & speak in chorus. When they get up & move singly it's rather like a nightmare Teddy Bears' Picnic, but I think that can be avoided. In repose they are quite impressive – not human at all.

To Mrs Peggy Butler at Maidenhall

Guthrie Theater, Minneapolis. 7 July 1967

Much preoccupied with *H of Atreus*, which looks stunning; but the last part (The Furies) is terribly far from ready and won't be as thoroughly prepared as the rest. Looks like there will be quite a convergence of friends & wellwishers to see it. Lola [Kipnis, New York writer] has been very ill, hopes to get over, also Gerda Wrede from Finland on way home from San Francisco where she has been visiting married daughter & seeing 9 grandchildren, also Tom Kerr from B. Columbia bringing wife & small son, named Tyrone for me.

I have just finished *The Newcomes* & before that *Martin Chuzzlewit*. Thackeray I find extremely congenial. Dickens is by far the greater but one does wish for less of the actor's passion to "entertain". Nice if his theatrical genius – Thornton [Wilder] always says that if Victoria the Good had been less pietistic and more of a Patroness of the Arts, Dickens would have been as great a playwright as Shakespeare – nice if his theatrical genius could have been combined with the serious thinking of Georgy Eliot, who, undiluted by the least wish to entertain and activated by sober passion for The Good of Mankind, is pretty ST*DGY.

Our landlady here, who is a rather grand, well-educated widow in her sixties, is A MYSTIC – "our little group" meets every so often, very quietly & decorously, downstairs – similar little ladies, The Colonel (a splendid, soldierly 70, just LOADED with Purple Hearts and Honorable Mentions of every kind), some artistic taxi-drivers, dreamy-eyed shoe salesmen and a handful of displaced Orientals who probably sell rugs & incense. Anyway she is just wild about Gurdjieff and also (though I don't see the connection) AE Russell, one of whose oeuvres she has just lent. I hadn't realised that he came from Lurgan!!! so, natch, his tiny pensées, heavily veiled in pink and amethyst mists, are expressed in the most florid excesses of the Celtic Revival – *dear* little thoughts but rendered almost unreadable by the BEAUTY of their expression.

To Mrs Peggy Butler at Maidenhall

Guthrie Theater, Minneapolis. 25 July 1967

Just a note to CONGRATULATE on arrival of grandson [Thomas Crampton].

House of Atreus opened last Friday to a packed & hugely attentive house. It couldn't have been a better audience & evoked a v.g. performance. *Furies* leaves a good deal to be desired; however it's not bad enough to sink the evening. To our great relief it's a huge "success". One and all are very tired but relieved & proud. It's been a considerable effort.

To Mrs Peggy Butler at Maidenhall

Annaghmakerrig. 17 August 1967

Becky is still alive. She is even smaller & whiter & perhaps a little less interested (if possible) in all outer affairs. But she still loves to talk about Old Times, still able to enjoy her own Bon Mots and still extremely interested in food. She is utterly frightful to, & about, Ethel who has, all things considered, stuck it out pretty nobly. It can't be much fun dancing ceaseless attendance upon a most demanding

& contrary invalid who makes not the least attempt to conceal a contempt which borders on paranoia. The kitchen is unbelievably cluttered & untidy & smells.

To Mrs Peggy Butler at Maidenhall
Annaghmakerrig. 1 September 1967

Becky still just alive; intermittently, we think, dimly, dimly conscious; not always apparently comfortable but absolutely not in pain.

Becky Miles, *née* Daley, Guthrie's former nanny, died a few days later at Annaghmakerrig.

To Mrs Peggy Butler at Maidenhall
Annaghmakerrig. 7 September 1967

Thought you'd like to hear about the obsequies, a day of vicious, vehement showers, but, as luck would have it, the sun came brilliantly out for "ashes to ashes". Quite a handsome turn-out of friends & well-wishers, though fewer came to The Viewing than were expected – sandwiches were cut up to feed 5000 and largely wasted. Naturally those great, fat, sly lumps Mesdames Hawthorne, McAdoo & Lee [Becky's nieces] were in great evidence when it was too late to be of use – they have, we think, been most negligent of Becky & selfish in not sharing more of the burden with Ethel.

There were nice wreaths "from the family" & Judy made (at Becky's oft-repeated request) a very bright wreath of scarlet geraniums. Rev. Brown conducted the ceremony & gave a really v.v.g. little "address", unsentimental, affectionate & shrewd. He said that "in other circumstances she might have been an important novelist or satirist".

Ethel is sleeping chez Lee [sister] but comes down daily. We have told her she need be in no hurry to leave [the free cottage] but in a week or so I shall suggest that she begins a very, very necessary clean-up. The sisters tidied up the kitchen & chapelle-ardente but did nothing about the 2 inner bedrooms which are in a state of scarcely believable mess & confusion & must be breeding mice. Ethel seems psychically incapable of throwing away anything – old paper bags, empty bottles & of course newspapers accumulate in frightening amounts. It's the odder because she is positively prodigal of fuel & constantly allows milk & meat to go bad. On the whole she has done her best with Becky who was often more than trying. She gets B's money, which is quite "a tidy sum" – several thousands of pounds.

John Gibson [BBC] comes here on Sunday in connection with a TV programme called "One Pair of Eyes" – my eyes – & Tanya comes on 9th to prepare *Volpone* for Nat. Theatre.

To Mrs Peggy Butler at Maidenhall
Annaghmakerrig. 23 September 1967

Sorry not to be able to meet in Dublin when you're there. But we are in midst of the BBC documentary thing & I have to be "on call". Most of it is being done just around here but there are "episodes" elsewhere – this aft., for instance, when we go to Maynooth to "do" the cardinal (who I hope will obey instructions & appear in the full glory of vermillion moiré) & 2 days next week in & around Belfast.

I had an interesting 2 nights in Germany seeing my future employers at Düsseldorf Opera (*Carmen* in April/May) & going thro' to Köln (35 minutes in MARVELLOUS comfortable FAST electric train) to see a much-praised *Trovatore* – v.g. singing & really first-rate conductor & efficient production but the décor was mittel Europa at its vulgarest – lots of black velvet with blobs of scarlet & emerald – sort of mourning -Xmas-card effect! & the acting, so called, very obvious and untalented.

A telegram came early this morning to say "Wendy Guthrie died y'day funeral uncertain probably Tuesday" signed "Orthodoy". Just that. I have no idea who Orthodoy can be, have you? It occurred to us it might be a telegraphic address, probably that of a lawyer or sump'n. If the film permits I'll try and hop over. You know how important all that is in Scotland. I have no idea who there is to mourn, poor little thing. It's been a sad and lonely life.

To J. Martin, Irish Farmhouse Preserves Ltd, Newbliss, Co. Monaghan
c/o George Chamberlain, 26 Wharton Street, London WC1. 1 November 1967

This is to give formal notice of my resignation from the Board of Irish Farmhouse Preserves Limited, to take effect from 31st

December 1967. As you know, this is no sudden decision and I have only stayed on until the matter of the loan was satisfactorily arranged. Naturally, my interest in the project is as keen as ever; and, unofficially, I shall endeavour to be as helpful as I possibly can. But, for some while now, and with so much of my time and energy committed elsewhere, I have been unable to give to IRISH FARMHOUSE the concentration which it requires. I shall be in Ireland between November 23rd and December 2nd: should we hold the Annual General Meeting at that period?

To Mrs Peggy Butler at Maidenhall

c/o George Chamberlain, 26 Wharton Street, London WC1. November 1967

We have seen quite a number of old friends. Had dinner with John Gielgud (with various "mutuals" also present) in his very lovely little old house in Cowley St., W'minster; and another night with Dame Sybil & Sir Lew [Casson] in their cosy mouse's nest in a *hidjus* great block in Chelsea. Geo, alas, is now, and at only 76, QUITE senile: can't remember recent events *at all*, & will ask the same series of questions – "What are you doing now?" – "Two plays at the National Theatre, George" – "Oh. The National Theatre" (in tone of great amazement) – "Yes" – "Which plays?" – "*Tartuffe*; and then *Volpone*" – "Oh. Who's in them?" – "John Gielgud and Robert Stephens in *Tartuffe*" – "Oh. Gielgud at the National Theatre?" – " Yes" – "And what are you doing now?".

And that can happen six or seven times on end. Annette is often near to screaming & isn't at all in good order.

Glad to hear of safe arrival of Master Adrian Fitz-Simon & will write.

To Lady Guthrie at Annaghmakerrig

c/o George Chamberlain, 26 Wharton Street, London WC1. Undated, November 1967

My visit with My Lord Goodman [Chair of Arts Council] was a great success. He is MOST interested in the plans for A'kerrig & thinks the Arts Council of G.B. would almost certainly be helpful. A dinner invitation will be extended for Nov 24 when he will be in Belfast. Please put into deah Dahwry.

Went last night to T.V. Centre & saw rough cut of *One Pair of Eyes*.[50] It's still twice too long; but a lot of the photography is excellent. I couldn't see anything that would be offensive to either sect.

Tartuffe is a great deal better than a week ago; slower, more grave & coherent & *Sir* John [Gielgud] really beginning at last to do some of it with a great deal of sense & authority. We have dress rehearsals tomorrow aft. & evening so I hope we shall get quite a bit of sorting-up of the potentially handsome but rather colourless fwocks. If laughs come the tensions will be strong; without laughs it will be a fright.

To Mrs Peggy Butler at Maidenhall

The National Theatre, London. 11 December 1967

Are you still thinking of NYC? In that case would you like – as an Xmas present – a little financial aid towards the cost? We had hoped to be home for Xmas but don't feel it right to go with Foot & Mouth situation as it is.[51] Chamberlains have George's brother (77 & has had several strokes!!) coming to stay so we shall clear out & are going to Diana Valk for 5 or 6 nights. She is a dear & the boys (William, 21 & at T.C.D.; Robin, 19, at York University) all clever, interesting & very nice.

[Irish] Arts Council now inclined to reconsider decision about A'kerrig, distinctly encouraging. I don't see that we can get far so long as you are assuming that it's all been my fault. I *have* been to blame; and do regret it and have "apologised" in sincere contrition. It's late. Am writing this after a long day of rehearsal & m' head is buzzing with *Volpone*, which I'm enjoying very much.

To Mrs Peggy Butler at Maidenhall

National Theatre, London. 13 January 1968

All well here. *Tartuffe* is long over (8 weeks) & we open *Volpone* next Tues. Dress rehearsal tomorrow 1.00 pm, followed by a (public) preview at 7.00 pm. I have no idea whether it's any good. Tanya has done spanking gold Venetian décor. Acting is v. broad & loud & fast

50   *One Pair of Eyes*, BBC TV documentary directed by John Gibson on Guthrie's recollections of his early life.

51   People living on farms throughout the British Isles were discouraged from travelling during an outbreak of foot-and-mouth disease.

& if thought funny will go great; if un-funny it will be red cheeks in the hugest way. I leave for Glasgow on the following morning to get up *The Anatomist* – 37 years after our original production. Lots of old friends & colleagues in the cast.

Judy has had flu, 6 days in bed & is now up & about but feeble and dying to "do things" without the energy to do the things she wants. It would be nice if you could send hr a wee note (to A'kerrig) if you felt like it.

Re. plans for A'Kerrig, I will endeavour to follow your "hint" and push things with Mervyn Wall [Secretary, Irish Arts Council]. But *he* really ought to be making the next move. It was agreed that he would hire an accountant to prepare a Budget. My impression is that he is *nice*, but a thoroughly slack, lazy, easy-aisy kind of character. What will turn the scale is the attitude of the British Arts Council, 'cos it has the dough. Present economic situation NOT favourable. But I'm endeavouring to work on My Lord Goodman [Chair, Arts Council of Great Britain] – a great, plump, loveable, roguey-de-poguey of a lawyer. It can't be dealt with fast – far too many committees concerned. One only hopes we shan't be Called Home before things are more settled. Meanwhile we're going ahead with central heating; estimates have been tendered and accepted, but here again it seems impossible to move at a pace other than that of the most lethargic elderly snail. One just hopes to be Spared long enough to outlast most of the delays. Keep writing. Letters are a lifeline.

In Düsseldorf for *Carmen*, the Guthries were impressed that so soon after World War II many Germans of Jewish descent were very much to the fore in the artistic world. From the same city Guthrie wrote to his sister about Judy's state of health, loyally shielding the fact that she was drinking excessively; but her friends, especially in Minneapolis, were discreetly aware and were helpful in keeping her busily entertained. His production of *Tartuffe* (Molière) at the British National Theatre was not hailed as a success; *Volpone* (Jonson) at the same venue was generally praised and *The Anatomist* (Bridie) – of which he had directed the original production in 1932 – at the Glasgow Citizens Theatre was exceptionally well received, giving no inkling that the director was in very poor health. In spite of this he was supportive in the most practical personal ways to the dying Leonid ('Lola') Kipnis who was translating Chekov's *Uncle Vanya* for Minneapolis.

To Lady Guthrie at Annaghmakerrig

Park View Hotel, Glasgow. 20 & 23 January 1968

> I think it's a very good cast & the play [*The Anatomist*] improves with the passing of the years, tho' of course that may just be the view of an aged body to whose bygone era it still has something to say. It's rather fun being with so many old friends. Rehearsals go well, I think. Burke & Hare are not very convincing as Irishmen & a valuable point is lost when the clash of dialects is no clash; & the Mary Patterson (Flora's old part) is very genteel but she is very handsome & will probably improve.

To Lady Guthrie at Annaghmakerrig

c/o Citizens Theatre, Gorbals, Glasgow. 31 January 1968

> Our little Scottish National Players group is dwindling fast. Robbie Wharrie died last Mon; the Remains were buried this morning. Charlie Brooker is a dear good man ruined by the demon rum. It's very sad. He's clever, sensitive, capable of great nobility but is now just a silly nuisancy old SOT. Jean Taylor Smith, Gibbie [James Gibson] & I are sole representatives in this production. It doesn't make me feel in the least sorrowful but one's nose is being rubbed in the mutability of human affairs and the fact that man is but grass. I wouldn't have it otherwise. Not that what one would, or wouldn't, makes any difference.

To Lady Guthrie at Annaghmakerrig

c/o Citizens Theatre, Gorbals, Glasgow. 6 February 1968

> Play going well. Am dining tonight with Henry Havergal, father of Giles [Theatre Director] who is in U.S.A. Henry and I had rooms on the same staircase in St John's [Oxford] & haven't seen him since. He's now the Head of the Coll. of Music & has married again – Giles' Ma died a few years back. He's a nice person but as a musician is rather stuck in the era of Elgar, Stanford & Parry & he's not a sufficiently progressive Head for the Coll.
>
> The Joe/Jam situation is disturbing and must be tackled.

To Mrs Peggy Butler at Annaghmakerrig

c/o Citizens Theatre, Gorbals, Glasgow. 6 February 1968

I didn't answer your letter sooner because it made me flustered and angry and I thought a calm answer was necessary.

I'm afraid I don't, in spite of what you write, feel that a little note to Judy to say that you were sorry she had been unwell and hope she would soon be better should be stigmatised as "play-acting", and, even if it were, don't you think that a certain amount of play-acting is all an absolute necessity when close relatives have become tarred and disjointed. I am not for a second implying that the disjointing has been exclusively the fault of one side or another. "Play-acting" – and well you know it – is a necessary leaven to ALL human relations. My character has many grave defects, but our two characters are very, very similar and the rift between us is not solely of my making.

The weather is cold, snow is lying, bitter winds scream over the slush. In spite of it all I find black, old Glasgow immensely congenial – oh so much more so than Edinburgh where I have just spent a pleasant weekend with Bingo Mavor (Osborne's son), now 43 with a much younger Danish wife & 3 children, and a grand (but, to my mind, highly impractical) mansion in Heriot Row. *The Anatomist* (by James Bridie, aka Osborne Mavor) goes well but I don't know what young people will make of it. To me it still seems lively and interesting. But the fact has to be faced that it is 40 years old: the equivalent of what Kipling, Swinburne, Burne Jones, Stanford and Parry were in our youth but YOUNG Persons better qualified to judge thought them unutterably dowdy.

To Lady Guthrie at Annaghmakerrig

c/o Citizens Theatre, Gorbals, Glasgow. 9 February 1968

I'm quite worried about Joe [Martin]. He has entirely evaded my queries about whether he has replaced me "on the board". I don't feel at all happy about Joe going to U.S.A. & maybe embarking on considerable contracts if, as I suspect, he has NO legal status. Tiresome.

To Lady Guthrie at Annaghmakerrig

c/o Citizens Theatre, Gorbals, Glasgow. 15 February 1968

The opening night was a succès-fou – packed house, and one and all had come prepared for An Occasion & to love it. The actors gave a spanking rendition.

I haven't been entirely well. Another little "Vascular Occlusion" as in Phila only not so bad. I've been in and out of grand doctor's rooms for last days. It's QUITE ALL RIGHT – the trouble has cleared up.

To Mrs Peggy Butler at Maidenhall

c/o Citizens Theatre, Gorbals, Glasgow. 15 February 1968

Anatomist opened on Tues with utmost éclat. It isn't often the time, the place and the loved one coincide so happily. I think it is very well acted; several old Scottish National Players still to the fore, tho' the grim reaper is mowing us down year by year. Meg Buchanan (remember her?) came to see me one evening; also Charlie Brooker – both over 80. I am taking tea with Elliot Mason's elder sister, Mabel MacKinlay, a brisk 93.

Off to Düsseldorf tomorrow for meetings rather too early; to Cardiff for a committee meeting on Monday; and home on Tuesday. Let's consider the playacting note CLOSED.

Memo dated 27 February 1968, to his New York agent with copy to Barrie Stavis, author of Lamp at Midnight, *written as from Annaghmakerrig.*

Sept. 30 rehearsals begin MN for *House of Atreus* [revival for NY]. Dec. 1 rehearsals begin for *Lamp at Midnight* [for US tour]. Feb. 17 1969 rehearsals begin for *Peter Grimes* at Met. Re. *Lamp at M*: I would prefer to forego percentage & take a straight fee of $7,500. Re. a lecture tour: If the Colleges will agree I should prefer to give readings – Irish Prose & Poetry. From my pt. of view it is a good deal less exacting than a lecture, & from theirs, I believe, I could make it a good deal more entertaining.[52] A group of Lyric Poems; two very brief excerpts from Swift & Shaw; & two short stories of Brian Friel.

---

52   Some colleges welcomed readings, others preferred lectures; Guthrie obliged with both.

To Mrs Peggy Butler at Maidenhall

Annagh-ma-kerrig. 14 March 1968

> Judy has a slight, only slight, temperature. Felt very cold & low day before y'day & temp rose in the evening. So she spent y'day abed which was disappointing as we were supposed to go to help Terence O'Neill [Prime Minister of Northern Ireland] declare open the (very handsomely designed) new halls of residence at Queen's. So she stayed at home while I dressed up and chatted with the nobs; and also saw the Dr. [Smyth in Belfast]. I had a little "episode" in Glasgow, suddenly couldn't see out of one eye. I was in no pain and not a bit frightened. Jack Smyth takes quite a calm view but I'm to go to a specialist "just as a precaution". Can read and see quite well except that there appears to be a sort of brown feather in front of left lens.
>
> Central heating nearly ready for the Grand Turn On at AK.

To Mrs Peggy Butler at Maidenhall

Annagh-ma-kerrig. 28 March 1968

> All well here. Rather more Events than one would really care for. We go to Portora (very nice headmaster) to "adjudicate" school plays; Whiteabbey, Co Antrim, on Monday to "Open" Civic Week; a Symposium in Sligo (Marist Brothers) on Tuesday, a Sale of Work in Dartrey on Wed. and Düsseldorf on Thurs!
>
> I've been thinking: mightn't Ethel Daley be rather a godsend to Julia as a mother's help? She's v.g. with children; honest as the day; and from her (Ethel's) point of view N.Y.C. would really be no more of a wrench than Dublin, Belfast or even Dundalk. Of course I won't dream of mentioning the idea to her or anyone else. But you might think it worth suggesting to Mrs Crampton.

To Mrs Peggy Butler at Maidenhall

Deutsche Oper am Rhein, Düsseldorf. 1 May 1968

> May Day; & a National Holiday; and a day of violent gusts & stinging icy showers. We have had three weeks of uninterrupted sunshine and balmy warmth; the trees have *burst* into a glory of new greenery; the cherries came and were instantly fried; now it's azaleas & tulips, lilac

& syringa, laburnum & wisteria. This is a city of lakes and avenues of Kastanien (chestnut to you), neatest of rosebeds, trimmest of shrubberies. The industry and order are AMAZING; imagination and originality are not, I think, the strong points.

I guess, as in Lancashire, the concentration of huge multitudes into small space creates many social virtues at the expense, maybe, of some personal ones. This is the Admin., financial, judicial legislative capital of the province of Nordrhein and Westphalen; the heavy industry (& is it heavy!) lies in the ring of huge towns which surround it, e.g. Duisberg (pop. about the same as Dublin), Essen, Wuppertal, Gelsenkirchen, Dortmund, Barmen, Elberfeld and an incredibly dense concentration of wealthy apts. Despite what was evidently fearsome bombing there are still evidences of the mediaeval city but nearly everything is *very* new and much of it very handsome.

Carmen comes on. Oh such a big lady sings C – quite decent, an Irish-American from Nashville, Tennessee. The voice is HUGE – thrilling at the top; rather ordinary, tho' still VERY LOUD, lower down. She acts – enough; enters into the rôle with great spirit, as they say; and is thoroughly pleasant and unpretentious. Work with the chorus (110 strong) is a bit of a chore, 'cos of language. My interpreter isn't quite in command of the Eng. Language to cope with anything idiomatic or anything not strictly literal. My exaggerations, like saying 20 million when you mean 5 or 6, utterly FOX him. Also he's too gentle and shy to catch, & hold, the attention of such a multitude. This wastes time & leads to some confusion. I find there's a tendency when I try to Blow them Up for them to think I'm making a joke; and then when I do essay a tiny jokelet, they blush and look at their boots.

I wish you could have had, in your life, the same pleasure that I think I have had from music. The conductor is called Fruheit de Burgos and is, as the name is no doubt intended to convey, half German half Spanish and inaccurately fluent in Italian, French, English and Swedish as well. He is very musical, very able and very reasonable. Partly because I'm old enough to be his grandfather and really rather too old to be his father, he has to treat me with "respect" & does so rather nicely – no suggestion that I am crumbling with senility; which, in fact, I rather am.

Carmen, directed by Guthrie, at Deutsche Oper am Rhein, Düsseldorf, 1968.

Lola Kipnis has been here on return journey from Kiev [to New York] where he had been to say farewell to his greatly loved sister (the father died last year aged 96) and to Russia. He – Lola – is mortally ill with cancer. He is splendidly stoic and philosophic about it all; but already in great almost incapacitating pain. His visit was an emotional ordeal but, in an odd way, an uplifting, even enjoyable, experience. He stayed 3 nights.

To Mrs Peggy Butler at Maidenhall

Deutsche Oper am Rhein, Düsseldorf. 18 May 1968

Carmen has had five successive orchestral rehearsals; tomorrow night is Dress Rehearsal mit Klavier (last chance to do anything about the acting & choreography); Tues is Hauptprobe; Wed Generalprobe; Thurs is Ascension Day & a State holiday! Fri is the Opening. Barring illness it will be ready. The climate here is very humid & rather cold. We had 3 divine weeks when we first came; after that it has been dismal & we both spend a lot of time choking & snuffling with stuffed tubes – what I call "Gray's Allergy in a country churchyard".

Our visit has been very marred by Judy's state of health. She has had no energy whatever; sleeps all night & all afternoon from lunch till 5.30 or so & can hardly keep awake in between; can't concentrate well; speaks very slowly & is apt to say the same thing (in different, very emphatic, words) 4 or 5 times in succession. One day she took a violent fit of trembling accompanied by dizziness. I sent for Dr. (recommended by singers) who came at once & in spite of linguistic difficulties was very helpful. Blood tests & x-rays of lungs & stomach, none of them provided a clue. So he gave her a Bottle (vitamins, I think, nothing more) & bowed out. It's all grieving & worrying & has greatly taken the shine out of the trip. Please refer to all above with *great caution* when you write.

Owing to illness we haven't been nearly as much to the Opera as I had planned – after all one gets in FREE. *Bartered Bride* v. good production rather spoilt by terribly heavy Germanic folklorical décor in crusted blood & peacock green. And, last Wed., Schönberg's *Moses & Aaron* which was much much the best thing we've seen & a great achievement. It couldn't be more Jewish in theme, music, décor & all. Yet no one seemed to mind – at all. The Intendant at the Opera is an obvious Jew but seems generally liked & greatly respected. It's a great pity that one's German doesn't begin to run to any serious talk, indeed is pretty inadequate even for the purchase of groceries. I've had a little talk with Dr Brenner (my aide & interpreter) but I suspect that he too is at least partly Jewish. Anyway it's not a topic which he seems to want to open up. As far as I can see, collective guilt is just lumped into a myth called Adolph Hitler & a group of mythical monsters called the Nazi Party, to which, apparently, NO ONE at any time belonged.

To Lady Guthrie at Annaghmakerrig

c/o All Arts Productions Inc., Suite 5G, 8 East 48th Street, New York City. 31 May 1968

Lola [Kipnis] is greatly failed – the swelling is now formidably huge, a great sticking-up lump; & his colour is now very bad & he's greatly thinner. He is hardly eating at all – the constant pills & injections destroy appetite. Mentally he is perfectly clear. He says Give me 10 minutes and I shall be better; and I go along with the pretence. Sonia [his wife] is said to be "doing her utmost" but is never around. She greeted me yesterday most charmingly & cordially & struggled with tears (victoriously; but evidently genuine) then just drifted away in a peignoir & watched the telly till 4 A.M.

Write fully about visit to [Doctor] Jack Smyth; & don't allow him just to say there's nothing that they can trace organically; maybe it's all "just nerves"; but the situation just can't be left as it is. Even "nerves" are a form of illness & treatment should be suggested.

To Lady Guthrie at Annaghmakerrig

c/o Kipnis, 181 South Compo Road, Westport, Connecticut. Undated, June 1968

Vanya is now copied; 3 (out of 4) have been carefully revised. An agent has been appointed; copyright is being arranged. By Wednesday all should be in order. Lola has had a rather better night & is consequently not so weak. But it can but be a "flutter"; the disease goes on working. Truly the atmosphere isn't GLOOMY. Stoic, I think is the word.

I want to hear about your report from Jack Smyth. Let him think you a tiresome hypochondriac. Too many people allow themselves to drift into serious disorder because they're afraid of being thought to be Making a Fuss.

Sonia never went near Lola all day. We offered to take her up with us [to the hospital] and she said she was too tired – after watching the Kennedy [assassination] affair on T.V! The carry-on here is quite, quite exotic. Shots on the T.V. in pastel shades of colour – sorry, color – of commuters' "reactions" as they got off trains & busses in N.Y.C.; silver daddies boo-hooing & sobbing; little Jewish battleaxes shaking their blue curls, rattling their gold chains, & saying "I just don't know how I can get through my day!" Incredible shots of Romanists in St. Pat's pretending to pray but peeping through their fingers at the camera. The whole event is reduced to a rather vulgar Drama. Even the shots of Ethel Kennedy & other mourners have the air of "effective" emotional intercutting. Some of it is a Drama & I suppose, to be fair, as History, incredibly vivid.

To Lady Guthrie at Annaghmakerrig

c/o Kipnis, 181 South Compo Road, Westport, Connecticut. 8 June 1968

Got your letter today describing visit to Jack Smyth. He evidently thinks the trouble is psychic. Perhaps it is. But this is no reason for not taking steps. Does he think you have been drinking too much?

Very relieved the Farmhouse [Jam] meeting passed off without much ill feeling.

I feel that the best possible thing for Lola is to keep him interested in *Vanya*, &, at present, he is; very much so. I am vexed to be missing the flowers, the quiet, the relative CALM of Ireland.

To Lady Guthrie at Annaghmakerrig

c/o Kipnis, 181 South Compo Road, Westport, Connecticut. Undated, 11 June 1968

Uncle Vanya, with its muted, humorous, philosophic emotion is a very good companion at this time; & though nothing has been said, I can see that Lola feels this too. What a funny, sad interlude this is being. One is forced to contemplate the transitory nature of existence – passing through nature to eternity & I think it is *by no means* a gloomy, rather an *uplifting* contemplation.

To Mrs Peggy Butler at Maidenhall

c/o Kipnis, 181 South Compo Road, Westport, Connecticut. 20 June 1968

This is being a strange, solemn, but by no means entirely SAD time. Lola is very frail & almost daily seems able to do less. But he is mentally quite lucid, & thanks to terrifying but marvellous and still brand new treatment, not in pain. He already looks more than half dead. I think he is genuinely not afraid to die & discusses the whole business with extraordinary calm & detachment. For instance, a day or two ago he was talking with Sonia, his wife, & they called me: "Tony, I vant you to vitness some of my last vishes"… then followed details of cremation, memorial ceremonies & disposal of property as though it were no more than the planning of a forthcoming social gathering. Friends & well-wishers are almost too pressing in their attentions & every afternoon from about 4 till 8 or 9 receps. are held at the bedside – vairy Rawssian & very, very Jewish. Lola has no belief in Resurrection, Eternal Glory etc etc but also no belief in a torment of Everlasting Fire. He had a strong attachment to his parents and the father died in Kiev last year aged 96.

Sonya is about 60, a graceful, rather charming but (I think) silly woman. She works very hard selling real estate & is seldom on hand.

The fort is held by Sonia's mother, a MONSTER of 87! The mother & daughter actively hate each other & Lola & the old lassie have had several frightful scenes over the years, including the exchange of buffets! She has been here more than 20 years, each minute of which has been fraught with jealousy, malice, covetousness and any other evil you care to mention. She has her own very charming & sunny rooms in this sweet old house (XVIIth century). She's as strong as an ox and WICKED.

While Lola rests & Sonia is out at her Real Estate office I type up the *Vanya* translation. The old girl and I are alone in the house & I get treated to reams of reminiscence in a weird German/English. It is fascinating stuff & full of bourgeois greed & Freudian malice. She was born a bastard & feels a grudge against all humanity. Her one redeeming feature is her love of animals. She has an old, old pussy cat to whom she talks while stirring horrible meaty messes over the stove; & a tame rabbit who miraculously survives motor cars & neighbouring dogs & cats.

To Mrs Peggy Butler at Maidenhall
Annaghmakerrig. 4 September 1968

We are, as Julia probably told you, having to leave for NY more than a week earlier than planned. Poor, dear, old Lola is STILL hanging on and wants to see us. But, while he is still conscious and still able even flickeringly to want a visit, naturally one HAS to go. How terrible it is, when the conscious wish is for nothing but to be dismissed in peace, the subconscious will for survival will not be gainsaid. One saw the same with Beckie.

We have Amie Gibson, John G's wife, a French "Lady" in the hugest way and three children of rather difficultly assorted ages, Joanna, a very intelligent and advanced fifteen, Matthew, a rather sensitive boy of nine, and Julie who is only three and has a will of iron. I can remember you at similar age, being a fearful drag, you had to be "in" everything and then when inevitably you couldn't "keep up" there were YELLS and grown-ups allowed us to feel that we were being "selfish".

Julia will have told you all about Terry Trench [Chair of An Oige, Irish Youth Hostel Association] lunch. She thinks a take-over by

An Oige is all but accomplished; and indeed they did seem eager and can manage with parts of the house that we can let them have sans inconvenience and without preventing the [Irish] Arts Council scheme being simultaneously feasible. But there will be MONTHS of delay while the legal and formal details are settled. Meantime the existing Arts Council is being, as I'm sure you know, considerably reorganised. Mervyn Wall writes that he "hopes and believes" that under the new arrangements the interest in our scheme [for an artists' workplace] will still be maintained; but, of course, there will naturally be still further delays. But I think they are going to get a bit more money; and also, with any luck, a rather more up and doing Secretariat! Mervyn is nice, but NO ball of fire!

We now go to M'polis for about two months – revival of *House of Atreus*. It will play for about sixteen performances, I think, then goes to N.Y.C. for a very "limited season" – two weeks, I believe, at Lincoln Centre, then maybe Boston and Ann Arbor but I'm not really au fait with the arrangements. Meantime I shall do three weeks of Lectures; then a new play by Barrie Stavis called *Lamp at Midnight* – it's about Galileo and will do a tour of universities and sort of "art houses" beginning at Richmond, Va. Then revival of *Peter Grimes* at the Met.

By then it will be March and that's that. Next year I am going to try hard to be at home. Have arranged to do Eugene McCabe's *Swift* play at the Abbey about this time next year, and Shiel's play *McCook's Corner* in Belfast, and that should about do until it's time to go to Detroit where for four months I am to be a rather highly-paid and leisured Temporary Professor at a JESUIT university. I haven't mentioned the dread name JESUIT at Queen's [Belfast] yet!

To Mrs Peggy Butler at Maidenhall

c/o Guthrie Theater, Minneapolis. 1 October 1968

Lola's last days & very, very peaceful demise were sad. The end of an interesting, happy, stimulating chapter. We have now to face an increasing number of chapter ends & a decreasing number of new chapters. And time seems to pass at such an accelerating speed. We had only been away from here for 14 months; but one's returns each year are more and more in the Rip Van Winkle Dept.! It does scare me to think how the last five or six years have just FLED. When one compares them, say, with the 5 or 6 years from 14 to 20, which feel like a whole long epoch; or even 33 to 39 when I was at the Old Vic, which seems like a HUGE slice of my professional life.

Interested to hear of planned alterations & improvements at M.Hall. And so very glad you like Dick so much. I only see him in circs which don't make for intimacy or very realistic assessments, but he has always seemed very agreeable and interested in many things, and to have about him a very likeable weight & solidity and real professional dedication. So many Americans make the right noises & faces & are very "easy" but one feels there is NOTHING behind the façade.

All going well at the theatre. It's the best season so far as regards attendances. The big hit is *Arturo Ui* (Brecht) which we may see tonight. *Atreus* rehearsals started y'day. The principals are all the same as last year but about ½ the chorus are new and it's the chorus which takes up most of the time at rehearsal. It's *very* hard to get the speech truly simultaneous and the choreography is quite complicated.

To Mrs Peggy Butler at Maidenhall

Annaghmakerrig. Undated, probably early October 1968

Eugene McCabe & wife come tonight for him to read his new *Swift* play of which we are going to give a Reading at the Queen's Univ. Arts Fest next month. I shall bring over 4 or 5 of the National Theatre Co & they'll sit round a table in "mellow" light!

I've made a very minuscule start on "cataloguing" the books – but it's never ending because New Additions create major displacement on shelves. Also one keeps havering between arranging by author, alphabetically (the only way to make sure of quick finding) or by subject (more logical and useful for comparative reference), &, at the same time, it's tempting to make pretty arrangements with books of similar size & elegant binding grouped for ORNAMENT!

Guthrie embarked on the lecture and readings tour in the US in order to bolster the finances of the jam factory in which he was still deeply involved though no longer a member of its board. This would be followed by the touring production of *Lamp at Midnight* opening in Richmond, Virginia.

To Lady Guthrie at Annaghmakerrig

Flint, Michigan. 2 November 1968

I hated leaving you to go off on that long flight feeling so groggy. I hope that wuzzy cat gives you a nice welcome; I'm quite sure that Mary, Bob & Seamus will do so.

Do nudge Joe in the BIGGEST way over gyfte pack [jam] publicity. It's just *idiotic* if we're late for Xmas two years in a row.

Do ring Eugene [McCabe] & ask him to send me a copy of *Swift* including the new Sir William Temple scene, as soon as poss. to Minneapolis as Tanya & I want to begin the prep.

To Lady Guthrie at Annaghmakerrig

Flint, Michigan. Undated, November 1968

Quite a strenuous day y'day – speech at 11 a.m. preceded by a "press conference" at 10, then A Lunch followed by "Questions" – quite interesting; then Seminar in which five amateur groups presented Scenes (very short) which I was supposed to "criticise" – 2½ hours in a very hot auditorium. Quite pleasant evening chez Mr & Mrs Shercher or Sticker or sump'n – rich, nice, bright Jews; & after dinner a gathering of theatre-minded friends, 60% Jewish, natch, sort of like a Habimah party only in this very costly, very nouveau, suburban Home.

Flint is a big, thriving city (motor industry) of 200,000 & growing fast. But TALK of provincial! Stratters, Ont., is Paris in the grand-siècle.

At 2 P.M. Dr Mahoney, my future boss at U of Detroit, is coming to fetch me down there (about 60-70 miles) for Talk, & I fly thence tomorrow for Concord, Mass.

To Lady Guthrie at Annaghmakerrig

Detroit, Michigan. 3 November 1968

Writing this from a not entirely charmless little motel in deepest, flattest, noisiest, hideousest De-troyut. Was fetched y'day aft by Dr Mahoney (pronounced Ma Hoeney) the head of the Eng Dept & my boss this time next year, accompanied by a rather nice little academic gel whose name "I couldn't quite catch". Mahoney is kind & decent

I'm sure, but pretty dim – anyway on first impression; he may turn out to be Socrates with a dash of Voltaire thrown in. A lovely drive, oddly enough. Eventually, in a marvellous misty sunset, we debouched into this flat flat endlessly industrial Gehenna where the motor is father, mother, King and Lord God Almighty. The source, one way or another, of just about everyone's bread & butter & the *indispensable* method of covering the vast distances. We principally discussed how my schedule [1969] could be rearranged so that I could direct Vanya in M'polis. The other object of the visit was for me to see a University production of *Death of a Salesman* in a nice little theatre "converted" out of a lecture hall. We saw the play very reasonably well done – fluffy & sentimental but "thoughtful".

To Lady Guthrie at Annaghmakerrig
Concord, Massachusetts. 5 November 1968

This is a charming old town, surprisingly unspoilt. I am writing this in a Break between my Speech & First Question Period. Then I have quite a long break & hope to visit the Alcott house.

Today is Election Day here & Everyone is in a high state of [undecipherable word]. The School is solidly for Humphrey but hear Nixon will be elected.

To Lady Guthrie at Annaghmakerrig
Salt Lake City, Utah. 12 November 1968

Have had a simply spellbindingly interesting stay in Mormonland, incl. two marvellous drives in the mountains; an organ recital on the gigantic organ in the GIGANTIC tabernacle; a televised ½ hour by the Tabernacle Choir (marvellous noise, contemptible programme); a Mormon service; Mass in a Trappist monastery in a sort of Alpine monastery farm in a valley 10,000 feet up; & a great deal of interesting talk. My health is standing up O.K.

It is a MILLION pities that Joe did not have the jam package publicity ready. "Everyone" expresses an interest & would gladly give it a try. I'm keeping names & addresses but it's NOT the same thing as being instantly & personally able to produce the necessary information.

To Lady Guthrie at Annaghmakerrig

Pittsburg. 13 November 1968

Have given my lecture in Pittsburg – oh so rich & ignorant & desperately dispiriting. It all explains Oliver Rea so eloquently. A hateful female appeared (in mauve tweed, natch) & said "I'm Ingrid Rea, Oliver's a cousin of my husband. I hear he's run away with one of the young actresses in your company." I can tell you she left with a good big flea in her lug.

Dear knows an evening like tonight with all these rich ignoramuses makes one realise how one must CLUTCH at a sensible scale of values. I'm sort of fascinated & simultaneously horrified by America – the SPLENDID endeavours, the crass ignorance, the gross materialism & then, in the same second, sweetly simple, gentle kindness. It has the charm & the utter awfulness of gawky adolescence; and, just as with "real" adolescents, one does sort of recognise that the utterly hopeless thing is to condescend. It's one of the things about growing old: one must do so with humility. Their energy and consuming desire for self-betterment are so touching, so admirable. The answer, I suppose, is to laugh at the awfulness, but charitably; & – this is hard – without condescension. I've had enough enough-enough of America but would miss it dreadfully if one were never to be part of it again.

To Lady Guthrie at Annaghmakerrig

North Central Airlines, between Sioux City & Kansas City. 22 November 1968

I am now embarked on final week of tour. It is very tiring but I am "standing up to it" well. My luggage got lost at Chicago on way here & I had to "appear" in dirty check shirt & green "sneakers" &, of course, the books from which I'd planned to read were in lost case which turned up at ½ past midnight.

I have had extremely interesting, rather touching, weekend chez Ibbs [in San Antonio].[53] They are very unsettled & homesick.

---

53   Ronald Ibbs, whose *Hamlet* Guthrie had directed in Dublin in 1950.

To Lady Guthrie at Annaghmakerrig

Minnesota Theater Company. 29 November 1968

Plans! Tanya would like to come to us, travelling with me & staying over Xmas, in order to complete sets for *McCook's Corner* [George Shiels]. I cannot attend Senate (Queen's University, Belfast) on Dec. 17th but can, & will, be at graduation Dec. 18th. Have written to [Dr.] Jack Smyth suggesting he sees us both on Dec. 18th. I suggest we all stay in Belfast night of 8th. If you agree, will you confirm?

Atreus looks like it will work quite well in proscenium. We have last rehearsal at noon today.

To Mrs Peggy Butler c/o W. & N. O'Sullivan, Foxrock, Dublin.

Annaghmakerrig. 30 December 1968

We've both had flu – rather badly; and though now quite a good deal better are still creeping about with NOENERGYWHATEVER and no desire for anything but the deep, deep peace of the sepulchre. It will pass; indeed I'm a bit better already – couldn't have attempted this letter y'day. I was supposed to go back to New York today to start work on a new piece but Dr Gunn of Cootehill has said that's totally out of all question – and indeed it is. So agitated messages have flown along the electric wires and "arrangements" are being made by the Management; and I shall just await developments in a rather passive frame of mind.

Tanya has been here for Xmas and hasn't had a very lively time with both the host and hostess either bedded or in the last stages of flopsy bunnydom. T. has made models of sets of the Shiels play we are doing in Belfast in May. We have played a lot of gramophone which has been a huge solace; so, incidentally, is the central heat which quite transforms the house – all passages now delightfully warm, and damp really beginning to be a thing of the past.

Did you see *One Pair Of Eyes* [BBC documentary] on Telefís Éireann? We didn't feel equal to looking but various neighbours seem to have quite liked it. Mammy McGorman definitely emerges as the star turn … puts The Cardinal and Taoiseach and dirt like that well in place.

The imminent collapse of Irish Farmhouse Preserves, Guthrie's philanthropic project to provide employment in the neighbourhood of Newbliss, Co. Monaghan, and attempts to bolster its finances through sponsorships and fundraising lecture tours, colours much of his correspondence on highly successful theatrical activities abroad.

To Mrs Peggy Butler at Maidenhall

Annaghmakerrig. 3 January 1969

I'm off to NYC tomorrow – NOT really quite able for it, I think; but I've already missed a week of rehearsals for a new play, *Lamp at Midnight* by Barrie Stavis, and shrieks of despair and anxiety have come from both management & author, so I feel utmost efforts are owed. Don't know how long I'll be away; but hope not much more than three weeks, then back here for a brief while before returning to revive *Peter Grimes* at the Met and do a very brief other lecture tournée.

Was in Dublin yesterday with Joe [Martin] tying, I hope, final knots in the arrangements whereby a grand firm [Albright & Wilson] takes over the marketing of Irish F'house Preserves which henceforth we shall only be concerned with making. Rather liked the grand business gents – they gave us lunch in the Dun Laoghaire Yacht Club which is a lovely, frail survival of Other Days – waitresses of seventy-eight, fully as grand as Georgina, Duchess of D, but full of (patently assumed) respect for "Members"; a beautiful early-Victorian dining room with huge bow window onto terrace in the harbour. The business gents were headed by an Englishman of chauffeur class, but very highly intelligent and, I thought, sensitive and interested in other things than the sale of tinned beef and jam – e.g. Christ

Church Cathedral. The other senior one was from Cork and rather grand and travelled. The younger ones were interestingly the nouveaux Irlandais – golf club accents, terribly expensive ultra-Edwardian suits, but bright and well-mannered … a little, I suspect, what Joe [Hone] might be, had he stayed in Ireland, perhaps less brilliant and certainly less louche, but rather similar.

Surprised you found *One Pair of Eyes* so black. I quite agree it's more for export (made by B.B.C.) than for local consumption. It's been shown in Canada and several friends have written to say they liked it and especially commenting on the charm of the landscape and interior shots. It seemed when I saw a rough-cut to be very well photographed – esp shots of Yours Truly and old Jimmy Dickson of Drumkeen leaning over a gate.

To Lady Guthrie at Annaghmakerrig

c/o R. Gans, Suite 111, 36 West 44th Street, New York City. Undated, January 1969

Atreus had a very bad notice in the all-important Times. Other press apparently good. Biz is no better than so-so. Pity. I haven't seen any of them 'cos too tired of an evening to go out. Max [Schaffner, Guthrie's host in Brooklyn] & I listen to a leetle Good Music & go to bed v.v. early.

To Mrs Peggy Butler c/o W.& N. O'Sullivan, Foxrock, Co. Dublin

Lodgings in Milburn, N.J. 9 January 1969

I've been out here for a week now. It's about 20m from N.Y.C. and one takes a new tube [subway] from 33rd Street (under Gimbel's actually) to Hoboken and thence a suburban train – just under an hour in all. It must once have been charming country – steep, wooded hills. Now all woods are cut down or full of dainty dormitory villas. I have a nice bedsitter with windows facing s. & E. for $6.00 b.& b. The landlord is called Frank (Francisco) Sortiera, born in Italy, now at about 62 crippled with what they *will* call Arthuritis, plus diabetes, plus a threatened clot in the "good" leg, and, from the look of him, not very long for this world. Mrs Sortiera is German-born, an ugly, fuzzy, heavy-set rouged person of great energy and a great chatterbox. She's a semi-retired hairdresser aged 66. There seems to be loads of money – electric this, that and t'other, big car, coloured TV.

The house is quite big & roomy and could be rather charming but is done up in typical German petit-bourgeois taste – masses of knick-knacks, little china top hats, china high-heeled boots, ferns in fancy pots; very huge chairs in which you press a secret button and extra shelves fly out or arms tumble down to form a Put-Yew-Up in emerald rexine. There's a sideboard loaded with silver of the most evidently spurious character; pictures in dozens bought from Rexall representing galleons on a sunset sea or quaint streets rather a long way after Utrillo; and roses, roses everywhere in paper, plastic, rubber, velvet, wax, in psychotic profusion.

The play [*Lamp at Midnight* by Barrie Stavis] has been an uphill fight against time and incompetent, cheeseparing management. I don't think it's a v. good effort. Pity, 'cos the script is rather fine, about Galileo & very apropos to current struggles against R.C. Authority.

To Lady Guthrie at Annaghmakerrig

c/o R. Gans, Suite 111, 36 West 44th Street, New York City. Undated, January 1969

We have to light the play & there's a dress rehearsal, the one and only, at 8. Some of the fwocks are said not to be ready; no one has seen the set. It's all chaotic. Mr [Morris] Carnowsky who is a very nice, splendid old gentleman, won't know, *really* know, his words [as Galileo] for another 10 days. He obviously knows them pretty well when Mrs C. "cues him through" at night, but when it came to Doing the Actions with other, much younger, persons waiting to get on, then he gets in a stew & can't remember a thing. As he is in every scene (ex. 2 quite short ones) out of a total of 19 it makes the performance a total hash. I endeavour, I think successfully, to keep calm & confident. But it's really being a horrid experience. Luckily Barrie hardly notices the deficiencies he seems to live in a dream of bliss; from which, I fear, he may be rudely aroused tomorrow night. Oh dear.

The Stavises have very kindly & generously invited us to go with them as their guests to Martinique or Guadalupe or one of those, between end of rehearsals for this and beginning of rehearsals for Met. Do you want to do this? Please wire what you feel but in such terms that I can show the wire to Barrie. They've been so kind & enthusiastic about it that we have, if we're not going to accept, to practice a little diplomacy.

To Lady Guthrie at Annaghmakerrig

No address, probably Richmond, Virginia. 14 January 1969

The play opened last night – pretty ghastly but not quite the shambles I had feared. We rehearse at 2 today – over and over till the (very nice) old gentleman can say more than three words on a breath. The set is excellent but the costumes bear ALL the stigmata of cheeseparing. It's all been a very tiresome, exhausting & quite unrewarding experience. Barrie Stavis is being Oh so kind & truly good but he *is* a frightful BORE.

To Lady Guthrie at Annaghmakerrig

No address, Richmond, Virginia. 17 January 1969

Well, our opening night (Tues & Wed were classed as Previews & were pooty disgwayceful) passed off not too badly. The good old gentleman has struggled, & is still struggling, heroically. The management is hopeless – incompetent & untruthful: this is the Papermill Management whose exact involvement neither Barrie nor I can fathom. Gans is incompetent but I think well-intentioned. The actors have, as usual, behaved splendidly. But I don't envy them the tour which will mostly be in vast university auditoria, or worse, gyms. There's still talk of my lighting the play at Columbus, Ohio, on Jan 30, but I've said firmly to do this I want to be paid my full expenses plus the regulation fee, which is quite high. I'm pretty sure they'll not be prepared to pay.

I'm having nice restful day reading Gordon Craig book, I suppose he has been A Great Influence but it's been exerted less thro' solid work than thro' the windy, pretentious effusions of self & fluent friends.

Guthrie stayed with *Lamp at Midnight* for two days after the very successful official opening in Columbus, Ohio. The subsequent tour was described by one critic as 'a triumphal progress'. He flew home to Annaghmakerrig, returning to New York two weeks later to direct Benjamin Britten's *Peter Grimes* at the Metropolitan Opera and then undertake another lecture tour at $1250 per appearance plus travel and subsistence expenses, in aid of Irish Farmhouse Preserves.

To Lady Guthrie at Annaghmakerrig
Minneapolis Airport. 28 March 1969

Tour has not been well arranged. I dare say there are excellent reasons but I have big long journeys, & expensive ones, & a 3-night "stopover" at Williamsburg which will probably be quite pleasant but I'd rather have been working.

Have you seen Joe? How did the great [jam] labelling fortnight work out? I do hope he was able to fulfil the contract without too much sturm & drang – "upset" to the lower classes.

Please make a point of seeing [Dr.] Jack Smyth at earliest opportunity. Tell him fully about the symptoms & follow his instructions to the letter – vitally important if you are not to fall into deadly alcoholic dependence. I don't know if you realise what danger you are in; & hate to "nag" about it & make it an "Issue". My being a bore about it can do more harm than good. But you have never indicated whether you realise the implications of too great dependence upon artificial stimulants. You must tell Jack Smyth all about this & be prepared for a long difficult battle with yourself.

To Mrs Peggy Butler, c/o W. & N. O'Sullivan, Foxrock, Co. Dublin.
Annaghmakerrig. Easter Saturday, 1969.

Home again; & very glad to be so.

Julia & Dick [Crampton] came with me to Opening of *P. Grimes* + a sandwich beforehand. They looked v. well and are clearly excited about impending move to Charlottesville. It *is* rather a thrill.

My tour was very brief but during 2 weeks I travelled twice to far west, once to L.A., once to Logan, Utah. Latter is lovely, a very flourishing & serious university in this *exquisite* valley (Cache Valley 'cos trappers used to assemble there & sell their furs) right up in the Rocky Mts – the valley is 7,000 feet above sea level and the mountains are like the rim of a cup (a very jagged rim) to another 4,000 feet. I reached it by Air Taxi from Salt Lake City: a wee, wee plane (3 of us on board and a lot of parcels) which threads its way between great towering crags. Thrilling. It was brilliantly sunny & warm with a sort of "edge" on the air, like champagne in an iced glass. "They" took me right up one of the canyons to summit where there was a wonderfully remote, still, frozen lake and a view over mountains *for ever* – NW into Idaho, Wyoming. We didn't actually see, but passed near, a juniper tree which is said (by Forestry Dept who have a big research station nearby) to be 10,000 years old & the oldest known living thing on earth.

Also spent 3 days in Williamsburg, VA, where Rockefeller Foundation has done a 20 year job of Restoration of Colonial Williamsburg – very interesting but rather too beautiful at present – will be all right in another 100 years when it all settles in & looks a bit used & worn. The guides, vergers, boatmen, ticketsellers etc wear William & Mary *Fancy Dress* in v.v. cheap furnishing fabrics – sprigged cretonne in pastel shades! & then of course, they have no wigs, just their own hair-do's.

To Mrs Peggy Butler at Maidenhall

Annaghmakerrig. 4 May 1969

The political situation in N.I. is hideous; the change in P.M. is NOT for the better.[54] I think the new idea will be to impose Law & Order by means of oppressive measures & "deterrent" punishments. Inevitable these will be said, & probably truthfully, to be applied to R.C.s more than the rest. English intervention will be madly resented by both sides. Withdrawal of U.K. support would cause great hardship and tend to throw dissident Ulster into the arms of Eire. The points at issue really aren't what they seem. They're atavistic and just aren't soluble by means of sweet reason. Right now things are quiet because recent events in Derry were so hideous & gave everyone a fright. But at any moment new provocations can arise.

JAM. We are now "distributed" by a very large firm in Dublin. It's going very well indeed. They hope to start distrib. in N.I. in July & in England next year. Meanwhile, & quite coincidentally, our customers

54   Terence O'Neill resigned; James Chichester-Clarke appointed.

in U.S.A., Canada, France, Italy & - wait for it! – ARABIA have all put in greatly increased orders, so now we're having to put in a lot of new machinery to enable output to be increased. Of course this is *lovely*. But, as always, new developments produce new problems, of which the largest is how to get enough fruit. Local plantations are increased tenfold but it's not nowhere near enough. Luckily 41% of total production is of marmalade, with oranges imported from Malaga. Right now we produce 1,000 cases every day (i.e. 12,000 pots of jam) but this isn't keeping pace with demand. We're looking for someone to advise local powers & stimulate new growers. The County Advisor is 140 years of age and (we suspect) has had his palm crossed with silver by Robertson's of Glasgow. Ask Hubert if he knows of a suitable candidate – personality & integrity more important than training and botanic qualifications.

This week Tanya & I had to go to Dublin to see Abbey Theatre re. Eugene MCabe's *Swift* play. We caught the Enterprise at 5.30 from Belfast where we're doing Shiels' *McCook's Corner*, Eugene met us at Amiens Street (sorry, Connolly!) & we had an hour and a half collogue with Abbey followed by a sumptuous Irish stew chez Mother MacLiammoir. Eugene & Margot drove us up here at 1 a.m. arriving just before 3. *Swift* goes into rehearsal June 30, opens July 26 – MacLiammoir=Swift – not, I think, quite what the dear Dean was "really like"; but that's less important than having a big, rich, loudly expansive "Personality".

To Mrs Peggy Butler at Maidenhall
Annaghmakerrig. 21 June 1969

Tanya arrives Friday to stay (off & on) till we have achieved Eugene McCabe's *Swift* at the Abbey – opens Aug 4, try & be there. And on Tuesday we have the Co Monaghan Blind Association annual Outing here to tea – 60 blind people, about the same number of friends & well-wishers, and, at a guess, another 20 committee members, clergy and the like. Fortunately we aren't really dependent on the weather as poor loves can't see the Beaut anyway. The Feature, and what they like best, is to move from group to group picking up threads from former rencontres. So I guess all we can do is place chairs in rather flexible arrangements so that no one gets stuck all afternoon in uncongenial company.

We had quite an interesting few days in Eng. I had to lecture at Lancaster Univ., one of the absolutely brand new ones – quite interesting to see & architecturally impressive. They sent us then by car driven by impeccable ex-Sgt who is the university chauffeur, across the Pennines to Sheffield, for opening of Tanya-designed *Caucasian Chalk Circle* (Brecht; & a fierce bore). Had time to view Sheffield Cath., bombed & most splendidly restored. & a SPANKING exhibition of Cartier Bresson photographs. I longed for you to see them. They were very much our cup of tea.

Guthrie's mother having been blind for the latter part of her life, he took a special interest in the Monaghan Blind Association and was particularly sympathetic towards MacLíammóir's condition.

To Mrs Peggy Butler at Maidenhall
c/o Abbey Theatre, Dublin 1. 17 July 1969

> I'm hard at work at the Abbey. It's being an uphill fight because poor Michael [MacLíammóir] has cataracts in each eye as well as acute & very painful conjunctivitis & can't read *at all*. This makes the learning of the words a fearful struggle – it's just waste of time to rehearse until he knows the words of a scene. As he [Swift] never leaves the stage & talks practically non-stop our progress is that of a paralytic snail. After nearly 2 weeks we are a good deal short of ½ way through & not one single scene is really ready. It's alarming; & I think there'll be no alternative but to postpone for a week. This the management, understandably, is very reluctant to do because there'd be a great deal of "interest at the box office" & the first week is booked practically solid.

To Mrs Peggy Butler at Maidenhall
c/o Abbey Theatre, Dublin 1. 9 August 1969

> Having a frustrating time with *Swift* 'cos MacLiammoir, in addition to cataracts, has been laid aside with Brownkitis – hopes to be back

tomorrow; 2 other actors "off", one with pleurisy, the other with screwmatics. If M.M. is on deck tomorrow we should be OK. Cast is a curate's egg; play v. interesting; but not, I think, quite what the audience will take to its heart. We shall see.

To Mrs Peggy Butler at Maidenhall

c/o Abbey Theatre, Dublin 1. 10 August 1969

The play is being postponed by 2 weeks. A *great* relief. Michael will, I think, be v.v. good when he knows it, and is admirably willing, nay eager, to play a genuine *old* man, and does so excellently. I'm finding Eugene McCabe very pleasant and a person of considerable sensitiveness & depth. We have old Padraic Colum (now 86) around – he comes a good deal to rehearsal – interested 'cos Swift is one of his topics. He looks like the very oldest King of the Gnomes but is still extremely alert mentally.

To Lady Guthrie at Annaghmakerrig

c/o 37 Palmerston Road, Dublin. Undated, September 1969

Jam. Had a most interesting but fairly disquieting evening [with factory inspector]. There are several alarming features of which far the worst seems to be the unsatisfactory (both mechanically & hygienically) condition of the refrigeration system. I think it essential that he talks frankly with Joe [Martin]; & have asked him & wife to lunch next Sunday. I do realise it may make us a very large party & wouldn't land them on you if I didn't think it essential vis-à-vis Joe whom they have numbered as an incurable optimist who is going to get a grilling & be subjected to a rather trying situation; it's better that this should occur on neutral ground & in rather social circumstances (they can retire to the Morning Room à deux while we hold the guests in elegant play elsewhere!).

So: rehearsals at this stage, are an Agony 'cos of the cataracts. He [MacLíammóir] really can't read at all but is fearfully game & alert, & has made a tape so that he can learn it aurally. It's dreadfully flustering for Eugene, who is behaving, as we would expect, in a very grown-up way. Set is going to "work", I think.

To Mrs Peggy Butler at Maidenhall

Guthrie Theater, Minneapolis. Undated, September 1969

> *Swift* has been rather a sad & disappointing experience. Poor old
> M.M. struggled most gamely & good-humouredly; but it was too
> much for him. He didn't really know it & on 1st night gave a weary &
> monotonous paraphrase of a stylish text. The press was kind & implied
> that Mr MacLiammoir did wonders with a rather dull & verbose
> play. For the most part it was well beyond the range of a very so-
> so company of actors. I'm sorry for Eugene McCabe who at 40 now
> needs the confidence, as well as the cash, of a "success".
>
> Rehearsals [*Uncle Vanya*, translated by Leonid Kipnis][55] start today.
> It is now 9 a.m. We begin at 12 & go to 5.30, odd hours but designed
> to suit those who are acting at night. I'm mugging up G.B.S. for my
> Detroit nonsense. He is unbelievably brilliant in a fairly frivolous way.
> Yeats' metaphor of a sewing-machine is very witty & accurate, I think
> – but he's a marvellous entertainer & a truly kind, generous person. I
> think a course of him will be quite good for totally humourless, crew-
> cut, blonde boy-Jesuits in pebble specs.

To Mrs Peggy Butler at Maidenhall

Tyrone Guthrie Theater, Minneapolis. Undated, September 1969.

> We are invited out by Pierce Butler The Third (don't you love that
> American way of claiming aristocracy? What about all the PBs before
> PB The First – way back to Neandeththal PB?). In fact, this man is
> quite grand & very pleasant. He's a lawyer & a member of the theatre
> Board; also a member of the Butler Socy. The object of the Dinner
> isn't clear beyond the fact that there *is* an object over & above mere
> hospitality. One thinks that it concerns a Patk. Butler who is a very
> wealthy resident of St Paul & a (distant) cousin of Pierce. And one
> *thinks* that one is intended to wheedle money out of poor Patrick but
> whether it's for the theatre or for the Butler Socy. did not emerge.
>
> Last time Pierce & I were similarly employed we lunched at the
> St Paul Club (straight out of Scott Fitzgerald) with a very nice old
> gentleman called Mr O'Shaughnessy. By the end of luncheon the poor

---

55   'Lola' Kipnis had died the previous year shortly after Guthrie had worked with him
on the script in his home in Westport, Connecticut.

old love had signed a cheque for $30,000. That was for the theatre. It's done by tickling their stomachs with a feather.

U Vanya "opens" tomorrow night & plays a Preview tonight – "They" pay something less than full price to see a D. rehearsal. But it is absolutely ready. On Wed. a.m. we leave for hidjus Detroit.

Detroit. Jesuits – so far – are making no attempts to convert! & seem very open-minded. By no means are a majority, either of Faculty or Students, in Holy Orders or even of the R.C. faith. There really are very few "reminders", whether on campus or in classrooms, that we are in a Catholic institution. One of the (few) attractions of Detroit is proximity of Canadian border. We hope to hop over more than once to visit Stratters, & friends in Toronto.

To Mrs Peggy Butler at Maidenhall

University of Detroit, 4001 W. McNichols, Detroit. 25 October 1969

A very easy routine – I only lecture 2ce on Mon and 2ce on Wed so am writing a book , a slim volume on ACTING commissioned by an English publisher called (regrettably) STUDIOVISTA (!!). The money is not v.g. but I think I can make good economic use of various bits & pieces for magazines & radio.[56]

Detroit is pretty extraordinary. It's grown almost inconceivably fast. Till Henry Ford got going in the early years of the century it was just a small lakeside city on the Canadian border – the trains from Chicago to Toronto & Montreal passed thro'. Now it's the size that London was at the beginning of this century. Without a car it's a little diff. to get about. The Motor Industry totally dominates every aspect of Municipal Life and they have so far succeeded in suppressing any serious attempts at public transport. The U of D has this apartment for the use of visiting Profs. & it's just within walking distance of the campus – 1½ miles – quite OK in good weather but, come ice & snow, I shall have to do it by bus, a very infrequent service. "Downtown" is 6 miles away & McNichols is 24 miles long – city all the way.

The contrasts between wealth & poverty are said to be startling. The drug problem is said to be acute in the schools. But I can't help

---

56   *Tyrone Guthrie on Acting* (London 1971).

feeling that if it were all that bad one would see more wrecked & ruined students on campus. And I don't. My undergraduate class of 60 couldn't be more eager, clean-cut, all-American, except for one or two lethargic, glandular [girls] who sit in fleshy heaps apparently absorbed in their gum but then they suddenly ask rapier-sharp questions. The graduate class is much smaller – only 17 – of whom 2, maybe 3, are priests – they wear mufti so it's hard to know – and 2 nuns, also in mufti – the rest are all teachers & the bright ones are all Jews.

To Mrs Peggy Butler at Maidenhall
University of Detroit. 13 November 1969

We seem to have just arrived here and Lo! It's time to be planning to leave. I have just "done" G.B.S.'s *Black Girl in Search of God* with my junior class. I read it when it first came out, about 1932, but had forgotten what a charming & poetical fable it is, and how beautifully illustrated (in woodcuts) by John Farleigh. I have got so "fond" of Shaw. Like Dr Samuel Johnson he's a wonderfully vivid & eccentrically real personality. Not that the works aren't wonderful too. Some authors one can do nicely without having met or even having known much about them personally. I don't feel drawn to know Dickens or Thackeray. Am *glad* to have missed Ruskin or Swinburne, Shelley or Meredith. But I'd give a lot to have encountered Currer Bell and hear her lay London hostesses flat on their backs with her answers to their compliments.

To Mrs Peggy Butler in Las Palmas, Canary Islands
Annaghmakerrig. 27 December 1969

I think our first ever Christmas à deux. We had no guests this year. It was rather cosy. After a (considerably reduced & simplified) dinner we put on *The Messiah* recording and listened to it with enormous satisfaction. One thing: the gramo does let one get to know the works very thoroughly. I now, for the first time, realise what the words are trying to say & how very thoughtfully the librettist, as well as the composer, has done his work. A propos, I've embarked on reading the Holy Bible cover to cover. Fascinating – so far. But I'm only in Exodus, I anticipate some tough reading in Leviticus, & tougher still round Hosea!

On a brief visit to Australia in 1965 Guthrie had accepted an invitation for an extended stay some time in the future: this resulted in five months in 1970 directing *Oedipus* in Sydney and *All's Well That Ends Well* in Melbourne. His medical consultant, Jack Smyth, advised against the trip, but if determined to go he must travel by surface.

To Mrs Peggy Butler, c/o M. & E. Burgess, 'Mulberries', Boreham, Essex
Annaghmakerrig. 6 January 1970

> I'm sorry you take such a sniffy tone about Antipodean trip! I won't now go into all the reasons & pros & cons, but don't you think it vastly preferable to go pop in an Australian aeroplane with a herculean crimson stewardess in strident attendance rather than to make a perhaps more dignified departure in one's own centrally heated & flower-decked death chamber? And as to the disposal of the remains, I'm not in the least averse to the idea of lying toothless on a slab under the mocking gaze of Australian med. students.

To Mrs Peggy Butler, c/o M. & E. Burgess, 'Mulberries', Boreham, Essex
Musgrave Clinic, Belfast. 17 January 1970

> For some months I've been troubled by breathlessness – puffing & panting after the least exertion. Jack Smyth examined me & sent me in here to be "under" Dr Pantridge, the chief heart person in the hospital and, I gather, a very highly regarded expert. X-rays, cardiogram, the works have been brought to bear & I am to be released tomorrow. BUT *complete* rest is ordered and I am "on a diet" in order not to put on weight when deprived of exercise. I feel the resting business is fairly absurd. At 70 I shall never get back to anything like where I was even 6 months ago. I think I'd rather go on doing what I can do usefully & pleasurably, even if it shortens my span.
>
> Judy is being very steady & supportive. We have both known for some time that I was "dicky" (what can be the origin of that expression?) & half suspected this verdict. I'm not in the least agitated or even depressed, but do seem to have aged ten years overnight. Alas, vigour has not been replaced by wisdom; but I believe I have to quite an extent achieved the serenity (or is it just callousness?) of eld.

To Mrs Peggy Butler at Maidenhall

Annagh-ma-kerrig. 7 February, no year but certainly 1970

Thank you for telephone enquiries. I really *am* better; much less breathless and après-flu symptoms decreasing daily. Walked y'day round Tom's Lane where there are Big Changes. They [Forestry Commission]'ve made it into a hard & excellent road; the trees are being greatly thinned and those left seem enORmous monarchs of the forrest. It was ve'y ve'y beautiful with the sunlight slanting thro' the "stems", and marvellously silent till one rounded the bend (above the bog) & there were the limousines of the workers and the most terribly noisy machines – power saw & "stripper" which tears off the bark of a tree like you might remove the wrapping from a chocolate.

An old man (the head of the party) worked the saw; two rather sly & secretive youths (his grandsons I think) were in charge of two gentle old horses & were pulling out all the felled trees. The grandfather then cut them into about 6' lengths & then an incredibly handsome, strong, dextrous young fellow from near Monaghan stripped them. He expects to do 96 TONS per week for which his average weekly take-home is just under £40. Of course it's tremendously hard work and one can't possibly grudge them the snappy Jaguars & MGs in which they arrive & depart! They had a nice little fire going & were about to partake of family Afternoon Tea with chocolate biscuits. But in wet weather (or as today, sleet driven on a bitter blast) it wouldn't be quite so pleasant.

Do come again for a night (or several); if we all keep our heads PERHAPS WE CAN Live Down the hateful years of estrangement & recrimination.

To Mrs Peggy Butler at Maidenhall

Annaghmakerrig. 18 February 1970

We're organising the books and yesterday Seamus, Micky Maguire & Frank MacDermott manhandled the ENORMOUS new bookcase I bought in Dublin last summer & set it up in the morning room. It looks very well & offers accom. for large number of waifs & strays. I did nothing but carry books from place to place. But it evidently was TOO MUCH – had a bad night & feel poorly today. Not serious.

We have also sold some furniture. The only things you might "miss" are the hunting pictures on the stairs. He [a dealer] offered £1,000 for the Chippendale "breakfront", £1,000 for the two snuff boxes and £1,500 for the Philadelphia silver teapot & sugar bowl. I refused to be tempted; but it's nice to know that, worst come to worst, they are valuable, & presumably won't get less so.

I've resigned as Chancellor of Q.U.B. Didn't feel I could face those constant journeys. It's not "announced" yet, so this is entre-nous.

To Mrs Peggy Butler at Maidenhall

Annaghmakerrig. 12 March 1970

Wexford. I didn't think the opera a bit good [Mozart: *La Finta Giardiniera*]. *Wonderful*, of course, if you keep saying to yourself "it's only poor little Wexford", but I think that's so condescending. By any absolute standard it was 2nd rate. Eyetie singers and obviously local amateur chorus, a B+ orchestra and a production that was "really rather charming, *considering*" the stringent limitations, budgetary & architectural. Irish cultural endeavour will never get much better while everyone is so absolutely thrilled by the idea of Endeavour. Their effort is partly, if not primarily, to increase their own BIZ. If so, let's hope they get a good reward for trying to rise above the vulgarity of a mere Beer Festival!

Went to Belfast on Tues to see Jack Smyth (doctor) who gave me a GOOD REPORT. But I must go on keeping v. quiet, & be patient. Australia will be OK if we travel both ways by boat & *curtail* the work. 'Strylians may, in this event, feel the visit hardly justifies the expense. Have written them fully & must wait to hear.

Have finished 1st draft of my dreary wee book. Starting now on long (13,000 word) article on *Theatre, Art of* for new Encyclo. Britannica, which is now a totally American enterprise located in Chicago. Have also "Invitation" to write & narrate for TV on Gilbert & Sullivan.

To Mrs Peggy Butler at Maidenhall

Annaghmakerrig. 4 April 1970

Can you come up here for a night or two, soon, if possible, because after April 20 we start to get rather full up. We have John & Hazel

Lewin, M'polis author who "did" version of *Oresteia* & comes to prepare one of *Oedipus Rex* for Sydney later this year. And on April 24 Dr & Mrs M. Dewhurst – enough said. And at beginning of May little Miss Mildred Stock from N.Y.C., busy as a bee collecting "data" about Tyrone Power. She's ferretted out heaps of "facts" & is pursuing various noble Lords (Waterford[57] & somebody else) whose archives may yield honey. Then, later in May, other M'polis friends who have spent the winter in Florence & are on their way home.

I spend the days writing, writing, writing & don't like what I write. The Encyclo. piece is just what I can't do. It should be brief, fact-packed, learned. It is diffuse, flighty, empty.

To Mrs Peggy Butler at Maidenhall
Annaghmakerrig. 20 April 1970

I seem to be rather pressed by literary endeavour. I'm trying to improve the very poor opening chapters of m'slim volume. Have prepared a 40 minute programme for steam-radio in Belfast next Wed. & am in closing stages of Enclyclo Brit piece, but await instructions from the Gestapo in Chicago.

We have let A'kerrig for 4, possibly 5, weeks in July/Aug to John Gibson's wife. John will be abroad filming but she wants to come with their two younger children & her brother, his wife & 3 children, frogs from Rheims called Schleimberger (pronounced Schloombairglay), they are French Protestants, make Champagne and are very, very rich, but quietly, respectably, responsibly rich.

To Mrs Peggy Butler at Maidenhall
Annaghmakerrig. 5 May 1970

Dewhurst [cousins] visit is taxing our endurance *to the limit*. One tells oneself to be nice and remember that this will be the LAST TIME and there must be no unseemly impatience & irritation. Molly is thinner & whiter than tissue paper, almost wholly deaf & perpetually tangled in the wires of her "aid", also almost wholly blind – one eye looks dimly from behind "pebble" lens, the other concealed behind a piece

---

57   A persistent oral tradition cites Tyrone Power (Tyrone Guthrie's great-grandfather) as the illegitimate son of a late eighteenth-century Marquis of Waterford.

of lavatory-window ground glass. Her face is paralysed, which means that the false teeth cannot be held in place, also that one can't hear what she says. That doesn't matter because, after one has what-whatted & "slower, Molly, dear, I'm sorry to be so stupid" it turns out to be that John and Norah [children] liked something, or didn't like something, when they were small; or that when she was cutting the loaves for the Old Peoples' sandwiches she made a mark on the bread-board – oh no, that was last year; this year we gave them biscuits.

Michael is even feebler, but not so sensationally so. He hirples around on two sticks *shouting* in an assumed ton of joviality; and complains – very impertinently – about the bedding, the heat, the inefficiency of Irish electrical fittings, the fact that their orange juice (taken to bed at night) isn't prepared "just so". The sherry should be *dry*. We went to church yesterday & he left his sticks behind. This was not discovered till we got back here. Then he wanted to fetch them himself in their hired car, which, natch, wouldn't start. By the time he'd fiddled & fuddled and finally said would Molly & I go fetch them, 20 minutes had gone by, so when we got back to Aghabog the church was triple locked, the gate chained, etc. So we had to fly all over the countryside to get keys from the sexton who lives up an all but impassable lane (exquisite with primroses) way over by Wright's Mill! The whole ploy took an hour but was, in fact, quite fun!

At night we play the gramophone, which does at least relieve the need to Make Talk. I don't think poor old Molly can hear a thing. The pair of them sit side by side on the sofa, stiff and white like a pair of corpses. It's eerie, and makes one ashamed to be irritated. Then, just as one is resolved to be saintly, peevish complaints begin about the orange juice as though they were paying heavily to be waited on by lodging-house keepers who badly needed the lodgers!! 'Twill pass.

To Mrs Peggy Butler at Maidenhall

Annaghmakerrig. 14 May 1970

A visit from you on 18th or later would be perfect – not earlier 'cos Lewins leave on 18th & you wouldn't find them extra congenial – intelligent but sickly, nervous; hopelessly urban Americans who eat too much & think about their stomachs! He is achieving a fine

Oedipus Rex so NO complaints. Dewhursts depart this afternoon. Phew!!! Ugly scenes have twice only just been averted. We both feel glad to have made the effort. Was allowed all the time to feel that one was keeping a Boarding House that didn't quite "do"

We leave May 25 [for Australia]. Lewins leave next Mon. & thereafter the coast is clear exc for possibility of Friels for a night. You would like them very much, I think.

To Mrs Peggy Butler at Maidenhall

U. of N.S.W. 'Strylia. 9 July 1970 (on Lloyd Trestino letterhead)

The voyage was very very very comfy & ditto ditto ditto dull. Fellow (first class) passengers mostly elderly dullards in search of sunshine & "relaxation", majority Italian & Australian but a sprinkling of Seth Efricans (OH their accent!), Dutch, Scandinavian & some fearsome Germans who stamped about usurping the best chairs, scowling at those whom they felt they could intimidate, fawning on those whom they felt might be useful or dangerous! Very few British – "We always go P&O"! We are sumptuously housed on the first floor of a house owned by Aust. Natl. Trust. It's a white little country house of 1840 on a peninsula called Point Darling which juts out into the harbour. The view is MARVEE & FAB. – the sunshine pours in 'cos we face *North*! – very confusing, one has to remember that we are underneath the rest of the world & that, if it weren't for an incomprehensible miracle called GRAVITEE, would be crawling upside down on the ceilings like flies.

The garden ends in a ha-ha with two very small palms in Victorian urns which stand out against the sparkling but hazy waters of the harbour. The pinky haze is, we are told, v. "Sydnee". Right between the palms & not more than 200 yards out in the water sits a v. large battleship. To the left, & away from the sea, is the centre of the city and the Bridge, under which full scale ocean-going ships can pass. We were up at sunrise this morning to see sunshine illuminating the windows of the skyscrapers – rose quartz flashes in the pinky mist. Across the water the ground piles up in a series of tree & villa covered hills – trees mostly non-deciduous gums and Moreton Bay figs, a very beautiful juicy-looking relative of the ilex.

Have met Co [Old Tote Theatre Company] who seem to be nice & look like they'll all be reasonably suitable. Today we attend a grand Luncheon given by Aust Council for the Arts & in the p.m. an eNORmouse cocktail partee given in our "honour". Tomorrow I go to Melbourne (11 hours by train) to meet employers & Co [Melbourne Theatre Company] there. After that will settle down to work. Manners are extremely democratic but the free-&-easiness is tempered by sunburnt, smiling jollity – none of the ferocious pushing & grabbing & scowling & PANIC of N.Y.C.

Think this 5 months in 'Strylia is going to be extremely interesting & enlightening. Sydney, when I was first here 21 years ago, was still an English suburb – a rose-red city half as old as Sevenoaks incongruously sited on palm-fringed sub-tropical creeks. Now it is a huge cosmopolis, growing faster than any other and beginning to search (too excitedly, like King Oedipus) for its own identity. It is now extremely "out" to refer to England as "Hawm".

The 'Strylian accent is the biggest pain in the neck – it causes every snobbish & musical antipathy. Isn't it odd? It's a real barrier between the community & the educated portion of ours. I keep telling myself not to be a snob but I still find it almost insufferably ugly and crude. It's like Cockney but not by any means exactly like, and contrives to be at once lazy and perky. Great hulking Diggers (male & female) shove past one in corridors or leave one's table in a restaurant or pass one on the stairs & they all say "Sceeze me ploys" in silly weak little rough voices – Brutes! And they're so kind & friendly in general; their naïveté would amuse were it not also extremely vexatious!

To Mrs Peggy Butler at Maidenhall

The University of New South Wales, Kensington, NSW. 1 August 1970

Oedipus is coming along. I can't expect it to do well; but I do think it's rather well done. I leave daily at 9.30 and get back around 5. Not a long day; but I am now old enough not to want to do any more than have a light super & Retire with a book. J. has made acquaintance with various neighbours in addition to people we knew before, so is adequately provided with society. We are being taken this p.m. for a drive up the coast northwards; and next Sat go quite far N to see Brenda Robertson Davies' sister Mysee (Maisie) who is now married to a splendid (I think) painter called Russell Drysdale. The younger and predominantly abstract painters find his "Australiana" rather old hat but he is very much my cup of tea & a very nice person.

Oedipus turned out to be an unprecedented success, described by the adapter John Lewen as 'a deeply personal and valedictory religious event'. While in Australia the Guthries' frequent health needs were exceptionally well looked after by concerned friends. When they returned to Ireland they were considerably refreshed – for what was to be Guthrie's last Christmas.

To Mrs Peggy Butler at Maidenhall

c/o John Sumner, Melbourne Theatre Co., Russell St Theatre, Melbourne. 10 August 1970

Very nice friends took us a heavenly drive thro' a National Forest about the size of Hampshire or 2ce Monaghan – 15 miles from the middle of the city. We looked at aboriginal rock carvings at least 10,000 years old & the wild flowers & bushes were "beaut" – very aromatic & tender pinks & blue & cream & mauve, looking touchingly springlike in the greeny-grey of the bush. It's all high up, maybe 6700 foot precipitous drops to strange melancholy but very booful inlets from the ocean – just the ticket for kiddies' bathing-picnics, 'cept the *second* little Horace or Edie put their toes in the water a shark bites off their legs – at the waist.

We viewed large sharks in a superb aquarium at Manly reached by a fascinating trip by ferry. They were seven feet long, an infinitely sinister colour (bluey-browney-black, like a mouldy undertaker) and the silliest little faces like C of E curates, wee round eyes like trouser-buttons and the receding teeth which make their bite so deadly ('cos the prey can only go downwards), it gives them a gentle-Jesusy smiling look over a receding chin.

On Sat we lunch with Patk. White, who is as near as dammit a great novelist – do you know his work? Sunday we leave for Canberra, where I have to Declare Open some Art Seminar; leave the next day for Melbourne.

To Mrs Peggy Butler at Maidenhall

c/o John Sumner, Melbourne Theatre Co., Russell St Theatre, Melbourne. 13 September 1970

We are enjoying Melbourne. Nothing as spectacular as Sydney's harbour, but also nothing so HIDJUS as Sydney's scarlet, scarlet suburbs. M gives a feeling of being older (it isn't) and much more gracious and digni. (which it is). This is a very well managed & run theatre by an Englishman called John Sumner whom apparently Yours Truly recommended for the job 20 years ago. I'd entirely forgotten. His wife is a senior lecturer in physiology at the Yeunee; & they live in a v. charming old (1870) house on the sea-front. We have now for 3 days been ensconced in a nice flat in a sort of small apt. block operated by the Yeunee for stray dons & such. I count as "And Such" because the theatre originally operated under the university auspices until it outgrew their premises.

The theatre now has a membership of 20,000 subsc. ticket holders & has almost outgrown Russell St, which is not large. In a year or two the whole shebang moves to a grand new Arts Centre now under construction, it looks like a giant fortress (extremely forbidding!) & holds the Art Collection (very fine, I hear), collections of Aboriginal art, treasures of Oceania, etc. & will have a concert hall, opera house, theatre & a small experimental theatre.

The Zoo is marvee; we went there on Sat. & spent most of the time gasping at Australian cockatoos which live in a vast enclosure, 40 or 50 foot high & about 50 yards long with trees & perches galore, & the parrots fly screeching about & come & hang upside-down & "talk" to visitors & seem to be very content. My favourites are quieter in colour – chastely white with sulphur crests. The noise is stupefying. The brightest are scarlet with yellow trimmings & emerald & sapphire backs. I suppose it's to make them, in the dazzling sunlight, melt into the landscape. The emus are amazing – the full grown ones stand 7 foot tall with tiny, silly, supercilious faces & expressionless ginger-coloured eyes.

I'm writing this in the theatre, having arrived early – there's a transport strike, so I had to walk. Strikes are rife. Don't really know the ins & outs, but I can't feel it's right that the entire community should be victimised because a few (comparatively small) groups feel they aren't getting a square deal. There are no trams, no electric light, no gas, no trains – which brings the city to something very like a standstill.

Tomorrow I fly to New Zealand (Christ Church) for 3 or 4 days to meet a group who want me, maybe, to go there in 1972. If spared, it might be nice.

To Mrs Peggy Butler at Maidenhall
Melbourne Theatre Company, Russell Street Theatre, Melbourne. 4 October 1970

We are going Out to Lunch – this is Grand Week – Friday it was to meet Sir Robt. Menzies; today it's Sir Roy & Laydye Grounds. Roy is a rather jolly architect (knew him here before) who has designed the new Arts Centre. Sir R. Menzies is the G.O.M. of 'Strylian politics. He's now retired & about 80, still a much (& rightly) respected Monument. He has stood for White Australia, Queen & Country, Law & Order, No Nonsense & similar Conservative notions; but he is a cultivated, humane old *gentle*man – oh so much grander than politicians usually come. He is Chancellor of Melbourne Yewnee & this was a University Do., informal, no speeches, just a v. v. good quiet luncheon which was quite enjoyable – a leetle spoilt by the presence of Dame Somebody Something who is a U. Senatress & the Very Spirit of Pretentious Toorak – Toorak is Melbourne's Ailesbury Road, & Dame Something was a dread combination of Fuzz Buzz & Battleaxe in a very handsome, and I suspect real, diamond & emerald "clip".

Apart from such elegant beanos, *All's Well* goes on rather satisfactorily. It opens Oct 21 & we leave Oct 25 by train (2,000 miles) for Perth.

To Hubert Butler at Maidenhall
University of New South Wales. 11 October 1970

This will only be a short note because I haven't much to say nor time to say it. *All's Well that Ends Well* is coming to the boil, we move into the (very large) theatre tomorrow with attendant technical complications of carpentry, lights, costumes, props and *not* very expert or efficient technicians.

I wanted to say how very sorry I feel that the Saints book has had this set back. Obviously a large work of potential importance, but which cannot reasonably be expected to achieve large sales even in very long term, isn't an easy proposition to market. On the other hand, it should not lose by waiting as would a topical work which, like puff pastry, must be consumed on the instant.

The Pope is to visit Australia and plans to hold an "Ecumenical" service in Sydney. *Before* invitations had been issued the Prot Archb announced in most firm if civil tones that he did not intend to join with His Holiness in worship of Almighty God. All over the continent nutty anti-papists screamed their approval of loyal protestant gesture. Now there's talk of inviting Ian Paisley to come out and head the opposition to Popery. No less "nutty" Liberals are screaming that he be not admitted to the shores of the Commonwealth. The papers are fizzing with letters from Pro Bono Publico, Mother of Nine and other Old Faithfuls of the Correspondence Columns.

To Mrs Peggy Butler c/o M. & E. Burgess at 'Mulberries', Boreham, Essex
Annaghmakerrig. Christmas Eve, 1970

So glad to have your economy letter-card, I'd wanted to write & couldn't recall "Mulberries". I've given your love to the Burns, who are well. Mary has taken to dye her hair (in rich chocolate) & looks 10 years older. The boys are both in the Jam Factory; Jim engaged to a v. nice girl called Cynthia Hawthorne (sole heiress to a snug farm near Drum). Maureen arrives tonight from Cardiff where she is a factory-gel. Christine (Mrs William Dickson) has just produced her seventh – Eric William.

Tanya arrived on Tues. Eugene McCabe came over, "did" the index for my book very kindly – it's a fiddly job, rather fun if you have Patience (not my strong suit). Seamus McGorman & Co are all very well – children in a perfect stew about "Santa". Frank McDermott is married to a Miss Rosemarie Quelquechose from near Aghabog Chapel; they reside in Garron (Mountain Hill), a v. nice house, & Frank commutes by car & has midday meal with his mum in Crappagh.

There has been a church vestry meeting & we're going to do the heating (which was totally conked out) at a cost of £100. I have undertaken to circulate Former Parishioners so in due course you may expect a tout & I shall expect 10/-.

To Mrs Peggy Butler c/o M. & E. Burgess at Mulberries, Boreham, Essex
Annaghmakerrig. 29 December 1970

Was in Belfast today. The Arts Council there wants me to do 2 plays later in the year. Quite a lot of Govt. money to celebrate the 50th anniversary of N.I. *Not* quite the moment for jubilation. I'm trying to persuade them not just to get up a couple of plays for a short & expensive season in Belfast but to invest a little *more* money – well, a great deal more – with a view to a longer term, more spiritually profitable investment. Am not expecting to get anywhere; but the attempt has to be made. It's the dashing of hundreds of such waves upon the rocks of apathy which finally smashes them down. The Pyramid rises on the blood & crushed bones of a million anonymous slaves; and if one's keen enough on Pyramids one doesn't mind too much being one of the slaves.

LAST TESTAMENT AMONG THE ELGIN MARBLES

Guthrie had no overseas engagements during the early months of 1971 though a Canadian production of *The Marriage of Figaro* was scheduled for July. He directed *The Barber of Seville* for Phoenix Opera in Brighton in April-May. It is clear that he was becoming increasingly conscious of the debts of Irish Farmhouse Preserves, amounting to about £200,000, though he never admitted this to relatives; nor did he admit that Judy's constant bouts of 'influenza' were a cover for alcohol dependency. After a delay of three years the Irish Youth Hostel Organisation (An Oige) failed to respond to his proposal to create a hostel at Annaghmakerrig, but the Arts Councils in Dublin and Belfast jointly became more positive about his offer, proposed by Hubert and Peggy Butler, that the house should become an international centre for artistic endeavour; and finally the Department of Finance agreed to the project.

To Mrs Peggy Butler in Las Palmas, Canary Islands

Annaghmakerrig. 14 January 1971

> Glad to get your p.c. depicting a simply fearfully gloomy landskip. I hope you never leave the shelter of the red and yellow umbrellas & the Coca-cola Kiosks. Hope the sun & change are doing Hubert good. PLEASE don't go rushing into those terrible mountains, full, one can't doubt, of snakes and Berbers and sharp cacti. Just stick around and sit on public benches wheezing and looking with unseeing eyes out to sea and towards a big greasy high tea in the Boarding House with the Browns from Greenock and the Greens from Brownville and little Frau Relling from Pigstrandt and big Frau Snelling from Hogstrandt.

Guest have all gone. A Mr Jack White is expected from Dublin tomorrow night. I know him only as the author of what *I* thought a very funny and wise and witty play (none of the other judges[58] thought likewise). We're to spend an evening discussing what, if at all, might be its future. On Monday we are giving a select Dinner – Dr and Mrs Gunn from Cootehill, whose parlour is lousy with Infants of Prague and such repository rubbish but also loud with Verdi, Bach and Beethoven on a super-hyper-ultra-stereophonic machine; Baldwin Murphy [solicitor] who, since his wife dropped dead as a stone while mowing the lawn, is sadly lonely and bereaved; and the Rev and Mrs Lumley, now Incumbent and Queen-consort of Ballybay. All are "owed hospitality" and all are reasonably to be relied on to lift the talk above the weather and the Sale of Work but not to drag it into regions so controversial that actual blows are likely to be struck. If that looks likely, Verdi's Requiem can be spun on good and loud.

To Mrs Peggy Butler in Las Palmas, Canary Islands

Annaghmakerrig. 3 February 1971

Christopher Scaife arrives this afternoon for a week or two which is very nice. He gets off the Dublin train at Dundalk & I board it for Belfast! Not an ideal arrangement but I have a TV at 9 a.m. tomorrow & rehearsal tonight. And the fee makes acceptance imperative.

Did a lot in England. Visits on biz to Leeds & Sheffield. Stayed in London c/o Geo & Annette whose case is simply deplorable. Geo's[59] memory has totally gone and he's also deafer than 9 posts. Annette is "on duty" 24 hours out of 24. She won't organise baby-sitters (tho' many are eager to help) & won't do lots of sensible things which could ease the situation. But "won't" is really "can't" because of the psychological context. It's all very sad & wholly frustrating.

I went, by invitation of the young Drama Master, who turns out, fortuitously, to be a v.v. far out relation on the Kirk side, to Wellington Coll. & stayed as a guest of the Headmaster. It was all quite interesting & oddly unchanged – it's not even much bigger – but the "ethos" is

58   *Today the Bullfinch*, by Jack White, in the Dublin Theatre Festival play competition; subsequently produced Abbey Theatre, 1971.

59   George Chamberlain, former administrator, Old Vic Theatre.

now *quite* different. Last year only 4 boys went into the army & the whole military background has receded. Young fellows with Clapham accents and hair to the shoulders were MODELLING in CLAY, rotten little cissies!

Visited at Glencullen [Fitz-Simon home, Dublin] last week. Simon keeps going marvellously but his entire life (body & soul) is devoted to a hopeless struggle to maintain a status quo that, quite apart from Ailish's illness, became completely insupportable 30 years ago. A. lay corpselike except for desperate heartrending panting, on a sofa, but was marvellously cheerful & un-self-absorbed. We cd. tell them 1st hand news of Nickie & his rather impressive Architect bride [in Australia]. They knew it all already, but the facts weren't quite the point.

The Melbourne Theatre Co have sent a smashing "Presentation" – two walloping great Vols, profusely & splendidly illustrated, about Australian Painters. I think you'll enjoy it very much.

To Mrs Peggy Butler in Las Palmas, Canary Islands

Annaghmakerrig. 24 February 1971

Christopher Scaife's visit was a huge success. I think he enjoyed it just as much as we did. He's a very easy guest with plenty of occupation of his own yet agreeably willing to join in whatever's offered. We had nightly sessions with the gramo to everyone's great pleasure. I'm endeavouring to "study" *Figaro* and *Barber* from recordings. In neither case is the music alone much guide to planning movements and business, but, of course, infinitely better than if one had to rely on what one could fiddle out for oneself from the piano score.

Got back last night from two tiring but quite satisfactory days and a night in London. Had to shew up my prep to Thames T.V. for Brit. Museum programme – happy to say They seemed to like the script v. much; see Mario Bernardi, conductor from Ottawa, who will be doing *Figaro* when I go there in July; and Tanya to see prelim drawings for *Barber of Seville*, & Geo & Annette just out of friendship. The sun was streaming into their room and there was an air of content and calm which was rather conspicuous by its absence last time I was there.

So glad to hear of Hubert's benefitting by the change and the sunshine. The black volcanic beach sounds simply fiendish. I imagine spring flowers will quite be beginning. We have had snowdrops out since Jan 15. All trees beginning perceptibly to thicken and the alders round the lake are getting that interesting purply-rose-madder glow.

Saw Joan Lennox-Conyngham & D & M. They came over to an architectural "Do" at the Comprehensive School in Cootehill. Young architects, full of enthusiasm but sadly lacking in practical grasp, wanting to preserve & use the stables (1840) at Dartrey. Joan [Hubert Butler's sister] looked well. Young M, with whom I had just a word, seemed to be sad at giving up whatever he was doing (would it be farming?) at one of his various "seats". I thought he was rather nice but lost a bit. Paddy [Lord] Rossmore was also there, wandering round like a gentle ineffectual ghost. Really these declining relics of the Upper Orders are rather a fright – the young ones especially. We *have* declined; our sun has all but set; but the thirty year old nobles – where can they go? What can they do? My Lord of Caledon seems to manage reasonably well. They sold most of the ancestral library & used the money to make the enormous (& very beautiful) house watertight. They live in a small flat in warmth & comfort; have done the big main rooms up – rather well – & use them for occasional parties. He farms with energy – I don't know how much skill; & Milady dusts & mends the pillowslips & the Little Lordlings go to Eton whence they return with the accents of the sons of Lancashire stationmasters who are Etonians by dint of winning scholarships; "they" comprise over 50% of the intake; the 49% of little Noblemen only eat when Daddy sells another Gainsborough or a Caxton 1st Edition.

To Mrs Peggy Butler in Las Palmas, Canary Islands

c/o Thames TV, London. 11 March 1971

[Letter pencilled on back of TV script] Writing in the Brit. Museum during one of the interminable pauses in filming. The Museum is the perfect "field" for anthropological observation. Dotties of all nationalities, all ages, all sexes and all classes troop through in myriads, mostly *deeply* eccentric in dress & demeanour. Hubert would seem like a stockbroker on the 9.05 from Bagshot. Children are herded through by anxious pedagogues, watch in hand, counting heads all the time – very pretty to see the complete desegregation?? as the little nippers hold hands & share caramels with the Master Race. I think the BM must be Under Entirely New Management – it's marvellously busked up with new, beautiful Entrance Hall, newly arranged exhibits, and, clearly, a VAST public.

We have to make this programme [*The Greeks*] in 2 days – the BBC would allot a month. But this is ITV so Art is very subordinate to money. However, the director is a very nice chap, most philosophic in adversity & nice with one & all, including old Yours Truly who can only endeavour not to waste more time by forgetting the words or muffing the positions. I work today & tomorrow here (BM); & how we shall get through the whole thing I really can't imagine. I was here before 9 a.m. – it's now 2 p.m. & we've done 2 short scenes.

Judy, whose b'day is today, was to have come over and she & Geo (who is 80) were to have shared a small birthday beano. But the night before last she was smitten with one of these (currently very prevalent) "lightening" flu bugs. Probably won't travel till tomorrow. Sat. is devoted to *Barber of Seville* – auditions, I think, & conferences about set & frocks, which Tanya has got ready & the designs look delightful.

After our demise, Min of Finance have agreed to accept responsibility for house [Annaghmakerrig]. And, in consideration of establishment of a "Trust", to run it on lines broadly indicated in my will. Will remit estate duty, which should leave enough to operate it, at least thro' early years of inevitable "teething troubles" without expense to the taxpayer. I have left to Julia the portraits of g-grandfathers Power & Guthrie, the Alibone silver, & (very valuable) Power snuff-boxes; also grandfather's medals [Sir W.T. Power]. I am leaving for her a request, but not an injunction, that she make the snuffboxes available, one to the National Theatre Museum of G.B., & t'other either to the Abbey or Natl. Museum of Ireland. But if they got into low water financially she could still sell them if she wished.

Looks like they're going to be ready for me at any moment so I'll be drawing to a close. Have you ever had so *long* a letter? Have you ever had a letter written, as 'twere, from amongst the Elgin Marbles?

NEXT INSTALMENT: Brit. Museum, March 12th. Well, Judy turned up y'day afternoon, none the worse of the journey; & is completely OK today. I was here at 9.00 & we've done the first "shot" of the day. I've been out in the portico in lovely sunshine watching the visitors assemble (in hundreds) for the 10 o'clock opening. The Museum has its own "community" apart from the staff (over 1,000, hundreds of guards, an army of cleaning women) there are Habitual Visitors. I think it must have many of the qualities of a mediaeval Religious House – part mental hospital, as well as many other functions – a place where rather lonely individuals can find both occupation & a sufficient companionship without having to surrender treasured anonymity. No doubt by the early-middle XVI century the monastic life of western Europe had become corrupt & decadent, but what a DISASTER to root it out rather than attempt to reform. I imagine that some time, perhaps not very far into the future, there will be a similar root & branch destruction of industrial giants, like Ford & ICI, who have become decadent & who offer to newer powers (e.g. military dictatorship) a moral excuse to source & plunder enormous treasure.

Can't send this quite yet – it's my only copy of The Script & I have to make a transcript which Collins will publish and pay money for so doing. It ought to have been done already but I haven't felt "equal". The news, tho' stale, may still entertain.

To Lady Guthrie at Annaghmakerrig

c/o George & Annette Chamberlain, 26 Wharton Street, London WC1. Easter Sunday, 1971

We finished the British Museum programme on Thurs. There were only 3 or 4 camera set-ups & I swiftly galloped through reams of "voice off" to which 4 hours had been allotted but which took under an hour. Yesterday I visited with Commander Cross [Joan Cross], reasonably mobile on one stick but I felt under a brave façade & rather heavy discouragement. She would like to retire (or says so) but cannot afford not to work. Her civil list has been granted; but I didn't like to ask how much it amounts to. A spanking tea was served ("Indian, sir, or China?") with toast & gent's relish & a chocolate cake from Gunter's. The room is very charming with aft. sun streaming through long Regency windows. I felt she had aged & was pulled down & depressed though NO BREATH of complaint. I stayed over an hour with talk going a mile a minute & no longueurs.

Geo is TOTALLY deaf. Annette thinks it is due to accumulations of wax. Right now Geo only hears if you put your mouth right up to his ear & speak ve-ry slow-ly. Annette is no good at this. She SCREAMS at him, long, rapid, half jokey, half virago tirades. Geo of course gets utterly moidered & very cross & snappish. I *think* my being here is a help – not sure; but I think if one went elsewhere she'd mind very much. I try to give minimal trouble & to amuse Geo a bit – nothing holds his attention more than a moment or two.

We start *B of Seville* tomorrow in St Martin's church hall. Any jam developments? I do hope no hideous revelations but feel there may well be.

To Mrs Peggy Butler at Maidenhall

c/o Geo & Annette Chamberlain, 26 Wharton Street, London WC1. 16 April 1971

I can't think why I was such a *goat* as to open the topic of the will business again. It only seems to lead to total misunderstanding & rather pointlessly distressing recrimination. Our spirits move on such a similar course (wave-length?) that the inevitable difference due to many years of extremely diff. environment, experience & companionship, are more painful. Let's try not to wound one another by each defending our own point of view, but rather be thankful that we have, even so, so very much in common.

To Lady Guthrie at Annaghmakerrig

c/o Geo & Annette Chamberlain, 26 Wharton Street, London WC1. 16 April 1971

Barber is relentlessly high-spirited but I *think* I'm enjoying it. Any jam developments? I have from time to time nasty little fears that further "revelations" will emerge of a kind discreditable to Joe [Martin]. I do hope not.

To Lady Guthrie at Annaghmakerrig

c/o Geo & Annette Chamberlain, 26 Wharton Street, London WC1. 18 April 1971

Am distinctly enjoying rehearsals of *B of S* though the synthetic gaiety & worked-up excitement of the piece are NOT interesting.

Don't you think it pretty shaming that An Oige still stands where it did? I thought Terry Trench's little handwritten P.S. implied crimson cheeks.

Have had a message from Damey Thorndike suggesting that we meet so I think I may propose myself for aft. tea today.

To Mrs Peggy Butler at Maidenhall

Old Ship Hotel, Brighton. 5 May 1971

Happy to hear that Hubert was home [after brief hospital stay] & trust that he will now "pick up" & not be too flattened by – whatever it was, I gather some intestinal virus, tho' having said that, is one any the wiser? but amazing that Drs, even reliable ones, STILL announce with sage nods that one is suffering from INFLUENZA – the evil influence. I've had no voice for days & have been really quite poorly; but today I can speak, if hoarsely, & feel, for the first time, that I'd quite *like* to get better.

This is a v.g., not quite de luxe, hotel & the great comfort is quite helpful; even more so is the divine weather, "Dr Brighton" at his/her very best. It is now 2 p.m. We spent the morning lolling about in the sun; came back to a v. good lunch & now, when I've written this, I shall take 40 winks. Judy is going out to get a present (maybe tiny booties) for the newest McGorman (No.6). At 5 Alec Guthrie comes for a nip – can't remember who he is other than one of Uncle Sandy's grand or great-grandsons. 'Twill be revealed. James & Louise Forsythe (he's a writer) comes a little later for a snack & to go to 1st Perf of *Il Barbiere*, which had quite a ready dress rehearsal last night before a ¼ full house of friends & friends' friends. We go to Forsythes (near Cuckfield) on Wed night; & to Angela Fox, recently widowed, near the same place, for next night. She has Robert Morley, a great friend of her husband, to lunch on Sat. We shall stay for that & catch plane from Gatwick (quite near) to Belfast. Should be home around 9 p.m.

To Mrs Peggy Butler at Maidenhall

Annaghmakerrig. 12 May 1971

Got back on Sunday night – a leetle exhausted but all right. The weather is lovely & cherries, azaleas, bluebells & crimson r'dendrons make a positively technicoloured impresh.

The jam is ironic & very sad. For the last six or seven months we have been selling really well & advance orders would have ensured a good year. But the "liquid capital" was impossible. We couldn't finance the fulfilling of the orders and had debts that couldn't wait. If Joe had been in really good health I think we'd have fought on; but he has a gall bladder (I think) affection & is in poor order. Liquidation seemed the only possibility. Afraid the creditors will only get a very poor dividend.

Barber of S went off quite well. The last 10 days or so were rather a struggle because I wasn't well & finally lost my voice. Attempting to direct an opera in a whisper is no fun at all – one feels utterly powerless &, oddly enough, invisible as well as inaudible.

Have a few weeks now here, & with v. few engagements. Leave for Canada June 5 – from Cobh. Back July 26 & go straight into rehearsal at the Abbey with that play you read.[60]

No more. Want to transplant snowdrops & then listen to *Figaro*.

That is the last known letter written by Sir Tyrone Guthrie. He died on May 15 (his mother's birthday) 1971 in the morning room at Annaghmakerrig while reading his mail. The story circulated was that he suffered a stroke on learning of the huge liability of Irish Farmhouse Preserves but he was already aware of these and the post actually brought him news of a tax rebate on theatre earnings. He was buried in the family enclosure at Aghabog Church following a service conducted by the Bishop of Clogher. The chief mourners were Judith, Lady Guthrie and Mrs Peggy Butler. A memorial service was held in St Paul's Church, Covent Garden, London, on 16 June at which the chief speaker was Sir Alec Guinness; Dame Sybil Thorndike read Shakespeare's Sonnet CXVI and Lord Olivier read a passage from *The Pilgrim's Progress*. Judith Guthrie died at Annaghmakerrig the following year. The house was accepted for the nation by the Minister for Finance and after a delay of ten years a board of management was created by the two Arts Councils in Ireland. Annaghmakerrig became The Tyrone Guthrie Centre; as a workplace for writers and artists it has enjoyed immeasurable international success. Tyrone Guthrie died as he had lived – organizing a professional transatlantic trip, listening to the opera that was to be his next production and planting woodland flowers.

---

60   *The Devil at Work* by Constantine Fitzgibbon.

Annaghmakerrig in 1961.

SELECT BIBLIOGRAPHY

Brown, Ivor and Quayle, Anthony, *The Shakespeare Memorial Theatre* (London 1948)

Forsyth, James, *Tyrone Guthrie* (London 1976)

Guilfoyle, Peg, *The Guthrie Theater* (Minneapolis 2006)

Guthrie, Tyrone, Davies, Robertson and MacDonald, Grant, *Renown at Stratford* (Toronto 1953)

Guthrie, Tyrone, *A Life in the Theatre* (London 1960)

Guthrie, Tyrone, *A New Theatre* (New York 1964)

Guthrie, Tyrone, *In Various Directions* (London 1965)

Guthrie, Tyrone, *Guthrie on Acting* (London 1971)

Hale, Lionel, *The Old Vic 1949–50* (London 1950)

Rossi, Alfred, *Astonish Us in the Morning* (London 1977)

Surridge, Jennifer and Derry, Ramsay, *A Celtic Temperament* (Toronto 2015)

Vickers, John, *The Old Vic in Photographs* (London 1947)

Williams, Harcourt, *Old Vic Saga* (London 1949)

Williamson, Audrey, *Old Vic Drama* (London 1948)

ACKNOWLEDGMENTS

I wish to thank Julia Crampton for drawing my attention to her uncle Tyrone Guthrie's letters, written to her mother, Peggy Butler, from all parts of the world, which are preserved at her family home, Maidenhall. When I responded positively to the suggestion of a book she and her husband Dr Richard Crampton gave me every possible encouragement throughout the research period. I would particularly like to thank the Chairman and Board of the Tyrone Guthrie Centre at Annaghmakerrig – of which I had been a founding member in 1981 – for allowing me to reproduce letters, written by Guthrie to his mother and his wife, which the Centre subsequently placed on permanent loan in the Public Records Office of Northern Ireland; I wish to thank the Director at Annaghmakerrig, Robbie McDonnell, and members of the staff, especially Ingrid Adams and Mary Clerkin, for their invariably productive response to enquiries. At PRONI my researches were helpfully guided by Dr Bethany Sinclair and later by Lorraine Bourke; my admiration is due for the highly professional way in which the PRONI staff have catalogued and preserved the material. The Scottish Theatre Archive at the University of Glasgow, and particularly its Chief Library Assistant, Claire McKendrick, provided essential background information regarding Guthrie's work in Edinburgh and Glasgow, and Dr Michael Makower supplied a list of his productions with the Scottish National Players. I also thank the staff of the Burnley Public Library, Lancashire, and especially its Library Assistant, Neil Marshall, for access to material relating to Guthrie's residence with the Old Vic Theatre Company, the Sadler's Wells Opera and the Sadler's Wells Ballet at the Royal Victoria Theatre, Burnley, during the Second World War. Research would not have been possible without a substantial travel grant from the Arts Council of Northern Ireland, to whose Literature and Drama Officer, Damian Smyth, I extend special thanks. Ms Jo Holcomb, Senior Dramaturg and Librarian at the Guthrie Theater, Minneapolis, has generously provided pictures of Guthrie's signature work there. Others who have helped enormously include Paul Cusack, Joe Dowling, Judy Friel, Kieran Hoare, the late Joe Hone, John Sheehan, Ellen Ödhal, the Rev. Dr Robert Tobin and Professor Brian Walker. My wife, Anne Makower, has been enormously supportive, especially with her ever-relevant and judicious comments on the selection of letters. Professor Terence Brown read the first draft and provided encouragement to an unexpected degree. Finally I wish to thank the publisher, Antony Farrell, for recognizing the significance of these letters and for adding yet another handsome book to his now vast list of publications at the Lilliput Press; Djinn von Noorden, surely the most skilful editor and proofreader ever; and Niall McCormack, for his arresting yet eminently sensitive design.

PICTURE CREDITS

Most of the illustrations in this book have been taken from family collections in which personal and professional photographs abound with very little indication as to their provenance. Guthrie would undoubtedly have sent production pictures to members of his family to illustrate his work but in almost all cases without the names of photographers. Where names are given it has been found that the majority of firms have gone out of existence. Every effort has been made to discover picture origins and apologies are extended where individuals or companies could not be traced. The ArenaPal Agency in London has been helpful in finding the sources of several of the Old Vic pictures numbered below. Appreciation is offered to the Crampton family at Maidenhall where almost all the family pictures were found; others were discovered in the Annaghmakerrig archive Thank you to Patrick Martin, Darac Conservation & Archival Picture Framing, Newbliss, Co. Monaghan, for the atmospheric photographs of the Irish Farmhouse Preserves enterprise taken by his mother Antonia Lofting. Individual pictures are gratefully credited with their page numbers: Frontispiece, Tyrone Guthrie Centre; 26, Wellington College; 43 and front cover, the British Broadcasting Corporation; 59, 67, Glasgow University Library; 96, J.W. Debenham; 105, Elizabeth Corcoran; 109, Anthony Photographer, London; 127, 139, 141, 148, 151, Burnley Public Library; 191, John Vickers; 213, Habima Theater, Tel Aviv; 227, 245 Svenska Teatern, Helsingfors; 258, 265, 269, drawings by Grant McDonald published by Clarke, Irwin & Company Ltd, Toronto; 291, The James Hardiman Library, NUI Galway, Siobhán McKenna Collection; 316, Darac, Newbliss; 349, 359, Antonia Lofting; 361, Guthrie Theater, Minneapolis; 367, Reg Watson, The Queen's University of Belfast; 390, Mrs Anne Friel; 392, 397 and back cover, Donald Getzug, Guthrie Theater Collection, Minneapolis.

INDEX

Names of persons mentioned incidentally in the letters are not included.
Numbers in italics indicate illustrations.